JONES & BARTLETT LEARNING INFORMATION SYSTEMS SECURITY & ASSURANCE SERIES

Auditing IT Infrastructures for Compliance

MARTIN M. WEISS AND MICHAEL G. SOLOMON

JONES & BARTLETT
LEARNING

World Headquarters
Jones & Bartlett Learning
5 Wall Street
Burlington, MA 01803
978-443-5000
info@jblearning.com
www.jblearning.com

Jones & Bartlett Learning books and products are available through most bookstores and online booksellers. To contact Jones & Bartlett Learning directly, call 800-832-0034, fax 978-443-8000, or visit our website, www.jblearning.com.

This publication is designed to provide accurate and authoritative information in regard to the subject matter covered. It is sold with the understanding that the publisher is not engaged in rendering legal, accounting, or other professional service. If legal advice or other expert assistance is required, the service of a competent professional person should be sought.

Production Credits
Chief Executive Officer: Ty Field
President: James Homer
SVP, Chief Operating Officer: Don Jones, Jr.
SVP, Chief Technology Officer: Dean Fossella
SVP, Chief Marketing Officer: Alison M. Pendergast
SVP, Chief Financial Officer: Ruth Siporin
SVP, Business Development: Christopher Will
VP, Design and Production: Anne Spencer
VP, Manufacturing and Inventory Control: Therese Connell
Editorial Management: High Stakes Writing, LLC, Editor and Publisher: Lawrence J. Goodrich
Reprints and Special Projects Manager: Susan Schultz
Associate Production Editor: Tina Chen
Director of Marketing: Alisha Weisman
Associate Marketing Manager: Meagan Norlund
Cover Design: Anne Spencer
Composition: Mia Saunders Design
Cover Image: © ErickN/ShutterStock, Inc.
Chapter Opener Image: © Rodolfo Clix/Dreamstime.com
Printing and Binding: Malloy, Inc.
Cover Printing: Malloy, Inc.

ISBN: 978-0-7637-9181-0

6048
Printed in the United States of America
16 15 14 13 12   10 9 8 7 6 5 4

Contents

Preface

Purpose of This Book

This book is part of the Information Systems Security & Assurance Series from Jones & Bartlett Learning (*www.jblearning.com*). Designed for courses and curriculums in IT Security, Cybersecurity, Information Assurance, and Information Systems Security, this series features a comprehensive, consistent treatment of the most current thinking and trends in this critical subject area. These titles deliver fundamental information-security principles packed with real-world applications and examples. Authored by Certified Information Systems Security Professionals (CISSPs), they deliver comprehensive information on all aspects of information security. Reviewed word for word by leading technical experts in the field, these books are not just current, but forward-thinking— putting you in the position to solve the cybersecurity challenges not just of today, but of tomorrow, as well.

Part 1 of this book identifies and explains what each of these compliance laws requires in regard to safeguarding business and consumer privacy data elements and the design and implementation of proper security controls. Once these safeguards and security control requirements are defined for your organization, the yardstick of measurement for conducting an audit of your IT infrastructure for compliance can commence.

Part 2 presents how to audit an IT infrastructure for compliance based on the compliance laws themselves and the need to protect and secure business and consumer privacy data and have properly documented and implemented security controls within the organization. Auditing standards and frameworks are also presented, along with what must be audited within the seven domains of a typical IT infrastructure. Part 2 also discusses planning, conducting, and documenting what was identified during the audit and whether the compliance requirements are being met and complied with throughout the IT infrastructure. Specific security controls and countermeasures are presented for each of the domains of a typical IT infrastructure.

Part 3 provides a resource for readers and students who desire more information on becoming skilled at IT auditing and IT compliance auditing. This final chapter provides additional content on ethics, education, professional certifications, and IT auditing certifying organizations. In addition, professional codes of conduct are explored, along with an overview of auditing certification and accreditation bodies. This can provide information systems security practitioners with career opportunities in performing IT infrastructure audits given that public and private sector organizations are now under U.S.-based compliance laws.

This book not only addresses the tools and techniques used for auditing IT infrastructure for compliance, but it also examines the need. While much of the content is related to information security, the text considers the broader and higher-level principles around information governance and risk management. This text brings together the fields of auditing, which has traditionally been seen as a function of accounting, and information technology.

Learning Features

The writing style of this book is practical and conversational. Each chapter begins with a statement of learning objectives. Step-by-step examples of information security concepts and procedures are presented throughout the text. Illustrations are used both to clarify the material and to vary the presentation. The text is sprinkled with Notes, Tips, FYIs, Warnings, and sidebars to alert the reader to additional helpful information related to the subject under discussion. Chapter Assessments appear at the end of each chapter, with solutions provided in the back of the book.

Chapter summaries are included in the text to provide a rapid review or preview of the material and to help students understand the relative importance of the concepts presented.

Audience

The material is suitable for undergraduate or graduate computer science majors or information science majors, students at a two-year technical college or community college who have a basic technical background, or readers who have a basic understanding of IT security and want to expand their knowledge.

Acknowledgments

Thank you to those who helped both indirectly and directly. I am grateful to Carole Jelen for bringing me on board. Thank you to Larry J. Goodrich for helping get me off to a solid start. Thank you Kim Lindros for working with me throughout the process. Thanks to Jeff T. Parker for keeping me honest and providing much needed humor. Thank you Michael Solomon, as I couldn't have done this book without your help. Thank you Kathleen Rushall for handling the really important stuff! Thank you to the entire staff at the Woodbridge Starbucks, where I spent many evenings during the process. Thank you Erin Banks, a colleague and great friend, who provided tremendous support and insight. Thank you Heather Pizzarelli for all you do in helping around the farm. Finally, I'd like to thank my entire family (sorry I missed your birthday again, Tiffy), especially Kelly Cosgrove, who provided a lot of support and put the animals to bed every night. And of course, thank you Kobe, Max, and Ollie. (Don't forget to dedicate a book to your Dad when it's your turn.)

Martin M. Weiss

I would like to thank Jeff T. Parker, the book's technical reviewer, and Kim Lindros, who managed the project, reviewed, and ferried all the pieces that flowed between me and Jones & Bartlett. You two make this stuff so much easier and added a lot to the book. Also, thanks so much to Carole Jelen with Waterside Productions for working so hard to make this happen.

I would also like to thank my wife Stacey and my sons Noah and Isaac, who make everything I do possible and fun. I can never thank them enough. So, to my three best friends, thanks again.

Michael G. Solomon

To my Mom and Dad (since my book, Awesome Parents, *never got published)*
—Martin M. Weiss

To God, who has richly blessed me in so many ways
—Michael G. Solomon

About the Authors

MARTIN M. WEISS manages a team of information security gurus at RSA, the security division of EMC. He has over 15 years of experience in information security, risk, governance, and control. He is also on the Board of Directors of the ISSA Connecticut, and is a member of ISACA. Weiss holds a BS in computer studies from the University of Maryland and an MBA from the Isenberg School of Management at the University of Massachusetts Amherst. He holds several certifications, including the CISSP and SSCP. Weiss has also authored and coauthored over a half-dozen books on information technology. He currently resides between Boston and New York City and can be reached at marty.weiss@gmail.com.

MICHAEL G. SOLOMON (CISSP, PMP, CISM, GSEC) is a full-time security speaker, consultant, and author, and a former college instructor who specializes in development and assessment security topics. As an IT professional and consultant since 1987, he has worked on projects for more than 100 major companies and organizations. From 1998 until 2001, he was an instructor in the Kennesaw State University Computer Science and Information Sciences (CSIS) department, where he taught courses on software project management, C++ programming, computer organization and architecture, and data communications. Solomon holds an MS in mathematics and computer science from Emory University (1998), a BS in computer science from Kennesaw State University (1987), and is currently pursuing a PhD in computer science and informatics at Emory University. He has also contributed to various security certification books for LANWrights, including *TICSA Training Guide* (Que, 2002) and an accompanying Instructor Resource Kit (Que, 2002), *CISSP Study Guide* (Sybex, 2003), as well as *Security+ Training Guide* (Que, 2003). Solomon coauthored *Information Security Illuminated* (Jones and Bartlett, 2005), *Security+ Lab Guide* (Sybex, 2005), *Computer Forensics JumpStart* (Sybex, 2005), *PMP ExamCram2* (Que, 2005), and authored and provided the on-camera delivery of LearnKey's CISSP Prep and PMP Prep e-Learning courses.

PART ONE

The Need for Compliance

The Need for Information Systems Security Compliance

I N THE EARLY TO MID-2000s, many large corporations suffered public failures. Since then, a number of compliance laws have been introduced. Many of these laws and regulations place an increased responsibility on information technology (IT) staff. This increased responsibility ensures they have proper information system controls throughout the environment to provide the necessary security of customer data. In addition, they ensure the integrity of the systems upon which business processes run.

Compliance goes beyond just conforming to internal policies and standards. Compliance extends outside of the organization, mapping to external regulations and industry standards. Regular assessments and audits of the IT environment are important concepts to ensuring compliance. Failure to comply with external regulations and industry standards can carry severe penalties. As a result, it is increasingly important to understand the methods by which an organization can be evaluated and the relationship between compliance and risk management and governance.

Chapter 1 Topics

This chapter covers the following topics and concepts:

- What an IT security assessment is
- What an IT security audit is
- What compliance is
- How audits contrast with assessments
- What the importance of governance and compliance is
- What the consequences of not complying with compliance laws are

> ### Chapter 1 Goals
>
> When you complete this chapter, you will be able to:
>
> - Examine the role of an IT assessment
> - Examine the role of IT auditing
> - Compare the differences between an audit and an assessment
> - Summarize compliance and explain why it is important

What Is an IT Security Assessment?

Assessing IT security is typically part of a larger security program within an organization. Specifically, an IT security assessment is a key activity that involves the management of **risk**. Information systems provide numerous benefits and efficiencies within organizations. However, the benefits come with risks as a result of operating these systems. A risk-based approach to managing information security involves the following:

- Identifying and categorizing the information and the information systems
- Selecting and implementing appropriate security **controls** to be applied to the systems
- Assessing the controls for effectiveness
- Authorizing the systems by accepting the risk based upon the selected security controls
- Monitoring the security controls on a continual basis

This approach is a continual cycle as organizations evolve and as activities such as assessments and monitoring reveal gaps and ineffective controls relevant to requirements and acceptable levels of risk.

The benefits provided to organizations as a result of information technology involve complex systems and processes. These systems not only benefit organizations, but they have also become critical components to the success of the organization. As a result, the continued and secured operation of these systems contributes largely to that success.

To understand their effectiveness, organizations must assess security controls. Security controls include the physical, procedural, and technical mechanisms to safeguard systems. First, are they implemented? Second, are they functioning as expected? If so, are they producing the required results based on the security policy of an organization?

You should not use a security assessment simply as a method for proving the strength of system security or as a reason to immediately provide greater security. Rather, a security assessment should produce information required to do the following:

- Identify weaknesses within the controls implemented on information systems
- Confirm that previously identified weaknesses have been remediated or mitigated
- Prioritize further decisions to mitigate risks
- Provide **assurance** so that associated risks are accepted and authorized
- Provide support and planning for future budgetary requirements

A number of personnel can often conduct security assessments. The personnel can be internal or external to an organization. Although the procedures for assessments may vary widely by organization, the **National Institute of Standards and Technology (NIST)** provides a framework to build effective security assessment plans in NIST Special Publication 800-53A. This publication defines a recommended assessment procedure, which includes a set of assessment **objectives**. Each objective has a set of assessment methods, including examination, interview, and test. In addition, each objective has a set of assessment objects, including specification, mechanism, activity, and individual.

An assessment objective includes one or more statements that are directly related to a corresponding control to determine the validity and effectiveness of the control. For example, consider a common control that most users of computer systems have experienced: being locked out of an information system or application after too many unsuccessful logon attempts. The following illustrates the relationship between the control and the assessment objectives, methods, and objects.

Unsuccessful Logon Attempts

Control: The system enforces a limit of four consecutive invalid access attempts on the same username within a period of 15 minutes. The system automatically locks the account for 30 minutes. Subsequently, four more consecutive invalid access attempts within a period of 15 minutes lock the account indefinitely, which requires manual intervention by the system administrator.

Assessment objectives:
- Determine if the system enforces the defined threshold of consecutive invalid access attempts.
- Determine if the system enforces the delayed logon after initial account lock.
- Determine if the system enforces the defined threshold for locking the account indefinitely.

Assessment methods and objects:
- Examine access control policy statement and procedures addressing failed logon attempts.
- Examine associated information system documentation and configuration settings.
- Examine associated information system log records.
- Test the automated mechanism implementing the access control policy for failed logon attempts.

 TIP

NIST Special Publication 800-53 Appendix F contains a catalog of assessment procedures. You can tailor the assessment procedures for use in performing a security assessment. Appendix H provides a summary worksheet of all assessment procedures contained in Appendix F.

Methods for Conducting a Security Control Assessment

You can use several methods to conduct an assessment of security controls:

- **Examination**—Verify, inspect, or review associated assessment objects to understand or obtain evidence to support the existence and effectiveness of the security control. Examples include reviewing security policies and procedures and observing physical security mechanisms.

- **Interview**—Discuss associated assessment objects with groups or individuals to understand or obtain evidence to support the existence and effectiveness of the security control. Interviews can include senior officials, information system owners, security officers, information system operators, and network administrators.

- **Test**—Put associated assessment objects under specific conditions to compare actual behavior with what is expected to obtain evidence to support the existence and effectiveness of the security control. "Objects" can include hardware or software mechanisms or system operations or administration activities. Examples include testing actual security configuration settings and conducting penetration tests.

Assessment objectives should be part of your organization's IT security assessment plan. After executing the plan, you can create a report. The IT security assessment report documents the findings of the assessment and provides the information necessary to determine the effectiveness of the controls. Senior management uses the report to provide assurance that risks are appropriate to the goals of the organization and to help create, if necessary, another document for an action plan based on the results of the assessment.

 TIP

It's helpful to create an executive summary document that quickly highlights the key findings and recommendations in a security assessment report.

Not all IT security assessments need to be comprehensive to cover all security controls or even all information systems. In fact, often times, security assessments are performed partially across controls and information systems. Although this chapter has laid out a best-practice framework for a comprehensive IT security assessment, security assessments vary in scope, depth, and breadth. The following is a list of some sample assessments you might encounter:

- Network security architecture review
- Review of security policies, procedures, and practices
- Vulnerability scan and testing
- Physical security assessment
- Security risk assessment
- Social engineering assessment
- Application assessment

▶ **NOTE**

Penetration tests are commonly referred to as "pen tests." The terms "black box," "white box," and "gray box" are also related. A black-box test makes no assumptions about the environment to be tested, whereas a white-box test provides complete knowledge and information, such as network diagrams, about the environment to be tested. Gray-box tests are variations between black-box and white-box tests.

Another common type of assessment, and one that seems to be more popularized in the media, is a penetration test. A **penetration test** is an assessment method that attempts to bypass controls and gain access to a specific system by simulating the actions of a would-be attacker. However, penetration tests operate under specific constraints and "rules of engagement." So they don't truly simulate the process a real adversary might take.

As a result, a penetration test is not necessarily the best means by which to judge the security of an information system. The test helps an organization understand its systems and gain insight into the level of effort an attacker might need to go through to penetrate the system. Penetration tests often reveal weaknesses or easily exploited vulnerabilities within a system. It is not uncommon for penetration tests to be a catalyst for selling management on the need to invest more money and/or effort in information security.

What Is an IT Security Audit?

An IT security **audit** is an independent assessment of an organization's internal policies, controls, and activities. You use an audit to assess the presence and effectiveness of IT controls and to ensure that those controls are compliant with stated policies. In addition, audits provide reasonable assurance that organizations are compliant with applicable regulations and other industry requirements.

Many people associate an audit as a function of accounting. This makes sense because audits are often a part of the examination of financial systems and records. Consider, however, how financial accounting has moved away from traditional paper ledgers and books to information computer systems. The integrity of information systems is vital to accurate financial reporting. In recent years, the integrity of information systems has gained additional attention to help prevent financial disasters that occurred at corporations such as **Enron** and **WorldCom**, as discussed in the case studies later in this chapter. Even beyond financial reporting, computer information systems have now become a valuable asset within organizations, and as a result need control and auditing.

There are many types of audits, such as the following:

- **Financial audits**—Determine whether an organization's financial statements accurately and fairly represent the financial position of the organization
- **Compliance audits**—Determine if an organization is adhering to applicable laws, regulations, and industry requirements
- **Operational audits**—Provide a review of policies, procedures, and operational controls across different departments to ensure processes are adequate

- **Investigative audits**—Investigate company records and processes based on suspicious activity or alleged violations
- **Information technology audits**—Address the risk exposures within IT systems and assess the controls and integrity of information systems

In addition, organizations are finding that integrated audits are more appropriate. Again consider the reliance on IT systems for transactions, storage of data, and communications across all operational aspects of an organization. Next, consider that many organizations—especially those that process payment cards and those that are publicly traded—are required to comply with numerous laws and regulations. As a result, it makes sense to be able to cover multiple regulations from a single audit event and prevent audit inefficiencies by treating compliance, financial, operational, and IT audits as silos. Aside from duplicating efforts, audit requirements can overlap between the various types of audits. As a result, it begins to make sense that an IT audit includes elements of a regulatory compliance audit or an operational audit includes elements of a financial and IT audit.

The scope of an IT audit often varies, but can involve any combination of the following:

- **Organizational**—Examines the management control over IT and related programs, policies, and processes
- **Compliance**—Pertains to ensuring that specific guidelines, laws, or requirements have been met
- **Application**—Involves the applications that are strategic to the organization, for example those typically used by finance and operations
- **Technical**—Examines the IT infrastructure and data communications

External or internal auditors typically perform IT security audits. In most large companies, the auditor is actually a team of auditors. An external auditor is independent of the organization and is often engaged from one of the big accounting and consulting firms. Publicly traded companies are required to engage external auditors. Internal auditors are employed by the organization that they audit. Unlike external auditors, internal auditors are not independent of the organization they audit. They directly report to the board of directors or a subcommittee of the board of directors. This is important so as not to be influenced by management and to ensure the integrity and honesty of their findings. Organizations often outsource their internal audit functions to an external consulting firm.

FYI

Who are the "big" auditors? That list is shrinking, but as of 2002, what was called the "Big Five" had become the "Big Four." These are the largest accounting and professional service firms. The Big Four includes PricewaterhouseCoopers, Deloitte, Ernst & Young, and KPMG. Arthur Andersen was dropped from the Big Five list as a result of the Enron collapse, for which they were the auditors. Arthur Andersen was indicted for obstruction of justice and subsequently ceased operations.

An effective IT security audit program should ultimately accomplish three goals:

- Provide an objective and independent review of an organization's policies, information systems, and controls.
- Provide reasonable assurance that appropriate and effective IT controls are in place.
- Provide audit recommendations for both corrective actions and improvement to controls.

In many cases, external auditors do not advise the client as would internal auditors. External auditors are typically limited to providing information about gaps discovered and leading the client to accepted principles. Internal auditors can provide recommendations for improvements; however, they should never be involved in the design or implementation of any system or control.

What Is Compliance?

Despite being a relatively simple term, the term "**compliance**" has become something of an enigma within many organizations. Different people view and define "compliance" in different ways. This is evident across different industries, within the same industries, and even within organizations.

The Merriam-Webster Online dictionary defines compliance as "the act or process of complying to a desire, demand, proposal, or regimen or to coercion." To comply is "to conform, submit, or adapt as required or requested." In regard to IT compliance, compliance pertains to two broad areas, internal and external. "Internal compliance" refers to an organization's ability to follow its own rules, which are typically based on defined policies. "External compliance" refers to the need or desire for an organization to follow rules and guidelines set forth by external organizations and initiatives. Although many external compliance mandates are regulatory in nature, other compliance initiatives also include standards and guidelines that must be followed as set forth by industry regulations.

The credit card industry is a prime example, which developed a set of security standards in an attempt to provide self-regulation. The majority of compliance mandates are, however, laws and regulations. Later in this book, you'll learn about numerous compliance mandates to which organizations may be required to adhere. In most cases, regulations do not provide specifics and are open for interpretation. Compliance frameworks, such as **Control Objectives for Information and related Technology (COBIT)**, and standards, such as NIST, help interpret how to comply with the regulations.

Unlike a simple traffic law, such as the requirement to stop at a red light, compliance laws and regulations are not always so clear. This is often another source of frustration for those with the responsibility of helping an organization comply. The general steps to meeting compliance include the following:

1. Interpret the regulation and how it applies
   to the organization.
2. Identify the gap or determine where the organization
   stands with the compliance mandate.
3. Devise a plan to close the gap.
4. Execute the plan.

> **NOTE**
> Meeting compliance often
> includes implementing mechanisms
> to prove that an organization
> has properly executed its plan.

Compliance is closely related to **risk management** and **governance** on all levels, be it
technical, procedural, or strategic. Risk management seeks to mitigate risk through
controls. For example, an organization identifies, evaluates, and takes action to lessen
its risk. Compliance helps risk management by verifying that the desired controls are
in place. Governance seeks to better run an organization using complete and accurate
information and management processes or controls. For example, a sound security policy
and comprehensive procedures are in place to implement the policy.

Compliance helps governance by ensuring such information and controls also satisfy
applicable standards or regulations. On a strategic level, compliance ensures an organization can effectively meet organizational goals and objectives as planned. This means
IT must ensure it is capable of delivering services to satisfy business needs and to stay
compliant with external laws and regulations.

How Does an Audit Differ from an Assessment?

Although there seem to be many similarities between an audit and assessment, there are
some stark differences. One is the mindset people tend to have of the word audit. "Audit"
brings to mind thoughts of distrust and punishment. Regardless of whether these feelings
are justified, these thoughts are based on several outcomes that can result from an audit:

- **Failure**—Audits are typically more clear-cut in the sense of pass or fail. It is possible
  to fail an audit, but most people don't think of an assessment in terms of pass or fail.
  Rather, you might see an assessment as an opportunity to assess the current state
  and make improvements as necessary.

- **Blame**—Audit findings might place blame on specific individuals or groups within
  an organization. Assessments, on the other hand, are nonattributive. That is, they
  don't place blame on an individual as being directly responsible for a poor finding.
  Many organizations use assessments to prepare for audits. Assessments provide
  a chance for improvement in a more comfortable and productive environment that
  helps facilitate the goals of the organization.

- **Consequences**—Audits can have consequences, many of which are negative.
  Consider that an organization can fail an audit and, subsequently, have blame
  attributed to an individual or group. In addition, noncompliance with regulatory
  and industry standards can carry stiff penalties. The consequences of failing
  an audit can create a sense of fear, whereas an assessment simply identifies gaps
  to improve security operations and achieve goals.

Security auditing, in general, must follow a more rigid approach and process over a security assessment. This is a key point, especially when you consider that an audit is an "assessment." Moreover, an audit contains the following unique characteristics:

* An auditor should never be involved in the auditing of processes, systems, or applications that they themselves designed or implemented.

* Audits are an independent evaluation. A security assessment may also be conducted independently, but it is not necessary. Many organizations use a combination of both.

* Audits follow a rigorous approach and are conducted according to accepted principles. This also requires that auditors are qualified. The approach taken for an assessment can fall across a wide spectrum, but in many cases, they have taken a cue from audits with well-defined approaches and frameworks.

* In the event an organization passes an audit, the organization typically receives some type of certification or confirmation. This is not the case for assessments.

* An audit is concerned about past results and performance, whereas an assessment considers previous and current results as well as expected performance.

You might find it helpful to evaluate a security audit and security assessment in more personal terms. Consider, for example, your own financial situation. When was the last time you personally assessed your financial state? Are you comfortable with your current situation? Are you on track to meet long-term goals? You can use many different tools and materials to do this yourself. Or you can hire a financial consultant or tax advisor to look at your situation, set goals, and identify gaps that exist in meeting those goals. Now imagine the U.S. Internal Revenue Service (IRS) knocking on your door to audit you. Granted, an individual IRS audit seems more adversarial. Keep in mind that is why companies go through audits in the first place. A successful audit enables a business or organization to be more profitable and/or successful without risk of penalties or being deemed incompliant.

Why Are Governance and Compliance Important?

Without proper governance in place, an organization can have neither effective risk management nor compliance. A common theme thus far has been the reliance on IT throughout the organization. As a result, IT can have a tremendous impact on either the success or failure of an organization. The interest in formally governing the use and application of IT should come as no surprise. IT is now woven into the fabric of business and has made organizations dependent on information and the systems that help generate and store information. In addition, IT will continue to provide opportunities for competitive advantage and reduction of costs throughout the organization. On the other hand, IT systems are subject to numerous threats that continue to evolve and seek to exploit vulnerabilities.

At a fundamental level, internal compliance to corporate policies is critical to the success of any business. Risk management means deeming some risks acceptable so a company may accomplish their business goals. Compliance, therefore, embraces the organizational mission, and noncompliance can harm or even impede business.

Regulatory compliance benefits organizations, consumers, and shareholders. Regulatory compliance protects the reputation and integrity of the organizations that are required to comply. It considers the interests of the consumer and shareholders. Regulatory compliance also has a farther-reaching economic impact on ensuring public confidence in organizations and capital markets.

Case Study: Enron

Enron Corporation was a U.S.-based energy company that at one point was the seventh-largest company in the United States and the largest trader of natural gas and electricity in the country. Enron came about in the mid-1980s, focusing on the natural gas market. By the 1990s, it had pursued a diversification strategy to achieve growth. Subsequently, Enron got involved with trading and ownership in electric, coal, steel, paper, water, and broadband capacity.

Enron collapsed in 2001 and filed bankruptcy, which at the time was the largest bankruptcy in history. The collapse was a result of a complex and methodical accounting scandal. The fallout was massive, resulting in thousands of employees who were laid off and who lost their life savings plans that were tied to the company's stock. In addition, shareholders saw a loss of $11 billion. Economically, the disaster perpetuated a lack of trust in the stock market and eroded public confidence.

Enron's auditing firm, Arthur Andersen, had attested to Enron's financial health for years, despite widespread fraud and hidden losses at Enron. In addition, the auditing and consulting firm assisted Enron in deal structuring and other consultative practices. Enron paid Arthur Andersen a combined $52 million in consulting fees in the year 2000 alone. Arthur Andersen was eventually convicted of obstruction of justice as a result of shredding paper documents and destroying electronic documents related to their client. Arthur Andersen's involvement with Enron also led to the discovery of other audit discrepancies, including those at WorldCom.

NOTE

WorldCom would go on to surpass Enron as the largest bankruptcy. Ultimately, it was the Enron fiasco that led to the downfall of Arthur Andersen as one of the largest auditing and consulting firms.

Although complex and occurring over a period of many years, investigative findings discovered that Enron used several complicated and questionable accounting methods:

- Reduced their tax payments and inflated their income and profits
- Increased their stock price and credit ratings
- Hid losses in off-balance sheet subsidiaries
- Funneled money to themselves and acquaintances
- Misrepresented Enron's financial condition in public reports

The Enron Board of Directors was faulted on several accounts. One of these was not being involved in the examination of terms related to moving debt off the company's balance sheets. They missed the chance to uncover fundamental flaws in the accounting practices at the company. A report written by the special committee investigating Enron described what went wrong with management: "We found a systematic and pervasive attempt by Enron's management to misrepresent the Company's financial condition." Enron's culture was one that seemed to cast aside traditional controls. In fact, the investigating committee also stated that Enron had an "across-the-board failure of controls and ethics at almost every level of the company." The report continues, stating "a flawed idea, self-enrichment by employees, inadequately designed controls, poor implementation, inattentive oversight, simple (and not so simple) account mistakes, and overreaching in a culture that appears to have encouraged pushing the limits."

Enron has become in many ways the premier symbol of fraud, corruption, and audit failure. The scandal also resulted in a host of new regulations and legislation being enacted, including the **Sarbanes-Oxley Act**, which is covered in depth in Chapter 2. As you will discover, this act addresses many of the shortcomings and lessons learned from the Enron scandal.

The following are some questions for further thought and discovery:

- How do a company's acquisitions relate to risk management and governance?
- The Enron scandal resulted in steps to improve standards, controls, and accountabilities. How much do morals contribute to such events and what can be done to address this issue?
- What financial incentives may have been in place for Enron's consulting firm to perhaps have lax auditing standards?
- Given the large sums paid on consultancy fees, is it possible that talented auditors are focused on consulting while less-experienced employees audit?
- How might a control framework for IT that is more closely aligned with business processes have prevented this?
- How could adequate controls on IT systems and financial applications have helped?
- Do you think that controls designed to prevent or detect fraud were in place? How important is the monitoring of such controls, and how should access be controlled?

Case Study: WorldCom

Prior to filing bankruptcy in 2002, WorldCom was the second largest telecommunications company in the world. It handled Internet data traffic globally and accounted for more international voice traffic than any other company.

WorldCom grew quickly from its modest beginning in 1983, and achieved its tremendous growth through 65 acquisitions. In the 1990s, the company had made some large acquisitions, including MCI Communications. Through this period, WorldCom had spent approximately $60 billion and accumulated approximately $41 billion in debt. The MCI acquisition was the largest merger in U.S. history at the time.

The market value of WorldCom continued to grow substantially through these acquisitions, and high expectations continued to be placed on the company. This generated pressure to keep the stock price at elevated levels, which in turn allowed WorldCom to continue its acquisition spree. A proposed merger in 2000 with Sprint would have eclipsed the merger with MCI; however, the merger was disapproved and WorldCom started to unravel. In an attempt to maintain its earnings, WorldCom liberally interpreted accounting rules to make its financial statements seem profitable. The company soon moved from liberal interpretation into outright fraud by creating false entries.

A team of internal auditors became suspicious over numerous financial oddities and began investigating, but the auditors encountered problems. They tried to discuss financial irregularities with WorldCom's external auditors, Arthur Andersen, who did not fully cooperate. Responsible to the WorldCom chief financial officer (CFO) at the time, the internal audit group raised issues with the CFO but was pressured to stop. The internal auditors persisted and eventually uncovered what would become the largest account fraud in U.S. history.

How could this have happened, and what were some of the events and situations that led to this mess?

- The board of directors became simply a "rubber stamp."
- The board of directors allowed the chief executive officer (CEO) and CFO of WorldCom to have unfettered power.
- WorldCom acquired many companies without a strategy for linking them properly.
- The board of directors approved deals worth billions of dollars with little discussion.
- Little oversight of debt accumulation existed.
- Little oversight of company loans made to the CEO existed.
- The company lacked internal controls and transparency.
- External consultants failed to apply techniques consistent with their risk rating of the company.
- Internal auditing was underqualified and focused on nonauditing activities.

Consider the questions previously discussed in the Enron case. What parallels can you draw between these two disasters? How can information technology be used as a tool across all lines of business within an organization? How can IT better align with the organizational processes?

Resulting regulations have had far-reaching impacts on information technology—specifically controls and the auditing of those controls. These controls include general controls, which are embedded in IT services, as well as application controls, which are embedded in business applications. Why are these controls important? Why is the auditing of these controls important?

What If Our Organization Does Not Comply with Compliance Laws?

Of course you wouldn't break a law, right? But asking what if your organization doesn't comply with compliance laws is a fair question. Let's look at an example of an individual "compliance" issue to understand why.

It is a law to come to a complete stop at a stop sign, yet many people ignore it. This scenario is actually a form of risk management. Many people consider it an acceptable risk to approach slowly and continue on if there is no traffic, without coming to a complete stop. The threat of another car exists, yet many people feel safe enough with the slow approach and "rolling stop." There is always the threat of a police officer pulling you over and issuing a ticket. Yet how often is this enforced? If it were, what is the punishment? Given the likelihood of being pulled over by law enforcement, combined with what is likely a bearable fine, many people decide the risk is low and the benefit of noncompliance outweighs the risk.

> **NOTE**
>
> Don't forget about the other negative effects that noncompliance can have on an organization, beyond the threat of fines and imprisonment. For example:
>
> - Legal fees resulting from infringements contained within many regulations
> - Brand damage and lost revenue as consumers abandon a business
> - Negative effect upon stock price, hurting shareholder value
> - Increases in the cost of capital

Organizations have spent and continue to spend large sums of money to achieve and maintain regulatory and industry compliance. This is especially true as regulations have placed greater accountability on individuals within an organization. Noncompliance can result in huge fines as well as jail time. Some regulations are subject to strict liability. Strict liability means even if there wasn't intent, government agencies can levy huge fines on organizations and some individuals can spend years in prison. Even greater punishments are in store where intent can be proven!

In addition to financial and reputational consequences of noncompliance, organizations can also incur operational consequences. This can happen, for example, in the case of compliance standards imposed by the payment card industry. For example, potential consequences include payment-card imposed operational restrictions and even loss of card-processing privileges.

The **Payment Card Industry Data Security Standard (PCI DSS)** applies to organizations that process credit cards. Companies that meet a specific threshold for large volumes of credit card transactions are required to achieve compliance. This is done via an audit by an independent Qualified Security Assessor (QSA). You'll learn about this standard in detail in Chapter 2.

Case Study: TJX Credit Card Breach

Imagine being the chief information officer (CIO) of one of the largest department store chains in the United States. Now imagine your CEO publicly announces that the company has just become the victim of the largest known theft of credit card data in history. This is a nightmare situation for any IT security professional, and this is what happened to The TJX Companies.

The TJX Companies, Incorporated is a large off-price retailer of apparel and home fashion. The company operates under several brands, including the T.J. Maxx and Marshalls stores. On January 17, 2007, TJX announced it had become a victim of an intrusion into portions of its information systems that process and store customer transaction data.

An unauthorized intruder first accessed systems in July 2005, and unauthorized access continued through mid-January 2007. On December 18, 2006, TJX discovered suspicious software on its systems, and immediately initiated an investigation along with leading computer security firms. Within a few days, TJX had notified law enforcement officials and met with the U.S. Department of Justice and the U.S. Secret Service to brief them on the discovery. Shortly thereafter, TJX notified contracting banks and payment card processing companies. Before the public release of the incident, the company had notified the U.S. Federal Trade Commission (FTC), the U.S. Securities and Exchange Commission (SEC), and the Canadian authorities.

At the time, this had evolved into the biggest credit card breach in history. Conservative estimates initially put the number at over 45 million credit and debit cards breached, as well as the personal information of hundreds of thousands of customers, including Social Security numbers and driver's license numbers.

Although the exact details of the breach aren't clear, what is known is that the breach initially occurred as a result of the attackers targeting the wireless network of one of TJX's retail stores. The wireless network used Wired Equivalent Privacy (WEP) as an encryption method, which even at the time had proven inadequate. The alternative was Wi-Fi Protected Access (WPA), which was introduced to replace WEP. Once the attackers penetrated this weak link, they eavesdropped on usernames and passwords used to log on to TJX's main systems in Framingham, Massachusetts. Eventually, the attackers created their own accounts on the main system and collected sensitive data.

 NOTE

Initially, the TJX attackers accessed only historical data. To capture live transaction data, the attackers installed software that recorded the traffic. This enabled the attackers to steal credit card data as customer transactions were occurring in the store.

In the aftermath, TJX has become the poster child for credit card breaches. The incident has also generated a lot of conversation and debate around adequate security controls for confidential personal information. Much of the blame for this incident was placed on the poorly secured wireless networks, but what type of defense in depth or compensating controls existed? The FTC charged TJX with failure to maintain proper security controls, specifically citing the lack of firewalls, wireless security, failure to patch vulnerabilities, and failure to update antivirus signatures.

The following are highlights of the fallout resulting from the breach. TJX:

- Agreed to pay $9.75 million to settle state investigations.
- Settled with the FTC. As a result, TJX had to create a comprehensive security program to protect the confidentiality of personal information it collects. In addition, TJX must submit to a third-party audit of the program every two years for the next two decades.

NOTE

The TJX breach has since been eclipsed in size. Heartland Payment Systems announced a breach in 2009, which resulted in 130 million compromised payment card records. The attacker of Heartland Payment Systems was indicted in August of 2009, and was also the leader of the TJX breach.

- Settled lawsuits brought by consumers and banker groups. Customers were provided with a special, three-day sale and vouchers as a result of settlement of class-action lawsuits.
- Settled with Visa and MasterCard for almost $41 million.
- Was required to implement a data-security program to ensure that this type of incident could never happen again.
- Offered three years of credit monitoring to about 450,000 people who needed to provide their driver's licenses for transactions that occurred in the stores.
- Set aside $250 million for breach-related costs. Many analysts believe this number could ultimately be much higher.

Unlike the collapse of Enron and WorldCom, TJX did not break any laws but was simply not compliant with stated payment card processing guidelines. Court documents filed by the banks that sued TJX indicated that TJX did not comply with 9 of the 12 broad provisions within the standard established for the payment card industry. Although the breach has been costly for TJX, it is a multibillion dollar retailer that has survived and made appropriate adjustments. Smaller organizations, however, might not have survived.

Although it costs money to implement proper controls and procedure for compliance, noncompliance and security breaches have their own costs. You learned fines can be levied for noncompliance, but what about the costs of a breach? Forrester Research puts the cost *per record* breached at anywhere between $90 and $305, depending on the type of breach and how regulated of an industry the breach occurs within. Consider the following categories from where costs can occur following a breach:

- **Discovery, notification, and response**—Legal counsel, mailings, call center support, discounted product offers
- **Lost productivity**—Employees' attention diverted or put on other tasks requiring attention
- **Opportunity cost**—Loss of customers and attaining new customers
- **Regulatory fines**—FTC, PCI, Sarbanes-Oxley
- **Restitution**—Money set aside for payment
- **Additional security and audit requirements**—Those levied as a result of a breach
- **Other liabilities**

The following are some questions for further thought and discovery:

- Consider the reasons why TJX might have had the weaker WEP encryption configured. Was this the internal standard? Did retail equipment perhaps not support newer, more secure methods? If so, should compensating controls have been in place, and what types?
- Do you feel that TJX properly handled the incident upon discovery of the breach? Consider how incident-response procedures are important to the IT security program.
- Had TJX collected and retained unnecessary personal data? What are the risks of holding onto data?
- Did TJX understand where customer data resided, how it was transmitted, and whether it was encrypted?
- If the data was encrypted, could the breach have been possible? Is it enough to just encrypt sensitive data? What about the cryptographic keys that perform the encryption/decryption of the data? How and where are those stored? Is this defined in a policy? If so, how is it audited?
- What were the results of TJX's payment-card processing audits and third-party vulnerability audits?
- Were weaknesses and vulnerabilities within TJX discovered and documented through internal security assessments?

CHAPTER SUMMARY

Conducting audits and assessments of IT environments has increasingly become more important and visible since the collapse of companies such as Enron and WorldCom in the early to mid-2000s. Although they might share similar qualities, the differences between an audit and an assessment can be great. Likewise, internal auditors and external auditors have much of the same functions, yet some important differences in their roles and expectations. Regardless, assessments, audits, and auditors are all key components to ensuring a successful risk management and compliance strategy. Adequate governance and oversight of these activities helps ensure that businesses don't follow the path that Enron and WorldCom did, and also helps in preventing incidents such as what TJX went through.

KEY CONCEPTS AND TERMS

Assurance

Audit

Compliance

Control Objectives for
    Information and related
    Technology (COBIT)

Controls

Enron

Governance

National Institute of Standards
    and Technology (NIST)

Objectives

Payment Card Industry Data
    Security Standard (PCI DSS)

Penetration testing

Risk

Risk management

Sarbanes-Oxley Act of 2002

The TJX Companies,
    Incorporated

WorldCom

CHAPTER 1 ASSESSMENT

1. A security assessment is a method for proving the strength of security systems.

   A. True
   B. False

2. Categorizing information and information systems and then selecting and implementing appropriate security controls is part of a _____.

3. Whereas only qualified auditors perform security audits, anyone may do security assessments.

   A. True
   B. False

4. NIST 800-53A provides _____.

5. Which one of the following is *not* a method used for conducting an assessment of security controls?

A. Examine
B. Interview
C. Test
D. Remediate

6. Which of the following is an assessment method that attempts to bypass controls and gain access to a specific system by simulating the actions of a would-be attacker?

A. Policy review
B. Penetration test
C. Standards review
D. Controls audit
E. Vulnerability scan

7. An IT security audit is an _____ assessment of an organization's internal policies, controls, and activities.

8. Which of the following best describes an audit used to determine if a Fortune 500 health care company is adhering to the Sarbanes-Oxley and HIPAA regulations?

A. IT audit
B. Operational audit
C. Compliance audit
D. Financial audit
E. Investigative audit

9. The internal audit function may be outsourced to an external consulting firm.

A. True
B. False

10. Compliance initiatives typically are efforts around all EXCEPT which one of the following?

A. To adhere to internal policies and standards
B. To adhere to regulatory requirements
C. To adhere to industry standards and best practices
D. To adhere to an auditor's recommendation

11. At all levels of an organization, compliance is closely related to which of the following?

A. Governance
B. Risk management
C. Government
D. Risk assessment
E. Both A and B
F. Both C and D

12. Which one of the following is true in regard to audits and assessments?

A. Assessments typically result in a pass or fail grade, whereas audits result in a list of recommendations to improve controls.
B. Assessments are attributive and audits are not.
C. An audit is typically a precursor to an assessment.
D. An audit may be conducted independently of an organization, whereas internal IT staff always conducts an IT security assessment.
E. Audits can result in blame being placed upon an individual.

13. Noncompliance with regulatory standards may result in which of the following?

A. Brand damage
B. Fines
C. Imprisonment
D. All of the above
E. B and C only

14. Which of the following companies engaged in fraudulent activity and subsequently filed for bankruptcy?

A. WorldCom
B. Enron
C. TJX
D. All of the above
E. A and B only

15. Some regulations are subject to _____, which means even if there wasn't intent of noncompliance, an organization can still incur large fines.

Overview of U.S. Compliance Laws

T O STAY COMPLIANT WITH REGULATIONS first means you must interpret the regulation. You must understand the gap between the regulation and your organization. The next step is coming up with a plan. Finally, you must execute the plan and implement measures to report compliance.

Without compliance laws and industry regulations, compliance means adhering to an organization's internal policies. However, it is likely that—whatever your industry—compliance laws exist to which you must adhere.

Many industry standards and government regulations affect IT operations. Remember each country has its own laws and regulations. Thus, the number of compliance laws and regulations expands greatly. In this chapter, you will learn about many of the major regulations. Keep in mind that you are only scratching the surface. Other compliance regulations exist and are often specific to a particular industry.

Chapter 2 Topics

This chapter covers the following topics and concepts:

- What public and private sector regulatory requirements are
- What the Federal Information Security Management Act is
- What the U.S. Department of Defense requirements are
- What the Sarbanes-Oxley Act, Gramm-Leach-Bliley Act, and Health Insurance Portability and Accountability Act compliance requirements are
- What the Children's Internet Protection Act and the Family Educational Rights and Privacy Act are
- What the Payment Card Industry Data Security Standard is
- What the Red Flags Rule is

Chapter 2 Goals

When you complete this chapter, you will be able to:

- Describe the goals and requirements for key acts of Congress
- Understand Department of Defense requirements and the importance of information assurance
- Describe the goals and requirements of the Payment Card Industry Data Security Standard
- Describe various regulations concerning protection of health, accounting, and other information

Introduction to Public and Private Sector Regulatory Requirements

Dealing with regulatory requirements is a hard task for many organizations. Troubles come from two directions. First, information technology personnel rarely have a legal background. Second, most requirements lack technical depth. This is because people drafting the regulations lack the information technology background. Many regulations are vague in their requirements. Therefore, proper technologies, depth of controls, and control frameworks become an important tool. Part 2 of this book provides an overview of different frameworks you can leverage.

Nevertheless, it is first important to understand why these requirements exist. In addition, you must have a broad understanding of which requirements exist.

technical TIP

Your internal policies should execute the regulatory policies with which you need to comply. Policies should follow a framework or complete structure. Having a framework demonstrates a company's planned approach. Meanwhile, the policies demonstrate a company's drive and support to be compliant. Take the time to properly build your internal policies. This rids you of many headaches in the event you must undergo an audit. In other words, ensuring your policies follow a solid framework to comply with different regulations really pays off.

WARNING

There is an irony in regulatory compliance laws. Although the laws might appear complicated, they make high-level points that are simple to understand. A problem occurs when people interpret regulations in different ways.

 WARNING

If you do business in other countries, you need to consider the requirements and compliance laws of those foreign countries. In addition, many U.S.-based companies rely on foreign, third-party service providers. This could result in noncompliance with U.S. regulations.

Regulatory requirements exist at different levels. Those levels include state, federal, and international. In addition, industry consortiums propose requirements. It is important to know which regulations apply to your organization. This helps you ensure you stay compliant and prevents trying to solve the same problem twice. In most cases, you should consult corporate counsel or legal to help identify which regulations apply.

So what sources do people consult for IT compliance requirements? In 2005, the Burton Group asked attendees at one of its conferences this very question. The results were as follows:

- Text of laws, 28 percent
- Administrative code, 13 percent
- External auditors, 23 percent
- Internal auditors, 18 percent
- Industry associations, 13 percent
- Third-party guidelines, 5 percent

Regulatory Acts of Congress

Congress enacts major legislation known as "statutes." The president of the United States signs these **acts of Congress** into law. Examples of such acts include the E-Government Act of 2002, the Sarbanes-Oxley (SOX) Act, and the **Health Insurance Portability and Accountability Act (HIPAA)**.

After such acts become law, various government agencies create and enforce the federal regulations authorized by those acts. Some examples of these government agencies are the Food and Drug Administration (FDA), Environmental Protection Agency (EPA), U.S. Securities and Exchange Commission (SEC), Federal Trade Commission (FTC), and Federal Communications Commission (FCC) to name a few.

Congress first typically passes a statute to address a problem, such as social or economic. These are considered enabling legislation. It allows the **regulatory agencies** to create the necessary regulations to implement the law. For example, the FCC creates regulations under the Children's Internet Protection Act (CIPA). The SEC creates regulations under the Sarbanes-Oxley Act.

Regulatory compliance is nothing new. However, government oversight and strong compliance regulations greatly increased in the early 2000s. This was mainly due to corporate scandals—Enron, WorldCom, and others. Consider how quickly the Web and other information technologies advanced. Then, the increased focus on IT and IT security becomes more apparent. Yet regulatory requirements and industry standards are not without their critics. Critics accuse requirements regulating publicly traded companies of putting U.S. corporations at a disadvantage. At the same time, they discourage listing on the U.S. stock exchanges. Further, critics describe laws regulating federal information systems as bureaucratic without helping security. Furthermore, consider the payment card standards. Critics call these standards unfair for small businesses, and criticize the standards for failing to provide enough security.

Federal Information Security Management Act (FISMA)

The **Federal Information Security Management Act of 2002 (FISMA)** is contained within the E-Government Act of 2002, Public Law 107-347, as Title III. This act grants the importance of sound information security practices. It also controls the interest of national security and the economic well-being of the United States.

The purpose of FISMA is to do the following:

- Provide a framework for effective information security resources that support federal operations, data, and infrastructure.
- Accept the interconnectedness of IT. Ensure effective risk management is in place.
- Ensure coordination of information security efforts between civilian, national security, and law enforcement communities.
- Facilitate the development and ongoing monitoring of required minimum controls to protect federal information systems and data.
- Provide for increased oversight of federal agency information security programs.
- Recognize that information technology solutions may be acquired from commercial organizations. Leave the acquisition decisions to the individual agencies.

The need for FISMA started during the 1990s. Government agencies became more like commercial organizations. They started to transition from traditional mainframe computing to internetworked systems. As the Web became commonplace, federal agencies started to develop their own Web sites and offer online services. There was a sudden awareness that systems were more open and vulnerable than before. This eventually got the attention of Congress.

FISMA tasked the National Institute of Standards and Technology (NIST) to develop and set standards and guidelines. These apply only to federal information systems. Standards help categorize information and the systems. They are based on a risk-based approach. They include the minimum information security controls. For example, standards include the management, operational, and technical controls to apply to the information systems.

In support of FISMA, NIST developed the following publications:

- FIPS Publication 199, "Standards for Security Categorization of Federal Information and Information Systems"
- FIPS Publication 200, "Minimum Security Requirements for Federal Information and Information Systems"
- NIST Special Publication 800-18, "Guide for Developing Security Plans for Federal Information Systems"
- NIST Special Publication 800-30, "Risk Management Guide for Information Technology Systems"
- NIST Special Publication 800-37, "Guide for the Security Certification and Accreditation of Federal Information Systems"
- NIST Special Publication 800-39, "Managing Risk from Information Systems: An Organizational Perspective"
- NIST Special Publication 800-53, "Recommended Security Controls for Federal Information Systems"
- NIST Special Publication 800-53A, "Guide for Assessing the Security Controls in Federal Information Systems"
- NIST Special Publication 800-59, "Guidelines for Identifying an Information System as a National Security System"
- NIST Special Publication 800-60, "Guide for Mapping Types of Information and Information Systems to Security Categories"

To comply with FISMA, the appointed inspector general of the agency performs a separate, annual evaluation. The evaluation first tests the value of the IT security policies, procedures, and practices. A subset of the information systems within the particular agency is tested. If no inspector general exists, an independent external auditor performs it. The external auditor submits the results to the Office of Management and Budget (OMB).

The OMB is a cabinet-level office within the Executive Office of the President of the United States with oversight responsibilities. The OMB compiles the data from each agency. The OMB then prepares an annual report to Congress on compliance with the act.

At first, it appears only federal agencies need to worry about compliance, but this is not true. Federal agencies, for example, must care about their own systems as well as the systems of other contractors or organizations supporting the agencies. Any company or organization that expects to conduct business with the federal government needs to concern itself with FISMA.

 TIP

The annual reports submitted to Congress from the OMB concerning FISMA compliance are publicly available online. You can find them at *http://www.whitehouse.gov/omb/legislative_reports*.

U.S. Department of Defense (DoD) Requirements

The United States Department of Defense (DoD) is a federal department. It is responsible for all agencies of the government relating to national security and the military. The DoD imposes many requirements upon the management of their information systems for both DoD-related systems. The same goes for organizations that work with, contract, and provide services for the DoD. These requirements are within many federal laws and regulations. These laws span over a period of decades. Given the fast-paced change around information technology, requirements have been rapidly evolving. This is especially true as systems have moved from traditional mainframe computing to more distributed and interconnected computing.

Information resource management (IRM) is the process of managing information resources to improve performance and accomplish the mission of defense agencies. The Paperwork Reduction Act of 1980 introduced IRM into law. This act provides the OMB with oversight concerning IRM. This oversight assumes that within the OMB's policies, individual agencies can maintain their own IRM.

In later years, various amendments strengthened the original implementation of the law. Most notably, agencies needed to develop processes to acquire, control, and assess information systems. In spite of these laws, the 1990s saw a large rise of distributed networking technology. This only created more IT management issues for the DoD.

In 1996, Senator William Cohen led further reform. The reform streamlined the process of acquisition of IT resources. The position of chief information officer (CIO) was formed within federal departments and agencies. This CIO position was previously the senior IRM official. Now the title was more like the civilian role and reported directly to the agency head. This gave it a more strategic focus with greater accountability to solve the IT problems plaguing the agencies.

There are many laws and regulations to the DoD. These laws are both external and internal. They guide the operation, management, and protection of information systems. A summary of the key laws, regulations, and policies include the following:

- **Paperwork Reduction Act of 1995**—Furthers the goal of the original act to have federal agencies take more responsibility and be held more publicly accountable in reducing the paperwork on the public

- **Clinger-Cohen Act of 1996**—Formerly the Information Technology Management Reform Act, it improves the acquisition, use, and disposal of federal IT resources

- **House of Representatives Report 104-450 Conference Report**—Contains provisions for acquisition and management issues related to IT

- **OMB Circular, A-130, Management of Federal Information Resources**—Includes procedural guidelines for the management of federal information resources

- **OMB Circular A-11, Section 53, Information Technology and E-Government**—Allows the agencies and OMB to review and assess IT spending across the federal government to provide for more effective operations, including ensuring privacy and compliance with other acts

- **Designation of the Chief Information Officer of the Department of Defense memorandum**—Designates the role of CIO within the DoD

- **10 U.S.C. Section 2223, Information Technology: Additional Responsibilities of Chief Information Officers**—Assigns additional responsibilities for CIOs

- **10 U.S.C. Section 2224, Defense Information Assurance Program**—Provides for protection and defense of DoD information and information systems, and ensures availability, integrity, authentication, nonrepudiation, and rapid restoration of information and information systems

- **Federal Information Security Management Act of 2002 (FISMA)**—Establishes a framework for effective information security in regard to information resources that support federal operations

- **E-Government Act of 2002**—Improves the management of electronic government services by establishing a framework that requires using the Internet and related technologies to improve citizen access to government information services

- **DoD Directive 5144.01, Assistant Security of Defense for Networks and Information Integration/DoD Chief Information Officer**—Assigns responsibilities, functions, relationships, and authorities to the DoD CIO

- **DoD Directive 8000.01, Management of the Department of Defense Information Enterprise**—Provides guidance for creating an "information advantage" for the DoD and those that support its mission

Certification and Accreditation (C&A)

As part of FISMA, all federal systems and applications must adhere to well-known security requirements. These requirements are documented and authorized. This process is known as **Certification and Accreditation (C&A)**. It is essentially a process of auditing federal systems before putting them in a production environment. C&A recertifies every three years. The C&A process ensures that efforts are made to mitigate risks. Security controls on information systems must be properly implemented and maintained. It supports risk-management activities. At a high level, C&A allows the government to conduct consistent and repeatable assessments of security controls. They also gain awareness into risks and allow authorized officials to more confidently accredit or validate a system. The accreditation aspect is an accountable process. An official reviews the applied security controls. Then, the official approves or accepts risks to the system and organization.

Accreditation holds you accountable for the decision. Therefore, it is important to make the decision after reviewing documentation and supporting evidence. All must be complete, valid, and accurate. This is the certification part of C&A. Certification includes the technical controls as well as the management and operational controls.

Certification and Accreditation use three methodologies:

- DoD Information Assurance Certification and Accreditation Process (DIACAP)
- National Information Assurance Certification and Accreditation Process (NIACAP)
- NIST Guide for the Security Certification and Accreditation of Federal Information Systems

Of the three, most agencies, including civilian organizations, embrace the NIST methodology.

All three methodologies are similar in their intent and require a thorough review of the systems. The information system owner submits a package of documents or accreditation package. The accrediting authority audits the package. A decision is made about accreditation for the information system. An accreditation package includes the following documents:

FYI

DIACAP, the first C&A methodology discussed, replaces the DoD Information Technology System Certification and Accreditation Process (DITSCAP) as the chief process for evaluating and accrediting Department of Defense information systems. At the time of this writing, DoD agencies and military branches are currently switching over. For example, the Department of the Navy expects their transition to be complete in fiscal year 2012.

- **System security plan**—The requirements, agreed security controls, and supporting documents. Examples are network diagrams, data flows, and risk assessment.
- **Security Assessment report**—The evaluation results of security controls. This report might also include recommendations.
- **Plan of action and milestones**—The details mitigating controls. You may plan or apply controls to reduce vulnerabilities. You can also plan or apply measures to correct any deficiencies.

Conducting the C&A process requires four phases. Assigned individuals carry out the various tasks in each phase. Figure 2-1 illustrates the following four phases:

- **Initiation**—Before certification begins, initiation ensures all parties are in agreement with the plan. Initiation also ensures that appropriate documentation is completed.
- **Security certification**—Security certification involves the process of actually assessing the security controls on the information system. It assesses controls to ensure they are implemented and operating as planned. A subsequent plan notes and addresses any deficiencies for remediation. When the assessment is done, the security certification documentation is created.
- **Security accreditation**—With the security certification information, the system might receive accreditation. Remaining system vulnerabilities are considered. If the resulting risk is acceptable, accreditation results in one of three ways:
  - Authorization
  - Denial of authorization
  - Interim authorization
- **Continuous monitoring**—Continuous monitoring provides ongoing assurance that the security controls stay in place. Configuration management and security monitoring alerts the authorizing authority if changes affect systems.

FIGURE 2-1

Four phases of C&A.

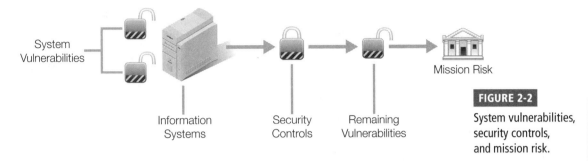

Security certification and accreditation pertain to a specific information system. They don't determine the risk level to the agency. To determine risk at the higher agency level, you must take a more holistic view. This must consider all information systems. Figure 2-2 shows how information system controls and vulnerabilities relate to the agency's mission risk.

Information Assurance (IA)

Department of Defense Directive 8500.1 establishes policy and assigns responsibilities under Section 2224 of title 10 USC. They achieve DoD **information assurance (IA)** through defense in depth and integrating personnel, operations, and technology. IA includes all DoD-owned and DoD-controlled information systems that use DoD information. This is regardless of sensitivity. Information assurance is the controls that protect and defend information and information systems by ensuring **confidentiality**, **integrity**, and **availability**. It also provides authentication and nonrepudiation.

DoD needs to protect information and the systems that support that information. Information assurance grasps the natural vulnerabilities in systems that transmit, store, or process data. The vulnerability stems from the following:

- Reliance upon commercial information technology solutions and services
- Increased complexity through interconnectedness
- Fast pace in which technology changes
- Distributed and nonstandard management structure of a global network
- Low cost of entry for attackers

Protecting the confidentiality, integrity, and availability are common security objectives for information systems. This forms the foundation for information assurance.

- **Confidentiality**—Ensuring that information is not disclosed to unauthorized sources. Loss of confidentiality occurs when data is open to some unauthorized entity or process.
- **Integrity**—Ensuring the protection against unauthorized modification or destruction of data. Integrity also includes the quality of an information system regarding logical completeness and reliability of the hardware, software, and data structures.
- **Availability**—Ensuring the timely and reliable access to data and services for authorized users.

> **NOTE**
>
> Confidentiality, integrity, and availability (CIA) are often referred to as the security triad or the CIA triad.

Figure 2-3 shows these three security objectives as a protective triangle. If any side of the triangle fails, security fails. In other words, threats to the confidentiality, integrity, or availability represent risk.

In addition, the DoD considers authentication and nonrepudiation as two additional measures. These two are joined along with confidentiality, integrity, and availability. Authentication establishes the substance of a transmission, message, and originator. It also verifies an entity that has authorized access to information. Nonrepudiation provides assurance of proof of delivery and proof of identity. This way, neither party can later deny having processed or received the data.

You can easily describe implementing information assurance as a system for managing risk. It is built upon five principles defined within DoD Directive 8500.2, "Information Assurance (IA) Implementation," These five competencies are as follows:

- The ability to assess security needs and capabilities
- The ability to develop a purposeful security design or configuration that adheres to a common architecture and maximizes the use of common services
- The ability to implement required controls for safeguards
- The ability to test and verify
- The ability to manage changes to an established baseline in a secure manner

In 1996, a U.S. federal law called the Information Technology Management Reform Act of 1996 was passed. The goal was to improve how the federal government acquires, uses, and disposes of information technology. The act is now called the Clinger-Cohen Act (CCA), named after its cosponsors. The CCA worked with other related legislation to spawn the DoD's Acquisition of IA strategy, DoD 5000.02 to ensure compliance. The Acquisition Information Assurance Strategy provides the groundwork for Certification and Accreditation. However, it is a separate process, which requires compliance. Information assurance compliance is required for any IT system, including those IT-based processes that are outsourced.

FIGURE 2-3

The CIA triad.

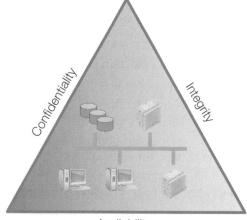

Availability

Beyond Information Assurance—CIIA

Information assurance as a concept has been around for a long time. It is the defined strategy for the Department of Defense since the early 2000s. However, emphasis on information systems and threats has risen. The idea of assurance of information has grown to better protect the DoD from current and future threats. In addition, it accelerates the secure change to a more network-centric setting. The new strategy calls for **Cyber, Identity, and Information Assurance (CIIA)**.

The Department of Defense sets up information assurance from "five pillars." The five pillars are assurance of confidentiality, integrity, availability, authentication, and nonrepudiation. One criticism might be that authentication and nonrepudiation are the only means of assuring the security triad. On the other hand, confidentiality, integrity, and availability are attributes of the information or information systems.

In 2009, the DoD issued new guidance replacing the DoD 2004 Information Assurance Strategy. This new strategy is all about information assurance. The strategy introduced two new levels of assurance. The two new levels are cyber assurance and identity assurance. Cyber assurance prepares network-centric missions and supporting infrastructure to respond to harmful events more quickly. Identity assurance is about maintaining identity, security, and privacy.

Sarbanes-Oxley Act (SOX)

The Sarbanes-Oxley Act of 2002, also known as Sarbox or SOX, is a U.S. federal law. It is the result of the Public Company Account Reform and Investor Protection Act and Corporate Accountability and Responsibility Act. Sarbanes-Oxley dramatically changed how public companies do business.

The bill stems from the fraud and accounting debacles at companies such as Enron and WorldCom. Former President Bush characterized the act "as the most far reaching reforms of American business practices since the time of Franklin Delano Roosevelt." The act's primary purpose was to restore public confidence in the financial reporting of publicly traded companies. As a result, the act mandated many reforms to enhance corporate responsibility, enhance financial disclosures, and prevent fraud. Sarbanes-Oxley consists of the following 11 titles:

- **Title I, Public Company Accounting Oversight Board (PCAOB)**—It establishes the PCAOB. The PCAOB has several responsibilities, including overseeing public accounting firms, defining the process for compliance audits, and enforcing SOX compliance.
- **Title II, Auditor Independence**—It establishes the conditions of services an auditor can perform while remaining independent. For example, a public accounting firm that performs external auditing services cannot provide financial information systems design or internal audit outsourcing services.

- **Title III, Corporate Responsibility**—It requires the formation of audit committees. It also establishes the interactions between the committee and external auditors. Perhaps one of the more notable mandates of SOX is contained in Section 302, which requires the chief executive officer (CEO) and the chief financial officer (CFO) to take individual responsibility in certifying and approving the integrity of the company's financial reports.

- **Title IV, Enhanced Financial Disclosures**—It addresses the accuracy and features of financial disclosures. For example, this title specifically addresses and prevents what Enron did, such as selling liabilities on its balance sheet as assets to Special Purpose Entities (SPEs). This title also contains the controversial Section 404. Section 404 requires companies to report the adequacy of their internal controls.

- **Title V, Analyst Conflicts of Interest**—It fosters public confidence in securities research. This title defines code of conducts between firms.

- **Title VI, Commission Resources and Authority**—It provides greater authority to the SEC to fault or bar a securities professional from practice. This title also addresses the prevention of fraud schemes involving low-volume, low-price stocks.

- **Title VII, Studies and Reports**—It requires the comptroller general and the SEC to conduct studies and report their findings. Examples include studying the effects of the consolidation of public accounting firms as well as studying previous corporate fraud and accounting scandals.

- **Title VIII, Corporate and Criminal Fraud Accountability**—It provides the ramifications for corporate fraud and addresses the destruction of corporate audit records. This is a direct response to the auditing firm, Arthur Andersen, for shredding documents.

- **Title IX, White Collar Crime Penalty Enhancement**—It reviews the rules and penalties regarding white-collar criminal offenses.

- **Title X, Corporate Tax Returns**—It simply states that the CEO should sign the company tax return.

- **Title XI, Corporate Fraud Accountability**—Also known as the Corporate Fraud Accountability Act of 2002, this title provides additional guidelines regarding consequences of corporate fraud. It also provides the SEC with the authority to freeze the funds of companies suspect in violating laws.

Sarbanes-Oxley is quite large and contains many reforms to rally public confidence. It also improves corporate accountability and helps to avoid corporate fraud and dishonesty. Two sections receive much of the attention, especially of IT. The first is Section 302, "Corporate responsibility for financial reports." The second is Section 404, "Management assessment of internal controls." These two sections place vast constraints on IT security. Although neither section mentions IT or IT security, financial accounting systems rely heavily on IT infrastructure. Thus, it has strongly driven the subject of IT security into the boardroom.

Section 302 requires the CEO and CFO to personally certify the truthfulness and accuracy of financial reports. They start and make internal controls. Then, they must assess and report upon the internal controls around financial reporting every quarter. Section 404 goes a step further. Section 404 requires the company to provide proof. Again, they must assess the effectiveness of their internal controls, to which a public accounting firm must audit and attest. They then publish this information in the company's annual report.

SOX is lengthy and is specific in many areas, for example, criminal penalties for noncompliance. It still is very high level and leaves a lot of room for interpretation, especially concerning IT controls. SOX does not directly address IT control requirements. As a result, you need to become familiar with a couple of publications. These include the auditing standards created by the PCAOB and the SEC's release on management guidance—17 CFR Part 241. In this codification, the SEC issued further interpretation and guidance regarding Section 404. It provides "an approach by which management can conduct a top-down, risk-based evaluation of internal control over financial reporting." PCAOB also made a formal process to further define the criteria within Section 404. This process became Auditing Standard No. 2. This standard supersedes Auditing Standard No. 5. Some notable changes to provide greater clarity and a more prescriptive approach include the following four areas:

- Aligning Auditing Standard No. 5 with the SEC's management guidance, mostly in regard to prescriptive requirements and definitions

- Adjusting the audit to account for the particular circumstances regarding the different size and complexities of companies

- Encouraging auditors to use professional judgment, particularly in using a risk-assessment methodology

- Following a principles-based approach to determining when and to what extent the auditor can use the work of others to obtain evidence about the design and effectiveness of the control

The standard also states that the auditor should use the "same suitable, recognized control framework" as the management of the company they are auditing. Furthermore, it even goes as far to suggest a suitable framework. That framework is the Committee of Sponsoring Organizations (COSO) of the Treadway Commission. Chapter 4 explores frameworks such as COSO and others in greater depth.

Gramm-Leach-Bliley Act (GLBA)

Also known as the Financial Modernization Act of 1999, the **Gramm-Leach-Bliley Act (GLBA)** repeals parts of the Glass-Steagall Act from 1933. The Glass-Steagall Act prohibited banks from offering investment, commercial banking, and insurance services all under a single umbrella. GLBA deregulates the split of commercial and investment banking.

Pretexting

Pretexting is a method of social engineering. It is more about human interaction than about technology. For success, you must manipulate others to divulge sensitive information. The root of pretexting is pretext, or a situation or reason that is deceptive or false. For example, investigators often use pretexting—at least in the movies! It typically involves some type of con or clever ruse.

Consider, for example, how to guess a password. You might use some programmatic mechanism to guess a password. Now consider how much easier it is to ask someone for the password, presumably under a pretext. This is one example of why companies so often reiterate that they will never ask you for your password. A famous recent example involved Hewlett-Packard (HP). At the time, contracted private investigators determined the source of an information leak. To do so, the investigators operated under a pretext. They impersonated HP board members or journalists from popular news outlets to obtain phone records.

There are countless examples of why pretexting occurs. The GLBA Pretexting provision protects consumers from evildoers trying to obtain personal financial information under false pretenses. Identity theft is the greatest risk to consumers should their information be compromised.

GLBA also provides provisions for compliance within Sections 501 and 521 to protect the financial information held by the industry. This protection is on behalf of the consumers. GLBA generally applies to financial institutions or any organization "significantly engaged" in financial activities. Examples include banks and securities firms. More examples are firms dealing with mortgages, insurance, tax preparation, debt collection, and much more. The FTC maintains and enforces GLBA.

To protect personally identifiable information (PII), GLBA divides privacy requirements into three principal parts. Those parts are the Financial Privacy Rule, Safeguards Rule, and Pretexting provisions:

- The Financial Privacy Rule governs the collection and disclosure of customers' personal financial information.
- The Safeguards Rule requires financial institutions to develop, maintain, and implement policies. These policies should tell how they will protect customer information.
- The Pretexting provisions protect consumers. This protection is from both individuals and organizations that obtain personal financial information under false pretenses.

The Financial Privacy Rule requires financial institutions to provide notices to their customers. The notices explain their privacy policies, specifically covering the information collection and sharing practices of the company. The consumer is also given control over limiting the sharing of their information or opting out. If the financial institution changes its policy, they must provide another notice to the consumer.

The Safeguards Rule requires financial institutions to develop an information security policy to consider the nature and sensitivity of the information they handle. The plan must include and the company must comply with the following:

- Designate at least one employee to coordinate an information security program.
- Assess the risks to customer information within each pertinent area of the company's operation. Evaluate the effectiveness of the current safeguards and risk controls.
- Implement a safeguard program. Regularly monitor and test it.
- Choose service providers that can maintain appropriate safeguards, and govern their handling of customer information.
- Evaluate and adjust the security program in view of events and changes in the firm's operations.

Likely, most organizations will protect against pretexting as part of their information security program. The best defense against pretexting is not technical, but rather awareness and training. Training is for both employees and customers. The Pretexting provision makes it illegal to do the following:

- Make a false, fictitious, or fraudulent statement or representation to obtain customer information from the financial institution or from their customers.
- Use forged, counterfeit, lost, or stolen documents to obtain customer information from the financial institution or from their customers.

Health Insurance Portability and Accountability Act (HIPAA)

U.S. Congress enacted the Health Insurance Portability and Accountability Act (HIPAA) in 1996. The primary purpose of the statute is twofold. First, it provides for helping citizens maintain their health insurance coverage. Second, it improves efficiency and effectiveness of the American health care system. It does so by combating waste, fraud, and abuse in both health insurance and the delivery of heath care. The U.S. Department of Health and Human Services (HHS) is responsible for publishing requirements and for enforcing HIPAA laws. However, the Office of Civil Rights, a subagency of HHS, administers and enforces the Privacy Rule and Security Rule of HIPAA. These laws are divided across five titles, which include the following:

- Title I, Health Care Access, Portability, and Renewability
- Title II, Preventing Health Care Fraud and Abuse, Administrative Simplification; Medical Liability Reform
- Title III, Tax-Related Health Provisions
- Title IV, Application and Enforcement of Group Health Plan Requirements
- Title V, Revenue Offsets

 WARNING

Hippo has the letter "P" in it twice—not HIPAA. Surprisingly, many vendors that sell HIPAA solutions and even the government are guilty of misspelling the acronym for the legislation incorrectly in printed literature and on Web sites.

Much of the focus around HIPAA is within the first two titles. Title I offers protection of health insurance coverage without regard to pre-existing conditions to those, for example, who lose or change their jobs. Title II provides requirements for the privacy and security of health information. This is often referred to as Administrative Simplification. The broader law calls for the following:

- Standardization of electronic data—patient, administrative, and financial—as well as the use of unique health identifiers
- Security standards and controls to protect the confidentiality and integrity of individually identifiable health information

As a result, the HHS has provided five rules regarding Title II of HIPAA. These include the Privacy Rule, the Transactions and Code Sets Rule, the Security Rule, the Unique Identifiers Rule, and the Enforcement Rule. These five rules impact and affect information technology operations within organizations. Specifically, the Privacy Rule and Security Rule affect information security. HIPAA is primarily concerned with **protected health information (PHI)**. PHI means individually identifiable health information. PHI relates to physical or mental health of an individual. It can also relate to the delivery of health care to an individual as well as payment for the delivery of health care.

The Privacy Rule went into effect in 2003. It regulates the use and disclosure of PHI by covered entities. A covered entity, for example, includes health care providers, health plans, and health care clearinghouses. In many ways, the Privacy Rule drives the Security Rule. Under the law, covered entities are obligated to do the following:

- Provide information to patients about their privacy rights and how the information can be used.
- Adopt clear privacy procedures.
- Train employees on privacy procedures.
- Designate someone to be responsible for overseeing that privacy procedures are adopted and followed.

The Security Rule followed the Privacy Rule. Unlike the Privacy Rule, however, the Security Rule applies just to electronic PHI (ePHI). The Security Rule provides for the confidentiality, integrity, and availability of ePHI, and contains three broad safeguards. These safeguards include the following:

- Administrative safeguards
- Technical safeguards
- Physical safeguards

Each of the preceding safeguards consists of various standards. All are required or addressable. Required rules must be implemented, but addressable standards provide flexibility. This way, an organization can decide how to reasonably and appropriately meet the standard. Bear in mind, however, that addressable does not mean optional.

Administrative safeguards primarily consist of policies and procedures. They govern the security measures used to protect ePHI. Table 2-1 provides a summary of the administrative safeguards, including the required and addressable standards.

TABLE 2-1 HIPAA administrative safeguards and implementation specifications.

SAFEGUARD	IMPLEMENTATION SPECIFICATION	REQUIRED/ ADDRESSABLE
Security management process	Risk analysis	Required
	Risk management	Required
	Sanction policy	Required
	Information system activity review	Required
Assigned security responsibility	Not applicable	Required
Workforce security	Authorization and/or supervision	Addressable
	Workforce clearance procedure	Addressable
	Termination procedures	Addressable
Information access management	Isolating health care clearinghouse function	Required
	Access authorization	Addressable
	Access establishment and modification	Addressable
Security awareness and training	Security reminders	Addressable
	Protection from malicious software	Addressable
	Logon monitoring	Addressable
	Password management	Addressable
Security incident procedures	Response and reporting	Required
Contingency plan	Data backup plan	Required
	Disaster recover plan	Required
	Emergency mode operation plan	Required
	Testing and revision procedures	Addressable
	Applications and data criticality analysis	Addressable
Evaluation	Not applicable	Required
Business associate contracts and other arrangements	Written contract or other arrangement	Required

Physical safeguards include the policies, procedures, and physical controls put in place. These controls and documentation protect the information systems and physical structures from unauthorized access. The same goes for natural disasters and other environmental hazards. The physical safeguards include the four standards shown in Table 2-2, along with the implementation specifications.

Technical safeguards consist of the policies, procedures, and controls put in place. These safeguards protect ePHI and prevent unauthorized access. Table 2-3 lists the five safeguards and corresponding implementation specifications.

Although covered entities must comply with the previously listed safeguards and implementation specifications, there isn't a safeguard listed that should surprise organizations. In fact, most of these safeguards are addressed through best practices for any sensitive information.

In 2006, the Final Rule for HIPAA was issued—the Enforcement Rule—and set the penalties to be levied as a result of HIPAA violations. The Enforcement Rule also established the procedures for investigations and hearings into noncompliance. The potential for increased enforcement of noncompliance to HIPAA was later introduced in 2009 when the **Health Information Technology for Economic and Clinical Health (HITECH) Act** was signed into law. HITECH was signed in as part of the American Recover and Reinvestment Act (ARPA). In addition to laying the groundwork for increased enforcement, HITECH also adds requirements for a breach notification. The notification is what an organization puts in action should PHI becomes disclosed in a readable, that is, nonencrypted, format.

TABLE 2-2 HIPAA physical safeguards and implementation specifications.

SAFEGUARD	IMPLEMENTATION SPECIFICATION	REQUIRED/ ADDRESSABLE
Facility access controls	Contingency operations	Addressable
	Facility security plan	Addressable
	Access control and validation procedures	Addressable
	Maintenance records	Addressable
Workstation use	Not applicable	Required
Workstation security	Not applicable	Required
Device and media controls	Disposal	Required
	Media reuse	Required
	Accountability	Addressable
	Data backup and storage	Addressable

TABLE 2-3	HIPAA technical safeguards and implementation specifications.	
SAFEGUARD	**IMPLEMENTATION SPECIFICATION**	**REQUIRED/ ADDRESSABLE**
Access control	Contingency operations	Required
	Facility security plan	Required
	Access control and validation procedures	Addressable
	Maintenance records	Addressable
Audit controls	Not applicable	Required
Integrity	Mechanisms to authenticate ePHI	Addressable
Person or entity authentication	Not applicable	Required
Transmission security	Integrity controls	Addressable
	Encryption	Addressable

Children's Internet Protection Act (CIPA)

The **Children's Internet Protection Act (CIPA)** is a federal law introduced as part of a spending bill that passed Congress in 2000. The FCC maintains and enforces CIPA. This act addresses concerns about children's access to explicit content online, such as pornography at schools and libraries, by requiring the use of Internet filters as a condition of receiving federal funds. CIPA is a result of previous failed attempts at restricting indecent content. The Communications Decency Act and the Child Online Protection Act faced Supreme Court challenges over the United States First Amendment. The reason was the act violated the right of free speech contained within the Constitution.

CIPA does not provide for any additional funds for the purchase of mechanisms to protect children from explicit content. Instead, conditions are attached to grants and to the use of E-Rate discounts. "E-Rate" is a program that makes Internet access more affordable for schools and libraries.

CIPA requires schools and libraries to certify compliance to implement an Internet safety policy and implement "technology protection measures." This means having technology in place that blocks or filters Internet access that is either obscene, harmful to minors, or represents child pornography. This includes implementing a safety policy and controls that address the following:

- Access by minors to "inappropriate matter" on the Internet
- The safety and security of minors when using electronic communication such as e-mail, chat rooms, and instant messaging
- Unauthorized access and unlawful activities by minors
- Unauthorized disclosure, use, and dissemination of personal information regarding minors
- Measures restricting minors' access to harmful materials

Prior to implementing the policy and controls, however, the law also requires schools or libraries to first provide public notice and to hold a public hearing to address the proposed Internet safety policy.

You might have noticed that the term "inappropriate matter" could be considered vague and controversial. As a result, the act is clear in stating that the government may not establish the criteria for making such a determination. The act states that the determination is made at the local level by the school board, local educational agency, or library.

Finally, schools and libraries must comply with one more step before they can receive the E-Rate. They must certify they have an Internet safety policy in place meeting the preceding requirements. Noncompliance with the law occurs if there is a failure to submit for certification. In this case, the institution will not be eligible for services at the discounted rate. In addition, failure to ensure the use of the computers in accordance with a certification will be required to reimburse all funds and discounts for the certification period.

Family Educational Rights and Privacy Act (FERPA)

The **Family Educational Rights and Privacy Act (FERPA)** of 1974 is a U.S. federal law. FERPA protects the privacy of student education records. It also provides parents certain access rights to the student's educational records. Parental access rights stop once the student enters post-secondary education or the student turns 18 years old. The regulation applies to educational institutions that receive federal funding from the U.S. Department of Education.

Educational agencies or institutions should notify parents or eligible students of their rights under the law annually. The notice includes the right to do the following:

- Review the student's educational records. Under most situations, the school is not required to provide copies. They may charge to provide copies.
- Seek correction or revision of the educational records if believed to be inaccurate or a violation of privacy. If the school doesn't make any amendments, a formal hearing may be requested. If the school still doesn't make any changes, the parent or eligible student may place a statement regarding the content in question.

- Consent to disclosure of educational records. Schools, however, may disclose "directory information." However, schools must give parents or eligible students opportunity to restrict disclosure of the information. Disclosure of educational records and nondirectory information without consent is provided under certain conditions of the law.

- File a complaint with the department in regard to failures to comply with the act.

As the name implies, directory information is personal data that you can find in publicly available sources. For example, a publicly available source could be a phone book or yearbook. Such information is not considered a harmful invasion of privacy. Examples of directory information include the following:

- Name
- Address
- Telephone number
- Date and place of birth
- Honors and awards
- Date of attendance

> **WARNING**
>
> You may never disclose Social Security numbers as directory information, under the FERPA regulations. You cannot even use the last four numbers of your Social Security number, which is common across other industries.

Nondirectory information, on the other hand, includes, for example, Social Security numbers and transcripts.

In 2008, two relevant documents were published. The first was "Joint Guidance on the Application of the Family Educational Rights." The second was the "Privacy Act (FERPA) and the Health Insurance Portability and Accountability Act of 1996 (HIPAA) to Student Health Records." Many schools and universities operate health clinics. Thus, it is important that educational and health records kept at health facilities on campus are only subject to FERPA and not HIPAA. If the institution is a post-secondary school that provides health care to nonstudents, the health information of the nonstudent patients is subject to HIPAA.

Compliance with the law is typically the responsibility of the registrar's office, which in turn works with legal counsel. However, IT professionals should be involved in the process and understand FERPA to ensure compliance. The act was originally drafted in 1974, so distributed, networked computer technology was not around yet. Therefore, interpretation of the law is sometimes needed. Recent changes do help accommodate this technical evolution. Consider that the real meaning of FERPA is access and confidentiality. Access in that parents or eligible students must be permitted access to their records. Confidentiality in that education records must be protected and not released without written consent. Then, consider the number of electronic records relating to students that are likely to be stored on file servers and within databases. It is more difficult because IT makes tasks so easy, such as submitting and retrieving grades electronically, Web-based financial aid, and course registration.

> **NOTE**
>
> In the past, FERPA did not allow student ID numbers to be disclosed as directory information because they are used to both identify and authenticate the student. If a student identifier is not used to access records or used for authentication, such as a password, it may be treated as directory information.

Under the FERPA Final Rules issued in 2008, FERPA does address further requirements and guidelines around information systems.

The changes also recommend "educational agencies and institutions to utilize appropriate methods to protect education records, especially in electronic data systems." The update also addresses several examples of data breaches and the unauthorized disclosure of information. It also expresses concerns that data may be compromised as a result of failure to implement proper security controls. Yet the update does not dictate how to properly safeguard electronic records, but instead offers additional resources, for example, NIST, on how to protect the information.

FERPA now provides suggestions on what to do in the case of an inadvertent release of data on the Internet or other unauthorized disclosure. In case of unauthorized disclosure, FERPA doesn't require notification. That is, the school does not have to issue direct notices to the parents or students. However, it does require the school to maintain a record of the disclosure. FERPA advises that direct notification should occur if the unauthorized disclosure might lead to identity theft. Nevertheless, other laws might still require institutions to provide direct notification.

Payment Card Industry Data Security Standard (PCI DSS)

Chapter 1 introduced you to TJX, a company that suffered a serious breach in which it had millions of credit card numbers stolen. TJX was not the first, however, nor are they the last. Individual credit card companies started formulating programs to prevent breaches from occurring. These programs ensured that merchants meet baseline security requirements for how they store, process, and transmit payment card data.

The five leading credit card companies—Visa, MasterCard, American Express, JCB, and Discover—came together and formed the **Payment Card Industry Security Standards Council (PCI SSC)** in 2004. To help organizations that process card payments prevent credit card fraud, PCI SSC created the Payment Card Industry Data Security Standard (PCI DSS). PCI DSS is a set of requirements that prescribe operational and technical controls to protect cardholder data.

Adhering to PCI DSS requires three ongoing steps:

- **Assess**—Identify cardholder data as well as all related IT infrastructure and processes. This involves making sure adequate controls are in place and testing for vulnerabilities.

- **Remediate**—Eliminate the storage of unnecessary data and fix discovered vulnerabilities.

- **Report**—Submit validation records and compliance reports.

FYI

Compliance with PCI DSS is required for merchants and credit card processors. However, the PCI Security Standards Council also provides guidance for software developers of payment application systems and for manufacturers of PIN transaction systems. PCI PIN Transaction (PTS) Security Requirements are geared to the management of the devices used to protect cardholder PINs. Payment Application Data Security Standard (PA-DSS) is for the software developers of payment applications.

PCI SSC manages the overall program. However, card vendors have their own programs for compliance and enforcement. Determination of requirements depends upon the volume of card transactions that take place. Any organization, however, that holds, processes, or passes cardholder data must undergo annual assessment. The assessment is required regardless of amount. In general, organizations that process a smaller number of transactions might only need to complete a Self-Assessment Questionnaire (SAQ). Organizations with high-volume transactions must meet other requirements, such as assessment by an independent firm. The firm must be designated as a **Qualified Security Assessor (QSA)**. In addition, requirement 11.2 requires vulnerability scans. The scans are done quarterly and are performed by a PCI **Approved Scanning Vendor (ASV)**.

 TIP

There are many acronyms, but PCI DSS, SAQ, QSA, and ASV are some good acronyms to become familiar with. A list of qualified QSAs and ASVs is located at the PCI SSC Web site at *http://www.pcisecuritystandards.org*. The Web site also has procedures on how to become one.

PCI DSS is unlike most regulatory laws in one way. It is very specific in regard to requirements and expectations. The requirements generally follow security best practices and use the 12 high-level requirements, aligned across six goals, as shown in Table 2-4. Each requirement listed in the table consists of various subrequirements. Also included are procedures for testing. These must be documented as either being in-place or not in-place.

Consider requirement 8, for example. It requires a unique ID to be assigned to each person with computer access. Within the security standard, this requirement actually consists of 21 subrequirements. Many of them are very specific, for example:

- Incorporate two-factor authentication for remote access.
- Set first-time passwords to a unique value and change immediately after first use.
- Remove or disable inactive accounts at least every 90 days.
- Require a minimum password length of at least seven characters.

Since PCI DSS started, the Security Council has released several supplemental documents, including the following:

- **Information Supplement: Requirement 11.3 Penetration Testing**—This provides clarification around penetration testing. It also discusses the difference from the PCI DSS-required vulnerability assessments.

- **Information Supplement: Requirement 6.6 Code Reviews and Application Firewalls Clarified**—This recognizes the complexity and the possible unfeasibility of the original requirement. It provides further guidance regarding the intent and alternatives.

- **Navigating the PCI SSC—Understanding the Intent of the Requirements**—This provides further discussion regarding the purpose of each of the requirements.

- **Information Supplement: PCI DSS Wireless Guidelines**—This document provides further guidance and suggestions for deploying 802.11 wireless local area networks (WLANs).

TABLE 2-4   Goals and high-level requirements for PCI DSS.

GOALS	HIGH-LEVEL REQUIREMENTS
Build and maintain a secure network.	1. Install and maintain a firewall configuration to protect cardholder data.
	2. Do not use vendor-supplied defaults for system passwords and other security parameters.
Protect cardholder data.	3. Protect stored cardholder data.
	4. Encrypt transmission of cardholder data across open, public networks.
Maintain a vulnerability management program.	5. Use and regularly update antivirus software or programs.
	6. Develop and maintain secure systems and applications.
Implement strong access control measures.	7. Restrict access to cardholder data on a need-to-know basis.
	8. Assign a unique ID to each person with computer access.
	9. Restrict physical access to cardholder data.
Regularly monitor and test networks.	10. Track and monitor all access to network resources and cardholder data.
	11. Regularly test security systems and processes.
Maintain an information security policy.	12. Maintain a policy that addresses information security for employees and contractors.

Red Flags Rule

Based upon the Fair and Accurate Credit Transactions Act of 2003, the **Red Flags Rule** was created to establish procedure for the identification of possible instances of identity theft. The FTC along with the credit union and banking regulatory agencies created the Red Flags Rule. They are also responsible for enforcing it. The Red Flags Rule requires all financial institutions and creditors to implement an Identity Theft Prevention Program. The goal is to detect warning signs or "red flags" of identity theft.

 NOTE
The FTC works for the consumer to prevent fraudulent, deceptive, and unfair business practices in the marketplace. In addition, they provide information to help consumers identify, prevent, and stop such activity.

The law applies to financial institutions, such as banks, savings and loan associations, or credit unions. The law applies to any entity where a consumer has an account that conducts payments or transfers, such as a checking account. In addition, the law also applies to creditors. Creditors extend, renew, or continue credit. Examples include finance companies, mortgage brokers, utility companies, and automobile dealers. In both cases, the law only applies to financial institutions and creditors with covered accounts. Creditors use a covered account when there is a foreseeable risk of identity theft. A common example is an account used for household purposes. This includes such things as credit card accounts, mortgage loans, broker margin accounts, checking accounts, and so on.

To comply with the Red Flags Rule, financial institutions and creditors must follow the four basic elements. These involve having appropriate policies and procedures in place to do the following:

- Identify red flags for covered accounts.
- Detect red flags.
- Respond to those red flags.
- Update the program periodically.

Financial institutions are first responsible for identifying red flags for covered accounts. The regulation does not demand specific red flags. Instead, it requires the financial institution or creditor to identify and create a list of red flags on its own. The regulation offers guidelines, however, in identifying red flags. Table 2-5 lists the five categories provided by the regulation and includes an example of each.

After creating the list of relevant red flags from the preceding categories, the institutions must then put programs and procedures in place to be able to detect the red flags. The regulation provides very little guidance on how to do this, other than saying what most institutions are already doing. For example, guidance might include getting unique information, verifying the person opening the account gives accurate and real information, and ensuring transactions are monitored. For many organizations, effective detection relies upon technology solutions that specifically focus on solutions around authentication and fraud monitoring.

TABLE 2-5 Red Flag categories and an example of each.	
CATEGORY	**EXAMPLE**
Alerts, notifications, or other warnings received from consumer reporting agencies or service providers, such as fraud detection services	A recent and significant increase in inquiry volume
The presentation of suspicious documents	A photograph or physical description on an identification not consistent with the applicant or consumer presenting the identification
The presentation of suspicious personal identifying information, such as a suspicious address change	A Social Security number (SSN) that has not been issued or is listed as the number of a deceased individual
The unusual use of, or other suspicious activity related to a covered account	A notification to the financial institution or creditor that the customer isn't receiving paper account statements
Notice from customers, victims of identity theft, law enforcement, authorities, or other persons regarding possible identity theft in connection with covered accounts held by the financial institution or creditor	A notification from the customer to the financial institution or creditor of unusual activity

Next, the financial institutions and creditors must respond to the red flags. This prevents and lessens identification theft. Organizations must respond accordingly. For example, this ranges from contacting the customer to notifying law enforcement.

Finally, financial institutions and creditors should know that risks to customers and themselves are constantly changing. On one hand, business changes can affect its risk tolerance. Examples include mergers and acquisitions as well as changes in the type of accounts offered to customers. On the other hand, methods of identity theft and how it's detected and prevented are constantly changing. A game of cat and mouse is the best way to describe the relationship among fraudsters, law enforcement, and vendors that provide prevention and detection tools.

CHAPTER SUMMARY

In addition to private industry standards, such as PCI DSS, companies must be concerned with and comply with many laws. Such requirements might affect only specific industries, whereas others can span across industries. PCI DSS, for example, generally affects any organization that holds, processes, or passes payment cardholder information, regardless of industry. HIPAA, on the other hand, primarily affects the health care industry, and Sarbanes-Oxley pertains to any publicly traded company.

Although compliance to regulations can touch many different groups within an organization, IT departments are increasingly discovering they need to stay abreast of the latest regulations as IT has become pervasive throughout organizations. It might seem overwhelming to keep up with the requirements of all the regulations, not to mention new ones. However, a sound governance, risk-management, and compliance program within organizations using a well-defined framework can make the process much more efficient and effective.

KEY CONCEPTS AND TERMS

Act of Congress

Approved Scanning Vendor (ASV)

Availability

Certification and Accreditation (C&A)

Children's Internet Protection Act (CIPA)

Confidentiality

Cyber, Identity, and Information Assurance (CIIA)

Family Educational Rights and Privacy Act (FERPA)

Federal Information Security Management Act of 2002 (FISMA)

Gramm-Leach-Bliley Act (GLBA)

Health Information Technology for Economic and Clinical Health (HITECH) Act

Health Insurance Portability and Accountability Act (HIPAA)

Information assurance (IA)

Information resource management (IRM)

Integrity

Payment Card Industry Security Standards Council (PCI SSC)

Pretexting

Protected health information (PHI)

Public Company Accounting Oversight Board (PCAOB)

Qualified Security Assessor

Red Flags Rule

Regulatory agencies

CHAPTER 2 ASSESSMENT

1. Which of the following acknowledges the importance of sound information security practices and controls in the interest of national security?

   A. FISMA
   B. GLBA
   C. HIPAA
   D. FACTA
   E. FERPA

2. What organization was tasked to develop standards to apply to federal information systems using a risk-based approach?

   A. Public Entity Risk Institute
   B. International Organization for Standardization
   C. National Institute of Standards and Technology
   D. International Standards Organization
   E. American National Standards Institute

3. Certification and _____ is an audit of federal systems prior to being placed into a production environment.

4. Which of the following organizations was tasked to develop and prescribe standards and guidelines that apply to federal information systems?

   A. NIST
   B. FISMA
   C. Congress
   D. PCI SSC
   E. U.S. Department of the Navy

5. What section of Sarbanes-Oxley requires management and the external auditor to report on the accuracy of internal controls over financial reporting?

   A. Section 301
   B. Section 404
   C. Section 802
   D. Section 1107

6. Sarbanes-Oxley explicitly addresses the IT security controls required to ensure accurate financial reporting.

   A. True
   B. False

7. Which of the following was established to have oversight of public accounting firms and is responsible for defining the process of SOX compliance audits?

   A. COSO
   B. Enron
   C. PCAOB
   D. Sarbanes-Oxley
   E. None of the above

8. Which of the following is *not* one of the titles within Sarbanes-Oxley?

   A. Corporate Responsibility
   B. Enhanced Financial Disclosures
   C. Analyst Conflicts of Interest
   D. Studies and Reports
   E. Auditor Conflicts of Interest

9. Which one of the following is *not* considered a principal part of the Gramm-Leach-Bliley Act?

   A. Financial Privacy Rule
   B. Pretexting provisions
   C. Safeguards Rule
   D. Information Security Rule

10. Which regulatory department is responsible for the enforcement of HIPAA laws?

    A. HHS
    B. FDA
    C. U.S Department of Agriculture
    D. U.S. EPA
    E. FTC

11. Which one of the following is *not* one of the safeguards provided within the HIPAA Security Rule?

A. Administrative
B. Operational
C. Technical
D. Physical

12. In accordance with the Children's Internet Protection Act, who determines what is considered inappropriate material?

A. FCC
B. U.S. Department of Education
C. The local communities
D. U.S. Department of the Interior Library
E. State governments

13. While the Family Educational Rights and Privacy Act prohibits the use of Social Security numbers as directory information, the act does permit the use of the last four digits of a SSN.

A. True
B. False

14. PCI DSS is a legislative act enacted by Congress to ensure that merchants meet baseline security requirements for how they store, process, and transmit payment card data.

A. True
B. False

15. To comply with Red Flags Rule, financial institutions and creditors must do which of the following?

A. Identify red flags for covered accounts.
B. Detect red flags.
C. Respond to detected red flags.
D. Update the program periodically.
E. Answers B and C only
F. All of the above

What Is the Scope
of an IT Compliance Audit?

AUDITS COME IN ALL SHAPES AND SIZES. Regardless of size, audits represent a systematic and measurable assessment of the environment of an organization. Auditing for IT compliance is part of the ongoing process to ensure an organization is putting in place and maintaining effective security policies and controls. The audit makes use of various tools, but is primarily concerned with how the security policies are actually used. The IT environment is vast, and can be broken down into manageable and auditable chunks or domains. This chapter explores what is required to achieve and sustain compliance across different scopes of the IT environment.

Chapter 3 Topics

This chapter covers the following topics and concepts:

- What your organization must do to be in compliance
- What you are auditing within the IT infrastructure
- What your organization must do to maintain IT compliance

Chapter 3 Goals

When you complete this chapter, you will be able to:

- Understand what organizations need to do to achieve and maintain compliance
- Explain why protecting privacy data is important for achieving compliance
- Understand the process for selecting security controls
- Compare the different domains of IT infrastructure

What Must Your Organization Do to Be in Compliance?

Achieving compliance with external standards and regulations must be your first consideration in assembling a policy infrastructure. Second, being in compliance means making sure the organization meets the expectations of the policy by enforcing the infrastructure put into place. Policy and, thus, compliance are not just about technical measures, but they must also consider nontechnical methods. There is no definitive answer or solution an organization can purchase that will provide it with compliance. Each organization must determine what is appropriate for it. To do this, an organization must consider current laws and industry standards along with the organization's mission.

Organizational policies provide general statements that address the operational goals of an organization. The role of information technology is to help accelerate the business. At the same time, consider security and compliance with laws and regulations to safeguard data. Specifically, IT and IT security policies provide the same high-level directives. They are also concerned, however, with protecting the confidentiality, integrity, and availability of information and information systems. Specifically, this includes sensitive intellectual property of the organization and privacy data.

Complying with an organization's internal policy requires standards. Standards describe mandatory processes or objectives that align with the goal of the policies. Establishing both policies and standards is critical for ensuring the success of the organization as well as compliance to the myriad of regulations with which organizations need to comply.

A good starting place is with a solid organizational governance framework. This framework considers the applicable laws and regulations, and then sets the high-level requirements to secure and control the IT infrastructure. Frameworks such as Control Objectives for Information and related Technology (COBIT) provide a blueprint for implementing high-level controls within an organization. Further, control standards such as ISO/IEC 27002 and NIST 800-53 provide more specific security controls. Chapter 4 covers frameworks and control standards in greater depth.

Once policies and control framework are in place, organizations can then start implementing specific controls. These additional controls can further address risks to the organization. Perhaps one of the greatest challenges is determining what specific controls to apply. Always consider what is reasonable and appropriate for your organization. Too often, organizations spend too much time and money implementing controls that go beyond the requirements. This can even have the negative result of impeding the mission of the organization. On the other hand, many organizations may get compliance tunnel vision. That is, they lose sight of really addressing risk, and are only concerned with being compliant.

Finally, consider that organizations will often be required to comply with many different regulations. Many of these often have overlapping goals and intent. Therefore, what you want to avoid is chasing each one individually. By having sound policies in place and a framework for the application of controls, you will be able to map existing controls to each regulation, including future regulations. Thereafter, organizations perform a **gap analysis** to identify anything that is missing. From that gap analysis, the organization can then address the gaps separately.

Although compliance with internal policies and compliance with legal requirements should be closely tied together, each of these can be divided into two high-level control objectives. In fact, they are included as control objectives within ISO/IEC 27002. These include:

- Compliance with legal and regulatory requirements
- Compliance with security policies and standards and technical compliance

 WARNING

If your organization uses penetration tests and vulnerability assessments to check technical compliance, be careful as these could have a negative effect on the systems (for example, bring them down). Additionally, vulnerability and penetration tests are not a substitute for risk assessments.

Compliance with legal requirements includes controls such as identifying all applicable legislation, respecting intellectual property rights (IPR), ensuring proper use of cryptographic controls, preventing misuse of information-processing facilities, and protecting organizational records as well as data and the privacy of personal information. Compliance with security policies and achieving technical compliance includes controls for complying with security policies and standards and for technical compliance audits.

Protecting and Securing Privacy Data

In general, it is understood that privacy data must be protected. What is not so clear, however, is what constitutes privacy data. Depending upon the environment in which an organization operates, privacy can take on different meanings. The American Institute of Certified Public Accountants (AICPA) defines **privacy management** as "the rights and obligations of individuals and organizations with respect to the collection, use, disclosure, and retention of personal information." Thus, privacy is about personal information, which might be used to identify an individual. Examples include:

- Name
- Social Security number (SSN)
- Home address
- E-mail address
- Physical characteristics

Personal information can also be considered sensitive. Consider, for example, sensitive financial or health information. When combined together with personal information, this information becomes personal *and* sensitive. The protection of this data as a result becomes increasingly important when you consider the risks posed to this data, such as inadequate access controls, improper use, or unauthorized disclosure to name a few.

For both individuals and organizations, the collection of personal data provides many benefits. Organizations, for example, benefit from increased market intelligence and competitive advantage, whereas individuals benefit from things such as personalized services and targeted offerings. On the other hand, individuals might be subject to spam and **identity theft** if that data is not protected properly. The organizations also are subject to litigation, negative publicity, and even financial loss.

There are numerous methods used to protect privacy data. For example, organizations can:

- Develop appropriate privacy policies.
- Establish the position of a **privacy officer**.
- Conduct training and awareness around data handling, identity theft, and **social engineering**.
- Consider adequate controls around data retention and data destruction.
- Conduct regular risk assessments of access controls.
- Limit data to only that which is required.
- Consider security technologies such as encryption.

> **▶ TIP**
>
> It is difficult through tools to test the effectiveness of training and awareness campaigns. Consider social engineering, for example. An auditor might want to conduct an assessment in which he or she impersonates an executive to obtain personal or sensitive data, simply by asking for it.

Privacy laws and regulations vary not just by industry, but also by areas in which business is conducted. In North America alone, there are many laws concerning privacy. Popular examples include:

- **Health Insurance Portability and Accountability Act (HIPAA)**—The Privacy Rule within Title II of the act is concerned with the security and privacy of health data.
- **Gramm-Leach-Bliley Act (GLBA)**—The Financial Privacy Rule within the act is concerned with the collection and disclosure of personal financial information.
- **Children's Online Privacy Protection Act (COPPA)**—This act contains provisions for Web sites collecting personal information from children under 13 years of age.
- **National Do Not Call Registry**—This registry provides a choice for consumers as to whether they receive telemarketing calls at home.
- **SB1386**—This California law regulates the privacy of personal information.
- **Electronic Communications Privacy Act of 2000**—This act regulates and protects the privacy of e-mail and other electronic communications.
- **The Privacy Act of 1974**—This act imposes limits on personal information collected by U.S. federal agencies.
- **The Fair Credit Reporting Act (FCRA)**—This act regulates the use of consumer credit information.
- **Personal Information Protection and Electronic Documents Act (PIPEDA)**—This Canadian law addresses how organizations collect, use, and disclose of personal information.

As a result, it is necessary for IT compliance audits to consider privacy data and the application of an appropriate privacy control framework within organizations. First, consider the laws and regulations across multiple boundaries in which business is conducted. Further, the coordination between both general counsel and IT is necessary to understand both the legal and security repercussions.

Finally, organizations should consider a privacy audit. Most audits are concerned with the privacy oversight, privacy policies, and privacy controls within an organization. A privacy audit focuses on the following:

- Which privacy laws apply to the organization?
- Are the organizational responsibilities defined and assigned (for example, that of the privacy officer and responsibilities of the legal department)?
- Are policies and procedures for creating, storing, and managing privacy data applied and followed?
- Are specific controls implemented, and are compliance tasks being followed? For example, is privacy data encrypted? Are there privacy statements and an opt-out mechanism on the organization's Web site?

Designing and Implementing Proper Security Controls

Information security is largely about managing risk. This means that IT controls are implemented depending upon the risk they are designed to manage. Although the focus is on mitigating risk by implementing appropriate security controls, there are other ways to deal with risk. Risk can also be avoided, transferred, or accepted. For example, driving a vehicle poses many risks. Consider the risk of loss due to theft or an accident. Most people choose to transfer the risk by purchasing insurance. Others might accept the risk by not purchasing insurance. Still others might avoid the risk altogether by choosing not to drive.

Every day you make personal decisions that consider controls in relation to risk. Being human naturally makes you vulnerable to many different threats, which can have a tremendous impact upon you. Many people wear a seat belt while driving, for example.

> **NOTE**
>
> Assessing and prioritizing risk doesn't just provide security. It also prevents wasted time and money on unnecessary controls that might have a negative impact on the goals and missions of the organization.

Now think about how you might choose to protect your family while at home. Door locks are a good place to start. Door locks are also a relatively simple control. Yet some people have alarm systems, whereas others don't. The same concept applies to the threat of an assailant with a gun. Why doesn't everyone wear a bulletproof vest?

Managing risks involves making tradeoffs. A solid understanding of the risks and proper consideration of the tradeoffs results in the controls you select for your personal security and for the protection of information. It becomes necessary to properly assess and prioritize risk.

The process of selecting security controls needs to be part of an overall framework for risk management. For example, the following activities consider the implementation of controls within the context of such a framework:

- Discover and classify data and information systems. First, consider the confidentiality, integrity, and availability of the data and information systems. Next, examine the potential impact on the organization should confidentiality, integrity, or availability be compromised.

- Select security controls. Once you consider the impact, select appropriate security controls based on the risk to the systems.

- Implement security controls. After selecting controls, put the controls in place to ensure risks are reduced to an appropriate level.

- Assess security controls. Perform an evaluation of the effectiveness of the controls. The assessment provides the necessary information to ensure they are implemented correctly and meeting the security requirements.

- Authorize the controls. After considering the system in relation to the assessment of the controls, determine that the residual risk is at an acceptable level.

- Monitor the controls. Once controls are set, put a system of continuous monitoring in place. Changes within the organization or the information system, for example, might result in the need to update the security controls. In addition, an event involving the identification of a new threat or an event resulting in a breach will require an immediate assessment and possibly a change to the applied security controls.

COBIT is a popular and widely used control framework for IT in general. A high-level control objective with COBIT as related to the IT process is to "ensure systems security." This objective includes the following:

> **NOTE**
> Chapter 4 addresses COBIT in greater depth.

- Management of IT Security
- Security Plan
- Identity Management
- User Account Management
- Security Testing, Surveillance, and Monitoring
- Security Incident Definition
- Protection of Security Technology
- Cryptographic Key Management
- Malicious Software, Prevention, Detection, and Correction
- Network Security
- Exchange of Sensitive Data

Although this framework provides a sound overall foundation of control objectives, other frameworks or standards provide guidance that is more detailed. Selecting security controls is best approached by first adhering to a common set of basic or baseline controls. Next, you might need to apply additional controls that are specific to the system or application. Finally, you might need to apply **compensating controls**. Compensating controls are necessary when a baseline security control cannot be implemented, for example.

TABLE 3-1 Family of security control baselines and corresponding examples.

CONTROLS FAMILY	CONTROL EXAMPLES
Access Control	Account Management; Separation of Duties; Least Privilege
Awareness and Training	Security Awareness; Security Training; Training Records
Audit and Accountability	Audit of Record Retention; Auditable Events
Security Assessment and Authorization	Plan of Action and Milestones; Security Authorization
Configuration Management	Baseline Configuration; Configuration Change Control
Contingency Planning	Contingency Training; Alternate Storage Site
Identification and Authentication	Identifier Management; Cryptographic Module Authentication
Incident Response	Incident Handling; Incident Monitoring; Incident Reporting
Maintenance	Controlled Maintenance; Maintenance Tools
Media Protection	Media Access; Media Marking; Media Storage
Physical and Environmental Protection	Physical Access Controls; Visitor Control; Fire Protection
Planning	System Security Plan; Privacy Impact Assessment
Personal Security	Personnel Screening; Personnel Termination
Risk Assessment	Security Categorization; Vulnerability Scanning
System and Services Acquisition	Allocation of Resources; Security Engineering Principles
System and Communications Protection	Denial of Service Protection; Boundary Protection
System and Information Integrity	Malicious Code Protection; Spam Protection; Error Handling
Program Management	Enterprise Architecture; Risk Management Strategy

Some common control baselines from the National Institute for Standards and Technology (NIST) are listed in Table 3-1. Controls described in the table are from NIST Standard 800-53. The controls are categorized by a high-level control family and include various controls that apply to each group. Within each family, the policy and procedures are always considered.

In another example, SANS (SysAdmin, Auditing, Network, Security) created a list of 20 critical controls primarily addressing the technical control area. Of these controls, 15 are subject to automated collection, measurement, and validation, whereas the remaining 5 are not directly supported by such automation. These five should be validated manually. The first 15 include:

1. Inventory of authorized and unauthorized devices
2. Inventory of authorized and unauthorized software
3. Secure configuration for hardware and software on laptops, workstations, and servers
4. Secure configurations for network devices, such as firewalls, routers, and switches
5. Boundary defense
6. Maintenance, monitoring, and analysis of security audit logs
7. Application software security
8. Controlled use of administrative privileges
9. Controlled access based on need to know
10. Continuous vulnerability assessment and remediation
11. Account monitoring and control
12. Malware defenses
13. Limitation and control of network ports, protocols, and services
14. Wireless device control
15. Data loss prevention

You can implement all of the preceding controls through technical solutions and you can verify and monitor them through technical solutions as well. The five additional controls that require manual validation include:

16. Secure network engineering
17. Penetration tests and red team exercises
18. Incident response capability
19. Data recovery capability
20. Security skills assessment and appropriate training to fill gaps

TABLE 3-2 SANS summary of attacks correlated to top critical controls.

ATTACK SUMMARY	RELATED CONTROL
Attackers continually scan for new, unprotected systems, including test or experimental systems, and exploit such systems to gain control.	Inventory of authorized and unauthorized devices
Attackers continually scan for vulnerable software and exploit it to gain control of target machines.	Inventory of authorized and unauthorized software
Attackers exploit weak default configurations of systems that are more geared to ease of use than security.	Secure configuration for hardware and software on laptops, workstations, and servers
Attackers exploit and infiltrate through network devices whose security configuration has been weakened over time by granting, for specific short-term business needs, supposedly temporary exceptions that are never removed.	Secure configurations for network devices, such as firewalls, routers, and switches
Attackers exploit boundary systems on Internet-accessible DMZ networks, and then pivot to gain deeper access on internal networks.	Boundary defense

Stop for a moment, review these top-20 SANS controls, and compare them with the controls listed in Table 3-1. How different are they? Is it possible to map many of the controls to controls of the other? Interestingly, the SANS top-20 controls map to about one-third of the NIST controls, with the goal of addressing the most critical based upon an attack-based analysis. This basic control document was created based upon the most prevalent types of attack. Table 3-2 contains the first five controls along with an example of the attack summary to which it relates.

What Are You Auditing Within the IT Infrastructure?

Across the infrastructure, an audit should focus primarily on the following three objectives:

- Examine the existence of relevant and appropriate security policies and procedures.
- Verify the existence of controls supporting the policies.
- Verify the effective implementation and ongoing monitoring of the controls.

Examining risk and IT controls throughout the IT infrastructure can be complex given the breadth of components across organizations. There are, however, a lot of similarities between different IT departments. It is helpful to define and, if necessary, break up the scope of the audit into manageable areas or domains of security responsibility. Figure 3-1 illustrates these seven domains, which include:

NOTE

Chapters 8 through 14 explore the seven domains from a compliance perspective.

- **User Domain**—The end users of the systems, including how they authenticate into the systems
- **Workstation Domain**—The end users' operating environment
- **LAN Domain**—The equipment that makes up the **local area network (LAN)**
- **LAN-to-WAN Domain**—The bridge between the LAN and the **wide area network (WAN)**
- **WAN Domain**—The equipment and activities outside of the LAN and beyond the LAN-to-WAN Domain
- **Remote Access Domain**—The access infrastructure for users accessing remote systems
- **System/Application Domain**—Systems on the network that provide the applications and software for the users

Within these seven domains, IT consists of hardware, software, network communications, protocols, applications, and data. Additionally, each domain is implemented within a physical space and includes people interacting with logical and physical aspects of the system. Breaking the audit into domains helps to define clear boundaries, and determines the extent by which interconnected systems will be examined. An attacker needs to only exploit a vulnerability in one domain; however, each domain needs to be examined carefully. It only takes a weakness in one domain to exploit the others.

Although it is possible to separate these domains logically, there are many similarities concerning what is audited. For example, the following questions apply across these domains:

- Are there adequate policies and procedures in place?
- Are operating system security systems in accordance with standards and best practices?
- Are auditing logs configured, and are they being reviewed?
- Are appropriate authentication mechanisms in place?
- Are access control lists (ACLs) in place and configured correctly?
- Are systems patched from known vulnerabilities?
- Is a disaster recovery plan and failover plan in place?
- What change control processes are in place, and are they followed?

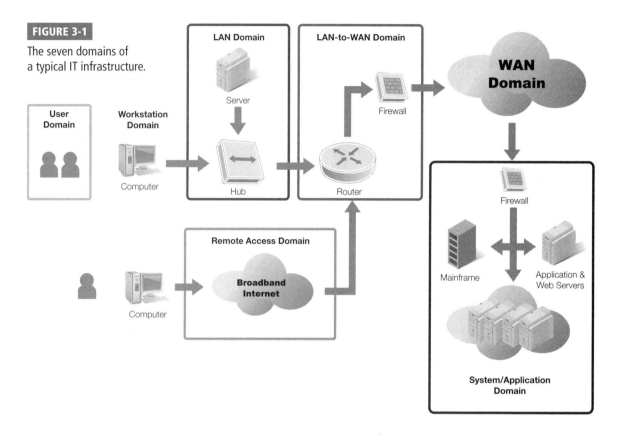

FIGURE 3-1

The seven domains of a typical IT infrastructure.

This list represents only a small sample of questions to be asked and areas to be assessed. What is important to understand is that although each domain has its own unique characteristics, there are many overlapping requirements and controls.

User Domain

An audit of the User Domain should be considered for anyone accessing the organization's information systems. This includes not just employees but nonemployees as well, such as contractors or consultants. This domain considers the roles and responsibilities of the users. It should examine all policies that relate to them, specifically access policies.

The policies that apply might include the following, for example:

- Acceptable use policy (AUP)
- System access policy
- Internet access policy
- E-mail policy

Additionally, the User Domain also includes the method by which the user authenticates to resources. Depending upon the organization's policy, users can authenticate in a number of ways. Regardless of the method used, the intent is to ensure that the user is indeed who they claim to be.

Workstation Domain

The Workstation Domain comprises the desktop environment of an end user's computing environment and includes:

- Desktop computers
- Laptop computers
- Printers
- Scanners
- Handheld computers and devices
- Modems
- Wireless access points

Each of the above devices should be first authorized to access and connect to the organizational network and information resources. Thereafter, an audit of this domain would also ensure proper procedures and controls around maintaining the system hardware and software. Any desktop operating system, for example, should comply with the standards defined by the organization. The audit would take into consideration those security controls already applied. Standard operating systems and patch levels are typically mandated as well as specific configuration controls and the presence of anti-malware, desktop firewalls, and other security controls.

LAN Domain

A LAN is typically made up of computing and networking equipment in close proximity, such as a single room or building. LANs provide each computer on the network access to centralized resources, such as file servers and printers. In addition, they provide an easy method by which all the computers can be administered. Various other elements compose the LAN Domain, including the physical connections required, such as the wiring, and networking equipment, such as hubs and switches. An audit of the LAN Domain can examine various elements, such as the following:

- Logon mechanisms and controls for access to the LAN
- Hardening and configuration of LAN systems
- Backup procedures for servers
- Review of power supply for the network

Each individual device on the network must be protected or all devices can be at risk. A LAN is generally considered a trusted zone. Communications across the LAN are not usually protected as thoroughly as they might be if they were sent outside the LAN. A malicious person, for example, might be able to capture data going across the network quite easily. This is more easily done if hubs are used instead of switches. The attacker could simply plug into any network port in the building and capture valuable data. On the other hand, switches would require an attacker to have physical access to the switch. To prevent this, switches must be placed in secured rooms or secured closets.

LAN-to-WAN Domain

Although the LAN is typically made up of a smaller defined geographical area, a WAN provides for long-distance communication to extend a network across a wider geographic area. Thus, a WAN is able to connect multiple LANs together. The transition from the LAN to the WAN typically involves equipment such as a router or a firewall. A router is used to forward data between different networks. A firewall is another common component. A firewall is placed between networks and is designed to permit authorized access, while blocking everything else.

The WAN Domain is considered an untrusted zone. It might be made up of components outside the direct control of the organization, and is often more accessible by attackers. The area between the trusted and untrusted zone is protected with one or more firewalls. This is also called the boundary, or the edge.

The public side of the boundary is often connected to the Internet and has public Internet Protocol (IP) addresses. These IP addresses are accessible from anywhere in the world and attackers are constantly probing public IP addresses looking for open ports and vulnerabilities. A high level of security is required to keep the LAN-to-WAN Domain secure.

An audit is critical to ensure that the environment is controlled correctly to prevent unauthorized access. There are many components and controls that work together to provide security. Organizations should carefully manage the configurations of all devices, such as firewalls, routers, and intrusion detection systems, for example.

WAN Domain

The WAN Domain provides the end-to-end connectivity between LANs. Like the LAN-to-WAN Domain, this environment includes routers, firewalls, and intrusion detection systems, but also has many more telecommunications components.

Examples include Channel Service Unit/Data Service Unit (CSU/DSU), codecs, and backbone circuits.

For many businesses, the WAN is the Internet. A business may, however, lease semiprivate lines from telecommunications companies. These lines are semiprivate because they are rarely leased and used by only a single company. Instead, they are shared with other unknown companies. Again, the Internet is an untrusted zone. Any host on the Internet with a public IP address is at significant risk of attack, and you should expect any host on the Internet to be attacked even if that just means it is scanned for open ports and vulnerabilities. A significant amount of security is required to keep hosts in the WAN Domain safe. WAN audits help ensure the WAN is operating and configured as expected and is conforming to corresponding policies and standards.

Remote Access Domain

The Remote Access Domain is made up of the authorized users who access organization resources remotely. Access often occurs over unsecured transports such as the Internet. Other unsecured transports include dial-up via a modem. Mobile workers often need access to the private LAN while traveling or working from home, for example. Mobile workers are granted this access using remote access solutions.

Remote access solutions, such as a virtual private network (VPN), are able to create an encrypted communications tunnel over a public network such at the Internet. Because the Internet is largely untrusted, remote access might represent a significant risk. Attackers can access unprotected connections. They might try to break into the remote access servers as well. Using a VPN is an example of a control to reduce the risk. VPNs, however, have their own vulnerabilities. For example, how does a user authenticate to the VPN? An attacker can gain access via the secured encrypted tunnel back to the corporate data just by knowing or guessing the credentials of the authorized user.

An audit should carefully consider the governing policies and procedures as well as the type of access provided.

3

What Is the Scope of an
IT Compliance Audit?

---

technical TIP

A common control applied to VPN authentication requires the use of two-factor authentication. Two-factor authentication requires, for example, something the user knows and something the user has. This typically means a user is provided with a physical token that generates a new token code every minute. To authenticate, the user would provide his password or PIN as well as the token code. An ATM card used at an automatic teller machine to get cash uses a similar process. The user provides a PIN and inserts the card. The user requires possession of one item and knowledge of the other.

> **technical TIP**
>
> You should lock down or configure a server using the specific security requirements needed by the hosted application. Shutting down unnecessary services or software is a great first step in keeping a system secure. In addition, each application might require a new set of security measures or controls. An e-mail server requires one set of controls, whereas a database server requires a different set.

System/Application Domain

The System/Application Domain is made up of the many systems and software applications that users access. This, for example, includes mainframes, application servers, Web servers, proprietary software, and applications. Mail servers send and receive e-mail. Database servers host data that is accessed by users, applications, or other servers. Domain Name System (DNS) servers provide name-to-IP address resolution for clients. Knowledge within this domain can be very specialized as operators may focus on one specific aspect, such as mail servers, and be quite familiar with associated security ramifications. On the other hand, that same person might know very little about databases.

Like the desktop operating system, server operating systems should be hardened to authorized baselines and configured according to policies and standards with the appropriate controls.

What Must Your Organization Do to Maintain IT Compliance?

Simply achieving compliance is not enough. Compliance is an ongoing process that should be treated as a continuous function within the organization. Change is constantly occurring. The following are primary examples of why organizations must maintain IT compliance as an ongoing program:

- Organizations are dynamic, growing environments. As they adapt and grow, things change and compliance must be assessed against the changes.

- Threats evolve. Threats to organizations, like organizations themselves, constantly change and adapt. Organizations must respond and adjust appropriately to these threats.

- Laws, regulations, and industry standards continue to evolve, and new ones are introduced. Organizations are required to exercise due diligence. These efforts evolve as due care rises. What was good enough one day might not be enough the next.

- Many regulations require annual audits, ongoing reporting, and regular assessments against the environment.

Maintaining compliance requires a well-defined programmatic approach that involves process and technology. This program needs to be monitored on an ongoing basis. At a minimum, the program should include:

- Regular assessment of selected security controls
- Configuration and control management processes
- Change management processes
- Annual audit of the security environment

Conducting Periodic Security Assessments

Regular security assessments should be part of the ongoing security strategy for any organization. Security assessments provide valuable metrics for maintaining compliance. In general, an assessment should address people, operations, applications, and the infrastructure throughout the organization. Because security assessments are conducted more often than an annual security audit, for example, the purpose and the scope of a **risk assessment** can vary widely. Generally, a security assessment is grouped into different types:

- **High-level security assessment**—Provides an overall view of the information systems and is useful when examining across a broader scope
- **Comprehensive security assessment**—Provides a more targeted, concise, and technical review of information systems; involves control reviews and identification of vulnerabilities
- **Preproduction security assessment**—Used for new systems prior to being placed in production; may also be used for systems after having undergone a significant change

In addition to undergoing any initial security assessment, organizations should also determine how often they conduct assessments thereafter. Some of the considerations that should factor into the decision for ongoing assessments include:

- Expected benefits
- Scheduling requirements
- Applicable regulations and industry standards
- System and data classification

High-impact systems, for example, that process or store sensitive information might require more frequent assessment than those that have a lesser impact. Also, consider when the last assessment was completed, as even a system having a moderate or low impact can present issues if the system has not been assessed in a long time. Often, the ongoing assessment process is driven by an organization's requirement to demonstrate compliance with regulations or standards.

Performing an Annual Security Compliance Audit

Regular security assessment should be supplemented with annual security audits. Although annual audits of specific functions are required for many organizations, an annual internal audit provides the organization with an independent review of the adequacy and effectiveness of IT security's internal controls. An audit should never be thought of as a one-time event.

In fact, as with security assessments, organizations have embraced the idea of continuous auditing. An audit completed less than once a year can offer only a narrow scope of evaluation. This results in not providing real value for the organization. Organizations with an internal audit function are in the best position to implement audits that are more frequent or a continuous audit program.

Defining Proper Security Controls

The environments of controls are made up largely of a basic set of principles that apply across the various domains. These basic principles are embedded throughout security operations and administration management. These include:

- Defined roles and responsibilities
- Configuration and change management
- Environments for development test and production
- Segregation of duties
- Identity and authentication
- Principle of least privilege
- Monitoring, measuring, and reporting
- Appropriate documentation

Once a basic control environment is in place, organizations can begin putting in place additional controls to continue reducing risk to acceptable levels. An important aspect to maintaining compliance is in defining and adjusting proper security controls. Although there are many different guiding documents for control standards, organizations must be careful in which specific controls they implement and how they put these controls into place.

Selecting and maintaining the right controls requires thought around completed risk assessments. This assessment must address real threats while considering the tradeoff between risk and benefit. If you start by implementing controls properly along with proper documentation, maintaining them shouldn't be as difficult. On the other hand, it might be easier to become complacent. As a result, organizations might not document the changes to controls and the implementation of new controls once a basic set are in place.

Creating an IT Security Policy Framework

IT security typically falls within an established IT policy framework. To maintain compliance, however, organizations should create a framework for IT security. A policy framework provides for a structured approach for outlining requirements that must be met. The framework can be thought of as a pyramid, as shown in Figure 3-2.

FIGURE 3-2

A policy framework.

That is, it starts on the top with very clear and concise objectives or requirements, and then continues downward exposing further details and additional guidance. At the topmost level is the policy. The policy regulates conduct through a general statement of beliefs, goals, and objectives. Next, standards support the policies. The standards are mandated activities or rules. Next, a guideline further supports the standard as well as the policy. Guidelines provide general statements of guidance, but are not mandatory. Here is an example of these three components:

- **Policy**—Users are required to use strong authentication when accessing company systems.
- **Standard**—Users are required to use two-factor authentication when accessing the remote network combining a physical one-time token code with a personal identification number.
- **Guideline**—Always keep your token within your possession, and be aware of your surroundings when entering your personal identification number.

In addition to these three items, a procedure can also be part of the framework. A procedure provides step-by-step instructions that support the policy by outlining how the standards and guidelines are placed into practice.

Implementing Security Operations and Administration Management

Information technology has become a big part of the way in which organizations operate and enables customers, partners, and suppliers to stay connected. As a result, this requires the organization to implement and evolve its security and operations management functions to handle rapid change in accordance with stated policies. This added complexity makes it even more challenging to ensure systems within the organization comply with security policies and standards. Consider that unauthorized changes are prevalent, and new vulnerabilities appear daily. In addition, mistakes are bound to happen with the configuration and deployment of new systems. The frameworks and tools discussed in Chapter 4 provide solid foundations upon which to base security operations and administration management.

Configuration and Change Management

Although **configuration and change management** isn't typically considered a function of IT security, it is very much related because of the implications upon IT security. Configuration and change management is a process of systems control throughout their life cycle making sure that the systems are operating correctly and as intended in accordance with security policies and standards. Additionally, configuration and change management involves the identification, control, logging, and auditing of all changes made across the infrastructure.

Configuration and change management is typically founded upon baseline configurations defined for systems. Subsequently, it ensures that authorized changes to the system do not affect their security. Additionally, change and configuration management provide a method for tracking unauthorized changes. Changes that are not authorized can negatively impact the system's security posture. Thus, a process for change and configuration management ensures that changes are requested, evaluated, and authorized. The following represents the high-level process:

1. **Identify and request change**—A need for a change is recognized, and a formal request is submitted to a decision-making group.

2. **Evaluate change request**—An impact assessment is done to determine operational or security effects the change may have on the system or related systems.

3. **Decision response**—A decision typically results in the request either being approved or denied.

4. **Implement approved change**—If the request is approved, the change can be implemented into the production environment.

5. **Monitor change**—Administrators ensure the system operates as intended as a result of the change.

A review board usually manages this five-step process. A committee from across multiple disciplines within the organization makes up this board.

CHAPTER SUMMARY

While the law requires audits, organizations find it more necessary to conduct regular assessments. Regular assessments help ensure that audits will be more successful as well as ensure the confidentiality, integrity, and availability of information and information systems. The protection of privacy data needs to be considered in addition to just the protection of intellectual property. Audits and assessments usually begin based upon a framework. Once a foundation is in place, companies are finding it easier and more effective to conduct regular audits and assessments. Various frameworks from which to implement a risk management and policy program as well as frameworks that guide audits and assessments are discussed next. Understanding and managing the scope of a compliance audit are critical for efficient audits as well. Later in this book, you will learn more about achieving compliance within the seven domains of IT infrastructure.

KEY CONCEPTS AND TERMS

Compensating controls

Configuration and change management

Gap analysis

Identity theft

LAN Domain

LAN-to-WAN Domain

Local area network (LAN)

Privacy management

Privacy officer

Remote Access Domain

Risk assessment

Social engineering

System/Application Domain

User Domain

WAN Domain

Wide area network (WAN)

Workstation Domain

CHAPTER 3 ASSESSMENT

1. After mapping existing controls to new regulations, an organization needs to conduct a _____ analysis.

2. Which of the following best describes the rights and obligations of individuals and organizations with respect to the collection, use, disclosure, and retention of personal information?

A. Security management
B. Compliance management
C. Privacy management
D. Personal management
E. Collection management

3. The process of selecting security controls is considered within the context of risk management.

A. True
B. False

4. If a baseline security control cannot be implemented, which of the following should be considered?

A. Compensating control
B. Baseline security standard revision
C. Policy revision
D. None of the above

5. Account management and separation of duties are examples of what type of controls?

A. Audit and accountability
B. Access control
C. Security assessment and authorization
D. Personal security

6. Which one of the following is *not* one of the seven domains of a typical IT infrastructure?

A. User Domain
B. Workstation Domain
C. LAN-to-LAN Domain
D. WAN Domain
E. Remote Access Domain

7. Which of the following policies would apply to the User Domain concerning the seven domains of a typical IT infrastructure?

A. Acceptable use policy
B. Internet access policy

C. Security incident policy
D. Firewall policy
E. Answers A and B
F. Answers B and D

8. Mitigating a risk from an IT security perspective is about eliminating the risk to zero.

A. True
B. False

9. Which of the following is an example of why an ongoing IT compliance program is important?

A. Organizations are dynamic, growing environments.
B. Threats evolve.
C. Laws and regulations evolve.
D. All of the above

10. Policies, standards, and guidelines are part of the policy _____.

11. Which one of the following is *not* part of the change management process?

A. Identify and request
B. Evaluate change request
C. Decision response
D. Implement unapproved change
E. Monitor change

12. What can be done to manage risk? (Select three.)

A. Accept
B. Transfer
C. Avoid
D. Migrate

13. Regarding the seven domains of IT infrastructure, the Workstation Domain includes which of the following? (Select three.)

A. Desktop computers
B. Laptop computers
C. Remote access systems
D. E-mail servers
E. Handheld devices

14. Adequate controls over privacy data helps prevent _____ theft.

PART TWO

Auditing for Compliance: Frameworks, Tools, and Techniques

Auditing Standards and Frameworks

CONDUCTING AUDITS AND ASSESSMENTS is challenging in the absence of a standard against which to audit or assess. Two concepts that are helpful include **control objectives** and **control activities**. Control objectives, despite the rapid evolution of technology, remain mostly constant. These tend to be high level and describe the goal for the organization. Control activities provide details on how to achieve the goals of the relevant control objective. There is no such thing as a one-size-fits-all framework or standard. Frameworks and standards simply provide the building blocks and guidance needed for organizations to tailor them to their specific needs. They are useful for guiding the control objectives and control activities. They are also useful for developing governance, risk management, and compliance. They provide auditors guidance from which to base their audit.

Organizations should create a methodology for governance, security, and compliance. Choosing from guiding control standards and frameworks is an ideal start. This chapter explores the importance of such standards and frameworks. This chapter also introduces several popular frameworks and standards in use today. There are still many more. Regardless, all have a common theme of putting in place sensible practices within organizations.

Chapter 4 Topics

This chapter covers the following topics and concepts:

- Why frameworks are important for compliance auditing
- Why standards are important in compliance auditing
- What ISO and IEC standards are
- What NIST 800-53 provides
- How to develop a hybrid auditing framework or approach

When you complete this chapter, you will be able to:

- Understand the importance in using a framework for audits
- Describe various strategies for using standards and framework for compliance auditing
- Understand COSO and how it relates to information technology
- Describe the key parts and importance of COBIT
- Understand the importance and benefits of a SAS 70 audit
- Describe the key ISO/IEC standards that relate to information security
- Describe the NIST 800-53 and 800-53A standards
- Understand the need for hybrid auditing approaches

Why Frameworks Are Important for Auditing

In general, a **framework** is a conceptual set of rules and ideas that provide structure to a complex and tough situation. Though a framework may be rigid in its skeleton, the idea is to provide flexibility. This textbook, for example, follows a framework to help guide the actual text and provide consistency. The framework includes distinct components, such as an introduction, learning objectives, headings, and a summary, for example. Yet the authors have flexibility as long as they are within the confines of this framework.

Information technology (IT) environments are different from one to the next. Despite many common similarities, each environment is different. Each company, for example, has different objectives. They have different ways of achieving goals. They have different risk profiles. IT departments exist to help support and drive the business. As long as no two organizations are exactly alike, neither will two IT departments be exactly alike.

An auditor must deal with multiple types of organizations. As a result, each audit is different. The size of the audit varies. The resources needed for the audit vary. The steps carried out for each audit also vary. A framework, however, provides a consistent system of controls to which IT departments can adhere. This system of controls also provides an auditor a consistent approach for conducting audits.

Controls tend to be either descriptive or prescriptive. A **descriptive control** framework provides for governance at a higher level. These control frameworks are important in helping to align IT with business goals. The challenge is that they don't provide a prescribed method for turning these objectives into action. A **prescriptive control** framework approach helps standardize IT operations and tasks, while still allowing for flexibility. Organizations often apply both approaches together within IT, and audits tend to make use of both.

A more governing and descriptive type of framework may dictate a control objective that each IT organization should ensure systems security. Such an approach typically provides additional controls, such as ensuring network security or ensuring identity management. A major component of ensuring network security involves using firewalls. How each organization actually applies this varies. What if there is not a local area network-to-wide area network (LAN-to-WAN) connection? In this case, there may not be a firewall at any border; there may only be firewalls between internal network segments. One company might use a software firewall. Another might use hardware. There are also different types of firewalls. An administrator might use an application-layer firewall in one situation and a network-layer firewall in another. For the auditor, the control objective stays the same, yet the audit procedure may vary because of the differences.

The Importance of Using Standards in Compliance Auditing

There is no shortage of frameworks and standards for IT departments and auditors to rely on. There are many different standards from varying organizations, each with its own set of strengths and weaknesses. However, they all have the same common goal of establishing prudent and good practices around IT control. Many organizations find that they need to use a blend of standards to accomplish their goals. Auditors tend to focus or specialize on particular standards, yet many organizations may seek an audit or assessment against a particular standard. Many organizations, in the beginning, often look to their peers and to the auditors for what framework and standards they should be using. It is important, however, to consider the needs of the specific organization.

While trying to determine a specific standard to adhere to, it is helpful to consider the high-level differences among them. Consider the following attributes that vary among different standards and frameworks:

- **Depth and breadth**—Some go far and wide, whereas others are narrow and deep. Guiding principles that cover a wide range might be most suitable to your organization. Alternatively, more prescriptive guidance around describing and assessing actual controls might be helpful.

- **Flexibility**—One standard might apply across the entire organization, whereas another might be limited to a specific department or team.

- **Reasoning**—Some standards provide stronger guidance about why they make a particular statement around controls. Sometimes, the reasoning can be important, as those putting in place and auditing controls understand how and why they apply.

- **Prioritization**—Although each organization determines acceptable risk, some standards can provide guidance for focusing on certain areas over others.

- **Industry acceptance**—Some standards are generally accepted more so than others. Acceptance also varies by industry.

Standards and frameworks are closely tied to the previous discussion of policies and standards. A framework should offer IT organizations a method for establishing an approach to managing IT risks. The use of a framework combined with an analysis of risk helps guide the development of appropriate written policies and standards within the organization. A high-level control from a framework might state, for example, that systems should be protected from unauthorized access. As a result, an organization develops several policies around enforcing authorized access to its systems. One such policy states that individuals are assigned unique user names and passwords for the system. In turn, a standard may dictate specific parameters, for example, user names must follow the format of first initial preceded by last name and be at least eight alphanumeric characters. Finally, a procedure indicates how to apply the requirements on a particular system.

Clear documented policies, standards, and procedures provide auditors with an obvious path upon which to base their audits. An unclearly documented policy structure makes the auditor's and auditee's jobs much more difficult. Audits go smoother when both parties work from closely aligned frameworks and accepted practices. If, for example, an auditor discovers a lack of clear policies, a standard provides a solid baseline upon which to base the findings. An audit deficiency that states password security, for example, should "be stronger" is less powerful than stating password requirements aren't up to a specific standard or "best practice."

Auditing against standards works best when the auditor and the organization agree upon a specific standard. Organizations first select frameworks most appropriate to their business. Then, it's the auditor's job to evaluate whether the company-selected standard is reasonable. The auditor must assess against the standard. The former is a reason why most companies go with recognized and mature standards. The following are some key recommendations when selecting a standard:

- **Select a standard that can be followed**—It also allows for others within the organization and auditors to embrace the standards. This allows the standards to be more easily put in place.

- **Employ the standard**—This reduces liability for having selected a specific standard, which is not actually put into place.

- **Select a flexible standard**—This provides the organization the ability to remain responsive to changing business environments, and consider their own risk profile.

 WARNING

A standard control framework provides a strong foundation for an internal policy structure. However, failure to act upon or meet what has been stated in an internal policy may result in an audit deficiency.

FIGURE 4-1

The hierarchy of
standards and personnel.

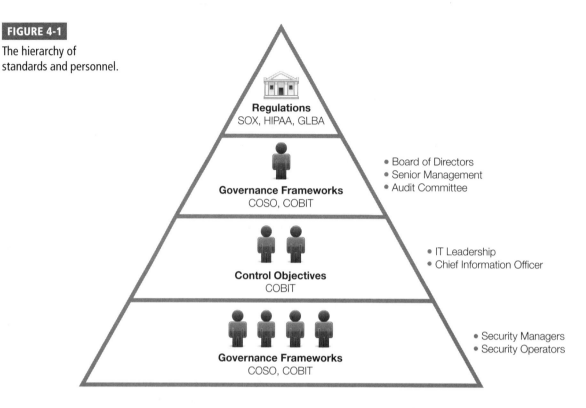

In the next sections, you'll learn about different frameworks and standards. Standards
are relevant to the individuals and groups within the organization. Figure 4-1 illustrates
the hierarchy of governance and controls. The diagram includes sample standards
as well as the people to which they apply.

Following are the high-level steps an organization may take to apply the use
of standards:

1. Educate personnel, beginning with senior management.
2. Choose the standards that the organization will follow.
3. Put the people in place and provide the needed resources to apply
   and meet the standard.
4. Confirm the standards are being met by using internal audit
   and outside resources as needed.

COSO

The **Committee of Sponsoring Organizations (COSO) of the Treadway Commission**
was founded in 1985 as part of a program to study the reasons that lead to fraud
in financial reporting. Today, the mission of COSO is to "improve organizational
performance and governance," as well as "reduce the extent of fraud in organizations."

This is achieved through thoughtful leadership and frameworks, as well as guidance on:

- Risk management
- Internal controls
- Fraud deterrence

Taken together, COSO issued a framework titled *Enterprise Risk Management—Integrated Framework*. This provides the structure to examine risk within the organization and apply risk-based processes.

The COSO **enterprise risk management (ERM) framework** consists of eight components across four objectives. The framework is geared to achieving an organization's objectives as defined by the following:

- **Strategic**—The high-level goals that support the overall mission of the group
- **Operations**—The effective and efficient use of the organization's resources
- **Reporting**—The reliability of reports
- **Compliance**—Adherence with applicable laws and regulations

Both reporting and compliance are within the control of the organization. ERM provides reasonable assurance of meeting these two objectives. On the other hand, strategic and operational objectives aren't always within the complete control of an organization. Both of these objectives are often influenced by external events. Thus, ERM can provide reasonable assurance that management is made aware in a timely manner of the degree to which the organization is moving toward achieving these two objectives.

The COSO framework identifies eight interrelated parts in connection with the management processes of an organization. These include:

 TIP

Many organizations choose COSO and see it as the only viable high-level, risk-management framework. The reason for this is that the Securities and Exchange Commission (SEC) recognizes COSO. It is specifically identified as a suitable framework within additional regulatory guidance around Sarbanes-Oxley compliance.

- **Internal environment**—Establishing a culture in a company that tolerates or even favors risk
- **Objective setting**—Setting objectives; this is first needed in order to later establish how negative events might affect achieving those objectives
- **Event identification**—Identifying external events that might affect the organization's ability to achieve its objectives
- **Risk assessment**—Analyzing risk by considering the likelihood of adverse events and the impact they would have upon the business
- **Risk response**—Considering the organization's appetite for risk, as well as the response to take to risks, such as avoiding them or accepting them

NOTE

COSO was updated in 2004. With this new update, it introduced three new components. These included objective setting, event identification, and risk response.

- **Control activities**—Establishing policies and procedures to ensure that risk responses are carried out
- **Information and communication**—Identifying and communicating information in a timely manner so that the people within the organization can perform their responsibilities
- **Monitoring**—Continuously monitoring and adjusting the ERM program, as needed

The COSO framework is quite broad, and applies across the functions of a company. Although IT security is not specifically addressed, COSO addresses risk management across the organization. COSO does not describe any controls, and is not prescriptive. The framework is targeted at senior management and board of directors. The chief information security officer (CISO) is likely to be involved in the risk-management process and in determining how controls are derived. IT departments should supplement COSO with a framework more specifically suited to IT. An excellent example is discussed next.

COBIT

Control Objectives for Information and related Technology (COBIT) is an IT control framework originally published by the **Information Technology Governance Institute (ITGI)** in 1994 with cooperation from **ISACA**. COBIT offers an IT-specific framework, and is an excellent supplement to COSO. COBIT provides corporate management, IT management, and auditors with an accepted set of processes and controls to develop IT governance and control within an organization. Specifically, COBIT allows IT management to develop clear policies and apply good practices. COBIT even considers other standards and considers those as it seeks to be the overarching IT governance framework. COBIT is business-focused, process-oriented, controls-based, and measurement-driven. COBIT considers risk and stays close to the business by focusing on the benefits associated with IT. COBIT helps to align IT with the business requirements by:

- Mapping controls to key business requirements
- Classifying IT activities into a process model
- Identifying the key IT resources to be controlled
- Defining the framework for control objectives

By providing business-focused alignment, management is able to better understand what IT does. In addition, COBIT provides additional benefits:

- Clear accountability and responsibility
- Acceptance from third parties, auditors, and regulators
- Fulfillment of COSO requirements in regard to the IT control environment

What Is ISACA?

ISACA was once an acronym for Information Systems Audit and Control Association. Today, ISACA goes only by the acronym in an effort to appeal to a broader range of groups. In the late 1960s, ISACA was formed by a group of like-minded individuals seeking guidance around the auditing of computer systems. This group initially became known as the EDP Auditors Association.

Today, ISACA has over 185 membership chapters in over 85 countries, with over 85,000 members. ISACA is behind several globally recognized professional certifications for information systems auditors, and IT security and governance professionals. ISACA also publishes a technical journal and hosts conferences worldwide. ISACA, along with its affiliated IT Governance Institute, provides several valuable resources to IT professionals. In addition to COBIT, the following frameworks are also available from ISACA:

- **IT Assurance Framework (ITAF)**—A framework for IT assurance, applicable to any formal audit or assessment.

- **Risk IT**—A framework based upon guiding principles to effectively manage IT risk. It is intended to complement COBIT. Risk IT provides the structure to identify, govern, and manage IT risk, whereas COBIT provides the set of controls to mitigate the risk.

- **Val IT**—A framework that governs IT investments, helping businesses get more value out of their IT assets. Like Risk IT, Val IT complements COBIT by focusing on the benefits.

Finally, ISACA also publishes additional standards, guidelines, procedures, and research for information system auditors and IT professionals. For students, ISACA offers a student membership program geared to those considering a career in IT.

COBIT serves as a valuable framework across different groups. For example, management can use COBIT to assess performance of IT processes by comparing business goals against the IT goals. Both types of goals are provided within COBIT. Those implementing COBIT as well as auditors can leverage the control requirements and assigned responsibilities from within COBIT. This framework can further be combined with detailed standards such as ISO/IEC 27002 by IT management to develop an overall approach to managing IT.

The COBIT framework is based upon the principle shown in Figure 4-2 and is stated here:

> To provide the information that the enterprise requires to achieve its objectives, the enterprise needs to invest in and manage and control IT resources using a structured set of processes to provide the services that deliver the required enterprise information.[1]

FIGURE 4-2

The basic principles
of COBIT.

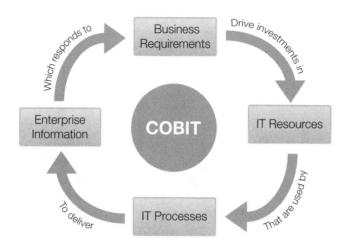

Prior to looking at the framework in depth, let's first explore some of the major parts of the overall structure. First, COBIT defines five areas of focus for IT governance. These areas, all centered on IT governance, include:

- **Strategic alignment**—Ensures IT is aligned with the business
- **Value delivery**—Enables IT to deliver benefits to the business
- **Resource management**—Ensures the proper management of IT resources and that they are used responsibly
- **Risk management**—Involves being aware of risks and the organization's tolerance for risk
- **Performance measurement**—Tracks and monitors the application of IT processes

The business focus of COBIT consists of three primary parts. First is the linkage of business goals to IT goals. Second, in order to meet business goals, COBIT has defined seven business requirements for information. These requirements include control criteria to which information must conform. Finally, COBIT defines a set of four IT resources that are used by processes to deliver the IT goals of the organization.

The general business goals provided by COBIT include 17 goals across four perspectives. The following list outlines these four perspectives along with an example from each:

- **Financial perspective**—Provide a good return on investment of IT-enabled business investments.
- **Customer perspective**—Improve customer orientation and service.
- **Internal perspective**—Provide compliance with internal policies.
- **Learning and growth perspective**—Acquire and maintain skilled and motivated people.

These examples as well as the other business goals not listed are then mapped to specific IT goals. COBIT includes a list of 28 general IT goals. These goals are then mapped to specific processes. A few examples of IT goals include:

- Respond to business requirements in alignment with the business strategy.
- Respond to governance requirements in line with board direction.
- Ensure satisfaction of end users with service offerings and service levels.
- Create IT agility.
- Account for and protect all IT assets.

The seven distinct yet overlapping areas of information criteria that are business requirements for information include:

- Effectiveness
- Efficiency
- Confidentiality
- Integrity
- Availability
- Compliance
- Reliability

IT needs to invest in resources to support a business function that helps the organization realize some type of benefit. The four IT resource areas defined by COBIT include:

- **Applications**—The systems and procedures that process information
- **Information**—The data that is processed and used by the organization
- **Infrastructure**—The technology that provides for the processing of applications
- **People**—The personnel needed to manage the information systems and services

The process- and controls-based focus of COBIT is made up of a model dividing IT into four domains and 34 processes. The four domains shown in Figure 4-3 include:

- **Plan and Organize**—Direction for how IT strategy can most effectively contribute to the goals of the business
- **Acquire and Implement**—IT solutions to be put in place to achieve the IT strategy
- **Deliver and Support**—The delivery of services required to support and maintain IT
- **Monitor and Evaluate**—The need to assess IT processes for effectiveness and compliance

Across these four domains are a total of 34 processes, which contain further, specific control objectives. These control objectives are statements of action to increase the value of IT or reduce risk. They consist mostly of policies and procedures, and provide reasonable assurance that business goals will be achieved. Table 4-1 shows the various processes within each of the four domains.

FIGURE 4-3

The four domains
of COBIT.

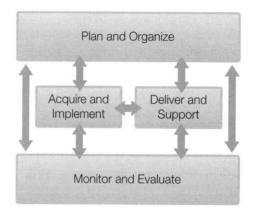

In addition to the various controls that apply to each process within the preceding table, COBIT also defines overarching processes and application controls. Understanding the roles for each process is critical to IT governance. Thus, COBIT provides a **responsible, accountable, consulted, and informed (RACI)** chart for each process. The RACI chart defines who is responsible, accountable, consulted, or informed of the process within the organization.

Finally, COBIT is measurement-driven. To make effective decisions regarding IT controls, organizations need to understand where they are and where they want to be. Thus, organizations need to answer the questions of what improvements need to be made. COBIT provides a maturity model for the management and control over IT processes. It also includes varying levels of goals and metrics. This maturity model is made up of six levels. The maturity model categorizes the process as one of the following six levels:

- **Nonexistent**—Processes are not applied.
- **Initial/ad hoc**—Processes are informal and disorganized.
- **Repeatable but intuitive**—Processes follow a regular pattern but with little communication of standard procedures.
- **Defined**—Processes are documented and communicated.
- **Managed and measurable**—Processes are monitored and measured.
- **Optimized**—Processes are based upon good practices and are automated.

Goals and metrics are defined in COBIT at three levels:

- **IT goals and metrics**—What the business expects from IT and how to measure it
- **Process goals and metrics**—What the IT process must deliver to support IT's goals and how to measure it
- **Activity goals and metrics**—What is required to happen within the IT process to meet the required performance and how to measure it

TABLE 4-1 The four domains and 34 processes of COBIT.			
PLAN AND ORGANIZE	**ACQUIRE AND IMPLEMENT**	**DELIVER AND SUPPORT**	**MONITOR AND EVALUATE**
Define a strategic IT plan.	Identify automated solutions.	Define and manage service levels.	Monitor and evaluate IT performance.
Define the information architecture.	Acquire and maintain application software.	Manage third-party services.	Monitor and evaluate internal control.
Determine technological direction.	Acquire and maintain technology infrastructure.	Manage performance and capacity.	Ensure compliance with external requirements. ✓
Define the IT processes, organization, and relationships.	Enable operation and use.	Ensure continuous service.	Provide IT governance.
Manage the IT investment.	Procure IT resources.	Ensure systems security. ✓	
Communicate management aims and directions.	Manage changes.	Identify and allocate costs.	
Manage IT human resources.	Install and accredit solutions and changes.	Educate and train users.	
Manage quality.		Manage service desk and incidents.	
Assess and manage IT risks. ✓		Manage the configuration.	
Manage projects.		Manage problems.	
		Manage data.	
		Manage the physical environment.	
		Manage operations.	

Now that you have an overview of the various pieces of COBIT, let's tie this all together and examine how the processes fit within the framework. Within the COBIT framework, each of the processes represented in Table 4-1 are represented by the following four sections, which provide the core of the framework:

- **Section 1**—Contains a description of the process, which summarizes the process objectives. This description follows this format: Control over the IT process of [*process name*] that satisfies the business requirement of [*summary of most important IT goals*] by focusing on [*summary of most important process goals*] is achieved by [*activity goals*] and is measured by [*key metrics*]. This section also includes a mapping of the process to the information criteria, IT resources, and IT governance focus area all discussed previously. These mappings are keyed as either being a primary relationship or a secondary relationship.
- **Section 2**—Contains the individual, detailed control objectives for the process.
- **Section 3**—Contains the process inputs and outputs. The process inputs are what the process owner requires from others. The process outputs describe what the process owner has to deliver. This section also includes the RACI chart. Finally, this section provides the goals and metrics for IT, the processes, and associated activities.
- **Section 4**—Contains the maturity model for the process.

For example, the control objective *Ensure Systems Security*, which is part of the Deliver and Support domain, is defined by COBIT within the first section as:

> The need to maintain the integrity of information and protect IT assets requires a security management process. This process includes establishing and maintaining IT security roles and responsibilities, policies, standards, and procedures. Security management also includes performing security monitoring and periodic testing and implementing corrective actions for identified security weaknesses or incidents. Effective security management protects all IT assets to minimise the business impact of security vulnerabilities and incidents.[2]

The primary information criteria are efficiency and confidentiality. The secondary information criteria are integrity, availability, compliance, and reliability. The process description is:

> Control over the IT process of *Ensure systems security* that satisfies the business requirement for IT of *maintaining the integrity of information and processing infrastructure and minimising the impact of security vulnerabilities and incidents* by focusing on *defining IT security policies, plans and procedures, and monitoring, detecting, reporting and resolving security vulnerabilities and incidents* is achieved by:
>
> - *Understanding security requirements*
> - *Managing user identities and authorizations in a standardized manner*
> - *Testing security regularly*
>
> And is measured by:
>
> - *Number of incidents damaging the organisation's reputation with the public*
> - *Number of systems where security requirements are not met*
> - *Number of violations in segregation of duties*[3]

The area of IT governance for this process includes risk management as a primary area; no secondary areas are specified. This process also applies to all four IT resources: applications, information, infrastructure, and people.

The second section for the Ensure Systems Security domain includes 11 control objectives, as outlined here:

- Management of IT Security
- IT Security Plan
- Identity Management
- User Account Management
- Security Testing, Surveillance, and Monitoring
- Security Incident Definition
- Protection of Security Technology
- Cryptographic Key Management
- Malicious Software Prevention, Detection, and Correction
- Network Security
- Exchange of Sensitive Data

The third section defines individual inputs, such as a risk assessment, technology standards, and assigned data classifications. It also defines outputs, such as a security incident definition, training on security awareness, and IT security plan and policies. The RACI chart then details who is assigned the following activities within the organization:

- Define and maintain an IT security plan.
- Define, establish, and operate an identity (account) management process.
- Monitor potential and actual security incidents.
- Periodically review and validate user access rights and privileges.
- Establish and maintain procedures for maintaining and safeguarding cryptographic keys.
- Apply and maintain technical and procedural controls to protect information flows across networks.
- Conduct regular vulnerability assessments.

Finally, the third section outlines many goals and metrics. For example, one goal of IT includes ensuring that confidential information is kept from those who should not have access. This is measured, for example, by the number of incidents with business impact.

The last section outlines the details of the maturity model. For example, a "nonexistent" process would indicate the organization doesn't recognize the need for IT security, whereas an "optimised" process would indicate that IT security is a joint action between IT management and the business, and it is integrated with corporate security business goals.

> **NOTE**
>
> The development of a newer version, COBIT 5.0, is under way as of this writing. A task force is working to bring all of ISACA's frameworks together. See the "What Is ISACA" sidebar for further information on these additional frameworks beyond COBIT.

4

Auditing Standards and Frameworks

SAS 70 Compliance

Most organizations these days outsource some function of their infrastructure to a third-party business. Imagine you are the owner of a company. Putting your company's sensitive data into someone else's hands is a difficult decision to make. You'll likely want to ensure that certain controls are in place before you take on such a risk. The functions provided by the third-party businesses are going to affect the user organization's records. This could be your customer's health or financial information, for example.

Statement on Auditing Standards No. 70: Service Organizations (SAS 70) is a widely recognized and accepted auditing standard. The **Auditing Standards Board of the American Institute of Certified Public Accountants (AICPA)** issues and maintains the auditing standard. It provides a framework for auditing and evaluating the controls of third-party service businesses that host or process data on behalf of their customers or the user organization. Examples of such service businesses include data centers, credit-processing companies, clearinghouses, or insurance claims processors. A SAS 70 indicates that an independent accounting and audit firm have examined the control objectives and activities.

Additionally, Sarbanes-Oxley (SOX) has placed increased importance upon SAS 70 audits. Recall from earlier chapters the goals of SOX. These include improving the accuracy and reliability of financial reporting, as well as restoring investor and public confidence. SOX essentially mandates establishing internal controls. Consider that many organizations outsource all sorts of activities that could have implications upon SOX. This includes payroll functions, for example, which are commonly outsourced. Ensuring adequate controls are in place is required regardless of whether that data is stored and processed in house or by an external party.

For a SAS 70 audit, the user organization must first prepare a statement of its goals. An independent accounting firm first determines if the controls are fairly stated. They then audit and assess the internal controls of the service organization. These professionals have a background in information security, accounting, and auditing. At the end of an audit, the auditor creates the service auditor's report.

A service auditor's report contains information and findings in the following areas:

- Operations and Equipment
- Control Environment
- Computer General Controls
- Control over Computer Operations
- Control over Access to Programs and Data
- Control over New Development and Changes to Existing Programs and Systems
- Information Systems
- User Responsibilities

Type I and Type II Service Audit Reports

There are two types of service audit reports. SAS 70 Type I covers a description of the controls at a specific point in time as well as an opinion on those controls.

TABLE 4-2 SAS 70 Type 1 and Type II report contents.		
CONTENTS OF REPORT	**TYPE I**	**TYPE II**
Independent auditor's report	Included	Included
Service organization controls description	Included	Included
Information from independent service auditor; description of auditor's test and results of operating effectiveness	Optional	Included
Additional information from service organization	Optional	Optional

SAS 70 Type II includes everything in the Type I report but adds a detailed testing of the controls over a minimum of a six-month period. Type II is also more thorough. It provides an opinion as to how effective the controls are for a longer period. For instance, if the Type II testing takes place for six months, the auditor will test the controls for that six-month period. Upon completion, the auditor provides the results back via the report to the service organization. Type I lists the controls but Type II tests the controls to ensure they are working.

Table 4-2 provides a comparison of the two types related to the contents of their reports. A SAS 70 Type II audit, according to SOX, is the only acceptable method a user organization can use to attest to a service provider's controls.

If a service organization chooses not to employ SAS 70, multiple audit reports may occur to establish a similar result. These multiple audits put an incredible strain on a service organization's resources and finances. Conversely, if the service organization moves forward with a SAS 70 commitment, it is stating that transparency and trust with its customers is its goal. The service organization is demonstrating that its control objectives and operations are effective and can be trusted. This trust may be a differentiator for the customer when making a decision as to which service company to employ. If a service organization chooses a Type II audit, it provides an opportunity to ensure its controls are effective or to know if changes are required. Once an organization has a service audit report, it can send the report to multiple customers who are interested in doing business with them.

4

Auditing Standards and Frameworks

FYI

Although a SAS 70 audit might be expensive and difficult for some service organizations, they might find they don't have a choice. Increasingly, a SAS 70 is required to conduct business with many user organizations. This is a result of SOX, Section 404, which requires management to certify financial controls even if they have been outsourced to a third party. Because a SAS 70 Type II can fulfill this obligation, organizations are demanding it of those they outsource their operations to.

WARNING

User organizations should not view a SAS 70 as a "rubber stamp" of approval for information security controls based upon recommended practices. The audit is an assessment of financial controls related to the service organization's stated objectives. User organizations should read each SAS 70 report carefully.

When a user organization employs a service organization that has received a SAS 70 audit, they receive information pertaining to the service organization's controls. The service organization provides the user organization with the independent assessment. The assessment includes the existence of controls. A Type II also states if those controls are operating effectively. It gives the customer a sense of security that their data has the appropriate controls applied. When preparing financial statements, the user organization uses the SAS 70 report as well. It is suitable for regulatory purposes. Furthermore, it removes the need for the user organization's auditors to go to the service organization and conduct audits for their own needs.

ISO/IEC Standards

ISO/IEC 27000 is a series of standards and related terms that provide guidance on matters of information security. This includes implementing, designing, and auditing an **Information Security Management System (ISMS)**. These standards were established by the **International Organization for Standardization (ISO)** and **International Electrotechnical Commission (IEC)**.

ISO is a nongovernment group that brings both the private and public sectors together and creates solutions for business and society. New standards are created by industries or ISO themselves. When a particular industry identifies a specific need, they inform a technical committee within the ISO to get standards developed. If a committee does not exist, a new one may be set up. To be accepted, though, the members of the ISO technical committee must establish majority support and a global relevance must be set. The technical committees within ISO are composed of experts from specific industries such as technical and business. Additionally, other entities such as laboratories, government agencies, consumer organizations, and academia may join the committee experts. Other popular series include ISO 9000 and 14000, which deal with quality management and environmental management, respectively.

TIP

It is common in speech as well as in print to find these standards preceded only by "ISO" rather than "ISO/IEC" used throughout this chapter.

Table 4-3 lists the published ISO/IEC standards in the information security series. The table includes both published standards and standards under development. The next two sections provide details on ISO/IEC 27001 and 27002. Both of these standards focus on information security systems and processes, and are complementary to each other. ISO/IEC 27001 is not a control standard. It focuses on management and processes, and relies upon other standards such as ISO/IEC 27002. ISO/IEC 27002 focuses on the specific controls to make ISO/IEC 27001 possible.

TABLE 4-3 ISO/IEC 27000 series.

PUBLISHED/PROPOSED STANDARD	DESCRIPTION
ISO/IEC 27000	Introduction to the family of standards and includes a glossary of all key terms
ISO/IEC 27001	Information security management system requirements
ISO/IEC 27002	Code of practice for information security management
ISO/IEC 27003	Information security management system implementation guidance
ISO/IEC 27004	Information security management measurement
ISO/IEC 27005	Information security risk management
ISO/IEC 27006	Requirements for bodies providing audit and certification of information security management systems
ISO/IEC 27007	Guidelines for information security management systems auditing
ISO/IEC 27008	Guidance for auditors on ISMS controls
ISO/IEC 27011	Information security management guidelines for telecommunications organizations based on ISO/IEC 27002
ISO/IEC 27013	Guidelines on integrated implementation of ISO/IEC 20000-1 and ISO/IEC 27001
ISO/IEC 27014	Information security governance framework
ISO/IEC 27015	Information security management guidelines for the finance and insurance verticals
ISO/IEC 27031	ICT readiness for business continuity
ISO/IEC 27032	Guidelines for cybersecurity
ISO/IEC 27033	Multipart standard on network security
ISO/IEC 27034	Multipart standard on application security

4

Auditing Standards and Frameworks

ISO/IEC 27001 Standard

ISO/IEC 27001 is a worldwide standard formally known as "ISO/IEC 27001:2005—Information Technology—Security Techniques—Information Security Management Systems—Requirements." It was established in October 2005 and replaced British Standards Institute Security Management Standard BS7799-2.

ISO/IEC 27001 contains accepted good practices and provides an accepted baseline against which IT auditors can audit. It specifies the auditable requirements for establishing, applying, operating, maintaining, reviewing, monitoring, and improving a control framework based on an organization's information security risk. Such risk applies to the information structure within the organization. This includes, for example, management responsibility and documentation. It also applies across all departments, such as human resources, facilities, and operations. It looks at the entire organization and its information assets and walks through a process to determine the associated risks. The process calculates the risk and impact to the organization. Then, it considers the steps needed to remove, reduce, or accept the risk.

The requirements established in ISO/IEC 27001 cover all styles of organizations, such as large enterprises to small- and medium-sized businesses. This also includes federal agencies and not-for-profit organizations. According to the ISO organization, using ISO/IEC 27001 allows an organization to:

- Formulate security requirements and goals.
- Ensure that security risks are cost-effectively managed.
- Ensure compliance with laws and regulations.
- Create a process framework for the application and management of controls to ensure that the specific security goals of an organization are met.
- Define new information security management processes.
- Identify and clarify existing information security management processes.
- Determine the status of information security management activities.

⚠ WARNING

Unlike many other standards and frameworks, the ISO standards are not free of charge. ISO charges fees for the standards, and ISO maintains a prohibitive copyright stance.

- Allow internal and external auditors to determine the degree of compliance with the policies, directives, and standards adopted by an organization.
- Provide relevant information about information security policies, directives, standards, and procedures to trading partners and other organizations with whom they interact for operational and commercial reasons.
- Put in place business-enabling information security.
- Provide relevant information about information security to customers.

The contents of ISO/IEC 27001 include:

- **Information Security Management System**—This section dictates the need for a documented ISMS.
- **Management Responsibility**—This section addresses allocating the appropriate resources to apply and operate the ISMS.

PDCA

The PDCA model used within ISO/IEC 27001 is also known by various other names. Other names include Shewhart cycle, Deming cycle, or Deming wheel. This approach is popular in varying situations focused around continuous improvement. It is also applied when defining a repetitive work process.

Although not invented by Dr. W. Edwards Deming, he certainly popularized its use. Dr. Deming, often called the father of quality management, is known for his work in quality improvement. He is credited with having been the driving force behind Japan's reputation of quality products. He later had a profound impact in the United States.

The four steps within PDCA are conceptually simple. Dr. Deming actually called this four-step process the "Shewhart cycle" after Walter A. Shewhart, an accomplished statistician. The key principle of the PDCA is iteration. With each cycle completed, the knowledge about the underlying system being studied improves. Repeating the process brings perfection closer.

- **Internal ISMS Audits**—This section is about conducting periodic internal audits to ensure the organization is continually addressing the ISMS.
- **ISMS Improvement**—This section is about the need to continually improve the ISMS and ensure its consistent effectiveness.

The standard also includes several annexes. Annex A provides a list of control objectives and associated controls, which come from ISO/IEC 27002. The first section just listed, the Information Security Management System, is the core of ISO/IEC 27001. This section is based on the iterative **plan-do-check-act (PDCA)** approach shown in Figure 4-4. This cycle signifies the importance of a continuous process with regard to improvement, and includes the following steps:

- **Plan**—Establish the ISMS.
- **Do**—Apply and operate the ISMS.
- **Check**—Continuously monitor and review the ISMS.
- **Act**—Maintain and improve the ISMS based on your findings.

ISO 27001 is a formal specification that mandates specific requirements. Organizations desiring to claim they have adopted ISO/IEC 27001 can be formally audited. As a result, they may obtain certification for ISO 27001 for being compliant with the standard. ISO 27001 certification and compliance is received via a third-party organization and is essential for some companies. Having such a certification has benefits to it in that it tells partners locally and globally that the organization has:

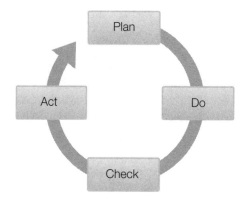

- Performed due diligence
- Ensured information security controls meet the organization's need on an ongoing basis
- Considered risks associated with the organizations

The certification process for ISO/IEC 27001 is similar to other ISO certifications. Although organizations are required to meet every requirement specified in ISO/IEC 27001 to become certified, the controls listed in the annex may be excluded if justified based upon the assessment of risk.

ISO/IEC 27002 Standard

ISO/IEC 27002 is formally known as "ISO/IEC 27002:2005 Information Technology—Security Techniques—Code of Practice for Information Security Management." Whereas ISO 27001 formally defines mandatory requirements for an ISMS, ISO/IEC 27002 provides the suitable information security controls within the ISMS. ISO/IEC 27002 is merely a code of practice or guideline rather than a certification standard. Thus, organizations are free to select and put in place other controls as they see fit.

Fifteen sections make up ISO/IEC 27002. The first four sections provide introductory material, whereas the rest of the sections provide the core recommendations and controls. Sections 5 through 15 provide the following framework:

FYI

ISO/IEC 27002 came from a UK government document originally published in 1995. The original document was republished as British Standard (BS) 7799. This was later republished by the ISO in 2000 as ISO 17799. This standard was updated in 2005 and finally renamed to bring it within the 27000 series of information security standards. The final document today is ISO/IEC 27002.

- Overview of organizational goals being addressed
- List of practical controls
- Guidance for how to put in place each of the controls
- Additional information including cross-references within the standards and other standards

The preceding framework applies to the key sections within the documents, which are summarized in the following list:

- **Risk Management**—Covers the management of risk, including the assessment and treatment of risk
- **Policy**—Covers management guidance and the need to have a documented information security policy and review process
- **Organization**—Covers the organization of information security, including internal organization and external parties
- **Asset Management**—Covers the discovery and classification of the assets
- **Human Resources**—Covers employment of employees and those associated with an organization specific to pre-employment checks and termination and change of employment
- **Physical and Environmental**—Covers secure facilities and equipment security
- **Communications and Operations**—Covers the largest range of areas, including operational procedures and responsibilities, outsourcing, system planning and acceptance, malicious and mobile, code, backups, network security management, media handling, information exchange, e-commerce, and monitoring
- **Access Control**—Covers business requirements, user controls and responsibilities, application level controls, mobile computing, and access controls for networks and operating systems
- **Acquisition, Development, and Maintenance**—Covers systems development and acquisition, including security requirements of systems, correct processing applications, cryptographic controls, system file security, development and support process security, and vulnerability management
- **Incident Management**—Covers information security incident management, including reporting of events and security weaknesses and improvements
- **Business Continuity**—Covers protecting critical processes from disruption
- **Compliance**—Covers complying with legal requirements, security policies, standards and technical compliance, and considerations for information systems audit

Each of the preceding key topics ISO 27002 are composed of many individual controls detailed in the standard. This standard provides wide coverage across the information security domain, and is quite specific in the prescription of controls. As a result, the security community has embraced it widely.

NIST 800-53

In Chapter 2 of this text, you learned about the Federal Information Security Management Act of 2002 (FISMA), and were provided an outline of various supporting documents from the National Institute of Standards and Technology (NIST). Recall that FISMA tasked NIST with developing security standards and guidelines for the federal government. Two documents that are addressed here include:

- NIST 800-53, Recommended Security Controls for Federal Information Systems
- NIST 800-53A, Guide for Assessing the Security Controls in Federal Information Systems

NIST 800-53 provides a comprehensive catalog of security controls. **NIST 800-53A** provides a framework for assessing the adequacy of in-place controls. Although both are targeted to the federal government, many organizations appreciate the depth and prescriptive nature of the NIST standards. As a result, they are widely used outside of government, even if used as a complement to other standards such as ISO/IEC 27002. NIST 800-53 addresses a wide range of controls. The controls consider multiple aspects, including management, technical, and operational. The catalog of controls is grouped into 18 families of controls, which include:

- Access Control
- Awareness and Training
- Audit and Accountability
- Certification, Accreditation, and Security Assessments
- Configuration Management
- Contingency Planning
- Identification and Authentication
- Incident Response
- Maintenance
- Media Protection
- Physical and Environmental Protection
- Planning
- Personnel Security
- Risk Assessment
- System and Services Acquisition
- System and Communication Protection
- System and Information Integrity
- Program Management

The framework for each of the preceding family of controls is composed of the following elements:

- **Control**—A descriptive statement of the security measure to be put in place
- **Supplemental Guidance**—Additional guidance for consideration
- **Control Enhancements**—Information on augmenting the control with additional functionality or increased security
- **References**—A listing of related federal laws, executive orders, directives, policies, standards, and guidelines related to the control
- **Priority and Baseline Allocation**—Listing of codes used for prioritizing decisions during security control implementation and control enhancements for systems of varying degrees of impact

NIST 800-53A provides guidance for building effective security assessment plans. This standard is an excellent complement to NIST 800-53. NIST 800-53A is designed to conduct assessments within a risk-management framework, and provides the following:

- Information about the effectiveness of security controls applied
- Proof of the quality of the risk-management process in use
- Information about the strengths and weaknesses of the information systems

This standard discusses in detail the process for conducting assessments. This includes topics on preparing for the assessment, developing the plans, conducting the assessment, and follow-on reporting, analysis, and other activities.

Developing a Hybrid Auditing Framework or Approach

Frameworks such as COSO and COBIT allow audited organizations to use the same approach for internal audits as they do for external audits. In addition, these frameworks allow traditionally operations-focused audits to combine with traditionally IT-focused audits. This provides the basis for hybrid or **integrated audits**.

The need for integrated audits is largely driven by Sarbanes-Oxley, which established the Public Company Accounting Oversight Board (PCAOB). The PCAOB oversees the rules that apply to publicly traded companies. Traditionally, auditors examined and expressed their opinions on a company's financial statements. However, the rules now require auditors to express an opinion regarding the organization's controls over financial reporting. For example, **Auditing Standard No. 5** states that as part of evaluating financial reports, the auditor should assess the following:

- The inputs, procedures, and outputs of the processes used to produce financial statements
- The amount of IT involvement in the financial reporting process

The standard also explicitly states that the "audit of internal controls over financial reporting should be integrated with the audit of the financial statements." The standard continues, "The auditor should design his or her testing of controls to accomplish the goals of both audits simultaneously." Auditing Standard No. 5 allows use of the work of others. This can save both time and resources. For the purpose of the audit of internal controls, external auditors may use the work of others. They may also receive direct assistance. This includes internal auditors, company personnel, or third-party organizations working under the direction of management or the audit committee.

Some of the key requirements to developing such an approach require organizations to:

- Select appropriate frameworks.
- Adopt risk-based approaches.
- Map business processes to IT processes.
- Have internal audits use the same approach as external audits.

COSO provides an excellent starting point. Consider that COSO provides a framework based upon risk and is an "integrated framework." COBIT is, then, a logical next step. COBIT, in turn, takes the COSO objectives and turns them into a framework applicable to IT.

CHAPTER SUMMARY

As you have seen, there are various standards and frameworks. Nevertheless, each of them has a common goal of establishing sensible practices within the organizations that use them. Standards and frameworks have different advantages and disadvantages. Some, such as COSO for example, appeal to senior-level positions. Others such as ISO/IEC 27002 provide controls that are more prescriptive and will appeal to those managing and implementing systems security. Because of the differences, organizations and auditors will find that a combination of standards and frameworks will be most appropriate. Both auditors and organizations benefit greatly from using well-known standards and frameworks. This includes reduced costs, and allows the auditor and the organization being audited to better understand one another. Finally, it provides the basis for integrated auditing.

KEY CONCEPTS AND TERMS

Auditing Standard No. 5

Auditing Standards Board of the American Institute of Certified Public Accounts (AICPA)

Committee of Sponsoring Organizations (COSO) of the Treadway Commission

Control activities

Control objectives

Control Objectives for Information and related Technology (COBIT)

Descriptive control

Enterprise risk management (ERM) framework

Framework

Information Security Management System (ISMS)

Information Technology Governance Institute (ITGI)

Integrated audit

International Electrotechnical Commission (IEC)

International Organization for Standardization (ISO)

ISACA

ISO/IEC 27001

ISO/IEC 27002

IT Assurance Framework (ITAF)

NIST 800-53

NIST 800-53A

Plan-do-check-act (PDCA)

Prescriptive control

Responsible, accountable, consulted, and informed (RACI)

Risk IT

Statement on Auditing Standards No. 70: Service Organizations (SAS 70)

Val IT

4

Auditing Standards
and Frameworks

CHAPTER 4 ASSESSMENT

1. A _____ is a conceptual set of rules and ideas that provide structure to a complex and challenging situation.

2. Frameworks differ in that they might offer varying levels of depth and breadth when compared with each other.

    A. True
    B. False

3. Avoiding the need for audits is one reason why organizations develop clearly documented policies, standards, and procedures.

    A. True
    B. False

4. Which of the following should organizations do when selecting a standard? (Select three.)

    A. Select a standard that can be followed.
    B. Employ the selected standard.
    C. Select a flexible standard.
    D. Select a standard that other organizations in the same geography are using.

5. The COSO framework is targeted to which of the following groups within a company?

    A. Executive management
    B. First-line management
    C. Security analysts
    D. Application developers

6. COSO is the acronym for which of the following?

    A. Compliance Objectives Standards Organization
    B. Committee of Sponsoring Organizations
    C. Compliance Organization Standard Operation
    D. Committee on Standard Objectives

7. Responding to business requirements in alignment with the business strategy is an example of an IT _____.

8. Which one of the following is *not* true of COBIT?

    A. It is business-focused.
    B. It is security-centered.
    C. It is process-oriented.
    D. It is controls-based.
    E. It is measurement-driven.

9. Which one of the following is *not* one of the four domains of COBIT?

    A. Plan and Organize
    B. Implement and Support
    C. Acquire and Implement
    D. Deliver and Support
    E. Monitor and Evaluate

10. SAS 70 Type I includes everything in a SAS 70 Type II report, but it adds a detailed testing of the controls over a specific time frame.

    A. True
    B. False

11. Organizations may be audited for both ISO/IEC 27001 and ISO/IEC 27002 and receive a formal certification for each.

    A. True
    B. False

12. ISO/IEC 27002 is a code of _____ for information security management.

13. What PCAOB standard states that the auditor should assess the amount of IT involvement in the financial reporting process?

    A. Auditing Standard No. 1
    B. Auditing Standard No. 11
    C. Auditing Standard No. 55
    D. Auditing Standard No. 5

14. Which of the following provides a framework for assessing the adequacy of implemented controls?

    A. NIST 800-53
    B. NIST 800
    C. NIST 800-53A
    D. NIST 800A

15. Which of the following does COBIT stand for?

    A. Control Objectives Beyond Information Technology
    B. Control Objectives for Information and Related Technology
    C. Compliance Organized By Information Technology
    D. Compliance Objectives In Technology

ENDNOTES

1. IT Governance Institute. *COBIT 4.1*. Rolling Meadows, IL: IT Governance Institute, 2007, p. 10.

2. Ibid, p. 117.

3. Ibid, p. 117.

Planning an IT Infrastructure Audit for Compliance

AUDIT PLANNING SHOULD NOT BE OVERLOOKED. What goes into the planning process directly affects the quality of the outcome. The planning stage is the first step and takes place before any of the detailed audit work begins. A proper plan ensures that resources are focused on the right areas and that potential problems are identified early. A successful audit first outlines what's supposed to be achieved as well as what procedures will be followed and the required resources to carry out the procedures.

Although each audit will vary, the plan and approach to each audit follow similar characteristics. Despite the best plans, however, circumstances do change, and plans need to be adjusted. As a result, flexibility must be considered. Significant errors, suspected fraud, and misrepresentation can all have a considerable effect upon the initial plan. Regardless, proper planning helps ensure an effective and timely audit.

Chapter 5 Topics

This chapter covers the following topics and concepts:

- How to define the scope, goals, and frequency of an audit
- What the critical requirements for an audit are
- How to assess IT security
- How to obtain information, documentation, and resources
- What the security policy framework definitions for the seven domains of IT infrastructure are
- How to identify and test monitoring requirements
- How to identify critical security control points that must be verified throughout the IT infrastructure
- How to create a project plan that organizes the IT infrastructure audit approach, tasks, deliverables, timelines, and resources

Defining Scope, Goals and Objectives, and Frequency

The **audit scope**, objectives, goals, and frequency are based on a risk assessment. Depending on the risk, the frequency of audits varies. Critical systems controls might need to be monitored more often than noncritical controls. In more high-risk situations, automated or continual audit tests might be considered.

Prior to performing an audit, the auditor should first define the audit scope. The scope includes the area or areas to be reviewed as well as the time period. Experienced auditors know it's just as important to define what will be audited as it is to define what will not be audited. If scope is not clearly defined, scope creep occurs, likely increasing the auditor's workload.

The **audit objective** is the goal of the audit. Both scope and objective are closely related. For the audit to be effective, the scope must consider the objectives of the audit. Defining scope requires consideration of the personnel, systems, and records relevant to the objective. Time is another consideration dependent upon the objective. The depth and breadth of an audit usually determines the time frame required to meet the objectives.

An external audit of financial controls, for example, will likely have a more narrow scope than an internal audit of information technology (IT) controls. When defining the scope, the auditor should consider the controls and processes across the seven domains of IT infrastructure. This includes relevant resources such as:

- Data
- Applications systems
- Technology
- Facilities
- Personnel

It is important for auditors to ensure the scope is sufficient enough to achieve the stated objectives. Restrictions placed upon the scope could seriously impact the ability to achieve the stated objective. Examples of restrictions that an organization may place upon an auditor that could have such a negative impact include:

- Not providing enough resources
- Limiting the time frame
- Preventing the discovery of audit evidence
- Restricting audit procedures
- Withholding relevant historical records or information about past incidents

Planned audit activities also have a defined rate of occurrence, also known as **audit frequency**. There are two approaches to determine audit frequency. Audits can occur on an annual basis or every two or three years, depending upon regulatory requirements and the determined risk. IT audits also are known for not following a predefined frequency, but instead using a continuous risk assessment process. This is more appropriate given the fast-paced change in technology as well as threats and vulnerabilities related to IT.

Project Management

An audit is a project. As with any project, proper planning is necessary. Auditors should be familiar with the Project Management Institute (PMI), which has created a standard named "A Guide to the Project Management Body of Knowledge (PMBOK)." This guide provides a well-known and applied framework for managing successful projects.

A project, such as an audit, has three important characteristics. First, a project is temporary. This means it has an identified start and end date. Unlike operations or a program, a project lasts for a finite time period. Second, a project is unique and produces unique results. At the end of the project, a deliverable is produced. Although projects might be similar, the process, resources, constraints, and risks, for example, will differ. Finally, a project is progressively elaborated. Because each project is unique, the process is more dynamic. Projects will occur in separate steps. As the process continues, the next phase becomes clearer.

Projects require someone to manage them. This position is often given the title of project manager. Large projects and even audits might have a dedicated project manager. Other times, the person managing the project might be the project expert. Project management requires the management of three competing needs to achieve the project objectives. Known as the "triple constraint," these include scope, cost, and time. Consider, for example, a project with a large scope, but with little time and cost. More than likely, quality will be compromised. A project manager must be aware of all three constraints at the start of and throughout the project.

Identifying Critical Requirements for the Audit

The risk assessment will influence the critical requirements for an IT audit. Overall, there are various types of IT audits. Aside from infrastructure audits for compliance, other examples include audits specific to IT processes, such as governance and software development. Another example includes integrated audits where financial controls are the focus.

Auditing IT infrastructure for compliance incorporates the evaluation of various types of controls. IT organizations today are concerned with controls around both security and privacy. Traditionally, privacy and information security activities are separate activities. The two, however, have become more interrelated, and coordination between the two has become a priority for many organizations. Two major factors contributing to this are regulatory issues and the rapid growth and widespread use of the Web. As a result, both privacy and information security are converging, specifically around compliance issues.

Implementing Security Controls

Before an evaluation of controls can begin, the auditor must first identify the critical controls. To do so, the auditor must consider the audit scope and objective along with the risk assessment. Documentation and any preliminary interviews also help to identify the requirements.

Controls can be classified into different groups to aid in understanding how they fit into the overall security of a system. Figure 5-1 illustrates the different dimensions of control classifications. Understanding the classifications provides auditors with a foundation to identify and assess critical controls.

A high-level classification of controls for IT systems includes general and application controls. General controls are also known as infrastructure controls. These types of controls apply broadly to all system components across an organization. Application controls apply to individual application systems. Types of application controls include various transaction controls, such as input, processing, and output controls.

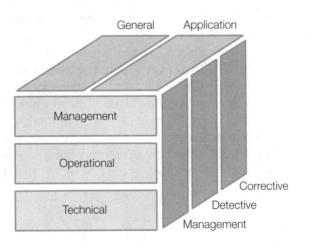

FIGURE 5-1

Control classifications.

Three IT security controls covered by the National Institute of Standards and Technology (NIST) include management, operational, and technical controls. The following list provides a description and examples of each of these:

- **Management controls**—Includes controls typically governed by management as part of the overall security program. Examples include:
  - Security policy
  - Security program management
  - Risk management
  - Security and planning the computer system life cycle
  - Assurance
  - Security and planning in the system life cycle

- **Operational controls**—Includes controls that are implemented by people rather than systems. These controls are often interrelated with both management and technical controls. Examples include:
  - Personnel and user issues
  - Contingency and disaster planning
  - Incident response and handling
  - Awareness, training, and education
  - Computer support and operations
  - Physical and environmental security

- **Technical controls**—Includes controls that are performed by the IT systems. Examples include:
  - Identification and authorization
  - Logical access control
  - Audit trails
  - Cryptography

Controls are further classified as being preventive, detective, or corrective. Preventive controls stop a particular threat in the first place. A door lock on a home is a simple example of a preventive control. A detective control identifies that a threat is present. A home alarm system, for example, is a common detective control. Some people even advertise they have an alarm system by putting a notice on the door or a sign in the yard. In this case, this also serves as a preventive control. Finally, a reactive or corrective control can lessen the effects of a threat. The home alarm system that also notifies the police department is an example of a reactive control. Antivirus software is a common control that spans all three. It can prevent a system from getting a virus in the first place. It can detect if a virus is on the system. Finally, it can react and correct the situation by removing or quarantining the virus.

Protecting Privacy Data

Audits of IT infrastructure around security are common. However, due to recent legislation regarding the need to protect personally identifiable information, audits specific to privacy are more commonplace than before. ISACA defines privacy within the context of information systems as "adherence to trust and obligation in relation to any information relating to an identified or identifiable individual (data subject). Management is responsible to comply with privacy in accordance with its privacy policy or applicable privacy laws and regulations."[1]

Privacy audits go beyond traditional IT audits in that the entire information life-cycle process needs to be considered. This includes not just the controls around how it was gathered and secured, but also how it is collected, used, and retained. Specifically, privacy audits address the following three concerns:

- What type of personal information is processed and stored?
- Where is it stored?
- How is it managed?

Table 5-1 outlines guidance for privacy audits established by the American Institute of Certified Public Accountants (AICPA) and the Canadian Institute of Chartered Accountants (CICA). This guidance is named **Generally Accepted Privacy Principles (GAPP)**.

A privacy audit should consider what privacy laws apply to the organization. Auditors should consider who has responsibility for privacy within the organization. This includes the roles of legal counsel and if a **chief privacy officer (CPO)** role is established. Finally, the policies and procedures specific to privacy should be examined.

Assessing IT Security

Examining IT security is a key component of auditing IT infrastructure for compliance. An audit can help identify fraud, ineffective IT practices, improper use of resources, and inadequate security. Assessing IT security is largely about ensuring adequate controls are in place. Controls cost money, however. The selection and implementation of controls need to be a result of a consideration of risk.

Suppose you want to build a fence to protect a cow. Building the fence will cost money. Exactly how much might depend upon the quality and size of the fence. How much might you be willing to spend? Of course, you should first understand why you want to protect the cow. How valuable is this cow to you? What are you protecting the cow from? Let's assume the cow has some type of value to you—otherwise there might be little reason to spend money on protecting the cow. Is a fence the only solution? Could you tie the cow to a tree instead? If you decide to build the fence, is it strong enough? Is it high enough? Now suppose you decide to have the security of your fence assessed. What you don't need is the auditor to come by and tell you what you already know—you have a fence in place. Rather, what would be useful is a determination of the lack of controls, the ineffectiveness of controls, or even the use of unnecessary controls. If your cow turns out to be a bull,

TABLE 5-1	The Generally Accepted Privacy Principles.[2]
PRINCIPLE	**DESCRIPTION**
Management	The entity defines, documents, communicates, and assigns accountability for its privacy policies and procedures.
Notice	The entity provides notice about its privacy policies and procedures and identifies the purposes for which personal information is collected, used, retained, and disclosed.
Choice of consent	The entity describes the choices available to the individual and obtains implicit or explicit consent with respect to the collection, use, and disclosure of personal information.
Collection	The entity collects personal information only for the purposes identified in the notice.
Use and retention	The entity limits the use of personal information to the purposes identified in the notice and for which the individual has provided implicit or explicit consent. The entity retains personal information for only as long as necessary to fulfill the stated purposes.
Access	The entity provides individuals with access to their personal information for review and update.
Disclosure to third parties	The entity discloses personal information to third parties only for the purposes identified in the notice and with the implicit or explicit consent of the individual.
Security for privacy	The entity protects personal information against unauthorized access.
Quality	The entity maintains accurate, complete, and relevant personal information for the purposes identified in the notice.
Monitoring and enforcement	The entity monitors compliance with its privacy policies and procedures and has procedures to address privacy-related complaints and disputes.

perhaps that fence isn't so effective. Is the fence effective against someone determined to steal the cow? To understand these issues, consider the following:

- Is a control even required?
- How much effort or money should be spent on a control?
- Is the control effective?

To understand the answers to these questions first requires thought about risk. This is why risk management needs to be a key part of organizations and any audit.

Risk Management

Managing and understanding risk is a key operating component of any organization. Risk is about uncertainty. Yet, there will always be uncertainties across organizations. Uncertainty presents both challenges and opportunities for companies. Risk management provides a method for dealing with the uncertainty. This includes identifying which ones to accept or which ones to control. The Committee of Sponsoring Organizations (COSO) of the Treadway Commission, which provides a framework for **enterprise risk management (ERM)**, identifies the following key components of ERM:

- **Aligning risk appetite and strategy**—Helps manage the uncertainty with consideration of the goals of the organization
- **Enhancing risk response decisions**—Improves the ability to make better decisions about how to manage risk
- **Reducing operational surprises and losses**—Enhances the organization's ability to identify potential events or threats and react appropriately
- **Identifying and managing multiple and cross-enterprise risks**—Helps consider related risks from across the organization and provides a unified response across the varying risks
- **Seizing opportunities**—Helps the organization recognize events from which new opportunities can be pursued
- **Improving deployment of capital**—Improves how organizations divide their financial resources to enhance performance and profitability

An example of an IT risk framework compatible with ERM is ISACA's Risk IT. The Risk IT framework is based on and complements Control Objectives for Information and related Technology (COBIT). Risk IT provides a comprehensive framework for not just assessing risk, but also guidance around governance and response. Whereas COBIT provides a framework of controls to minimize risk, Risk IT provides the framework for managing risk. Another example of an information security risk management framework is ISO standard **ISO/IEC 27005**. In addition to providing guidelines for information security risk management, this ISO standard also supports the concepts within ISO/IEC 27001.

The key component of risk management includes a risk assessment. Planning an audit of IT infrastructure is dependent upon this assessment. The audit plan should only be prepared after a risk assessment is complete. The key reason for this is that the audit will focus on those areas with the highest risk.

There are several methodologies for assessing risk specific to IT environments. **NIST 800-30**, "Risk Management Guide for Information Technology Systems," is one such example. This guide provides a practical nine-step process, as follows:

- **System characterization**—Identify and understand the systems and their operating environment.
- **Threat identification**—Identify potential methods or situations that could exploit a weakness.

- **Vulnerability identification**—Identify flaws or weaknesses that can be triggered or exploited, which might result in a breach.
- **Control analysis**—Analyze the controls to reduce the likelihood of a threat successfully exploiting a vulnerability.
- **Likelihood determination**—Determine the likelihood by considering the motivation and capability of the threat source, along with the nature of the vulnerability in relation to the current controls.
- **Impact analysis**—Determine the impact of a successful attack on a vulnerability by a threat. Consider the mission of a system, data criticality, and data sensitivity.
- **Risk determination**—Consider the likelihood, magnitude of impact, and adequacy of controls as an equation of risk.
- **Control recommendations**—Consider controls to reduce the level of risk to an acceptable level.
- **Results documentation**—Document for management the observations on threat/vulnerability pairs as well as risks overall and recommended controls.

To evaluate risk requires looking at the different parts of the risk equation. Effective risk management starts by identifying the IT assets and their value. Next, organizations need to identify the threats and vulnerabilities to these assets. A threat is any activity that represents a possible danger. A vulnerability is a weakness. An analysis or assessment of both threats and vulnerabilities is a key part of the risk-management process. Next, organizations need to identify the likelihood each threat will exploit a vulnerability. Finally, organizations need to consider the impact of the risk. Naturally, risks should then be prioritized, to permit attention to the most severe. Different methodologies are available, which provide clear frameworks for evaluating risk.

NOTE

Threats don't pertain to all organizations equally. This is part of what makes threat identification a difficult task. A simple example is the threat of a hurricane. Although a hurricane is a threat that can cause a loss, you wouldn't consider a hurricane a threat to a data center based in Iowa, for example.

Threat Analysis

Part of the risk assessment process requires an examination of those activities that represent danger. Threats to IT are numerous and can affect the loss of confidentiality, integrity, and availability in a number of ways. Analyzing the potential threats requires the identification of all possible threats first. This is called **threat identification**.

Threats can be grouped through a combination of the following:

- External or internal
- Natural or man-made
- Intentional or accidental

TABLE 5-2	Example of threats, motivations, and threat actions.	
THREAT	**MOTIVATION**	**THREAT ACTION**
Cracker	Challenge	Social engineering
	Ego	System intrusion
Criminal	Monetary gain	Computer crime
	Destruction of information	Fraudulent act
		Information bribery
Terrorist	Destruction	Bomb
	Exploitation	System penetration
	Revenge	System tampering
Espionage	Competitive advantage	Economic exploitation
	Economic espionage	Information theft
		Social engineering
Insiders	Curiosity	System bugs
	Ego	System sabotage
	Revenge	Unauthorized access
	Unintentional errors	Computer abuse

Information about threats such as natural disasters will be readily available and easily obtained by private and governmental resources. The threats that are more difficult to identify are those that pertain specifically to the organization. Table 5-2 provides a summary of man-made threats identified in NIST 800-30. The table includes a list of threats, motivations, and methods that might be used to carry out an attack. The methods are also known as **threat actions**.

All of the threats in Table 5-2 represent varying degrees of potential risks if they are accompanied by vulnerabilities. Each organization will identify its unique threats. Even businesses with multiple locations will have threats specific to that location. To really understand threats, think about your own personal situation. What threats are common to you and where you live? Do these threats change as you travel? What threats exist based upon your lifestyle and goals?

You need to consider likelihood when examining threats. Using the example of a hurricane earlier in this section, it is safe to say that the threat of a hurricane impacting the state of Iowa does not exist. As a result, organizations should develop a threat classification mechanism. A simple example may include a classification of low, medium, and high:

- **Low**—No previous history of the threat, and the threat is not likely to occur
- **Medium**—Some history of the threat, and the threat might occur
- **High**—Substantial history of the threat, and the threat is likely to occur

Vulnerability Analysis

After performing a threat analysis, you need to identify weaknesses or flaws. Specifically, you need to identify vulnerabilities that can be exploited by the previously identified threats. This is known as **vulnerability analysis**. There are many ways to identify vulnerabilities. Examples include:

- Vulnerability lists and databases published by industry organizations
- Security advisories
- Software and security analysis using automated tools

TIP

The MITRE Corporation catalogs vulnerabilities in the Common Vulnerabilities and Exposures (CVE), which includes over 40,000 items.

It is important to always consider the threats relative to the vulnerabilities. Think about operating system patches issued by Microsoft or Apple. Typically, these fix potential vulnerabilities, which were previously unknown and have been discovered. In most cases, these vulnerabilities affect a particular piece of the system. Say, for example, Microsoft issues a patch to fix a vulnerability for a particular service of the operating system. However, what if you don't use this service or the service is turned off? In this case, the vulnerability is not really vulnerable. What if the particular system you use does not and will never be connected to the Internet? In this case, the threat in question does not exist. This is why it is important to pair the threats with the vulnerabilities. Threats are matched with existing vulnerabilities to further understand the risk. Finally, likelihood and impact must be considered. What is the likelihood that a particular threat can exploit a specific vulnerability? Furthermore, if that occurs, what would be the impact?

Finally, keep in mind that consideration of all these elements involves tradeoffs. For example, you can do many things to remove or reduce specific threats and vulnerabilities in your personal life, but you might choose not to. You might even choose not to apply specific controls that can reduce the risks. Many of these decisions are based upon your goals and personal tradeoffs. As you consider these concepts, think about the following:

- Why do some people live in areas with higher crime rates?
- Why doesn't everyone wear a bulletproof vest?
- Why do you ride in or drive vehicles, when there are approximately 40,000 vehicle deaths per year in the United States?
- Why do some people spend more money on home security systems than others?

Risk Assessment Analysis— Defining an Acceptable Security Baseline Definition

Given the previous inputs, the final step is to determine the level of risk. When pairing threats and vulnerabilities, risk is determined primarily by three functions: 1) the likelihood of a threat to exploit a given vulnerability; 2) the impact on the organization if that threat against the vulnerability is achieved; and 3) the sufficiency of controls to either eliminate or reduce the risk. At this point, matrixes and other mechanisms are useful for quantitatively understanding risk. Such matrixes typically categorize the impact and the likelihood of threats as either being low, medium, or high. The product of this results in a risk being low, medium, or high.

Applying controls to a system helps eliminate or reduce the risks. In many cases, the goal is not to eliminate the risk. Rather, what's important is to reduce the risk to an acceptable level. Applying controls is a direct result of the risk assessment process combined with an analysis of the tradeoffs. Several examples of the tradeoffs include:

- **Cost**—Are the costs of a control justified by the reduction of risk?
- **Operational impact**—Does the control have an adverse effect on system performance?
- **Feasibility**—Is the control technically feasible? Will the control be feasible for the end users?

An effective risk assessment process helps establish known good baselines for IT systems. A baseline is the system in a known good state, with the applied minimum controls relative to the accepted risk. Baselines provide a solid and simple method from which to audit a system. Comparing a system against a baseline can help discover nonexistent controls that should be applied as well as controls that have been removed or disabled. Additionally, a baseline audit can help identify a system that has been compromised or otherwise altered.

 NOTE

The best security is layered. This means the information system is composed of multiple controls operating at different layers. This is similar to a castle and its location high on a hill surrounded by a moat, a series of walls, and then locks and guards.

An information system may possess security controls at different layers within the system. For example, an operating system or network component typically provides an identification and authentication capability. An application may also provide its own identification and authentication capability rendering an additional level of protection for the overall information system. As organizations select and specify security controls, they should consider components at all layers within the information system to provide effective security architecture and privacy.

In addition to the results of the risk assessment, numerous "best-practice" baselines exist to help organizations select appropriate security controls. This includes the many documented standards from NIST. Several of these are introduced later in this chapter.

Obtaining Information, Documentation, and Resources

The COBIT framework provides a good starting point for auditors to assess IT controls. Prior to beginning an audit, however, the auditor needs to first gather information from people and relevant documentation and identify required resources. The information the auditor needs to understand prior to performing an audit includes:

- Understanding of the organization, and what its business requirements and goals are
- Knowledge of how the security program is currently in place
- Industry "best practices" for the type of organization and systems

Documentation around business structure, configuration, and even previous audits should be gathered and reviewed. In many cases, auditors will need to request further documentation during the course of the audit. At any point, if the auditor is not given adequate documentation, the auditor should notify the responsible personnel.

Aside from just understanding what regulatory and industry requirements the organization must adhere to, auditors should have a much larger understanding of the business. General knowledge about the business can be gained by gathering information on business and reporting cycles, key business processes, and key personnel to interview. Strategic objectives of an organization reveal details about the organization in the future and how this will affect their information systems. In addition, information about the operational objectives for internal control provides relevant information to the current state of the organization.

> **NOTE**
>
> Documentation is also a good sign that an organization has a sound security program in place. Other documents should include standards, procedures, previous audit reports, risk assessments, and network diagrams.

An organization's written policies are one of the most important documents for an auditor. They provide a guideline from which to check the environment for gaps. More specifically, the auditor can determine if the organization is stating it is doing something that it is not.

There are many other types of documentation that should be gathered depending upon the scope of the audit across the seven domains of IT infrastructure. Examples include:

- Administrative documentation
- System documentation
- Procedural documentation
- Network architecture diagrams
- Vendor support access documents and agreements

Existing IT Security Policy Framework Definition

The results of an audit will reflect how well an organization is adhering to its security policy. However, risk management must be considered. How well an organization adheres to its own policy when combined with an assessment risk helps to identify any gaps. For example, are there control objectives not defined in the policy that should be?

Earlier in this book, you looked at several examples of frameworks. Frameworks exist to help with risk-management programs, security programs, and policy creation. ISO/IEC 27002, for example, provides a structured way for organizations to base their IT security policy. The accounting and audit firms traditionally had their own interpretations of security standards. They, however, have been increasing the use of existing frameworks for benchmarks. It is important for the auditor to know upon what framework an organization has based its policy. This allows better alignment between the organization's policy and the audit. Most internal audits, to ensure compliance across the IT infrastructure, will align with the comparable framework.

Many organizations now have taken steps to implement a security policy framework. However, there are still many instances in which the policy is not actually being enforced.

Additionally, information security policies are living documents. Business environments change. Technologies change. Risks change. As a result, companies with existing policy frameworks might discover that their policies are outdated. The IT security policy must be managed as an ongoing program to evolve with changing requirements and ensure adherence.

Finally, always remember that policies are fundamental to the organization's actions. The policies drive the behavior of the people within an organization and even the technologies acquired. One of executive management's responsibilities is to set goals. Management further supports these goals with a set of objectives. These objectives are communicated throughout the organization by policies. This applies not just to IT security policies, but also to policies across the organization. The policies set the standards, which help drive the business to achieve its goals. As a result, an organization's policies are quite important if they are expected to drive actions and behaviors from the top down. Therefore, high-level policies should be approved and signed by executive management.

NOTE

An IT audit doesn't just assess adherence to the security policy; it also uncovers situations in which the policy needs to be refined.

TIP

It is a good practice to have executive management approve and sign each high-level policy and provide a statement about the importance of the policy and how it helps support the objectives and goals of the organization.

Configuration Documentation for IT Infrastructure

The auditor will gather documents related to the configuration of the systems being audited. Although a single system component is possibly made up of thousands of configuration elements, the following are examples of items the auditor should gather from documentation:

- Host name
- Internet Protocol (IP) addresses
- Operating system
- Patch level
- Hardware specifications
- Installed software
- Protocols
- Service configuration
- User accounts
- Password settings
- Audit log settings

Applications that reside on the computer systems might also have their own configuration documents. These should be gathered as well. Finally, network documentation is required for the network segments pertaining to the applications and systems being audited.

Many organizations will have standard configuration documents for role-specific systems. Examples include the configurations for:

- Firewalls
- Web servers
- Mail servers
- Domain Name System (DNS) servers
- File Transfer Protocol (FTP) servers

Interviews with Key IT Support and Management Personnel—Identifying and Planning

Interviews play an important role in both the information-gathering process and during the audit. Interviews with IT management, for example, can reveal expectations about the organization to the auditor. Interviewing IT support personnel can reveal pertinent information that might not otherwise be discovered. These interviews can also provide greater focus in areas that need it. For example, those personnel doing the daily work can help identify weak controls and broken processes.

Properly conducted interviews might even reveal more serious violations such as fraud. Effective interviews often result in employees offering information around fraud and other serious activities even when hotlines and other reporting processes exist. These conversations should be an interview, however, and not an interrogation. A friendly and nonthreatening environment fosters openness and honesty with those being questioned. The Institute of Internal Auditors (IIA) defines the audit interview as "a specialized form of communication used to gain information and assist in evaluation."

Although interviews play a key role throughout the audit, they help define the scope further during the planning phase. Individual interviews alone might be reason enough to expand the scope. Interviews looked at collectively can provide the auditor with more information. Taken together, these interviews might reveal patterns. Interviews can aggregate enough data to reveal new information. Reasons to expand the scope from the initial interviews can vary, but common examples include:

- Lack of controls
- Override of controls
- Fraudulent activity

Some of the most valuable information for audits will be a result of the interview. As a result, the interview and how well it is performed can make a difference in the outcome of the audit. A simple framework for conducting effective interviews is composed of the following six steps:

- Preparing
- Scheduling
- Opening
- Conducting
- Closing
- Recording

Preparing for the actual interview is essential. It is important to be cognizant of the time of others and the other job functions they must continue to accomplish even during an ongoing audit. The auditor should prepare beforehand a list of questions or at least go into the meeting knowing exactly what it is he or she hopes to achieve or learn. Additionally, auditors should also think like a psychologist. Be aware of the positions and the types of personalities of those being interviewed. Preparation and scheduling can happen in parallel. It is important, however, to ensure enough time is given for preparation. When scheduling, the auditor should try to remain as flexible as possible.

The next two steps constitute the actual interview. The opening sets the tone for the remainder of the interview. Opening with a positive tone and clear expectations, combined with thorough preparation in step one, makes conducting the interview much easier. This leads us into the next step, which is asking the questions. At this point, however, it is not enough to have just well-thought-out questions. The auditor must be adept at listening as well. The auditor should understand lines of management and how they might influence the interviewee's responses. Closing the interview occurs after the auditor has asked all the required questions, or once time is up. The interview should ideally end politely and on an upbeat note. The auditor should thank the interviewee for his or her time, and suggest an agreed-upon protocol, should the auditor require anything else. This leads into the final step of recording. Taking notes is certainly acceptable during the interview process, but it can be disruptive to the interview flow. Even if notes are taken, after the interview, the auditor should immediately review the notes and organize them as needed.

NIST Standards and Methodologies

The previous chapter introduced two important and widely used standards from NIST. These included NIST 800-53 and NIST 800-53A. They provide a catalog of security controls and a framework to assess the controls, respectively. Like the ISO/IEC frameworks, many organizations are basing their policies on NIST. NIST provides many more standards, including low-level documentation that has proven useful for internal auditing and assessments.

The Computer Security Division (CSD) of NIST provides these popular publications along with many more. All of their publications are a result of their research on IT security issues. The publications they provide include:

- **Special Publications**—The 800 series publication provides general-interest documents to the IT security community. NIST also publishes the 500 series, which covers IT.
- **NIST Internal Reports (NISTIR)**—These are publications that describe niche technical research.
- **Information Technology Laboratory (ITL) Bulletins**—These publications provide an in-depth look at timely topics of importance.
- **Federal Information Processing Standards (FIPS)**—These are standards documents published by NIST and approved by the secretary of commerce.

Of the four different document types just listed, the Special Publications from NIST are more likely to be used for audits and assessments. The publications are known for their depth and prescriptive stance. In addition to the two standards listed at the beginning of this section, the following are examples of other NIST Special Publications:

- SP 800-50, "Building an Information Technology Security Awareness and Training Program"
- SP 800-57, "Recommendation for Key Management"
- SP 800-58, "Security Considerations for Voice Over IP Systems"
- SP 800-61, "Computer Security Incident Handling Guide"
- SP 800-68, "Guide to Securing Microsoft Windows XP Systems for IT Professionals"
- SP 800-95, "Guide to Secure Web Services"
- SP 800-115, "Technical Guide to Information Security Testing and Assessment"
- SP 800-123, "Guide to General Server Security"
- SP 800-70, "National Checklist Program for IT Products—Guidelines for Checklist Users and Developers"

The preceding list provides several examples of the many different publications from NIST. The last resource defines the **National Checklist Program (NCP)**. The NCP is a government repository of available security checklists or baseline configurations for operating systems and applications.

Organizing the IT Security Policy Framework Definitions for the Seven Domains of a Typical IT Infrastructure

The IT security policy framework includes policies, standards, and guidelines. Each of these includes technology, processes, and personnel. The seven domains of typical IT infrastructure need to be mapped into the framework. As a refresher from Chapter 3, the seven domains of typical IT infrastructure are as follows:

- User Domain
- Workstation Domain
- LAN Domain
- LAN-to-WAN Domain
- WAN Domain
- Remote Access Domain
- System/Application Domain

In some cases, policies might be very specific to only a single domain. For example, the User Domain maps specifically to human resources security. This encompasses controls relating to items such as pre-employment background checks and information security awareness and training. The seven domains also map across various high-level areas. Examples include access control and operations management.

technical TIP

It is helpful to map the infrastructure against the control objectives for the audit. This can provide a clear scope and ensure that every necessary element is addressed against the control objectives. A challenge for auditors is considering the components or pieces of the IT infrastructure that relate to a key issue. Consider the common example of financial reporting. It is not just the application controls that need to be assessed. Even a single financial reporting system may rely upon many supporting technologies, from across the various domains of IT infrastructure. As a result, it is important to understand when developing an audit plan to have the complete picture of all processes and technology across the infrastructure. A security policy framework can help with scope planning by defining boundaries. It also ensures that all relevant pieces such as interconnected systems are considered to achieve the audit objective. Organizing the security policy framework to the seven domains of IT infrastructure helps define appropriate boundaries for the audit.

Standards further help align the seven domains to the security policy. This includes, for example, access control requirements for networks, users, applications, and operating systems. Just as IT infrastructure needs to be organized within a policy framework, the infrastructure needs to be considered within the framework used for an audit.

The **IT universe** includes all the auditable resources or auditable components within an organization. Naturally, the seven domains of typical IT infrastructure are a large part of this IT universe. The IT universe may be defined as one or more domains of IT infrastructure or even a portion of a single domain. In addition, the IT universe may describe specific entities, locations, functions, or processes within the organization.

Identifying and Testing Monitoring Requirements

Perhaps one of the most important and beneficial elements of an IT security program for auditors is monitoring. All frameworks include a control objective for regularly assessing and monitoring IT systems and controls. For example, COBIT has an entire domain defined for monitoring and evaluating internal controls. COBIT states this domain helps provide answers to the following questions:

- Is IT performance measured to detect problems before it is too late?
- Does management ensure that internal controls are effective and efficient?
- Can IT performance be linked back to business goals?
- Are adequate confidentiality, integrity, and availability controls in place for information security?

Auditors are trying to answer the same questions. Therefore, auditors should identify the tools already put in place by organizations that they will be able to leverage to help answer these questions. Of course, one of the objectives of most audits, regardless of the IT domain being audited, is to identify and test monitoring requirements. Although organizations might have monitoring solutions in place, it doesn't necessarily mean that they are monitoring the right things.

In addition, many companies might be monitoring the right things, but might not have a process in place to make the data actionable. Computer logs provide a perfect example. Are logs being generated? Is the correct information being captured? Is that information being maintained correctly? Are system analysts examining the log data? After analysts examine the data, are any actions created to deal with identified problems? Depending upon the maturity of the organization, there are many systems that manage these events and information and even provide ways to correlate and make this data more manageable and actionable.

Identifying and testing that an organization has implemented a sound program for monitoring provides a lot of the information required by an auditor. Consider the following control objectives suggested by COBIT:

- Monitor and Evaluate IT Performance
- Monitor and Evaluate Internal Control
- Ensure Compliance with External Requirements
- Provide IT Governance

The outputs provided from these objectives are a valuable resource to auditors. Except in situations where these controls are nonexistent, auditors can derive usable data regardless of maturity.

Identifying Critical Security Control Points That Must Be Verified Throughout the IT Infrastructure

Adequate controls should be in place to meet high-level defined control objectives. The organizational risk assessment plays an important role in identifying the high-risk areas. Areas identified as being the most risky should be assessed as often as possible. Levels of risk across the IT infrastructure vary across organizations. This is a result of differing objectives and risk appetites. Regardless, most organizations do share common critical controls.

A great example is the **Consensus Audit Guidelines (CAG)** published by SANS in 2009. This guideline is also known as the SANS Top 20 Critical Security Controls. This includes 20 technical control areas deemed critical, which were introduced in Chapter 3. These 20 controls, although not prioritized in any order, do establish an overall prioritized baseline of security measures and controls that should be in place at most organizations. Of the 20 controls, 15 can in part or whole be monitored through automated means.

As a result, this provides not only a baseline from which to identify security controls, but also a way to verify them efficiently and continuously.

NIST Special Publication 800-53, unlike the CAG, provides a comprehensive library of security controls. The CAG, on the other hand, only provides a subset, but is focused more on what's believed to be the critical controls. Keep in mind that this is only a generalization. After the critical controls are addressed, further controls can be considered from the NIST document, for example.

TIP

The Consensus Audit Guidelines provide an appendix that maps the top 20 critical security controls to specific controls within NIST SP 800-53.

Building a Project Plan Organizing the IT Infrastructure Audit Approach, Tasks, Deliverables, Timelines, and Resources Needed

Having the appropriate people assigned as resources to perform an audit is critical. This impacts the effectiveness and efficiency of the audit. Consider that IT professionals could not possibly be experts across all seven domains of IT infrastructure. Thus, it is not feasible to expect an auditor to be able to perform an adequate audit across all areas. Depending upon the scope of an audit, appropriate resources need to be obtained to perform the audit.

Other helpful resources include tools to support the IT auditing process. Various tools are available to assist in developing and managing the project plan and associated elements, such as tasks, deliverables, and timelines. The Institute of Internal Auditors (IIA) lists several types of tools that can facilitate an audit. These include:

- **Electronic work papers**—Provides a document management system to help centralize and provide workflow management of the audit process.
- **Project management software**—Includes mechanisms for managing any project, including auditing projects. These software packages help track progress to established milestones. Project management software is helpful in defining the timeline of the plan and for reporting upon status.
- **Flowcharting software**—Provides a way to visually document processes.

FYI

Although resources and budgets can be tight, organizations need to ensure adequate auditing resources. The Public Company Accounting Oversight Board (PCAOB) Auditing Standard No. 2 states that "an ineffective control environment was a significant deficiency and a strong indicator that a material weakness exists."[3]

- **Open issue tracking software**—Allows for easy tracking of audit deficiencies and areas that still need to be addressed. In many cases, this function can be integrated or included within a document management system.

- **Audit department Web site**—Internal auditing departments typically have an intranet-based solution that provides for collaboration and communication. Even external auditors benefit from maintaining secured Internet-based portals that provide the same functions.

The previous list of tools is useful for the overall management of the audit. During the course of an audit, however, auditors will likely use additional tools to help with the efficiency and effectiveness of carrying out the audit. Various programs and utilities exist that can help automate tests during the course of the audit. In the next chapter on conducting an audit, you will learn about the many options available. Meanwhile, from a planning perspective, it's important to understand that identification of such tools should be included as part of the planning process.

CHAPTER SUMMARY

An audit plan is a necessary step prior to conducting the actual audit and reporting findings. Identifying and prioritizing risks is a key component of the audit plan. This provides the necessary information to make informed decisions about the scope and objectives of an audit and what resources will be required. Performing key tasks such as aligning the scope with the objectives and gathering all pertinent information beforehand makes the process of testing controls much easier.

The next two chapters look at conducting an audit of IT infrastructure for compliance and the subsequent audit report. Conducting the audit and reporting upon the results will be a direct reflection upon the approved plan.

KEY CONCEPTS AND TERMS

Audit frequency
Audit objective
Audit scope
Chief privacy officer (CPO)
Consensus Audit Guidelines
  (CAG)
Enterprise risk management
  (ERM)

Federal Information Processing
  Standards (FIPS)
Generally Accepted Privacy
  Principles (GAPP)
Information Technology
  Laboratory (ITL) Bulletins
ISO/IEC 27005
IT universe

National Checklist Program
  (NCP)
NIST 800-30
NIST Internal Reports (NISTIR)
Special Publications
Threat actions
Threat identification
Vulnerability analysis

CHAPTER 5 ASSESSMENT

1. Which one of the following can an audit help identify?

A. Fraud
B. Ineffective IT practices
C. Improper use of resources
D. Inadequate security
E. All of the above

2. Which of the following is the discipline of managing and understanding uncertainty?

A. Audit management
B. Metrology
C. Risk management
D. Cryptology

3. Threat is synonymous with risk and can be used interchangeably.

A. True
B. False

4. Identifying potential dangers to an organization is part of the process called _____ identification.

5. Which of the following is the best example of a potential vulnerability to an IT system?

A. Hacker
B. Terrorist
C. Unpatched operating system
D. None of the above

6. The results of a risk assessment help define the audit objectives.

A. True
B. False

7. When applying controls, which of the following is *not* an example of what needs to be considered when examining the tradeoffs?

A. Feasibility
B. Cost
C. Operational impact
D. Due diligence

8. The audit _____ includes the area or areas to be reviewed.

9. Which of the following defines the goals for an audit?

A. Audit objective
B. Audit scope
C. Audit frequency
D. Audit report

10. Which of the following is *not* a category of IT security controls defined by NIST?

A. Physical controls
B. Management controls
C. Operational controls
D. Technical controls

11. Which of the following documents should be included in the gathering process of an IT audit?

A. Policies and procedures
B. Previous audit reports
C. Network diagrams
D. Answers A and C only
E. Answers A, B, and C

12. Only security operations personnel need to follow IT security policies.

A. True
B. False

13. Fraudulent activity uncovered during interviews would be a reason to expand the scope of an audit.

A. True
B. False

14. Which of the following describes all the auditable components within an organization?

A. Cosmos domains of IT
B. Domains of applications
C. IT universe
D. Universal audit

15. Which one of the following is *not* an example of an audit facilitating tool defined by the IIA?

A. Project management software
B. Flowcharting software
C. Electronic work papers
D. Presentation software

ENDNOTES

1. ISACA, *http://www.isaca.org/Template.cfm? Section=Standards&Template=/ContentManagement/ ContentDisplay.cfm&ContentID=18719* (accessed March 22, 2010).

2. AICPA, *http://infotech.aicpa.org/Resources/ Privacy/Generally+Accepted+Privacy+Principles/ Introducing+Generally+Accepted+Privacy+Principles. htm* (accessed March 22, 2010).

3. Public Company Accounting Oversight Board (PCAOB) Auditing Standard No. 2, *http://pcaobus.org/Standards/Auditing/Pages/ Auditing_Standard_2_Appendix_E.aspx* (accessed March 22, 2010).

Conducting an IT Infrastructure Audit for Compliance

ONCE THE AUDIT TEAM COMPLETES an approved auditing plan, they can begin auditing the IT infrastructure for compliance. Testing for compliance is centered on the presence of adequate controls or countermeasures within the planned scope of the IT infrastructure. This includes verifying policies are put in place and appropriately followed.

The actual execution of an audit can vary widely based on the scope and objectives of the plan. Several methods, frameworks, and automated tools are available to assist in the process. The choices made will depend on the areas being assessed and the depth and breadth to which controls need to be examined.

Chapter 6 Topics

This chapter covers the following topics and concepts:

- What minimum acceptable level of risk and appropriate security baselines are
- How to identify documented policies, standards, procedures and guidelines in an organization
- How to conduct audits in a layered fashion
- How to perform a security assessment for the entire IT infrastructure and individual domains
- How to incorporate the assessment into the overall audit validating compliance process
- Which audit tools organize data capture—CAATTs, checklists, and spreadsheets
- Which automated audit reporting tools and methodologies are available
- How to review configurations and implementations in compliance with security policies, standards, procedures, and guidelines
- How to perform, verify and validate proper configuration and implementation of security controls and countermeasures
- What problems and issues arise when conducting an IT infrastructure audit
- How to validate security operations and administration roles, responsibilities, and accountabilities throughout the IT infrastructure

Identifying Minimum Acceptable Level of Risk and Appropriate Security Baseline Definitions

For an organization to develop security baselines, that organization must select proper controls. However, the decision to apply or not apply controls is based on risk. Specifically, the controls put in place manage the identified risks. As a result, the risk assessment discussed in Chapter 5 needs to be completed first.

It might seem easiest to apply a wide range of controls based on different recommendations. Remember, however, that costs are associated with these controls. For example, you can take many different steps to secure your home and minimize risks. Most people consider door locks as necessary. Beyond that, there is no universal rule of home security that everyone adheres to. Even door locks are available in varying strengths. Consider other measures a homeowner might take. Examples include bars on the windows, storm shutters, insurance, burglar alarms, smoke detectors, carbon monoxide detectors, cameras, safes, watchdogs, outdoor lighting, fences, and even weapons. These examples of home controls are similar to IT controls in that there is a cost associated with each of them. Depending on the type or mission of the business, the cost justifications vary. The controls are based on the level of risk the organization faces.

Payment Card Industry Data Security Standard (PCI DSS) provides an example of a concise set of baseline controls required for those organizations that process or transmit payment card information. Refer back to Chapter 2 for a listing of the PCI DSS high-level standards and associated controls. The requirements of PCI consider the general risks to payment card data and provide the baseline approach to safeguarding the sensitive data. The challenge for many organizations is the need to identify and deal with many different types of risks. This is compounded by a constant shift in threats, vulnerabilities, and technology change. The following questions are helpful in determining an appropriate set of baseline controls:

> ⚠ **WARNING**
>
> Effectively managing risks is a complex task. Be careful not to focus only on risk management and lose sight of the organizational goals. If organizations focus more on risk management, they are likely to underperform. You can apply this same principle personally as well.

- Does the organization have a program for IT governance and security management?
- Do IT policies exist?
- Are there tools and processes for assessing risk in place?
- Is the IT environment physically secured?
- Are authentication and access control mechanisms in place?
- Is software to prevent, detect, and respond to malicious code in place?
- Are firewalls used?
- Has a program for configuration and change management been put in place?
- Are systems automatically monitored and reviewed by IT staff?
- Do personnel have the appropriate skills to perform their job, and is an ongoing training and awareness program in place?

Remember that IT is not completely independent. IT exists to enable the business. Understanding the minimum level of acceptable risks and implementing baseline controls depend on IT being aligned with the objectives of the business.

Organization-Wide

Establishing a baseline based on a control framework needs to be relative to the **risk appetite** of the organization. The Committee of Sponsoring Organizations (COSO) defines risk appetite as "the degree of risk, on a broad based level, that a company or other organization is willing to accept in pursuit of its goals. Management considers the organization's risk appetite first in evaluating strategic alternatives, then in setting objectives aligned with the selected strategy, and in developing mechanisms to manage the related risks."[1]

Risk appetite is a broad-based look at the amount of risk an organization is willing to take to achieve its objectives. This should not be confused with **risk tolerance**. Risk tolerance is about the ranges of acceptance for specific risks. Identifying levels of risk tolerance allows the organization to stay within its defined appetite for risk.

IT supports the enterprise risk management (ERM) strategy in a few ways:

- ERM depends on accurate and timely information. Information systems process and store this information. Maintaining the integrity and availability of the data is needed. As a result, adequate controls need to be placed around systems.

- The IT environment supports not only the ERM function, but it also supports all other operations of the business. As a result, the IT environment and associated controls need to be aligned with the organization.

Aside from looking at individual controls, an auditor will ensure the IT environment is aligned with the organization's risk appetite. Additionally, the auditor assesses the framework of internal controls to ensure it is appropriate to allow the organization to remain within its risk tolerances.

Seven Domains of a Typical IT Infrastructure

After considering the organization's risk appetite and tolerance, further consideration of the following is needed:

- The value and importance of data
- Risks to the IT infrastructure
- The level of expected quality of service

> **NOTE**
>
> Most businesses today rely on the Internet as a facilitator for accomplishing their goals. The Internet is a prime example of an IT component that has a clear benefit for the organization, but introduces risk. As a result, basic security controls are applied to protect the organization from numerous threats.

The seven domains of a typical IT infrastructure are composed of people, processes, and technology. This includes employees, partners, and customers interacting with data and using software and applications across a hardware infrastructure. Looking across the seven domains of a typical IT infrastructure can reveal immediate vulnerabilities. For example, domains consisting of remote access, WANs, and cloud computing environments all reveal potential rogue Internet connectivity. Gathering the appropriate documents as discussed in Chapter 5 can provide an immediate view into the domains and inventory of the IT infrastructure.

Mitigating risk within the IT infrastructure includes the application of controls. Again, the risks organizations want to minimize are based on the value of the assets coupled with how a vulnerability being exploited by a threat would impact the confidentiality, integrity, and availability of the data and associated systems. Reducing the risk depends on what controls are available, how much they cost, and if they are cost efficient. As a result of this analysis, organizations typically take the approach to managing risk introduced in Chapter 5. A more detailed look at these strategies includes the following:

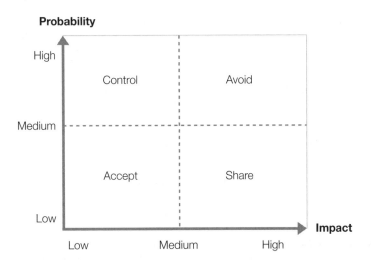

Probability

Impact

FIGURE 6-1

Applying risk-management strategies.

- **Accept the risk**—Do nothing and manage the consequences if the risk is realized.
- **Avoid the risk**—Seek alternatives or don't participate in the risky activity.
- **Share the risk**—Transfer or divide the risk with other parties.
- **Control the risk**—Apply mechanisms or countermeasures to minimize the effects of the risk.

Figure 6-1 provides a simple illustration of components or risk and how the preceding strategies might be applied. The approach an organization takes needs to consider the risk appetite of the organization. The risk might be so great, for example, that avoidance might be the best solution.

> ⚠️ **WARNING**
>
> Do not confuse risk acceptance with risk arrogance. Accepting a risk should be a result of careful planning and attention to an assessment of the risks and possible controls or other strategies for managing risk. "Risk arrogance" or "risk blindness" occurs when an organization does adequately plan and assess risks.

In the wake of the attacks on the World Trade Centers in 2001, a reporter asked Bruce Schneier, a security technologist, "How can we prevent this from ever happening again?" He replied, "That's easy. Simply ground all the aircraft."[2] This example of avoiding the risk might seem far fetched, but as Schneier points out, this is exactly what occurred in the hours following the attacks. Though few would argue with the enormous benefits of air travel, the situation at the time merited an extreme measure be taken.

Consider a simple example of the risk of worms and viruses from the Internet. Consider each of the previous strategies to determine how you might apply each of them to your use of the Internet at home:

- **Accept**—Browse the Web without applying any controls, and hope you don't get infected with malicious software. If you do, you will have to deal with the consequences, which might include losing all your data and having to pay expensive repair costs.

- **Avoid**—Disconnect your computer from the Internet. You will have certainly eliminated the possibility of being infected with malicious software from the Internet. On the other hand, you no longer receive the benefits of what the connection can provide. If you used the Internet primarily for research, for example, you can instead use other sources of information, such as books and encyclopedias.

- **Share**—Use the Internet from publicly available Internet kiosks or libraries. Although this might not be as convenient, this does provide a compromise between acceptance and avoidance.

- **Control**—Purchase antivirus software. This option, however, introduces costs. The costs might involve money and degradation of system performance, for example.

Although the preceding example is relatively simple, the decisions are not always so clear. Two additional concepts in selecting an approach include the introduction of new risks and compensating controls. The introduction of new risks is always a possibility when seeking to mitigate risks. Consider the third example from the preceding list. Do you incur a risk that might have otherwise not existed? Does driving daily to the library introduce the likelihood of being involved in an accident?

"Compensating controls" are alternative measures put in place to mitigate a risk in lieu of implementing a control requirement or best practice. Using the preceding example, suppose you don't want to spend the money on antivirus software and choose to accept the risks. You might take a compensating measure, such as not opening file attachments or only visiting reputable Web sites. Often, layering compensating controls is necessary. In addition to changing your habits, you might also back up your data regularly.

Armed with an understanding of risks within the IT infrastructure, the risk-mitigation strategies will be factored into the appropriate security baseline. An audit of the **baseline controls** will determine the following:

- Are the controls effective at reducing the targeted risk?
- Do the controls incorporate a mix of preventive, detective, and corrective controls?
- How are the controls monitored and audited in case of failure or breach?

Baseline controls are those countermeasures that apply broadly to the entire IT infrastructure. An exterior door lock on a home is an analogy of a common baseline control. Antivirus software is an example of a baseline control within the Workstation Domain. A firewall, which controls access between the organizational network and the public network, is a baseline control for the LAN-to-WAN Domain. In these examples, the controls are configurable depending on the level of risk. Depending on the sensitivity of the data or services, the organization can make further adjustments. For example, does the antivirus software perform periodic scans or does it scan files continuously? A firewall is flexible regarding the level and extent of services it controls. A firewall can place tight restrictions on point-to-point communications or limit what services or applications are able to traverse.

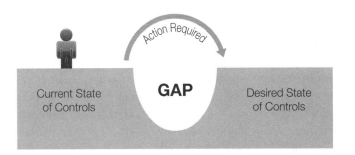

FIGURE 6-2

Control gap analysis.

Gap Analysis for the Seven Domains

A gap analysis is an examination of the current state of controls against the desired state of controls, as illustrated in Figure 6-2. The difference between the two indicates the required action. The ongoing risk assessment process determines the desired state. Thus, once a gap is closed, it does not necessarily stay that way. The results of a gap analysis determine the absence of baseline controls. Moreover, a gap analysis is ideally used once a baseline is established. It further defines the need for additional controls or enhancements to existing controls.

Analyzing gaps requires attention to the type of system and its value or criticality. Depending on the criticality of the system, different baselines may apply. The National Institute of Standards and Technology (NIST) provides baseline control recommendations across three different types of information systems: low impact, moderate impact, and high impact. NIST provides different baseline controls for different classifications.

Gap Analysis of Service Providers

Many organizations use and continue to expand their use of external service providers for operational, IT, and even IT security functions. The concept of a gap analysis can also be applied to these service providers. First, organizations should assess the security controls of any third party for which they outsource any of their IT or business functions. This might involve verifying the service provider has completed a SAS 70 audit. Organizations should also review the specific controls in place at the service provider. It is not unusual to find that a service provider's controls aren't up to the standards of their client organizations.

As a result, organizations can take several approaches. For example, they might decide that the use of the service isn't worth the risk. They might look for another provider that can support the required security controls. Other possibilities include negotiating with the service provider or examining contractual obligations of the service provider. Finally, an organization might employ further compensating controls within the organization if they continue to use the services and if the service provider cannot support the additional controls.

FYI

Multifactor authentication is analogous to using an automatic teller machine. To withdraw money requires a personal identification number (PIN) and a physical card. Neither component by itself is sufficient. Information systems typically rely upon a combination of two or more components for authentication. Typically, this includes something held, such as a card or a token that provides one-time passwords, along with something known, such as a password or PIN. Something inherent might also be included in the authentication process, including biometric features such as a fingerprint.

For example, users accessing low-impact systems might be required to identify themselves with a unique user name and authenticate with a password. This would meet a baseline requirement of an information system uniquely identifying and authenticating users.

Consider an example from NIST 800-53 for monitoring physical access in an information system environment. The control states that the organization should:

- Monitor physical access to the information system to detect and respond to physical security incidents.
- Review physical access logs.
- Coordinate results of review and investigations with the organization's incident response capability.

The previous points represent the baseline control for all systems regardless of the impact level. NIST further provides two more control enhancements for monitoring physical access. These include:

- The organization monitors real-time physical intrusion alarms and surveillance equipment.
- The organization employs automated mechanisms to recognize potential intrusions and initiate designated response actions.

Systems designated as being of a moderate impact would require not only the original baseline control, but also the first control from the previous two items. The high-impact system baseline control would require the original baseline control and both controls from the previous list. If an organization had broadly implemented the original baseline controls, but not the others, a gap analysis would reveal if the control enhancements are necessary. As a result, the organization would clearly understand where they currently stand with regard to monitoring physical access. They would also understand where they need to be and have clear guidance on what they need to do to fill the gap.

Identifying All Documented IT Security Policies, Standards, Procedures, and Guidelines

The organizational security policy framework is the foundation for the direction of information security management. This foundation provides direction and support internally and also provides direction for assessments and audits. The quality of the entire information security program is dependent upon policy. Fortunately, policies can be one of the least expensive controls. Unfortunately, they are often the most difficult to implement effectively. In fact, the first control objective within the International Organization for Standardization/International Electrotechnical Commission (ISO/IEC) 27002 standard states that management should set a clear policy direction by implementing and reviewing the security policy document. The policies provide reference documents for auditors and provide the statement of management intent throughout the organization. As a result, the policy framework, which also includes the standards, procedures, and guidelines, will help guide the organization and audits.

Although frameworks such as ISO/IEC 27002 provide guidance for policy development, the scope and maturity of policies vary widely across organizations. It is still not uncommon to find companies that lack any type of policy framework. Only slightly better are the organizations that have only a basic or boilerplate policy in place. In these situations, audit and compliance groups are valuable resources to help review the proposed policies, making sure they are realistic, in line with business objectives, and enforceable.

During the audit discovery, the governing policy document should have already been reviewed. During the course of the audit, however, this policy will help identify the standards, procedures, and guidelines needed to effectively understand and assess the IT environment. Although explicit audits against the documented policies and supporting documents are common, the existence and extent of such documentation should always be considered regardless of the type of audit. In other words, the auditor should always be identifying and evaluating policies, standards, and procedures. Even though ISO/IEC 27002 has a control objective dedicated to security policies, it references individual policies, standards, and procedures throughout all the other controls as well.

The IT infrastructure audit requires the auditor to rely heavily upon the documented policy framework. This helps identify the gaps for improvements to the policy as well as fulfill the responsibilities to evaluate adequate controls. Ultimately, the goal is to gain assurance around the strategic view and use of IT controls. Realizing this goal is built upon the security policy framework.

Conducting the Audit in a Layered Fashion

The auditor should conduct the audit according to the scope of the plan. This includes auditing the systems included in the plan within the specified time frame. Categorizing the audit into recognizable chunks by domains helps keep the audit focused with minimal reference to other systems. Although the scope may be defined to a specific domain, the auditor needs to recognize the various system inputs, processes, and outputs. This ensures that other domains necessary for an effective audit are covered as needed.

A layered audit approach across the domains of the IT infrastructure will be necessary when systems span the domains. This is especially evident in audits of a particular process. An external audit over financial reporting controls is a perfect example. A company's financial system can span across multiple domains and even include third-party providers such as payroll service providers. This means the auditor has to verify the controls considering the process and the infrastructure that the process uses.

Performing a Security Assessment for the Entire IT Infrastructure and Individual Domains

A variety of tools is used to perform a security assessment. The assessment may target the entire IT infrastructure, a single domain of the IT infrastructure, or anywhere in between. All assessments should follow a plan and be performed with a disciplined approach. There are different approaches to identify security weaknesses within an organization. Some of the approaches include the following:

- **Network scan**—Provides an automated method for discovering host systems on a network. Although it doesn't necessarily discover all vulnerabilities, it does determine which systems are active on the network and what services they offer or what ports are available. A **network scan** provides valuable information pertaining to the environment. A network scan can also provide an adversary with a footprint from which he or she can later conduct a more targeted attack. For this reason, network scans are an important part of defining the assessment process and understanding what an attacker might discover and target.

- **Vulnerability scan**—Provides the fundamental process for managing vulnerabilities. A **vulnerability scan** is an automated method for testing a system's services and applications for known security holes. Most vulnerability assessment scans also provide reports on the identified holes along with additional information for improving security. Unlike a network scan, which looks more broadly for available systems, a vulnerability scan is targeted to specific systems.

Vulnerability scans can be conducted across the entire infrastructure or specific components within the individual domains, such as:

- Operating systems
- Web servers
- Mail servers
- Databases
- File Transfer Protocol (FTP) servers
- Firewalls
- Load-balancing servers
- Switches and hubs
- Wireless access points

- **Penetration test**—This is most often associated with a security assessment. A penetration test, also known as a pen test, is an active hands-on assessment that uses methods similar to what a real-world attacker might use. A penetration test goes beyond simply looking for vulnerabilities. Once vulnerabilities are identified, attempts to actually exploit the vulnerability are attempted. The test helps determine how practical or viable specific attacks might be. This includes understanding what the impact might be of a successful attack.

The technical skill set required to conduct a security assessment depends upon the scope of the assessment and the types of tools or techniques used. Knowledge of basic security principles and technical fundamentals such as understanding **Transmission Control Protocol/Internet Protocol (TCP/IP)** is helpful.

All three of the preceding methods may be used independently or may be used together as part of the overall plan. It is common, for example, for a network scan to precede a penetration test. Both network scans and vulnerability scans are more easily automated on a regular basis than a penetration test. Penetration tests require more planning and coordination.

There are several popular frameworks for conducting comprehensive security assessments. Three examples include:

- **Open Source Security Testing Methodology Manual (OSSTMM)**—A method that takes a scientific approach to security testing. It is made up of five sections called channels, and each channel includes various modules.

- **Information Systems Security Assessment Framework (ISSAF)**—A method for evaluating networks, systems, and applications. It is divided into a three-phase approach, which includes a nine-step assessment process.

- **NIST 800-15**—A guide to the basic technical testing and examination functions of conducting an information security assessment. This NIST guide is composed of seven major sections and several appendixes.

TCP/IP

The language of the Internet and modern networks is the Internet Protocol Suite. This suite of protocols is more formally known as TCP/IP or Transmission Control Protocol/ Internet Protocol. TCP/IP is a result of a project of the Department of Defense (DoD) from decades ago. Research and development of the networking protocols continued. By the early 1980s, the DoD adopted TCP/IP as the standard for its military networks. The 1990s saw the coming of a new application protocol named Hypertext Transfer Protocol (HTTP). This protocol launched what today is known as "the Web." HTTP has been mostly implemented on top of TCP/IP. However, HTTP could make use of any reliable protocol. This networking application, along with others such as e-mail, has made TCP/IP the foundation of modern computer networks.

TCP/IP consists of four layers. At the top is the application layer, which provides support for the protocols necessary for technology, such as the Web and e-mail, but it also supports many other different application protocols. Next, the transport layer includes several protocols, including TCP. TCP allows communications between applications. The next layer down, the Internet layer, includes protocols such as IP. This protocol allows communication between computers. Finally, the data-link layer is the lowest layer. This layer includes the protocols for the physical and logical network connections used to connect systems on the network.

Protocols within the suite use a numerical identifier or port number to identity how hosts communicate across a network. The port first relies upon an **Internet Protocol (IP) address**. The IP address is a numeric label assigned to network systems. The IP address is analogous to your home address. The IP address is a numerical representation to identify and address a system on a network. On a side note, in the near future, you will see widespread adoption of a new IP address format to include hexadecimal representation. This new format will fix a current shortage of available addresses. For each IP address, there are thousands of ports. When a program sends or receives data over a network, the program uses a specific port assigned to a particular IP address. For example, the default port numbers for communications over the Web is 80. If an IP address is analogous to your home address, a port is the entry or exit point used depending upon the situation or "application." For example, visitors use the front doors, deliveries use the back door, trash is accessed via the side door, cars use the garage door, and a burglar uses an open window.

TABLE 6-1 Summary of major capabilities of review techniques.

TECHNIQUE	CAPABILITIES	SKILL SET
Document review	Examines policies and procedures for accuracy and completeness	General knowledge of information security and information policies
Log review	Provides data on system use, changes, and configuration	Knowledge of log events and ability to interpret log data
	Might reveal potential problems and deviations from policies and standards	Ability to use automated logging and log correlation tools
Ruleset review	Exposes holes in security controls based upon rulesets	Knowledge of ruleset formats
		Ability to correlate and analyze rulesets from different devices and different vendors
Network sniffing	Monitors network traffic to capture information such as active systems, operating systems, communication protocols, and services	Knowledge of TCP/IP and networking
		Ability to interpret and analyze network traffic
	Exposes unencrypted communications	Ability to deploy and use network-sniffing tools
File integrity checking	Identifies changes to important files and can also identify unwanted files that might be malicious	General file system knowledge
		Ability to use file integrity checking tools and interpret the results

Regardless of the method chosen, each uses similar techniques for conducting a security assessment. The remainder of this section uses the NIST methodology as a guide. NIST breaks the assessment down across three different types of primary techniques. These include:

- Review techniques
- Target identification and analysis techniques
- Target vulnerability validation techniques

Review techniques are composed of examining the components across the domains of IT infrastructure. Reviewing is a passive process, using noninvasive techniques, which has minimal impact to the systems. Table 6-1 provides examples of specific review techniques, along with the capabilities of the technique and the specific skill set required to use the technique.

After performing a document review, the next step involves the use of target identification and analysis techniques. The goal is to identify active devices along with their
available ports and services and look for possible vulnerabilities. The information
collected sets the stage for the next step of trying to exploit and validate the vulnerabilities.
Table 6-2 provides examples of the techniques involved, along with the capabilities
of the technique and the specific skill set required to use the technique.

TABLE 6-2 Summary of major capabilities of target identification and analysis techniques.

TECHNIQUE	CAPABILITIES	SKILL SET
Network discovery	Discovers active devices on the network	General TCP/IP and networking knowledge
	Identifies communication paths and facilitates determination of network architectures	Ability to use both passive and active network discovery tools
Network port and service identification	Discovers active devices on the network	General TCP/IP and networking knowledge
	Discovers open ports and associated service/applications	Knowledge of ports and protocols
		Ability to use port-scanning tools
		Ability to interpret results from tools
Vulnerability scanning	Identifies hosts and open ports	General TCP/IP and networking knowledge
	Identifies known vulnerabilities	Knowledge of ports, protocols, services, and vulnerabilities
	Provides advice on mitigating discovered vulnerabilities	Ability to use automated vulnerability-scanning tools and interpret the results
Wireless scanning	Identifies unauthorized wireless devices on the network	General knowledge of computing and wireless transmissions, protocols, services, and architecture
	Discovers wireless signals outside of an organization	Ability to use automated wireless scanning and sniffing tools
	Detects potential backdoors and other security violations	

TABLE 6-3 Summary of major capabilities of target vulnerability validation techniques.

TECHNIQUE	CAPABILITIES	SKILL SET
Password cracking	Identifies weak passwords and password settings	Knowledge of secure password composition and how operating systems maintain passwords
		Ability to use automated cracking tools
Penetration testing	Tests security using the same methods and tools that attackers use	Extensive knowledge of TCP/IP, networking, and operating systems knowledge
	Verifies vulnerabilities	Advanced knowledge of network and system vulnerabilities and exploits
	Demonstrates how vulnerabilities can be exploited iteratively to gain access to internal systems	Knowledge of techniques to evade security detection
Social engineering	Allows testing user awareness and if proper procedures are followed	Ability to influence and persuade people
		Ability to remain calm under pressure

Finally, with the information from the previous phase, potential vulnerabilities are probed further. The techniques shown in Table 6-3 are used to exploit the vulnerability.

An organization may use all of the preceding techniques as part of an overall security assessment or selected parts. Additionally, the techniques can be used across the IT infrastructure or they may focus on only specific domains. This is dependent upon the objectives of the assessment, which must consider available time and resources.

 WARNING

The techniques listed in Table 6-3 pose a greater risk during the assessment process than review and target identification and analysis techniques. Although there are benefits to testing out and exploiting vulnerabilities in an assessment, it is possible that these methods could impact the targeted systems negatively. Because of the likelihood and potential impact, you should never conduct these techniques without the expressed consent of senior management or risk owners.

Incorporating the Security Assessment Into the Overall Audit Validating Compliance Process

Some security assessment techniques were listed earlier in the section "Performing a Security Assessment for the Entire IT Infrastructure and Individual Domains." These techniques help determine the feasibility of successful attack against organizational resources. A security assessment is a component of a full IT security audit. Despite the technically focused nature of security assessment methods such as penetration testing and vulnerability assessments, they are not substitutes for an internal audit of IT security. An audit should also include a risk assessment and pay particular focus to internal controls.

The overall process of validating compliance should take a more holistic view. A penetration test, for example, might only reveal a limited number of vulnerabilities that are actually exploited, thus ignoring other vulnerabilities. As a result, these tools and methods should complement the overall audit process.

ISACA produces a series of auditing standards, guidelines, and procedures for information systems auditors. Its standard titled "Performance of Audit Work" states, "IS audit staff should be supervised to provide reasonable assurance that audit objectives are accomplished and applicable professional auditing standards are met."[3] The standard further states, "During the course of the audit, the IS auditor should obtain sufficient, reliable and relevant evidence to achieve the audit objectives." These statements justify the use of security assessment techniques such as penetration testing and vulnerability analysis. The security assessment should support the findings within the final audit report.

In fact, the ISACA procedural document "Security Assessment—Penetration Testing and Vulnerability Analysis" provides information system auditors with guidance. ISACA's suggested penetration test and vulnerability analysis procedures include:

- **Planning**—Defines the scope of the evaluation to include objectives, timing, and tools required
- **Skills required**—Identifies the skills and knowledge required
- **Agreements**—Provides guidance on the types of records to keep and contractual recommendations if external consultants are involved
- **Scope questions**—Offers guiding questions regarding the technical scope of the tests to be performed
- **Internet penetration testing**—Provides recommendations for system enumeration, vulnerability analysis, and vulnerability exploitation from outside the organization
- **Dial-in penetration testing**—Provides guidance for conducting assessments against dial-in technologies

> **FYI**
>
> In certain situations, an automated vulnerability assessment tool might be all that is needed to satisfy audit requirements for industry standards. PCI DSS, for example, qualifies companies that offer automated vulnerability assessment tools as approved scanning vendors (ASVs). In some instances, these solutions even offer the ability to automatically submit results to the required parties. This includes the mergers and acquisitions of banks in the example of PCI DSS.

- **Internal penetration testing**—Provides recommendations for system enumeration, vulnerability analysis, and vulnerability exploitation from within the organization
- **Physical access controls**—Provides recommendations to gain physical access to the network and procedures to perform once physical access is obtained
- **Social engineering testing**—Provides guidance for preparing and conducting social engineering attacks
- **Wireless**—Provides procedures for discovering and exploiting wireless networks
- **Web application**—Provides procedures for analyzing and attacking Web-based vulnerabilities
- **Report**—Recommends preparing the final report in accordance with auditing standards and conducting appropriate follow-up activities

In many situations, an information systems auditor might not have the required skills necessary to perform a security assessment. Additionally, there might be other limitations or constraints that prevent the auditor from performing such a technical analysis. In such situations, the auditor might consider using the work of other experts. The expert can be internal or external to the organization as long as independence and objectivity is preserved. Examples of experts provided by ISACA include:

- An information system auditor from an external accounting firm
- A management consultant
- An IT expert or expert in the area of audit who has been appointed by top management or by the information systems audit team

The auditor should determine that the expert's work is relevant to the audit objectives. The auditor should also obtain a letter indicating that he or she has the right to access the results from the work of others. Prior to incorporating the results of an assessment into the audit, the auditor should review all supporting documents and reports. This includes determining that the assessment supports the audit objectives. If necessary, the auditor might need to conduct additional testing for supporting audit evidence, if not covered in the assessment.

▶ NOTE

Publications and documents may use the acronym CAAT rather than CAATT. In general, the term can describe both tools and techniques. In addition, it is not uncommon to see the acronym use the term "aided" rather than "assisted."

Using Audit Tools to Organize Data Capture—CAATTs, Checklists, Spreadsheets

Auditors are able to increase their productivity through the use of **computer assisted audit tools and techniques (CAATT)**. These tools and techniques are simply computer applications auditors use to assist them in their job functions. Auditors are able to perform tests that otherwise might be difficult or even impossible to do manually. This includes doing an analysis of large amounts of data or being able to increase the coverage of the audit.

Although there are many specialized audit-specific tools available, even an office spreadsheet application is considered a CAATT. The tools and techniques include general audit software, audit expert systems, utility software, and even simple queries and scripts. CAATTs are used for many different functions, including the following:

- Testing transactions within applications
- Reviewing procedures
- Testing system and application controls for compliance
- Conducting automated vulnerability assessments
- Performing penetration testing

During the course of an audit, one of the objectives of the auditor is to produce evidence. Much of the process will still be manual. The use of CAATTs, however, is able to produce much more evidence than what would be possible manually. Prior to using an automated or computer-based tool, the auditor should first be familiar with the tool and have the necessary knowledge and skills required. The auditor should also take necessary steps to be successful and to limit the risk of using such tools during the process. Examples include:

- Establish any related resource requirements. This includes making sure the needed IT facilities, equipment, data, and personnel are available and accessible.
- Understand the type of data to be examined. This includes how much data, what type of data, and the format of the data.

Investigating the Use of Automated Audit Reporting Tools and Methodologies

Many organizations use automated audit reporting tools. Most systems, for example, are capable of producing many different types of audit logs. These logs detail various types of activity throughout the system, including security data. Examples include:

Event Correlation

Event logs can provide valuable information. Fortunately, most every type of system is capable of generating log data. Furthermore, there are systems able to bring all of these disparate logs together into a single location. Unfortunately, this creates a mountain of log data, which can be so overwhelming that eventually it all just gets ignored.

Event correlation enables organizations to better manage the vast amounts of data. Correlation of events provides a more effective means to mitigate threats and vulnerabilities, as well as respond more quickly to incidents. A terminated employee account, for example, can be associated with an attempt to log on to a system with that same account. Individually, this data would not have generated any alerts, but when combined, this becomes valuable information. In another example, multiple rules can be tied together. Consider the following example, which would detect a sequence and pattern of activity within the environment indicative of malicious code:

- If 10 instances are detected of IP spoofing or denied connections *or* successful connections without account data to any firewall ...
  - *and* we detect 10 instances of resource starvation to any IDS device all occurring from the same IP address as the previous rule, *and* this occurs ...
    - within 60 seconds ...
      - then perform some type of action, such as generate a visual alert and send an e-mail to IT security operations staff.

- Failed authentication attempts
- Technical policy changes
- Account changes
- Privileged use

Traditionally, the challenge is managing the voluminous amount of data generated by these systems. This problem is further compounded considering the number and different types of systems across an organization. The components within the seven domains of typical IT infrastructure, for example, are all capable of producing audit trails or log data. Making matters more difficult is that an event generated in one domain may likely contribute to other events being generated in the other domains. Yet by maintaining a silo approach to storing and managing this data, correlation of events is not easy and might be impossible.

Fortunately, automated solutions are available and in use by many organizations. These solutions aggregate all of this data centrally and provide mechanisms to correlate, alert, and report upon this data. These solutions can provide meaningful data from otherwise huge amounts of raw log data. From an organizational perspective, automated audit reporting tools or information and event management help simplify compliance, improve security, and optimize IT operations. Specific examples include:

- Meeting compliance regulations requiring the retention and review of audit records
- Identifying security incidents, such as policy violations and fraudulent activity
- Diagnosing and preventing operational problems
- Conducting forensic analysis
- Establishing operational, security, and performance baselines and being able to identify new trends and problems
- Reporting upon historical data

Table 6-4 provides a sample set of taxonomy for data collected and associated sample events. Security operations should regularly review the data, from which meaningful information can be abstracted. Additionally, operations should leverage programmatic alerts and correlation rules to help identify suspicious activity.

TABLE 6-4   Types of log data and information the data might reveal.

DATA CATEGORY	COMMON EVENTS	SUSPICIOUS ACTIVITIES REVEALED
Computer performance	Resource usage, errors, availability, shutdowns, and restarts	Unauthorized use, compromised systems, denial of service (DoS) attacks
Network performance	Traffic load, errors, network interface status, network scans	DoS and distributed denial of service (DDoS) attacks, information-gathering activities as a precursor to actual attack
Users	Logon and logoff data, privilege use and modifications, failed system access attempts	Brute force attacks on passwords, compromised accounts, privilege abuse
Applications	Application-specific events depending upon type, such as Web servers, firewalls, databases, remote access servers, and Domain Name System (DNS)	Attempts to exploit vulnerabilities, brute force attacks, information-gathering activities as a precursor to actual attack, DoS attacks
File system	Access to data, changes to access control lists, changes to file properties, file additions, and file deletions	System compromise, privilege abuse

Audit and logging systems need to be maintained to perform an efficient analysis of events. Whereas a single failed logon, for example, might not be a cause of concern, many rapid failed logon attempts should be. Maintaining and managing audit logs through the use of these systems also provides the organization with a great mechanism to respond to audit requests. This, of course, provides an auditor with a trove of available data to support the evidence-gathering process. Auditors can take, for example, a representative sampling of logs from the various systems across the IT infrastructure to ensure that automatically audited events comply with the stated policies and procedures.

Reviewing Configurations and Implementations in Compliance with Defined IT Security Policies, Standards, Procedures, and Guidelines

Managing the configuration of information systems is traditionally a function of IT operations. Configuration management, however, has a direct impact on information security and compliance. As a result, **security configuration management (SCM)** pertains more specifically to the configuration items that are directly related to controls or settings that represent significant risk if not managed properly. This includes the controllable parameters for hardware and software. Configuration management as a program is made up of several pieces, such as:

- **Configuration change control board**—A group of personnel with responsibility for governing configurations and configuration changes

- **Baseline configuration management**—The plan for establishing the basic standard of system configurations and the management of configuration items

- **Configuration change control**—A process for managing changes to the configuration standards defined for information systems

- **Configuration monitoring and auditing**—A process for identifying current configurations and testing configurations against established baselines

The configuration includes the specifics on a system's settings. Auditors can review the implementation of configuration items to ensure that prescriptive controls are put in place. The configuration can then be compared with standards and procedures. This task is difficult, however, in the absence of the previously mentioned components of a configuration management program. Even with a change control process in place, systems undergo unauthorized and untracked changes. These changes can directly impact the security of the systems. In addition to unauthorized changes, monitoring helps identify:

- **Misconfigurations**—Identifies authorized changes are correctly put in place and remain in place

- **Vulnerabilities**—Identifies missing system patches as well as configuration items related to a missing patch to determine and prioritize risk

- **Unauthorized systems and software**—Identifies systems not managed by a configuration monitoring solution as well as identify software not authorized for use on the managed system

What makes configuration management especially useful for auditors is that most of the data about the systems is contained with a **configuration management database (CMDB)**. The CMDB provides a central repository from which reports can be run. Thus, everything about all the systems at a particular point in time is stored in a database. Examples of configuration items include:

- Operating system type
- Service pack level
- Security patches
- Software installed
- Users
- Device drivers
- Hardware configuration
- Service and port status
- Access permissions
- Authentication controls
- Audit settings
- Protocols

Many configuration monitoring and auditing solutions are capable of providing predefined templates, from which the configuration items can be assessed. Many of these templates are based on industry-recommended practices such as those from NIST. In addition, organizations can configure auditing templates to align with their own internal policies and standards. The following are sample templates that can be programmatically run to assess parameters specific to the template:

- **Operating system**—Can include audit templates for each version of the operating system across UNIX, Linux, Macintosh, and Windows, for example
- **Database**—Can include audit templates for different types of databases that verify the database security and configuration parameters
- **Application**—Can include audit templates to assess applications for expected configurations
- **Network device**—Can include templates to verify appropriate settings across the network infrastructure, such as routers, switches, and firewalls
- **Best practice documents**—Can include templates to be run across different parts of the infrastructure to test for compliance based upon recommended practices from organizations such as NIST or the Center for Internet Security (CIS)
- **Regulations and standards**—Can include templates specifically targeted to assess against regulations such as the Health Insurance Portability and Accountability Act (HIPAA) or industry standards like PCI DSS

When systems aren't compared against acceptable baselines, the systems could be configured inconsistently a number of different ways. Configuration management and the use of monitoring tools ensure that systems stay configured as originally intended. This makes systems easier to troubleshoot and maintain and makes them more secure.

Performing Testing and Monitoring to Verify and Validate Proper Configuration and Implementation of Security Controls and Countermeasures

Auditing the security controls across the IT infrastructure involves testing the controls or countermeasures using available documents, interviews, and personal observation.

This section provides an overview of testing and validating controls based upon NIST SP800-53A, which provides an approach to assessing security controls. Regardless of the exact methods used, however, the principles are the same.

Each control to be tested should have an accompanying assessment objective. The objective provides the foundation or high-level statement to determine the effectiveness of the control. Based upon this, one or more assessment objectives are validated using a specific method. These methods, discussed in Chapter 1, include examination, interviews, and testing. The results of using these methods against particular assessment objects will produce the results, which are the determination as to the effectiveness of the controls. The assessment objects vary and include different types of elements. Three broad categories of objects include the following:

- **Specification objects**—Documents such as policies, procedures, plans, and architectural designs
- **Mechanism objects**—The specific hardware and software countermeasures installed and configured
- **Activity objects**—The security-related actions involving IT personnel

The effort required to assess controls will vary not just across the objectives. The auditor should also consider impact levels, or the sensitivity and importance of the information systems. The effort is directly related to the depth and breadth of the particular assessment. NIST's assessment framework uses the terms depth and coverage and also defines their associated values. A summary of these definitions includes:

- **Depth**—Addresses the thoroughness and level of detail in the examination, interview, and testing process
- **Coverage**—Addresses the breadth of the examination, interview, and testing process of objects

Depth and coverage each have three different values. The values that address depth include generalized, focused, or detailed. The values that address coverage include representative, specific, and comprehensive. Representative coverage makes use of a limited sample of assessment objects. Further, the goal is to determine that a security control is put in place and that there aren't obvious faults. More specific coverage builds upon this by increasing the scope to achieve greater confidence that the control is not only put in place correctly with no obvious faults, but also operating as intended. Finally, comprehensive coverage uses a much larger sample of assessment objects to achieve the results of representative and specific coverage. It also ensures the control is operating on an ongoing basis that is continually improved.

The varying levels of depth have the same relative expectations. This includes making sure controls are put in place and free of obvious errors. It also includes making sure that the controls are consistently operating as intended and are supported by continual improvement. Interviews and document reviews at a general level include high-level discussions and examination. A more focused assessment asks questions in greater depth and requires a more detailed analysis of documents. Finally, a detailed assessment includes asking deep, probing questions and performing thorough analysis of documents across a greater body of evidence.

In addition to interviews and document review, testing depth requires methodologies of varying degrees of knowledge about the environment being tested. This includes having no knowledge of the infrastructure or implementation of a control to having considerable and extensive knowledge of both the infrastructure and details about the control.

Based upon the tests of each control, an unbiased and factual determination is made as to the effectiveness of the control. The control should either satisfy or not satisfy the expected state. In some situations, the auditor will not be able to determine how effective a control is because of lack of information or other inability to test. In situations where the objectives of the control are not fulfilled, the auditor needs to understand and document how the control differs from what is expected. In addition, the auditor should note how these findings affect confidentiality, integrity, and availability.

Black, White, and Gray Boxes

Testing system controls with varying degrees of knowledge about the overall infrastructure and control is often classified within three boxes. These include black box, white box, and gray box. This terminology is frequently used when conducting penetration tests, software tests, and test of controls or countermeasures.

Black-box testing assumes no knowledge of the inner workings of a system. The idea being that no one can see inside of the box. White-box testing assumes complete and explicit knowledge of everything about the system. This explains why white-box testing is also known as glass-box or clear-box testing. It provides visibility or transparency. Finally, gray-box testing, as the name suggests, is somewhere in between a black-box test and white-box test. A gray-box test is more appropriately described as a translucent box.

When testing the adequacy of controls, the type of testing the auditor conducts is based upon depth. The three attributes of depth are related to these different boxes. Generalized testing is also known as black-box testing. Focused testing is also known as gray-box testing. Detailed testing is also known as white-box testing.

Identifying Common Problems or Issues When Conducting an IT Infrastructure Audit

An audit of an IT infrastructure should address the objectives stated within the plan. It should also comply with laws and professional standards of auditing. The audit seeks to discover evidence from which a conclusion can be made. This conclusion is based upon the analysis and interpretation of the evidence. Despite the best plans and intentions, however, issues can occur and things can go wrong.

To prevent problems from occurring, the auditors must start with the plan. Clear expectations are a common problem with many audits but are easily addressable. The appropriate parties should clearly understand three key points. First, they should understand why the audit is being conducted. Second, they should understand what the scope and objectives are. Finally, they should understand what happens upon completion of the audit.

In addition, interviews and interactions with IT staff are critical throughout the entire audit. Auditors should be careful not to neglect the concerns of the people within the organization. This occurs when auditors are focused entirely on the technology and the gathering of quantifiable data.

NIST defines several areas of potential challenges when conducting security testing and assessments. All of these areas could potentially apply to an audit as well. These areas include:

- **Time and resources**—The importance of a solid plan is critical to maximizing the use of available time and resources. Both are sometimes underestimated for many different reasons. For example, systems might not be able to be tested during normal business hours. Often, there is only a small window of opportunity each day. Because technology evolves so quickly, assessors and auditors might find that they don't have the requisite skill set to adequately perform specific actions.

- **Resistance**—IT personnel might be resistant to an assessment or an audit for many reasons. Operationally, IT personnel might have concerns about outages. On a personal level, individuals might be defensive and fearful for their jobs or fearful of being reprimanded.

- **Temporary behavior**—Users and operators might adjust their processes and systems they are responsible for prior to an audit or an assessment to comply with policies. Upon completion of the audit, however, systems and behaviors often return to the state prior to the audit or assessment.

- **Immediate response**—As weaknesses or audit deficiencies are uncovered, there might be a desire to immediately address the issue. Although generally acceptable and encouraged, changes need to adhere to the organization's policies and change management procedures.

- **Changing technology**—Technology and the tools used to assess technology are constantly evolving. As a result, auditors need to be committed to ongoing information technology education, including the use of new tools and techniques.

- **Operational impact**—There is always the possibility that tests might inadvertently disrupt the systems being tested. To limit any negative impact, the assessor or auditor should always maintain proper documentation, including a detailed list of actions being performed.

Validating Security Operations and Administration Roles, Responsibilities, and Accountabilities Throughout the IT Infrastructure

There are many different roles for security operations and administration across the IT infrastructure. Security operations and administration are responsible for implementing the policy framework to protect the confidentiality, integrity, and availability of the company's information and supporting technologies. The foundation of these operations is first based upon assigning, identifying, and classifying the information and information systems, and then implementing and maintaining the appropriate controls to protect the information and infrastructure.

The tasks include managing authentication and access controls, security hardware, and security software. Security operations and administration personnel are directly involved in the implementation and administration of controls designed to allow access only to those authorized. They also maintain the systems that prevent fraud, violations, and other malicious and even unintentional breaches of confidentiality, integrity, and availability. Security operations and administration personnel need to be held accountable over their responsibilities. Because of the important responsibilities of the security and administration staff, additional safeguards need to be in place to prevent inappropriate use and misconduct.

Those assigned to protect the assets are not above committing irregular or illegal acts. In fact, without the proper controls in place, such activities are easier to perform. This includes fraud, theft, suppression of information, and other legal violations. Examples of safeguards that need to be verified include:

- **Security operation policies**—Policies form the foundation for holding staff accountable. The policies define the expected behaviors that need to be complied with by security and administration personnel. Periodically testing the staff on the organization's policies helps increase accountability.

- **Assignment of responsibilities**—Those assigned with security and administration roles need to have clear expectations and responsibilities. This helps foster and enforce accountability within the individual roles.

- **Maintenance procedures**—These provide clear guidance for the security operations and administration staff in the performance of their duties to prevent misconfigurations and errors.

- **Segregation of duties**—Segregation of duties divides roles and responsibilities so a single individual or group can't undermine a critical process. From an IT perspective, this includes, for example, separating testing, development, and production environments to prevent unauthorized changes. Another example includes preventing the person who approves configuration changes from being the person who implements them. Segregation of duties is also referred to as "separation of duties" or "separation of responsibilities."

- **Rotation of duties**—**Rotation of duties** rotates employees into different functions, and helps mitigate collusion to circumvent what segregation of duties helps prevent.

- **Least privilege**—Least privilege involves users only having access to what they need to perform their duties.

- **Mandatory vacation**—For sensitive positions, a contiguous one-week vacation should be required. This reduces the opportunity for an employee to commit unethical or illegal acts. It allows others to fill in to support the position and verify the work being performed.

- **Screening**—Employees responsible for managing security and sensitive data within an organization should be carefully screened prior to employment. This includes background checks, for example, to ensure the individuals are appropriately suited for the position.

- **Training and awareness**—A continuous program of training is necessary to ensure employees understand their responsibilities associated with their duties and are adequately prepared to perform them effectively.

Security operations and administration personnel need to be held accountable. Strong accountability also serves the goal of preventing fraud and inappropriate use.

CHAPTER SUMMARY

Conducting an IT infrastructure audit for compliance first depends upon an adequate plan. Establishing baselines and identifying an acceptable level of risk across the environment provides a starting point for the actual audit. From there, the audit can follow common methodologies, while being flexible based upon the expanse of the audit. In addition to the documents gathered during the discovery phase, the auditor should continue to gather and use available resources during the audit. This includes continued interaction with the organization, the use of computerized audit tools, and available configuration information and audit logs. Upon completion of the audit testing, a final report should be prepared.

KEY CONCEPTS AND TERMS

Baseline controls

Computer assisted audit tools and techniques (CAATT)

Configuration management database (CMDB)

Information Systems Security Assessment Framework (ISSAF)

Internet Protocol (IP) address

Network scan

NIST 800-15

Open Source Security Testing Methodology Manual (OSSTMM)

Risk appetite

Risk tolerance

Rotation of duties

Security configuration management (SCM)

Transmission Control Protocol/ Internet Protocol (TCP/IP)

Vulnerability scan

CHAPTER 6 ASSESSMENT

1. The decision to apply or not apply controls is based upon risk.

A. True

B. False

2. Which one of the following is the best example of avoiding risk?

A. The IT department decides to install an antivirus device at its network border.

B. The IT department outsources its vulnerability management program to a third party.

C. The IT department disables the ability for end users to use portable storage devices.

D. The IT department installs data loss prevention software on all end users' workstations.

3. Which of the following is an examination of the current state of controls against the desired state of controls?

A. Control objective

B. Gap analysis

C. Baseline analysis

D. Log review

4. The purpose of a network scan is to identify as many vulnerabilities as possible.

A. True

B. False

5. A _____ is an assessment method that uses methods similar to what a real-world attacker might use.

6. Which one of the following is not an example of a review technique?

A. Password cracking

B. File integrity checking

C. Log review

D. Network sniffing

7. If required, an auditor is justified in the use of security assessment techniques, such as penetration testing and vulnerability analysis, and may consider using the work of other experts.

A. True

B. False

8. What does CAATT stand for?

9. Which of the following are examples of information provided by audit logs?

A. Failed authentication attempts

B. Account changes

C. Privileged use

D. All of the above

10. Which of the following benefits does an automated security information and event management log solution provide?

    A. Diagnosing and preventing operational problems

    B. Assigning appropriate responsibilities to security operations

    C. Management of a configuration change control board

    D. All of the above

11. A configuration _____ database provides a central repository of configuration items.

12. Which one of the following best describes an assessment objective for a control?

    A. A high-level statement to determine the effectiveness of a control

    B. A detailed statement on what activities need to occur to implement a control

    C. A definition of responsibilities to be assigned to security operations for the management of a control

    D. A statement to the required depth or coverage required to test a control

13. Which one of the following is *not* an example of a level of depth required to assess a control?

    A. Comprehensive

    B. Generalized

    C. Focused

    D. Detailed

14. Which of the following best describes documents such as policies, procedures, plans, and architectural designs?

    A. Specification objects

    B. Mechanism objects

    C. Activity objects

    D. Configuration objects

15. Preventing a user who approves a configuration change from being the person who implements the change is an example of which of the following?

    A. Rotation of duties

    B. Least privilege

    C. Segregation of duties

    D. Dual control

ENDNOTES

1. "IIA Information Controls." (The Institute of Internal Auditors, 2005). *http://www.scribd.com/doc/8340647/IIA-information-controls* (accessed April 19, 2010).

2. Schneier, Bruce. "The Psychology of Security." *http://www.schneier.com/essay-155.html* (accessed April 19, 2010).

3. "IS Auditing Standard, Performance of Audit Work, Document #S6." (ISACA, 2004). *http://www.isaca.org/AMTemplate.cfm?Section=Standards,_Guidelines,_Procedures_for_IS_Auditing&Template=/ContentManagement/ContentDisplay.cfm&ContentID=15388* (accessed April 19, 2010).

Writing the IT Infrastructure Audit Report

AFTER DOING AN AUDIT, the final report is arguably the most important part of the process. The report provides the means of communicating the project. The purpose of communicating the efforts effectively helps drive management to consider resources and appropriate steps to improve compliance across the IT infrastructure. The primary purposes of the audit report include the following actions:

- Communicate the results.
- Prevent misunderstanding of the results.
- Facilitate follow-up corrective actions.

Various entities and standards provide guidance on what should be included in the final report. These include, for example, the following:

- The American Institute of Certified Public Accountants (AICPA)
- The Institute for Internal Auditors (IIA)
- ISACA

The contents will be influenced by the scope, objectives, methods, work performed, use of other's work, and findings. Each of these items forms the basis of most reports. Other items may appear in the final report. These include a statement as to the independence of the report, if required, disclaimers, visual representations, restrictions, concerns, and audit opinions. Audit opinions generally are either unqualified or qualified. In short, an unqualified opinion means the auditor found no discovered exceptions, while qualified means the auditor notes one or more conditional exceptions were found.

Chapter 7 Topics

This chapter covers the following topics and concepts:

- How to write the executive summary of an audit report
- What a summary of findings comprises
- What to include in the IT security assessment results on risk, threats, and vulnerabilities
- How to write a summary of IT security controls and countermeasures implemented
- What to include in a finding on IT security controls and countermeasures gap analysis
- Important points to highlight in a compliance assessment
- What to include when summarizing compliance recommendations

Chapter 7 Goals

When you complete this chapter, you will be able to:

- Design the layout for a proper executive summary
- Understand audit findings and their importance to the audit report
- Understand the gap analysis and its importance to the audit report
- Identify the risk components part of an IT security assessment and audit report
- Understand how IT security controls identified in the IT audit report relate to the security policy framework and protection of privacy data
- Identify key areas from which a gap analysis should be documented
- Understand how to report upon a compliance assessment
- Understand how to craft meaningful compliance recommendations

Executive Summary

A final audit report is usually lengthy. In fact, the result may be a combination of several different reports. The report contains detailed issues, findings, and action plans. The **executive summary** provides a brief review intended for senior management or other decision makers. Many executives do not have the time to read the full report. Other executives might not have the technical expertise to understand it. The summary provides the necessary information for both types of executives.

> **technical TIP**
>
> Unlike introductory text, an executive summary must be able to exist on its own. Many executive summaries are standalone documents and may even have an accompanying presentation.

Unlike typical summaries, the executive summary should be bold and powerful. It should not be vague. It should include pertinent and valuable information. For example, it would not be suitable to provide a finding that states, "Important baseline controls were missing." Rather, it is better to state, "Over two dozen instances of malicious code were found on systems. And 65 percent of all systems did not have antivirus software installed or enabled." Although it isn't necessary to highlight every issue, the executive summary should include or clearly outline the most important issues.

An executive summary can be a single page in length or multiple pages. A good guideline is that the length of the executive summary should be about 10 percent of the final report. For example, a 1-page executive summary is adequate for a 10-page report. A 100-page report may have a 10-page executive summary.

The components typically used in the final report as well as the executive summary include:

- Introduction
- Objective and scope
- Methodology
- Findings
- Recommendations
- Action plan

All of these are covered in detail within the final report. The final format of the report and executive summary vary by organization. Most important to the executive summary is the review of major issues and findings. This includes making sure to effectively communicate the key issues. This will lead to positive changes within the organization.

Summary of Findings Within the Seven Domains of Typical IT Infrastructure, Gap Analysis

An audit **finding** is a documented conclusion. It involves deficiencies, abuse, fraud, or other illegal acts. The objective of the audit determines the extent of how findings need to be documented. As findings are discovered, further investigation might be required to satisfy the objectives, which will be summarized in the final report. The following four elements are what constitute a finding:

- **Criteria**—Identifies the expected or desired state. This provides the context for evaluating the evidence collected by the auditor and the subsequent procedures the auditor performs. The criteria might be based, for example, upon references to regulations, policies, standards, and external frameworks.

- **Circumstance**—Identifies the determined situation within the IT environment that exists.

- **Cause**—Identifies the reason for the gap between the circumstance and the criteria. The cause also provides a starting point from which the auditor can make a recommendation to correct the situation.

- **Impact**—Identifies the effect or potential impact to the IT landscape based on the difference between the circumstance and the desired state. Essentially, this includes consequences that might occur as a result. It might also reveal negative consequences that have already been occurring.

Within each of the different areas of IT, audit findings can get very specific. Providing a summary of findings across the seven domains of typical IT infrastructure should be broader. To do so in a meaningful, yet concise way requires an analysis of the gaps. This includes a measure of where the organization is and where it would like to be. This requires a complete understanding of the systems across the IT domains, as well as the level of control the enterprise needs. Factors that affect the level of control may include regulatory requirements and risk analysis. An auditor might also compare the organization against industry peers and other recommended practices.

Maturity modeling provides an excellent tool to evaluate the organization and identify gaps. The Control Objectives for Information and related Technology (COBIT) framework, for example, provides a maturity model that is applied across various IT processes. The model is based on a scale of 0 to 5. A rating of 0 means no processes exist. A rating of 5 means processes are optimized. Using such a model allows an organization to more easily understand where it stands today and where it wants to go. The resulting gap identifies the growth path the organization needs to take.

> **NOTE**
>
> The COBIT maturity levels are based upon the Capability Maturity Model (CMM) from Carnegie Mellon University's Software Engineering Institute (SEI) to improve software engineering.

Chapter 4 provides a generic description for the six ratings of the COBIT maturity model. Table 7-1 provides specific examples from "COBIT 4.1" for ensuring systems security. The details for each rating are provided by COBIT across 34 different control objectives.

You can use a maturity model to identify gaps across the IT infrastructure. Specific key facts and details should also be provided in the report as supporting evidence. This should include trying to address the problem and not just symptoms of the problem. With a thorough understanding of the problem, solutions are easier to consider and will be more effective. For example, pointing out critical systems that were infected with malicious code is important. However, knowing that antivirus software was disabled on the systems is more useful. Understanding why the control was disabled is even better. The report should provide enough evidence to support the stated findings. If there are any limitations in regard to evidence, this should be clearly noted.

RATING	RATING DESCRIPTION	DETAILS
TABLE 7-1	COBIT maturity model for the Ensure Systems Security control objective.	
0	Non-existent	The organisation does not recognise the need for IT security. Responsibilities and accountabilities are not assigned for ensuring security. Measures supporting the management of IT security are not implemented. There is no IT security reporting and no response process for IT security breaches. There is a complete lack of a recognisable system security administration process.
1	Initial/Ad Hoc	The organisation recognises the need for IT security. Awareness of the need for security depends primarily on the individual. IT security is addressed on a reactive basis. IT security is not measured. Detected IT security breaches invoke finger-pointing responses, because responsibilities are unclear. Responses to IT security breaches are unpredictable.
2	Repeatable but Intuitive	Responsibilities and accountabilities for IT security are assigned to an IT security co-ordinator, although the management authority of the co-ordinator is limited. Awareness of the need for security is fragmented and limited. Although security-relevant information is produced by systems, it is not analysed. Services from third parties may not address the specific security needs of the organisation. Security policies are being developed, but skills and tools are inadequate. IT security reporting is incomplete, misleading or not pertinent. Security training is available but is undertaken primarily at the initiative of the individual. IT security is seen primarily as the responsibility and domain of IT and the business does not see IT security as within its domain.
3	Defined	Security awareness exists and is promoted by management. IT security procedures are defined and aligned with IT security policy. Responsibilities for IT security are assigned and understood, but not consistently enforced. An IT security plan and security solutions exist as driven by risk analysis. Reporting on security does not contain a clear business focus. Ad hoc security testing (e.g., intrusion testing) is performed. Security training is available for IT and the business, but is only informally scheduled and managed.

TABLE 7-1 *continued*		
RATING	**RATING DESCRIPTION**	**DETAILS**
4	Managed and Measurable	Responsibilities for IT security are clearly assigned, managed and enforced. IT security risk and impact analysis is consistently performed. Security policies and procedures are completed with specific security baselines. Exposure to methods for promoting security awareness is mandatory. User identification, authentication and authorisation are standardised. Security certification is pursued for staff members who are responsible for the audit and management of security. Security testing is completed using standard and formalised processes, leading to improvements of security levels. IT security processes are co-ordinated with an overall organisation security function. IT security reporting is linked to business objectives. IT security training is conducted in both the business and IT. IT security training is planned and managed in a manner that responds to business needs and defined security risk profiles. Goals and metrics for security management have been defined but are not yet measured.
5	Optimised	IT security is a joint responsibility of business and IT management and is integrated with corporate security business objectives. IT security requirements are clearly defined, optimised and included in an approved security plan. Users and customers are increasingly accountable for defining security requirements, and security functions are integrated with applications at the design stage. Security incidents are promptly addressed with formalised incident response procedures supported by automated tools. Periodic security assessments are conducted to evaluate the effectiveness of the implementation of the security plan. Information on threats and vulnerabilities is systematically collected and analysed. Adequate controls to mitigate risks are promptly communicated and implemented. Security testing, root cause analysis of security incidents and proactive identification of risk are used for continuous process improvements. Security processes and technologies are integrated organisationwide. Metrics for security management are measured, collected and communicated. Management uses these measures to adjust the security plan in a continuous improvement process.

TABLE 7-2   Likelihood determination ratings and descriptions.

LIKELIHOOD LEVEL	WEIGHT FACTOR	DESCRIPTION
High	1.0	The threat source is highly motivated and sufficiently capable, and controls to prevent the vulnerability from being exercised are ineffective.
Medium	0.5	The threat source is motivated and capable, but controls are in place that may impede successful exercise of the vulnerability.
Low	0.1	The threat source lacks motivation or capability, or controls are in place to prevent, or at least significantly impede, the vulnerability from being exercised.

TABLE 7-3   Impact levels and descriptions.

MAGNITUDE OF IMPACT	WEIGHT FACTOR	IMPACT DESCRIPTION
High	10	Exercise of the vulnerability may result in the highly costly loss of major tangible assets or resources.
		Exercise of the vulnerability may significantly violate, harm, or impede an entity's mission, reputation, or interest.
		Exercise of the vulnerability may result in human death or serious injury.
Medium	50	Exercise of the vulnerability may result in the costly loss of tangible assets or resources.
		Exercise of the vulnerability may violate, harm, or impede an entity's mission, reputation, or interest.
		Exercise of the vulnerability may result in human injury.
Low	100	Exercise of the vulnerability may result in the loss of some tangible assets or resources.
		Exercise of the vulnerability may noticeably affect an entity's mission, reputation, or interest.

IT Security Assessment Results: Risk, Threats, and Vulnerabilities

A complete security assessment should include details about risk as part of the report. This includes full documentation on the identified threats, vulnerabilities, and resulting risks. The findings inform management of the resulting risk to the environment. This information provides management with the data necessary to make informed decisions to manage risk. The results will help drive how resources are allocated to address potential uncertainties.

The key components of the assessment should include the following:

* **Introduction**—Provides the purpose and scope of the assessment. This includes the systems, personnel, locations, and other details about the assessed environment.

* **Approach**—Describes the methods taken. This includes those involved as part of the assessment and the techniques and tools used to collect information. A description of the risk scale or matrix used should also be discussed.

* **System characterization**—Provides details about the infrastructure systems. This includes the hardware, software, data, interfaces, and associated users. A discussion of existing technical, management, and operational controls may be included.

* **Threat statement**—Lists a complete outline of potential threat sources and associated activities. Chapter 5 provides a sample output of identified threats, motivations, and threat actions.

* **Assessment results**—Provides details on vulnerability and threats, specifically, the pairing of threats with vulnerabilities that can be exploited.

* **Summary**—Provides a concise review of the observations, as well as risk levels. This may include any recommendations.

The report should describe the approach in detail. This includes the methodology used and details about the approach and definitions. A good practice is to use an established approach to assessing risks. The following four tables are adopted from NIST SP 800-30, "Risk Management Guide for Information Technology Systems." The final report should include a similar statement with accompanying background on the methodology. Table 7-2 provides the definitions for determining the likelihood of a threat.

The report should then describe the next step to determine the impact that would result from a vulnerability being exploited. Table 7-3 provides the impact levels and associated definitions.

Next, the report should provide a determination of the resulting risk. The resulting risk is based on the product of the threat likelihood and the impact the threat would have if successful. Table 7-4 provides the method to determine risk. It is based on multiplying the likelihood of a threat occurring by the impact the threat might have.

TABLE 7-4   Resulting risks as a product of impact and threat likelihood.

THREAT LIKELIHOOD	IMPACT LEVEL		
	Low (10)	Medium (50)	High (100)
High (1.0)	Low $10 \times 1.0 = 10$	Medium $50 \times 1.0 = 50$	High $100 \times 1.0 = 100$
Medium (0.5)	Low $10 \times 0.5 = 5$	Medium $50 \times 0.5 = 25$	Medium $100 \times 0.5 = 50$
Low (0.1)	Low $10 \times 0.1 = 1$	Low $50 \times 0.1 = 5$	Low $100 \times 0.1 = 10$

The resulting product of threat likelihood multiplied by the impact level provides a rating of risk. In this example, it would be categorized as Low, Medium, or High. Table 7-5 provides the description of the resulting rating. This also includes actions that must be taken as a result.

The results of the assessment should include a pairing of identified vulnerabilities with associated threats. For each pair, the report includes a brief description of the threat and vulnerability. It should also give a description of existing controls in place to reduce the risk. The results from the previous tables should also be included as summary items. This includes the threat likelihood rating, risk impact rating, and overall risk rating.

TABLE 7-5   Risk level descriptions.

RISK LEVEL	RISK DESCRIPTION
High	If an observation or finding is evaluated as a high risk, there is a strong need for corrective measures. An existing system may continue to operate, but a corrective action plan must be put in place as soon as possible.
Medium	If an observation is rated as medium risk, corrective actions are needed and a plan must be developed to incorporate these actions within a reasonable period of time.
Low	If an observation is described as low risk, management must determine whether corrective actions are still required or decide to accept the risk.

The following is an example of a vulnerability/threat pair analysis. "Weak passwords are vulnerable to hackers." These passwords are more easily guessed or cracked by automated programs. The existing control enforces passwords to be alphanumeric and at least five characters long. The likelihood, impact, and risk rating are all medium. As a result of the risk, a recommended control such as increasing password complexity or length should be documented.

IT Security Controls and Countermeasures Implementation

To identify and report on security controls implemented, a process needs to be in place to collect and manage this information. Many different types of electronic solutions are available to assist with the process, as well as various examples of control assessment reports. A useful form from the National Institute of Standards and Technology (NIST) is one example. The form can help you organize information related to security controls and countermeasures throughout the IT infrastructure.

This NIST sample form is composed of the following four sections:

- **Section I: Information Systems and Assessment Information**—Includes fields for the name of the information system, assessment dates, impact level, sites assessed, and components where security controls are employed. The components would include infrastructure such as firewalls, routers, and workstations.
- **Section II: Security Control Information**—Includes a field for the description of the security control as well as a field for guidance.
- **Section III: Assessment Findings**—Includes fields to identify the specific assessment objective, additional determination statements, as well as the assessment methods and objects. Each determination statement provides a column to indicate if the finding was satisfied or other than satisfied.
- **Section IV: Assessor Comments and Recommendations**—Includes fields for assessor comments and recommendations. The comments clarify identified weaknesses or deficiencies. Added recommendations can suggest how to correct or improve the implemented security control.

Per Documented IT Security Policy Framework

Are controls put in place as stated in the IT security policy framework? Control frameworks such as those from COBIT, NIST, and the International Organization for Standardization (ISO) are useful here. They provide an effective means to assess and document an organization's implementation of controls. This process is quite effective especially when the organization's framework is based upon a well-known external framework.

The organization might have mappings of their controls to well-known frameworks. If available, auditors may use these mappings but should verify them first. This should be included in the final report. In addition, it provides the method for conducting the analysis of any gaps. These gaps should also be documented. Documenting the gap analysis is discussed in the next section.

TABLE 7-6   Generally Accepted Privacy Principles and associated risks.

PRIVACY PRINCIPLE	RISK
Management	Lack of accountability can result in inadequate privacy protection as well as noncompliance with legislation.
Notice	If an individual cannot obtain the privacy policies, he or she may deny consent to use personal information.
Choice and consent	If consent is not obtained prior to collecting personal information, the organization can suffer reputational risk and loss of customer trust.
Collection	Collecting more information than is needed can result in increased retention and security costs and it introduces additional liability.
Use and retention	Personal information could be prematurely destroyed, resulting in information not being available to make important decisions.
Access	Individuals unable to access their information might not be able to correct incorrect information. This could result in a negative decision being made about the individual, resulting in legal liability.
Disclosure to third parties	Providing data to third parties with inadequate controls could affect customer retention and result in identity theft.
Security for privacy	Inadequate security controls could result in the authorized use of privacy data, causing harm to the individual.
Quality	Basing business decisions on inaccurate personal information could result in lost profits.
Monitoring and enforcement	Customer satisfaction and retention might be jeopardized if customer inquiries or complaints are not adequately addressed as a result of an ineffective monitoring process.

Privacy Data

Frameworks mentioned earlier include controls. These controls are essential to protecting privacy data. An audit may be concerned with assessing the protection of privacy data. Or it may be concerned with compliance with privacy laws. In both cases, the audit should report specifically on established privacy principles. Refer to the Generally Accepted Privacy Principles (GAPP) introduced in Chapter 5, if necessary. Also noteworthy are the organization's current implementation, related controls, and associated risks. Table 7-6 provides examples of related risks relevant to each privacy principle.

The risks to the organization for each of the privacy principles should be clearly documented in the audit report. IT security personnel in recent years have had to be more aware of privacy implications. The implications are due to the growing number of privacy regulations. IT controls for privacy go beyond just securing the data to prevent improper use. Most IT frameworks address privacy to a certain extent. In addition, the IIA and ISACA both publish guidelines. These guidelines establish common privacy controls and audit processes.

IT Security Controls and Countermeasure Gap Analysis

A gap analysis means comparing the "as is" to the "to be." For security controls, this involves comparing the present state of controls with a desired state of controls. Well-known frameworks help organizations set up a desired state. This process also helps better manage operational risk. This includes adherence to regulatory and industry requirements to protect sensitive systems and information as well as privacy data.

At a minimum, common baseline security controls should be in place. Any gaps to the following types of controls should be clearly documented:

- **Information security policies**—Provides direction for the entire organization regarding goals, risks, and applicable laws and regulations
- **Information security responsibilities**—Defines how staff will execute upon the policies, assign responsibilities, and promote accountability
- **Information security awareness, education, and training**—Defines the program to provide initial and ongoing security education across the organization
- **Correct processing in applications**—Prevents errors and unauthorized misuse of applications
- **Vulnerability management**—Reduces risk from known vulnerabilities being exploited
- **Business continuity management**—Provides methods to continue critical operations in spite of business interruptions
- **Security incident management**—Ensures security-related events are communicated and acted upon to allow corrective action to be taken by security staff

The report should clearly identify any major gaps. The report should also provide supporting documentation as to the overall implementation of controls, which includes noting any gaps. A simple method could include, for example, a spreadsheet with a list of controls and columns to identify a control that is in place, partially in place, or not in place. Another common method is to use a percentage. Table 7-7 provides an example of identifying gaps for security incident management controls management based on ISO/IEC 27002.

TABLE 7-7 Sample gap analysis of security incident management controls.	
CONTROL	**COMPLETION STATUS**
Report information security events as quickly as possible	100%
Report security weaknesses in systems and services	50%
Establish incident response responsibilities and procedures	100%
Learn from your information security incidents	0%
Collect evidence to support your actions	25%

> **⚠ WARNING**
>
> You should get legal counsel during the process of a gap analysis regarding regulatory requirements. Legal requirements vary from state to state and across different countries. Organizations that operate within a single country may still have to meet certain requirements based on the flow of information to other countries.

Compliance Requirement

Proper security controls are essential to maintaining and safeguarding the IT environment, which exist to help drive the organization's goals. You can group compliance broadly into two categories. This includes compliance to internal policies and standards and compliance to regulatory and industry requirements. Controls explicit to compliance should be included as part of a policy to ensure adherence with applicable legislation and internal governance.

At a minimum, organizations should have a program to manage compliance with internal policies and standards. Specifically, this includes identifying areas of noncompliance and methods for correction. Additionally, technical controls should be in place to ensure systems are compliant with standards. This would also include a program for penetration testing and vulnerability assessments. In addition, the organization should have a documented control program in place. This program should manage the audit requirements of information systems.

The final report should identify how the report and associated audit and assessment activities fit into the organization's control. Next, it should include the current state of compliance with legal requirements and compare this against where the organization needs to be.

Has the organization identified all legal, regulatory, and industry-specific requirements? Without these key controls, it will be difficult for the organization to implement and enforce further controls. Additionally, the organization should document the gaps for the following requirements:

- **Respecting intellectual property rights (IPRs)**—Organizations regardless of size depend on proprietary software and other intangible assets. Examples of intellectual property include those items protected by copyrights, trademarks, patents, and trade secrets. **Intellectual property rights (IPRs)** are the exclusive privilege to intangible assets.

- **Protecting and retaining organizational records**—Laws and regulations set time periods for which organizations must hold and protect specific types of data.

- **Protecting personal information**—Numerous laws have been enacted to protect the collection, processing, and storage of personal information. Chapter 2 provides several examples.

- **Preventing users from using systems for unauthorized purposes**—Because of legislation that provides protection against computer misuses, organizations are required to meet requirements for security monitoring access notification.

- **Managing the proper use and import or export of cryptographic controls**— Although laws have been relaxed in recent years, there are legal restrictions on the export of cryptographic technology to "rogue states" or terrorist organizations. In fact, strong cryptography for many years was considered munitions and was part of a list that included items such as firearms, tanks, chemical agents, and nuclear weapons.

Risk, Threat, and Vulnerability Mitigation Requirement

The documented gap analysis should include basic security controls introduced in the beginning of this section. It should also consider controls relevant to the risks of the organization. However, this depends on an organization's ongoing program for establishing security requirements, assessing security risks, and managing controls.

Compliance Assessment Throughout the IT Infrastructure

The results of a compliance assessment should clearly address whether specific requirements are met. For example, consider the following:

- **Compliant**—Indicates there is enough suitable evidence to show that a particular requirement has been met.

- **Noncompliant**—Indicates that enough suitable evidence was collected to show that a particular requirement has not been met.

- **Not determined**—Indicates that not enough evidence was collected or sufficient evidence wasn't collected to make an appropriate compliance determination.

- **Not applicable**—Indicates a requirement doesn't apply. For example, compliance requirements to wireless networks would not apply if the organization doesn't maintain wireless networks. In addition, this would be an appropriate response if a determination could not be made within the scope of the audit. This differs from not having enough sufficient evidence, in that a particular requirement may be dependent upon an activity or event. Consider the example where certain external organizations must be notified in the event of a breach. Making an appropriate determination would not apply if, for example, the organization has not encountered a breach.

TABLE 7-8   A sample documented PCI DSS compliance test result.

PCI DSS REQUIREMENT	TESTING PROCEDURES	STATUS	COMMENTS
Do not use vendor-supplied defaults for system passwords and other security parameters.	Attempted to log on to a sample of selected critical systems using the default vendor-supplied accounts and passwords taken from vendor documentation	Compliant	The point-of-sale systems do not support vendor-supplied default passwords.

The testing procedures used should be documented. This should also include comments regarding the determination. For example, consider compliance to the Payment Card Industry Data Security Standard (PCI DSS). PCI DSS requires vendor-supplied default passwords be changed before installing a system on the network. The report would include this along with the other requirements followed by the corresponding testing procedures and results. Table 7-8 provides an example of the documented results for this requirement.

Presenting Compliance Recommendations

Audits sometimes reveal major risks or compliance gaps. In those cases, the final reports may include recommendations supported by the audit findings. The recommended actions should be logically tied to a finding for which the problem has also been identified. A recommendation is more valuable to the organization when it is specific, sensible, and cost effective. Ultimately, the objective is to consider the processes and inputs up to this point and clearly communicate the following:

- Recommended actions to lessen control weaknesses
- Recommended actions to comply with applicable laws and regulations
- Comparisons and gaps to standards and accepted frameworks and recommendations to narrow the gap

Recommendations should be actionable. They should not include statements such as "controls should be strengthened." Tactical recommendations are important and needed. However, the report should also provide strategic recommendations. Specifically, these consider the broader picture of the organization objectives and how identified gaps or vulnerabilities affect the organization's ability to achieve those goals.

Management action plans and appropriate follow-up are critical to close the process. Recommendations provide the action management should take to deal with deficiencies. It is the documented action plan, however, that provides the guidance for correcting those deficiencies. This includes assigning responsibility for each recommendation and assigning deadlines. Agreed-upon actions should be documented within the recommendations if this information is provided by management prior to the final report.

As part of the document-gathering process of an audit, the auditor should consider previous audit results and past recommendations. Likewise, documented results and recommendations will be examined with the next audit. This provides a process for continual awareness to changing environments and constant improvement.

CHAPTER SUMMARY

Once the auditing team has completed the audit, an audit report will be issued to the organization. Depending upon the scope and objectives of the audit, this report can take on many different forms. Regardless, effective communication of the results is vital to prevent any misunderstanding. Proper communication of the results will also ensure adequate follow-up actions.

KEY CONCEPTS AND TERMS

Executive summary
Finding
Intellectual property rights
   (IPRs)

CHAPTER 7 ASSESSMENT

1. Which of the following is *not* a purpose of the audit report?

   A. Provide an action plan for auditors to implement controls.
   B. Communicate the results.
   C. Prevent misunderstanding of the results.
   D. Facilitate follow-up corrective action.

2. An abstract of an audit report provides a brief review intended for senior-level management who might not have the time to read and understand the entire report.

   A. True
   B. False

3. An executive summary should never be more than one page long.

   A. True
   B. False

4. Which of the following best describes an audit finding?

   A. The procedures used to find IT controls
   B. A documented conclusion that identifies deficiencies
   C. A verbal recommendation to improve controls
   D. The auditor's fee

5. Which rating description using the COBIT maturity model would be assigned to a business that does not recognize the need for IT security, nor has a recognizable system security administration process? _____

6. What is the formula for determining risk?

7. Which one of the following is *not* a privacy principle as identified by GAAP?

   A. Secrecy
   B. Choice and consent
   C. Collection
   D. Use and retention
   E. Disclosure to third parties

8. Which of the following best describes a business that is found to have unlicensed software installed throughout the environment?

   A. They have violated export restrictions on cryptographic software.
   B. They are not adequately protecting personal information.
   C. They have violated intellectual property rights.
   D. Answers B and C

9. Which of the following best describes when not enough evidence was collected to make an appropriate determination as to the compliance of a specific control?

   A. Not determined
   B. Not applicable
   C. Compliant
   D. Answers A and B

10. The final audit report includes recommended actions, which should be associated with which of the following?

   A. Findings
   B. Vulnerabilities
   C. Threats
   D. None of the above

Compliance Within the User Domain

COMPLIANCE IS MORE THAN just checking items off a list. It is a dynamic process of ensuring the items in each domain meet or exceed your goals. Because conditions can change in any organization, the status of how well you are meeting your goals can change as well. You should make all decisions related to security controls to satisfy your security policy and any other relevant compliance requirements. Ensuring compliance to your security policy keeps security-related actions headed in the right direction.

Chapter 3 discussed the seven domains of a typical information technology (IT) infrastructure. The User Domain defines the components in the IT infrastructure that directly interact with information system users. User Domain components both govern and are influenced by user behavior. The best User Domain controls direct and restrict user actions and result in compliant behavior. In short, your goal in the User Domain is to persuade users to act in a way that meets or exceeds your standards of behavior. You'll learn about different opportunities to affect user behavior and how that behavior impacts your organization's security.

Chapter 8 Topics

This chapter covers the following topics and concepts:

- How compliance law requirements and business drivers relate to one another
- Which items are commonly found in the User Domain
- What separation of duties means
- What least privilege is
- What need-to-know basis is
- What confidentiality agreements are
- What employee background checks are

- How acknowledgment of responsibilities and accountabilities relate to compliance
- How security awareness and training for new employees relate to compliance
- What information systems security accountability is
- How to ensure adherence to documented IT security policies, standards, procedures, and guidelines
- What best practices for User Domain compliance requirements are

Chapter 8 Goals

When you complete this chapter, you will be able to:

- Examine compliance law requirements and business drivers
- Compare how items found in the User Domain contribute to compliance
- Describe methods of ensuring compliance in the User Domain
- Summarize best practices for User Domain compliance

Compliance Law Requirements and Business Drivers

Information systems provide information to users. Without users, there would be no reason to invest in collecting, manipulating, and storing data. Information passes from the outside world to the information system through user actions. Keyboards, mice, and scanners are just a few of the common methods users employ to get information into the various systems. A secure system needs controls that limit the type of information users can provide and retrieve.

The User Domain is the initial domain in the IT infrastructure that formalizes how information flows in and out of computer systems. This domain defines components you need to control to ensure your environment is compliant with applicable requirements. Figure 8-1 shows the User Domain in the context of the seven domains in the IT infrastructure.

User Domain controls designed to help ensure compliance place limits on acceptable user actions. A User Domain "control" is any mechanism that interacts with a user and reacts when a user's actions meet certain conditions. The overall purpose of User Domain controls is to restrict user behavior to approved, or compliant, behavior. The control's reaction depends on what type of control it is. Controls generally fall into the following functional types:

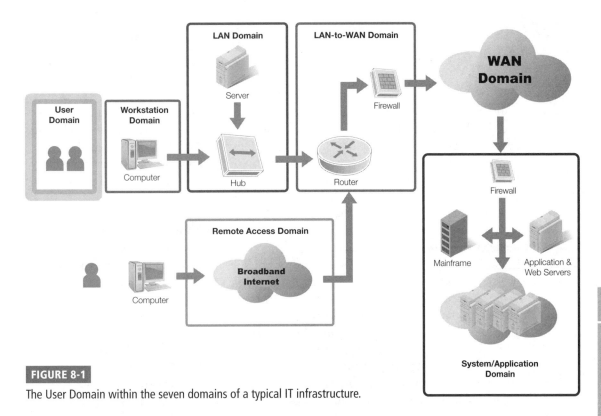

FIGURE 8-1

The User Domain within the seven domains of a typical IT infrastructure.

- **Preventive controls**—**Preventive controls** are mechanisms that keep an undesired action from happening, such as locked doors or computer access controls.

- **Detective controls**—**Detective controls** are mechanisms that recognize when an undesired action has occurred, such as motion detectors or usage log analysis tools.

- **Corrective controls**—**Corrective controls** are mechanisms that repair damage caused by an undesired action and limit further damage, such as the procedure to remove viruses or using a firewall to block an attacking system.

Figure 8-2 gives an overview of preventive, detective, and corrective controls.

By limiting what users can do, compliance-related security controls restrict users to appropriate actions. These restrictions can include limits on what users can access and what actions they can perform. Although limiting users to meet compliance requirements might be desirable or even necessary, they can make it more difficult to complete required business functions. One of the difficulties of ensuring security in the User Domain is designing secure controls that still allow and promote necessary business functions.

FIGURE 8-2

Types of security controls.

Preventive Controls	Detective Controls	Corrective Controls
• Stop actions	• Recognize actions	• Fix the result of actions

It is important that you implement compliance requirements in a way that minimizes the impact on **business drivers**. Recall that business drivers are the components, including people, information, and conditions, that support business objectives. Any negative impact on business drivers can also have a negative impact on your organization's ability to satisfy business objectives. Carefully research the impact to business drivers before you implement any compliance controls.

Remember that compliance requirements dictate how your organization conducts its activities. Whether the compliance requirement comes from legislation, regulation, industry requirements, or even your organization's standards, the end result is the focus. In most cases, your organization can control activities to ensure compliance in multiple ways. Always consider alternative controls to achieve the end result compliance requires. You'll likely find that some controls are less costly and less intrusive than others. Don't just accept the first control that does the job. Many times, alternate controls are just as good but intrude less on your organization's activities.

You can meet many compliance requirements using one of several controls. If one control has a negative impact on business drivers, consider another control. You can often justify eliminating one control if another control will achieve the same goal.

For example, Payment Card Industry Data Security Standard (PCI DSS) requires that you store credit card information as encrypted data. Implementing data-level encryption in a legacy application can be expensive and require a substantial effort. If you run Windows Server 2008, one possible alternative is to use Microsoft BitLocker Drive Encryption. BitLocker could be a compensating control for application-level encryption. Figure 8-3 shows a comparison of alternate controls using PCI DSS as an example.

FIGURE 8-3

Alternate controls.

PCI DSS Requirement—Encrypt Stored Data

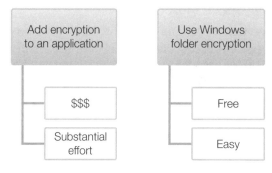

Protecting Privacy Data

Many User Domain compliance requirements relate to information access and privacy. The controls you implement will likely restrict what data and programs your users can access. Controls can also provide information on actions users have carried out. User Domain compliance focuses on accountability. Compliant systems monitor and control actions that relate to compliance.

Monitoring actions as they occur allows preventive controls to evaluate action requests and deny unsuitable actions. Operating system access controls fall into this category. The operating system denies a request to open a file if the user does not have sufficient permissions to open the file. The system can monitor access to many other objects as well. If the system uses a log file to track every access attempt, you can analyze the data. Logging object access is a type of detective control.

Implementing Proper Security Controls for the User Domain

Proper security controls in any domain take careful planning to develop multiple layers of controls. Control layers should complement other layers and work together to avoid exposing a single point of failure. In the User Domain, an **acceptable use policy (AUP)** for each type of user serves as a training guide and direction document for other controls. Simply put, the AUP is a statement of what actions are acceptable and which ones are not.

The AUP is not the only security control for the User Domain but it is an important one. Solid User Domain controls help ensure compliance with your organization's security policy. As you design controls, make sure you develop multiple layers to protect each resource. Your goal should be that an attacker must defeat several controls to compromise a resource. That way, no single control failure exposes a resource to an attack. But before you can design solid controls, you need to explore components commonly found in the User Domain.

Items Commonly Found in the User Domain

The User Domain contains several common items or components. You should consider each component when evaluating activities for compliance. People and documentation are the most common items in the User Domain. Each of the two broad categories includes several smaller types of items with unique characteristics. The following are different types of people in the User Domain:

- **Employees**—This group has the greatest stake in the organization. Most employees feel a greater sense of responsibility toward their employer than shorter-term personnel do. Employees generally have more privileges and access to organization resources. Although you can trust most employees, an unethical employee can cause substantial damage because of access to information and knowledge of the organization.

FIGURE 8-4

Common items
in the User Domain.

- **Contractors**—Contractors may bring specialized skills to an organization but they also pose potential risks. Because contractors may have access to sensitive information, you must monitor them and give them only enough access to do their jobs. Contractors may be less loyal to the organization than employees due to contractors' limited employment. All these reasons present contractors as a greater risk for security violations.

- **Guests/third parties**—Other parties might have no duties related to sensitive information but might still have access to an organization's network. Many organizations commonly provide Internet access to visitors. You should use strict controls to ensure guests do not have access to any sensitive information.

Figure 8-4 illustrates items commonly found in the User Domain.

The User Domain contains more than just people. It is important that people who are resources to an organization have formal directions for how they carry out activities. These activities should support meeting business goals. You need a collection of documents that outlines activities that support business activities to determine whether an action is acceptable or unacceptable. The User Domain also needs documented policies to direct the actions of people. The following are different types of documentation in the User Domain that affect compliance:

- **Human resources (HR) manuals**—HR acquires and manages an organization's personnel. Personnel management includes security awareness and education. Because many security incidents involve users, it is important to provide written documentation of an organization's policies and procedures. HR manuals provide information on how people within an organization should conduct themselves in any situation.

- **IT asset AUPs**—AUPs provide guidance for personnel on proper use of resources. They also define what constitutes improper use. An IT asset AUP covers the use of any IT asset, such as computers, wireless access points, networks, and printers.

- **Internet AUPs**—Internet AUPs define proper and improper use of an organization's Internet access.

- **E-mail AUPs**—E-mail AUPs define proper and improper use of an organization's e-mail capability.

A solid basis for compliant activity requires a well-organized User Domain with clear roles and expectations. In the following sections, you'll learn about important concepts to build a secure environment of compliant behavior.

Separation of Duties

A common theme in compliance requirements is to reduce the ability of any one element to compromise data security. In the User Domain, this means that no single person should have the ability to bypass security controls that protect data. Each computer user's role should limit the scope of permitted actions.

Most computer systems restrict access to deny unauthorized users. The first step in gaining access to data is to identify yourself to the information system and authenticate your identity. This process commonly involves providing a user ID and a password. Once you are identified and authenticated, the operating system grants authority in the form of permissions and rights. These permissions and rights are defined by your assigned roles. You can only accomplish what your assigned roles allow.

The concept of **separation of duties** requires that users from at least two distinct roles be required to accomplish any business-critical task. This means that users from at least two roles must collude to compromise data security. Although collusion is still possible, it is far less likely than if a single user could gain exclusive access to sensitive data without anyone else looking. Going further, separation of duties helps avoid conflicts of interest. For example, the role in charge of administering a system should not be the same role that audits that system for potential compliance violations.

Table 8-1 contains some examples of separation of duties in IT environments.
Figure 8-5 illustrates separation of duties in an IT environment.

8

Compliance Within
the User Domain

---

technical TIP

You can define User Domain roles at the operating system level to limit what users can and cannot do. One method of access control uses operating system groups to define access permissions for objects, such as files, folders, and printers.

Separation of Duties During the Cold War

You can find a common example of separation of duties in many movies. During the Cold War between the United States and the Soviet Union, the military of both sides operated silos that housed nuclear-tipped missiles. Because each missile could deliver multiple devastating warheads, it was imperative to avoid accidental launches at all costs.

Once a launch command made its way up the chain of command, the final actions to launch the missiles required two people to each insert and turn a unique key at the same time. Both keys were required for launch, and the keys were too far apart for one person to insert and turn them at the same time. This design reduced the possibility that a single person could initiate a launch because only one key wasn't sufficient to launch the missiles.

TABLE 8-1   Examples of separation of duties in an IT environment.

ROLE RESTRICTION	DESCRIPTION
Only grant limited access for external personnel to the computer and files they need for the current project.	External personnel can help complete projects but should have limited access to resources. This restriction helps reduce the number of people who have access to each part of a system and reduces the opportunities for data compromise.
Prohibit all access to production environments for developers.	Developers have the ability to write programs that access sensitive data and should not have the ability to bypass configuration management controls. Configuration management controls require a separate role to promote software from development to production.
Do not allow general administrative users to create backups of critical data.	It is easy to create backups on media that fit in a pocket. Create a role for backup operators and only allow a small number of individuals to create backups.

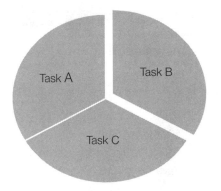

FIGURE 8-5

Separation of duties.

- Separate critical business processes into units of work
- A different person performs each unit of work

Least Privilege

The first step in implementing separation of duties is to remove unnecessary user privileges. Any unnecessary privilege provides an opportunity for a user to violate the AUP and perform unauthorized data access. It makes sense to use access controls to prevent unauthorized data access. The process of allowing only the level of access your users require might be tedious, but it is necessary to secure sensitive data.

The ultimate goal is to define access control where each user has the permissions to carry out assigned tasks and nothing else. This is the **principle of least privilege**. User permissions beyond what is required to carry out necessary tasks are excessive and potentially insecure.

Putting least privilege into practice can be challenging. Organizations with many users often use roles, or groups, to define access permissions. Administrators define roles that represent small tasks, such as "accounts receivable user" and "accounts receivable manager," and grant specific permissions to each role. Individual user accounts can belong to one or more roles and inherit the permissions from each of the roles definitions.

 TIP

When you define permissions based on roles, or groups, you allow object owners and administrators to grant access rights at their discretion. This type of access control is a **discretionary access control (DAC)** and is common in commercial environments.

Government organizations and some commercial organizations implement the principle of least privilege in a different way. They use a system not based on roles, but on data classification and user clearance. The operating system makes the decision to grant or deny access to any data object by matching the object's classification to the user's clearance. Because this method of access control is based on object and subject attributes and not on anyone's discretion, this is a **mandatory access control (MAC)**. Table 8-2 shows the classification system the U.S. government uses for MAC.

TABLE 8-2 U.S. government MAC clearance and classification levels.	
CLASSIFICATION	**DESCRIPTION**
Unclassified	No security label is needed—this object is accessible by anyone
For Official Use Only	Objects that should not be accessible by anyone outside an organization
Confidential	Objects that contain information that could cause harm to an organization or nation if divulged
Secret	Objects that contain information that reasonably could cause serious harm to an organization or nation if divulged
Top Secret	Objects that contain information that would likely cause extreme harm to an organization or nation if divulged

Nongovernmental organizations that need to protect information at different sensitivity levels can also use MAC to secure information. The ISO 27002 standard contains suggestions for five basic classifications. These classification levels are just suggestions for organizations that do not already have a classification strategy in place. Table 8-3 shows the ISO 27002 suggested classification levels.

TABLE 8-3 ISO 17799 suggested clearance and classification levels.	
CLASSIFICATION	**DESCRIPTION**
Public Documents	Objects in the public domain.
Internal Use Only	Objects that have not been approved for release to the public.
Proprietary	Objects that contain information that might be harmful to an organization if divulged to the general public.
Highly Confidential	Objects that contain sensitive information that is critical to an organization. Divulging such information could have a significantly negative impact on an organization.
Top Secret	Objects that contain extremely sensitive information that would cause extreme damage to an organization if divulged.

Need-to-Know Basis

Whereas DAC does support the detailed control necessary for least privilege, simple data classification and user clearances do not. You need an additional control to ensure users only possess the privileges they need to do their jobs. For example, a project manager needs access to documents related to the current project only. If the documents for several unrelated projects are all labeled as "highly confidential" and the project manager holds a "highly confidential" clearance, all project documents would be available.

Although this situation might seem reasonable, it does allow a project manager to access documents that are unrelated to the current project. This capability violates the principle of least privilege. Most systems that use DAC also use the concept of need to know. In addition to possessing a clearance level that matches or exceeds the classification label of an object, a subject must have the **need to know** for the object as well. Simply put, need to know means that you have a need to access an object to do your job. Adding the concept of need to know to DAC does provide full support for the principle of least privilege.

 NOTE

Need to know limits access to secure objects and limits damage in the case of a breach. Assume the project manager used in this section's example leaves the organization. If she chooses to violate ethics and disclosure regulations, she could disclose the contents of all objects to which she had access. The principles of need to know and least privilege protect the organization by limiting how much information a single individual can compromise.

Confidentiality Agreements

Employees who work with sensitive information can be a great asset and a great risk. A person who understands the inner workings of your organization can protect sensitive information or defeat your security controls. Someone who knows your organization could make violations difficult to detect. Contractors who have access to sensitive information can be just as dangerous. How should your organization protect sensitive information from insiders? The answer is to implement a defense-in-depth strategy. Solid access controls and the principle of least privilege are both important, but neither is enough.

Some information leaks occur because of simple ignorance or carelessness. If workers don't know that information is sensitive, they might treat the information with less care. When hiring personnel, you should communicate your organization's security policy clearly. The employee or contractor **confidentiality agreement** is a common document that accomplishes this. Another name for this document is a "non-disclosure agreement" (NDA).

NOTE

Two types of professional relationships involving sensitive information don't require a confidentiality agreement. Privacy laws cover relationships between clients and attorneys and between patients and doctors. These relationships do not need other agreements to keep information confidential.

⚠ **WARNING**

Binding confidentiality agreements should define time frames for the agreement. Confidentiality agreements are not valid forever. A good agreement specifies a date range within which parties must make disclosures and a date range within which disclosure restrictions are in force. A lack of either time frame could invalidate the agreement.

A confidentiality agreement is a legally binding document. By signing this document, each party agrees to keep certain types of information confidential. A confidentiality agreement is a necessary part of any relationship that involves sensitive information.

Confidentiality agreements allow organizations to disclose sensitive information to a small number of parties without concern that an information leak might cause harm. For example, these agreements allow organizations to share specifications of unreleased products to business partners. Sharing this type of information allows business partners to develop companion products before the release of original products. Most major software vendors, such as Microsoft and Apple, do this to allow their development partners to write software for new operating systems before the release date. The confidentiality agreement protects the operating system vendor by prohibiting partners from releasing information about the new product.

Another important feature of a confidentiality agreement is that it can protect patent rights. Publicly disclosing an invention can result in forfeiting any patent rights. An organization must keep information about the invention confidential until filing a patent application. Confidentiality agreements with anyone who has access to confidential information can protect your organization from a damaging public disclosure.

A confidentiality agreement defines the types of information parties can and cannot disclose. A confidentiality agreement also specifies how parties may use confidential information. The agreement defines expected behavior and the consequences of violating the agreement. A well-written confidentiality agreement lowers the risk of disclosing confidential information.

Employee Background Checks

Many organizations perform a **background check** on prospective employees before hiring anyone. The purpose of a background check is to uncover any evidence of past behavior that might indicate a prospect is a security risk. In reality, all personnel are security risks because they must be trusted with sensitive information. A background check can uncover information that indicates a person might be an undue security risk.

Background checks can vary in depth, for example simply verifying a Social Security number as authentic and belonging to the applicant. Another example is conducting a police criminal check and reviewing a prospective employee's complete history. Each organization sets the scope of background checks. The job description and the organization's desire to use a prospect's history to indicate future actions affect the scope of the investigation. You can conduct background checks using internal resources or by engaging external specialists. External resources can reduce your ongoing expense and may provide higher-quality information by using specialists. However, external resources who conduct background checks operate under additional restrictions.

The **Fair Credit Reporting Act (FCRA)**, which defines national standards for all consumer reports, also governs how you conduct background checks. FCRA governs background checks because they are labeled as consumer reports, even though a background check may consist of more than credit history information. FCRA sets time limits on negative information that investigators can include in their report. Although some states may lengthen FCRA time limits, investigators cannot include:

* Bankruptcies that are over 10 years old
* Civil suits or judgments that are over seven years old
* Paid tax liens or other negative financial information that is over seven years old

Background checks often include much more than just financial information. Most employers are more interested than ever in a prospective employee's general past and current behavior. In many cases, social networking sites, such as Facebook or MySpace, can provide information on a prospect's behavior. Fair or not, more and more employers are looking into past behavior to attempt to decide how trustworthy a prospect may be.

Although background checks are important and might provide interesting insight into a person's background, you must perform them with care. FCRA requires that you obtain permission from the subject of a background check before you begin the investigation. In addition, if you decide not to extend an offer due to information contained in the background check report, you must provide the reason and the contact information for the investigating organization. You must give the prospect the opportunity to dispute any negative information in the report. This safeguard helps prevent incorrect information from harming an unsuspecting individual.

Background checks can reveal quite a lot about a prospective employee. A prospect with prior criminal history might not be a good candidate for a role that allows access to very sensitive information. Knowing the background of prospective employees is an important step in granting authorization to sensitive information. Although a background check won't catch every potential attacker, it can help identify some of the most likely high-risk candidates.

Acknowledgment of Responsibilities and Accountabilities

As you've learned in previous chapters, auditing is the process of examining systems to verify they are in compliance with defined policies. In short, auditing ensures activities comply with policy. This process provides value only when it objectively reviews evidence of actions. An auditor who overlooks any evidence of noncompliance isn't very effective. Because of the potential of negative findings, it is important that all parties engaged in auditing activities understand responsibilities to the audit process.

▶**NOTE**

Repetitive auditing and taking action on the results of audits are proactive forms of continuous improvement. The general idea is that constantly adhering to policies results in higher-quality output—not just fewer violations.

Don't view auditing simply as a search for problems. Auditing is an opportunity to identify noncompliance issues before they escalate and possibly cause damage. This positive attitude toward auditing must start with upper management, who should share it with all affected parties. If upper management does not fully support the efforts of auditors, it is unlikely anyone else will.

Upper management can influence audit process quality by assigning responsibilities and accountabilities. Every employee bears some responsibility in the IT security audit process. Every agent of your organization must maintain the security of your information. Because the IT security auditing process verifies compliance with security policies, all employees bear responsibility for carrying out your policies.

Each task in the audit process has one or more people who are responsible or accountable for that task. Many organizations use a RACI matrix to document tasks and personnel responsible for the assignments. RACI stands for responsible, accountable, consulted, and informed. To create a RACI matrix:

1. List tasks along one axis and personnel or roles along the other axis.
2. Assign a level or responsibility for each role and task.
3. Assign each person or role a level of responsibility and accountability for each task.

The entries in the matrix will contain one of the following:

- **R (Responsible)**—Person who actually performs the work to accomplish the task; may be multiple people.

- **A (Accountable)**—Person who is accountable for the proper completion of the task; only one person is accountable for each task. The Accountable is likely the Responsible's manager.

- **C (Consulted)**—Person who provides input that is helpful in completing a task; may be multiple people.

- **I (Informed)**—Person who desires to be kept up to date on a task's progress; may be multiple people.

Table 8-4 shows a simple RACI matrix for an IT audit.

The RACI matrix clarifies the responsibilities and accountabilities for a set of tasks. A RACI matrix provides upper management a tool that communicates and conveys for tasks. Without the acceptance of audit responsibilities and accountabilities, the auditing process might encounter resistance. Management and other employees might view the audit process as punitive.

TABLE 8-4 Simple RACI matrix for an IT audit.

TASK/ROLE	MANAGEMENT	PROJECT MANAGER	AUDITOR	USER
Develop audit plan	A	R	C	I
Develop audit activities schedule	A	R	C	I
Conduct audit activities		A	R	C
Review audit results	A/R	R	R	C
Identify noncompliant elements	A	I	R	C
Develop plan to address noncompliant elements	A	R	C	I
Develop noncompliant mitigation activities schedule	A	R	C	C
Conduct noncompliant mitigation activities		A	R	R

Security Awareness and Training for New Employees

Employees often have the greatest access to an organization's critical resources. Your organization places substantial trust in its employees and takes on substantial risk in doing so. Many security incidents originate from internal personnel, including employees. Not all incidents are malicious attacks. Some are simply a failure to comply with the organization's stated security policy.

It is important to educate new employees on your organization's security policies and procedures. It is difficult for employees to comply with a policy if they are unaware of what the policy contains. Training employees on security matters can help avoid many security policy violations, including:

- Weak passwords
- Inappropriate use of the Internet
- Inappropriate use of e-mail
- Divulging confidential information

The HR department usually follows an established procedure when handling new employees. Security awareness and security procedures training should be a part of this process. You should provide training for each employee on security topics, including:

- Organization's commitment to information security
- Justification for security-related activities
- Important security procedures

Security training should include justification. It is important that employees understand the value of security to the health of your organization. Employees should acknowledge they have received security training and agree to abide by your security policy and procedures. Many organizations make use of the employees' acknowledgment to uphold the security policy requiring it as a condition of employment. Because the security of sensitive resources is important to your organization, it should be important to your employees.

Information Systems Security Accountability

Security-related activities often have lower importance than activities that directly make money. Unless upper management clearly states the importance of security, security personnel might find it difficult to obtain funding and support to maintain secure systems. Most important, an organization's upper management is responsible for protecting the security of the organization's resources. Management is responsible to the stockholders, regulatory agencies, government entities, and the public.

In addition, management should assign accountability for each security-related activity. Creating and maintaining a secure environment requires acceptance of accountability.

Requiring That Human Resources Take a Lead Role

HR is responsible for acquiring and managing all of your organization's personnel. This includes initial and recurrent training. Because HR is responsible for proper employee and other personnel training, the department should be accountable for ensuring each person receives training.

In fact, HR takes a lead role in the accountability of all personnel actions. Having HR take a lead role centralizes training delivery and employee-related compliance activities. HR also operates above functional management and protects the organization from role favoritism. HR ensures that the organization holds all personnel to the same set of standards.

Defining Accurate IT and IT Security Employee Job Descriptions

HR also holds the responsibility to define the activities of all personnel, including IT personnel. Accurate job descriptions are necessary to acquire the best employees for each position. Job descriptions also set proper expectations for all personnel. Accurate and up-to-date job descriptions allow HR to develop the most appropriate role-based training and to ensure all employees receive proper training to carry out their tasks.

Job descriptions also set and maintain the expectations and performance standards for each employee. These expectations provide a standard for employee performance measurement. Although specific performance numbers might be outside the scope of a job description, it does contain a framework of expected performance.

Incorporating Accountability into the Annual Performance Reviews for Employees

In addition to defining the job description, your organization should set performance criteria for evaluating employees. Each employee should have a set of performance criteria that compares performance to goals. These criteria can be valuable during annual performance reviews.

Performance accountability is important to motivate employees. A motivated employee tends to be happier and more productive. Performing simple tasks with no accountability can lead to boredom and even sloppy work. Your organization should encourage employee accountability and reward staff for taking on more responsibility and being more accountable.

Adherence to Documented IT Security Policies, Standards, Procedures, and Guidelines

User behavior is the focus of auditing for IT compliance in the User Domain. In the simplest sense, this consists of examining user actions and comparing those actions with security policies, standards, procedures, and guidelines. If you find any differences with organizational requirements, you should report the differences and analyze their impact.

It is important to train all internal and external users on acceptable behavior. Training should cover the contents of your organization's security statement documents and provide users with the knowledge to comply with the documents. Training that does not cover security expectations is insufficient. Users who hold a privileged role, such as system administrator, should receive additional, specialized training pertinent to their role.

 WARNING

It is difficult for untrained users to comply with your security policies. For example, as basic as it might seem, you shouldn't expect users to create and use strong passwords unless you train them how to do it and tell them they are required to use strong passwords.

Good security training should stress the importance of compliance and cover the important parts of these types of security documents:

- **Security policy**—A high-level statement that defines an organization's commitment to security and the definition of a secure system, such as the importance of changing passwords periodically

- **Security standard**—A collection of requirements the users must meet, typically within a specific system or environment, such as changing a Windows password every six months

- **Security procedure**—Individual tasks users accomplish to comply with one or more security standards, such as the steps to change a password

- **Security guideline**—A collection of best practices or suggestions that help users comply with procedures and standards, such as suggestions on how to create strong passwords

> **NOTE**
>
> Some security violations are obvious. However, User Domain auditing reveals many less-obvious noncompliant user actions.

Your access control policies should grant access to information systems depending on users upholding the organization's security policies, standards, procedures, and guidelines. Violation of any of these security elements should carry consequences ranging from a training refresher course to losing access.

Best Practices for User Domain Compliance Requirements

Identifying and influencing user behaviors that affect security are important to ensuring compliance within the User Domain. Behaviors that support or violate compliance with your security goals get the most attention. The following best practices do not guarantee compliance with all goals. However, they will lay the foundation to develop and maintain a secure environment:

- Document all laws, regulations, and standards that require User Domain compliance for your organization.

- Define AUPs for each type of IT service or equipment.

- Conduct background checks for all employees and critical contractors prior to engagement.

- Develop security awareness and procedures training for employees and contractors.

- Require security awareness and procedures training and assessment prior to engagement.

- Require users to sign confidentiality agreements prior to receiving access to any sensitive information.

- Establish unique logon credentials for each user and require strong passwords.

- Grant only the minimum privileges to each user required to accomplish that user's tasks.
- Require action by at least two separate users to complete any business-critical function involving sensitive information.
- Periodically audit user access privileges for compliance to stated goals.

CHAPTER SUMMARY

The User Domain defines information system users and the actions they carry out. A critical factor of maintaining secure systems is ensuring compliance of users to security goals. Because user actions result in accessing information, it is necessary to control and monitor user actions to maintain secure systems. Systems must uniquely identify users and allow access only to information for which they are authorized. Auditing activities should examine all access decisions and the rules that govern such decisions for compliance. Defining limits within the User Domain and validating user activities provide an important security layer in a defense-in-depth approach to system security.

KEY CONCEPTS AND TERMS

Acceptable use policies (AUPs)	Detective controls	Need to know
Background check	Discretionary access control (DAC)	Preventive controls
Business drivers		Principle of least privilege
Confidentiality agreement	Fair Credit Reporting Act (FCRA)	Separation of duties
Corrective controls	Mandatory access control (MAC)	

CHAPTER 8 ASSESSMENT

1. Which type of control only reports that a violation has occurred?

A. Preventive
B. Detective
C. Corrective
D. Restorative

2. The term _____ defines the components, including people, information, and conditions, that support business objectives.

3. Which of the following types of policies defines prohibited actions?

A. Access control policy
B. Password usage policy
C. Acceptable use policy
D. Violation action policy

4. Which of the following terms ensures at least two distinct roles must perform a series of actions to complete a task?

A. Separation of duties
B. Least privilege
C. Need to know
D. User clearance

5. When using DAC, a subject must possess sufficient clearance as well as _____ to access an object.

6. Which of the following terms defines a strategy in which you grant access that allows a user to complete assigned tasks and nothing else?

A. Separation of duties
B. Least privilege
C. Need to know
D. User clearance

7. Which type of agreement can protect the ability to file a patent application?

A. Relinquish ownership agreement
B. Security clearance waiver
C. Background check agreement
D. Confidentiality agreement

8. What condition must exist for a background check to be governed by FCRA?

A. The investigation includes credit history.
B. The investigation is performed by a third party.

C. The investigation is performed by the prospective employer.
D. The investigation includes criminal history.

9. Which of the following best describes the purpose of auditing?

A. Finds root causes of violation issues
B. Assists investigators in identifying blame for violations
C. Verifies that systems are operating in compliance
D. Searches for hidden unacceptable use of IT resources

10. Using a RACI matrix, which attribute refers to the party that actually carries out the work?

A. Responsible
B. Accountable
C. Consulted
D. Informed

11. Which department should take the lead in User Domain compliance accountability?

A. Information technology
B. Information security
C. Human resources
D. Security

12. A confidentiality agreement sets the expectations of each employee and sets job performance standards.

A. True
B. False

13. Which of the following is a series of individual tasks users accomplish to comply with one or more goals?

A. Policy
B. Standard
C. Procedure
D. Guideline

14. Which of the following is a collection of requirements the users must meet?

A. Policy
B. Standard
C. Procedure
D. Guideline

15. Discretionary access control is based on roles and granted permissions.

A. True
B. False

Compliance Within the Workstation Domain

COMPLYING WITH SECURITY-RELATED REGULATIONS, legislation, and other requirements means ensuring your organization protects the security of your information. In most cases, ensuring information security means ensuring users take appropriate actions and refrain from inappropriate actions. Although the directive seems simple, implementing it can be complex. In Chapter 8, you learned about compliance in the User Domain. You learned about the requirements of information system users and their responsibilities in ensuring the security of your organization's information.

If all users were perfect and completely compliant, there wouldn't be a need to consider any further security layers. Remember that users include both authorized and unauthorized users. Attackers fall into the category of unauthorized users. Because users are imperfect and often noncompliant, you must include additional layers of security controls to protect your information's security. The defense-in-depth philosophy provides the best strategy to secure information and remains the basic blueprint for designing security controls. In this chapter, you'll learn how to follow the defense-in-depth strategy to enforce compliance within the Workstation Domain.

Chapter 9 Topics

This chapter covers the following topics and concepts:

- How compliance law requirements and business drivers relate to one another
- Which devices and components are commonly found in the Workstation Domain
- What access rights and access controls in the Workstation Domain are
- How to maximize A-I-C
- How to manage workstation vulnerability

- How to ensure adherence to documented IT security policies, standards, procedures, and guidelines
- What best practices for Workstation Domain compliance requirements are

Chapter 9 Goals

When you complete this chapter, you will be able to:

- Examine compliance law requirements and business drivers
- Compare how devices and components found in the Workstation Domain contribute to compliance
- Describe methods of ensuring compliance in the Workstation Domain
- Summarize best practices for Workstation Domain compliance

Compliance Law Requirements and Business Drivers

Users generally access information from workstations. This is not always the case, but it is the most common access method that allows users to view and modify your organization's information. Because workstations provide access to information, they become an attack vector for unauthorized users. It is important that you ensure all items in the Workstation Domain are compliant. Figure 9-1 shows the Workstation Domain in the context of the seven domains in the IT infrastructure.

As with all domains, ensuring compliance in the Workstation Domain satisfies two main purposes:

- **Increases information security**—Because information is a material organizational asset, and in some cases, the primary organizational asset, ensuring the security of information equates to protecting the viability of the organization. It is just as important as protecting any other major assets of the organization. A loss of any important asset will likely disrupt your organization's ability to conduct normal operations. It is important to protect your organization's ability to do business.
- **Reduces liability**—If one or more attacks are successful against your organization's information, you might be liable to damages caused to third parties. If information loss or leakage causes damage to other people or organizations and the damage is a result of noncompliance, your organization might be liable for part, or all, of the damages. At the very least, disclosed successful attacks against your organization can degrade confidence in your commitment to security. An attention to compliance details and strong security can dramatically reduce your organization's exposure to liability clams.

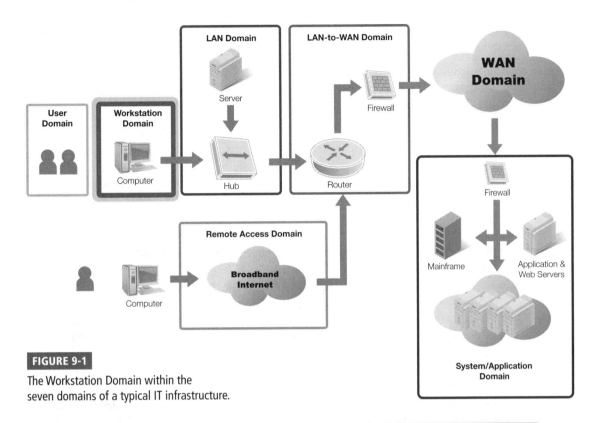

FIGURE 9-1

The Workstation Domain within the
seven domains of a typical IT infrastructure.

Due Diligence

Paying attention to compliance can reduce liability in direct and indirect ways. You can think of
it in terms of additional insurance. In the context of information security, the term **due diligence**
means the ongoing attention and care an organization places on security and compliance. You
can reduce your exposure to third-party liability by investing resources into establishing and
maintaining compliance. Demonstrating aggressive compliance activities can reduce the liability
potential if security incidents result in damages. In short, being compliant looks good in court.

Protecting Private Data

Many recent legislative and regulatory requirements extend the scope of threats to information to include all users. There is no assurance users will be compliant. Organizations
need additional layers of controls to protect information because not all threats come
from malicious users—some threats come from simple ignorance. For example, procedural changes might prohibit users from transferring protected files to remote workstations. Properly trained users should not attempt to transfer files to remote workstations,

but well-meaning users who are not aware of the new policy might unknowingly violate the policy. The proper way to handle this situation is to:

- Ensure all users receive updated training.
- Place access controls in the Workstation Domain to prohibit inappropriate actions.

You need both types of controls to secure information from all users.

Increased attention to security increases the need to hold employees accountable for security. Because employees generally have more access to information than other authorized users, they have greater ability to impact the information's security. Great ability to impact security means you need a greater scope of controls. The most common concern for information security that is reflected in most recent legislation is protecting information privacy. Although information integrity and availability are important, privacy is a primary concern of many regulations. All information system users are accountable for the privacy of the information they access. This puts a greater amount of responsibility and accountability on users.

A solid security strategy should include several types of controls to ensure user compliance. You've already seen some controls in the User Domain. The Workstation Domain is the domain that contains the devices and components to access information. Controlling activities in the Workstation Domain can provide an effective layer of information security. Workstation Domain controls should validate and support controls in other domains. Although controls in the User Domain are important, you need additional controls to ensure compliance with your security policy and any additional security requirements. Controls in the Workstation Domain should work with controls in other domains to ensure a high level of overall compliance.

Implementing Proper Security Controls for the Workstation Domain

Workstation Domain controls are security controls that prohibit, validate, or detect user actions. Users initiate actions in the Workstation Domain that generally involve some stored information. In short, users generally access information using some type of workstation device. It makes sense to place controls at the workstation level to ensure information access is compliant. Proper controls in the Workstation Domain should work with other controls in all domains to enforce compliance without interrupting normal operation.

For example, Payment Card Industry Data Security Standard (PCI DSS) prohibits merchants from storing the **Card Verification Value (CVV)** number. The CVV number is a three- or four-digit number that card issuers print on each credit card. The CVV number provides additional authentication when rendering payment for online transactions. One control to avoid storing the CVV is to remove any user prompts for the CVV. Although that complies with the PCI DSS data requirement, it also disables the merchant's ability to ask for the CVV to authenticate the transaction. You should not implement this control because it interrupts a necessary business function. Look for another control that balances security and business requirements.

E-mail Policy

Another example of multiple layers of controls is an e-mail policy. Every organization should have a policy on appropriate use of e-mail at work. E-mail messages can contain private information that employees can easily disclose using e-mail. It is important your employees carefully control destinations for private information to avoid unintended disclosure. Creating controls in multiple domains will help minimize private information disclosure. Controls may include security awareness training in the User Domain, e-mail client filters and rules in the Workstation Domain, and e-mail server rules and filters in other domains. Once again, multiple layers of controls in different domains greatly reduce the risk of disclosing private information and exposing your organization to potential liability.

A good strategy to identify the best Workstation Domain controls is to start with your security policy. Identify any requirements that directly relate to workstation components and create appropriate controls. The task of identifying controls is much easier if consulting ISO/EIC 27001, which provides a concise list of security controls. For more in-depth understanding of every control, ISO 27002 is the best reference. Once you have a list of potential controls, compare your list to the User Domain controls. The Workstation Domain controls should complement controls in other domains, but should specifically support User Domain controls. A good way to enforce this guideline is to create controls of different types for different domains. For example, suppose you want to enforce your password policy. You may have an administrative control in the User Domain that mandates user training on proper passwords. A good Workstation Domain control would be to enforce complex passwords on all workstations. This would be a technical control that enforces strong passwords by prohibiting weak passwords. Users should already know how to create strong passwords from their training class. However, forcing strong passwords using a Workstation Domain control ensures users follow the requirements. Once these controls are put into practice, they serve as countermeasures for the organization. Countermeasures are the controls you put in place to mitigate a risk. This is another example of a defense-in-depth strategy.

> **NOTE**
> Your Workstation Domain controls should not just duplicate User Domain controls, but should provide a second level of assurance.

Devices and Components Commonly Found in the Workstation Domain

The Workstation Domain connects users to local resources. You'll learn about how to handle remote users in Chapter 13. The Workstation Domain includes all local resources that support user functionality and allows users to interact with your information system. In some cases, Workstation Domain items collect and present information as well as process that information. In other cases, processing occurs in another domain.

FIGURE 9-2

Devices and components
in the Workstation
Domain.

Uninterruptible
Power Supply (UPS)   Desktop PC   Laptop   Netbook

Printer   Modem   External Hard Drive   Universal Serial
Bus (USB) Drive

In either case, users use the Workstation Domain to interact with the rest of your
environment, including your data. Each type of device or component in the Workstation
Domain presents potential vulnerabilities and security challenges. It is important that
you carefully consider each type of component when you design Workstation Domain
controls. Figure 9-2 shows the most common devices and components you'll find in
the Workstation Domain.

Uninterruptible Power Supply

An **uninterruptible power supply (UPS)** provides continuous usable power to one or more
devices. Some UPS models also provide the ability to protect data connections from power
surges that could damage computers or other hardware. A UPS can protect many types
of devices and may exist in several domains. Their primary purpose is to support the
availability of Workstation Domain devices. UPS devices generally provide several types
of protection, including:

- **Continuous power**—A primary purpose of a UPS is an integrated battery that
  provides power to connected devices when the AC power fails. When the AC power
  fails, or even falls below usable voltage, the UPS automatically switches to its battery
  to provide uninterrupted power to any devices connected to the UPS. This feature
  allows the connected devices to continue operating normally during power outages.
  Because the backup power depends on the UPS battery, the duration of the power
  is limited—generally around 30 minutes. Although larger UPSs include backup
  power generators that can provide power for extended periods of time, devices
  in the Workstation Domain generally do not require such measures. The ability
  to survive short duration power outages is generally sufficient.

- **Surge protection**—Nearly all UPSs condition the power supplied to connected
  devices. Conditioned power means that any voltage surges are removed before
  providing power to devices. This surge-filtering capability protects connected devices
  from potential damage from high voltage. Some UPSs include network connectors
  that protect networking connections from power surges as well as power connections.

- **Structured shutdown**—Many UPSs provide the ability to establish a communications connection to a primary computer. This connection allows the UPS to send a shutdown request to the computer when the UPS power is in danger of running out. When a power outage duration approaches the UPS power limit, the UPS can alert the computer and allow it time to shut down gracefully. This ability protects data integrity by avoiding uncontrolled shutdowns that could cause damage to open data files.

Desktop Computer

Desktop computers have historically been the most common type of Workstation Domain device. That trend is rapidly giving way to more portable computers. Desktop computers are designed to be stationary and are often physically connected to an organization's network to share information and devices. Because they are commonly connected to other network resources, it is important to carefully control access to these computers.

Most desktop computers have substantial local processing power and are often used to locally create and manage data. Although this ability can reduce the workload on other domain devices, it can also lead to data leakage. Users who are comfortable working with information locally on a desktop computer might not be diligent about backing up the information or perhaps about protecting the information.

Desktop computers have grown in power and storage capacity in recent years to the degree that they rival the capabilities of some server computers. This increase in power encourages users to install more and more software on their desktop computers. Allowing unsupervised software installations can lead to desktop computers that are difficult to support or even dangerous to your organization. Many computer problems relate to conflicts between programs that are competing for resources. Allowing users to install unapproved programs increases the likelihood of conflicts with approved programs.

Desktop Computers and Privacy

Many users think of their desk environment and desktop computers as private areas. When conducting security assessments, it is a common practice to examine desktop environments for confidential information. Far too many users write their passwords on sticky notes and place them on or around the computer monitor. Another favorite place to "hide" passwords is under the keyboard. This common practice punctuates two warnings:

- Don't make compliance with your password policy so difficult that users have to write down their passwords.
- Pay attention to physical controls that keep unauthorized people away from authorized users' desks.

A lack of desktop computer control also increases the likelihood users will unknowingly install malicious software. A desktop computer with malware is not only a threat to locally stored information, but also to all other devices connected to your network. It is important to understand the risks of allowing too much user freedom and implement the appropriate controls to protect your organization.

Laptop/Netbook Computer

As computers shrink in size and grow in capabilities, several new classes of computers now rival the desktop as the most popular type of workstation. Laptop computers are generally the larger, more powerful class of portable computers. Laptop computers can do nearly everything a desktop computer can do while maintaining a small enough profile to be very portable. Most laptop computers fit easily into briefcase-size bags and backpacks. Although laptop computers generally lack all of the capacity and power of desktop computers, laptops still can boast substantial capabilities that make them full-featured devices.

Netbook computers are relatively new devices that are smaller and lighter than laptop computers. Their smaller size and lighter weight means that they generally have fewer hardware options and limited capabilities. Netbook computers are generally designed to act as access devices to network devices and don't provide much local storage. Although they lack much local storage space, they still pose risks because of their support for network access.

As with desktop computers, it is important to control access to network resources and the ability to install unauthorized software. In fact, the need to control portable computers is more important than with desktop computers. The portable nature of laptop/netbook computers means these computers are likely transported and used at locations physically outside of your organization. In most cases, users connect portable computers to other networks when they are away from your organization's building. Connecting to unprotected networks can be extremely dangerous. Users can pick up infected programs when connected to other networks and then introduce them the next time they connect to your network. Your security policy should include specific standards for using portable computers to connect to your networks.

Local Printer

A local printer is any printer connected directly to a local computer. Many organizations use networked printers, which you'll learn about in Chapter 10. Local printers aren't shared by multiple users. Because these printers aren't connected to your organization's network, they aren't controlled from a central location. This means local users can print anything they want. Allowing users to access local printers without any controls can lead to several types of issues, including:

- **Personal use of the organization's resources**—Users can print any files to local printers. This can include personal information that might violate the acceptable use policy.

- **Disclosure of private information**—Users can print files with little or no control over content. There is always the chance that printed documents could end up in the wrong person's hands.

- **Printer buffer access**—Most printers retain copies of recently printed documents. It is not difficult to get a printer to reprint previously printed documents. It can be difficult to control this behavior on local printers.

Minimize local printer use in your organization. Printers should generally be networked and managed from a central location in another IT domain.

Analog Modem

Analog modems can pose serious threats to organizations. At first glance, they don't seem too dangerous, but they can provide damaging backdoor entryways into your network. Modems do have a place in a secure environment but not in the Workstation Domain. Modems provide a connection to another computer or network and belong in another domain where you can control them in a way that protects your network. Modems connected to Workstation Domain devices are almost always uncontrolled and installed to bypass network access controls.

Although many users consider modems to be harmless, they can be valuable tools for attackers. Many attackers still employ an old technique called **war dialing**. War dialing is instructing a computer to dial many telephone numbers looking for modems on the other end. The war dialing computer records any modems it finds for later analysis. Each modem that answers a war dialing computer is a potential target. Attackers will dial identified numbers and attempt to access the computer on the other end. Unauthorized modems are rarely secured well and are known to be fairly soft targets. The attacker attempts to access the computer to which the modem is attached and then move on to attack the organization's network.

> ⚠️ **WARNING**
>
> As innocent as it might seem, simply connecting an analog modem can potentially compromise your network. It is important that you search for rogue modems and ensure you either eliminate or carefully control each modem in the Workstation Domain.

Fixed Hard Disk Drive

Virtually all general-purpose computers have at least one internal, fixed hard drive. Computers primarily use fixed hard drives to store the computer's operating system as well as application programs and data. Some leading-edge or special-purpose computers use solid state memory to store programs or information, but most of today's computers use regular hard disk drives. Disk drives store files that contain data, instructions, or both data and instructions.

Privacy laws and regulations address both types of file contents. Compliance with different requirements often means restricting how you access certain types of information or how you must store information. For example, under the Health Insurance Portability and Accountability Act (HIPAA), you must protect all private medical information from unauthorized disclosure. That often means using centralized storage with carefully monitored access and storage controls. You implement centralized storage in another IT domain, not in the Workstation Domain. Continuing the example, assume you use your workstation to access private medical information. You decide to copy the information into a document and store it locally on your workstation while you edit the information. The decision to store the information locally potentially just violated HIPAA. The problem is that you have just placed private medical information in an area that unauthorized users can potentially access.

You must carefully control what devices in the Workstation Domain can do. The good news is that you do have some control when Workstation Domain devices "reach across" domains. You'll learn more about controlling access and storage in the LAN Domain in Chapter 10. Storing information from another domain is only one issue. You also need to control files stored on the hard disk that originate outside your organization's IT infrastructure. Outside programs and files often result from activity while you are connected to another network. In most cases, Internet access provides the inbound path for unwelcome files. Malicious files and software can infect unprotected computers and then spread to other computers and devices in your organization. Controls in the Workstation Domain for disk drive access can help prevent infections and protect the rest of your network.

Removable Storage Device

One last category in the Workstation Domain includes devices you connect to computers as you need them. You use most of the devices in this category to store files to transport to another computer. These devices include:

- Removable hard disk drives
- Universal serial bus (USB) flash drives
- Removable CD-ROM and DVD drives
- Removable tape drives

There are other removable storage devices, but these are the most common. In fact, the most common devices are USB flash drives. These drives are compact, are easily available, and can store from 128 MB to over 256 GB of data, depending on device capacity.

Because you can transport removable media easily and connect it to other computers, it is important that you control the files you transfer both to and from any such devices. In general, you should control two types of transfers:

- Control information you copy to a removable device to ensure you protect data privacy. This type of control keeps you from divulging private information.
- Control data you copy from a removable device to block malicious code or data. This type of control protects the rest of your environment from introducing malicious code.

Understanding the devices and components in the Workstation Domain is the first step to establishing controls to secure this domain. The next step is to understand data and device access controls. You'll learn about Workstation Domain access rights and controls in the next section.

Access Rights and Access Controls in the Workstation Domain

You learned in the previous sections how important it is to implement the correct controls in the Workstation Domain. Proper security controls limit access to objects based on a user's identity. Access control methods may be based on the permissions granted to a user or group, or they may be based on a user's security clearance. Either way, access rights start with knowing which user requests access to an object and what the user's identity permits him to do.

Most computers require you to log on before you can access any resources on the computer. Even systems set up to automatically log on are actually logging on to a predefined user account. The first step in logging on is to provide a user ID or username. Providing user credentials or claiming to be a specific user is called **identification**. Simply identifying yourself is not enough. If all you have to do is claim to be a user, anyone can claim to be a system administrator and gain permission to carry out potentially harmful actions. Operating systems require users to follow the identification step with authentication. **Authentication** is the process of providing additional credentials that match the user ID or username. Only the operating system and the real user should know the authentication credentials. The most common authentication credential is the password. Other options include security tokens and biometric characteristics. Once you provide the correct user ID and authentication credentials, you are logged on to your user account.

As the operating system logs you on, it looks up security **authorization** information and grants you access permissions based on your identity. There are two main approaches for authorizing users to access objects. Both approaches evaluate whether a user, also called a **subject**, has the permission to access some resource, also called an **object**. Access objects can be files, directories, printers, or any resource. There are other methods as well, but two methods are the most common ones you'll encounter.

The first access method uses **access control lists (ACLs)**, which are lists of access **permissions** that define what each user or security group can do to each object. Each object uses ACLs or permissions to define which users can access it. The object's **owner** can grant access permissions to any desired user or group. Because granting access is at the owner's discretion, this type of access control is called discretionary access control (DAC).

The second type of access control is not based on specific permissions but on the user's security clearance and the object's classification. Organizations that use this type of access control assign a specific classification to each object. Security classifications used by the U.S. government include Top Secret, Secret, Confidential, and Unclassified.

Authentication Types

There are three main types of authentication credentials—**Type I (what you know)**, **Type II (what you have)**, and **Type III (what you are)**. The credentials are described as follows:

- **Type I authentication (what you know)**—Information only a valid user knows. The most common examples of Type I authentication are a password or personal identification number (PIN).
- **Type II authentication (what you have)**—A physical object that contains identity information, such as a token, card, or other device.
- **Type III authentication (what you are)**—Physical characteristic (biometric), such as a fingerprint, handprint, or retina characteristic.

Type II authentication is generally stronger than Type I, and Type III is generally stronger than either Type I or Type II. You can make the authentication process even stronger by using more than one type at the same time. Using two types of authentication is called **two-factor authentication** and using more than two types is called **multifactor authentication**. Using more than a single authentication type strengthens the process by making it more difficult to impersonate a valid user.

Other governments and nongovernmental organizations use slightly different classifications but most classification schemes are similar. Each user receives a security clearance that corresponds to one of the classifications in use. The operating system grants access to objects based on a user's security clearance and the requested object's classification. For example, a user with a Secret clearance can access Secret, Confidential, and Unclassified objects but cannot access Top Secret objects. Because there is no discretion involved in granting access, this access method is called mandatory access control (MAC).

Regardless of the access control method you use, the end result is the ability to restrict access to objects by user account. Access control methods allow you to define an access control strategy that allows you to define controls to support your security policy.

Maximizing A-I-C

The overall purpose of compliance requirements is to enforce the basic pillars or tenets of security. Recall from Chapter 2 that secure environments satisfy the **A-I-C** properties of security. Although some compliance requirements might seem to be unnecessary, they all should work together to support the A-I-C properties of secure systems. As a review, here are the three tenets of information security:

A-I-C stands for **availability**, integrity, and confidentiality. The term is also commonly known as **CIA** (confidentiality, integrity, and availability), as described in Chapter 2. Some information systems security professionals refer to the tenets as the "A-I-C" triad to avoid confusion with the U.S. Central Intelligence Agency, commonly referred to as the CIA. Either abbreviation is acceptable, but if you use CIA, make sure people understand you're referring to "confidentiality, integrity, and availability."

- **Availability**—Assurance the information is available to authorized users in an acceptable time frame when the information is requested
- **Integrity**—Assurance the information cannot be changed by unauthorized users
- **Confidentiality**—Assurance the information cannot be accessed or viewed by unauthorized users

Figure 9-3 shows the A-I-C triad.

Notice that a central theme of the A-I-C properties is the difference between authorized and unauthorized users. The identification, authentication, and authorization process you learned about in the previous section provides the foundation for securing information in any domain. Maximizing the A-I-C properties is all about ensuring authorized users can access trusted data and unauthorized users can't.

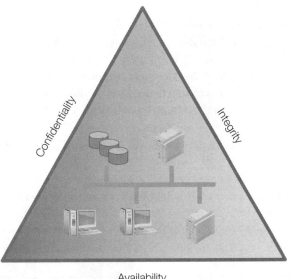

FIGURE 9-3

A-I-C triad.

Maximizing Availability

Secure information serves the purpose for which it was created. This means that secure information must be available when the information is requested. This requirement means that information should be available during normal processing, but also during and after unusual events. Unusual events include minor events such as short-term power outages up to major disruptions and disasters. There are two main areas in the Workstation Domain that can affect availability:

- Surviving power outages
- Executing a solid backup and recovery strategy

You should address each area when you create Workstation Domain controls.

Surviving Power Outages

The easiest way to ensure your computers and devices can continue operating in the event of a power outage is by using a UPS. The first step in implementing the right UPS is to list each of the computers and devices you want to protect. Consider any supporting devices you'll need along with computers. For example, if you want to stay online to the Internet during a power outage, you'll need to ensure you connect any network access devices to the UPS as well. Once you have a list of all devices, add up the power requirements for all devices you'll attach to the UPS. Then, search UPS manufacturers for a UPS that will satisfy your service and power requirements. An Internet search is a good place to start.

Backup and Recovery Strategy

A UPS is fine to keep your computers up and running when the power goes out for a few minutes, but what do you do in case of a disaster? What happens to the programs and data on your Workstation Domain computers if a fire in your office destroys the computers? Fire is only one type of disaster your computers might encounter. Information that burns up in a fire or is destroyed in a flood is not available when you need it. Because the information isn't available in this situation, it isn't very secure.

> **technical TIP**
>
> UPS devices come in many price ranges and provide varying levels of service. Lower-cost UPSs simply switch over to a battery when you lose full power. Higher-cost UPSs provide line conditioning and handle brownouts and blackouts in different ways. Higher-priced UPSs also tend to provide backup power for longer periods of time. Don't just shop for price—carefully examine the features on several different UPS models before purchasing one.

You must have a plan to periodically create secondary copies of your important information. This secondary copy is often called a backup. Creating a backup copy of information is an important step, but only one step in a plan to ensure availability. The real key to ensuring availability is to have a plan for restoring your information to the state in which it existed before a disaster. Your backup and recovery strategy should include the following:

- **Backup plan**—A plan to create frequent backup copies of important files. This plan includes identifying the files you need to back up, deciding on which backup utility to use, and setting a schedule for creating backups.

- **Safe media storage plan**—A plan to protect your backup copies. This plan includes procedures for transporting backup media to a protected location. In most cases, you want to keep copies of your important information in remote locations to keep them safe from disasters that might affect your primary office. Consider keeping backup copies far enough away from your primary office that a disaster won't affect them. For example, a flood or earthquake can affect a large area. You may need to store backup copies far away, even in a different geographic region.

- **Restore plan**—A plan to use the backup media to restore your environment to working order. This is often the plan most people overlook. You need backups, but you also need a plan that tells how to use the backups to build a working system.

The most important aspect of ensuring availability is to plan for situations that might disrupt your organization's activities and know what to do in those instances. Plan ahead and you won't likely be caught not knowing what to do when a disaster strikes.

Maximizing Integrity

The term "malware" refers to a collection of different types of software that share the goal of infiltrating a computer and making it do something. In many cases, malware does something undesired and operates without the explicit consent of the owner. This is not always the case, however. Some types of malware are downloaded and installed with the owner's full knowledge. Malware can be loosely divided into two main categories: programs that spread or infect and programs that hide.

Programs that spread or infect actively attempt to copy themselves to other computers. Their main purpose is to carry out instructions on new targets. Malware of this type includes:

- **Virus**—A software program that attaches itself to, or copies itself into, another program for the purpose of causing the computer to follow instructions that were not intended by the original program developer

- **Worm**—A self-contained program that replicates and sends copies of itself to other computers, generally across a network

Other malware hides in the computer to carry out its instructions while avoiding detection. Malware that tends to hide includes:

- **Trojan horse**—Software that either hides or masquerades as a useful or benign program
- **Rootkit**—Software that modifies or replaces one or more existing programs to hide the fact a computer has been compromised
- **Spyware**—Software that covertly collects information without the user's knowledge or permission

Understanding these five basic types of malware and how to protect your systems from them is important to a solid security plan. You install anti-malware software to protect Workstation Domain computers. There are many anti-malware software products from which you can choose. Carefully review suppliers and their products for costs, functionality, and support. The best place to look for specific anti-malware for your operating system is the Internet. Use an Internet search engine to search for "antivirus software" and "antispyware software."

Once you decide on one or more anti-malware products, you must develop procedures to ensure the products and their signature databases are kept up to date. With over 150 new viruses, worms, and Trojan horses being released every day, it is important your software be kept current to recognize as many new threats as possible. Up-to-date anti-malware software can help make your Workstation Domain computers more secure and able to ensure information integrity.

Maximizing Confidentiality

Because Workstation Domain computers may store sensitive or private information, it is important to protect the information from disclosure to unauthorized users. Two methods are commonly used to protect information confidentiality. Access controls can help ensure unauthorized users cannot access protected objects. The easiest way to deny access to anyone other than authorized users is through access permissions. If you only grant read and write access to authorized users, the operating system ensures the information's confidentiality. Regardless of your choice of access control methods, you can assign user accounts to enforce confidentiality.

There is a drawback with using operating system access control. It is possible for an attacker with physical access to a computer to boot the computer using alternate boot media. Most Workstation Domain computers have USB ports and CD/DVD drives. Either of these can support booting. If you insert a bootable CD/DVD or USB drive, many computers will boot from the alternate devices instead of the internal disk drive.

Booting from alternate boot media makes it easy to use tools to access files directly from the disk. If you boot from a CD/DVD or USB drive, you can bypass the operating system access controls and access any files you want. So, operating system access controls don't fully protect the confidentiality of your information. To protect private information

Whether a particular computer will boot from the CD/DVD drive or USB device before the internal disk drive depends on that computer's complementary metal-oxide semiconductor (CMOS) configuration. Most computers allow you to enter a setup mode to alter CMOS settings, including the device boot order by pressing the Delete key, F2, or F11 early in the boot process. Specific keys and options differ between computer manufacturers.

at all times, you need to protect it even when the operating system isn't running. Only encryption provides that much protection.

Encrypting data makes it unreadable to everyone without the decryption key. You can encrypt all sensitive information and only provide the decryption key to authorized users. Attackers can still boot your computer using alternate media; however, they will only see encrypted files and will be unable to read their contents.

 TIP

Each operating system supports encryption a little differently and some need third-party software to encrypt folders or entire drives. Explore how your operating system supports encryption and use it to secure private information.

Workstation Vulnerability Management

Because Workstation Domain computers and devices are commonplace and plentiful, they make good attack targets. Workstations generally are not located in areas that are secure as devices in some other domains. They also exist in sufficient numbers that there is a high probability of finding vulnerable computers.

Although you can't make every computer and device totally secure, you can make them secure enough to frustrate all but the most determined attackers. In general, your computer environment doesn't have to be totally secure—just more secure than the attacker's next target. If you can get an attacker to give up and go on to another target, you have been successful.

Operating System Patch Management

One of the first attack activities is to identify a target machine's operating system and look for any known vulnerabilities. There are multiple methods attackers use to identify, or fingerprint, a target machine. **Fingerprinting** a computer means identifying the operating system and general configuration of a computer. Attackers will fingerprint a computer and use that information to identify known vulnerabilities for that operating system version.

It is important to keep your operating system up to date and patched to the latest version of your operating system. Applying the latest security patches eliminates many of the vulnerabilities attackers are looking for when planning attacks.

 TIP

Explore options for automatically acquiring and applying operating system patches. Automatic updates can reduce the administrative workload by ensuring the latest patches get installed on Workstation Domain computers.

Application Software Patch Management

After fingerprinting, a computer attacker scans target computers for information on resident applications. Just like operating systems, applications may contain security vulnerabilities and provide attackers with an opportunity to compromise a computer. It is important to keep your applications up to date as well as your operating system.

Develop a plan to keep all applications up to date. Each application's provider may approach the update process differently. Some vendors provide automatic update notifications and others only report updates when directly queried. Know the update policy for each of your vendors. Create procedures to ensure you update all applications with the latest security patches. Keeping applications current will reduce the number of vulnerabilities on your computers and make it harder for attackers to succeed.

Adherence to Documented IT Security Policies, Standards, Procedures, and Guidelines

Workstation Domain computers and devices are often the most visible components to users. The majority of users access an organization's applications and information using Workstation Domain computers. That means Workstation Domain computers and devices tend to interact with users a lot. Many security issues result from user errors and can be addressed with proper training. However, training can only address some of the security issues related to users. Eventually, an untrained, unmotivated, or careless user will violate security policy and will take action that causes a security incident. The incident might be large or it might be very small and unimportant. Regardless, it is important to employ multiple layers of controls to ensure security does not rely on any single control. Even organizations with very effective training programs encounter problems that users create.

A solid security policy should define multiple layers of controls working together to keep your information secure. Your security policy should direct security activities and state standards that maintain compliance with legislation, regulations, and any other state requirements. Following procedures and guidelines should always result in fulfilling your security policy as well as any other organizational policies.

FYI

How your organization implements its security policy can specifically follow an auditing framework. For example, if the organization follows the Committee of Sponsoring Organizations (COSO) or Control Objectives for Information and related Technology (COBIT) auditing frameworks, the process of implementing the security policy and guidelines can be more aligned to that framework. This helps an organization compare "apples to apples" while auditing. Similarly, if an organization relies on outsourced services, it can make use of auditing standard SAS 70 to best assess the provider.

Periodically, an organization should assess its adherence. To accomplish this, an organization can perform a gap analysis to determine what holes might exist in how it enforces the security policy. Specifically, the organization compares the present situation with the desired situation. Once identified, the gap between is used to create actionable tasks.

Procedures define the steps necessary to fulfill the intent of the security policy. The Workstation Domain procedures can cover many aspects of maintaining computers and devices, but should include the following:

- Change password procedure
- Logon/logoff procedure
- Backup procedure, including handling backup media
- Recovery procedure
- Update operating system and application software procedure
- Maintaining private data procedure
- Malware alert procedure
- Grant/deny object access procedure

Procedures provide the step-by-step instructions for fulfilling the security policy but cannot include every variable. In some cases, you have to make decisions based on the information at hand. In these cases, guidelines help make decisions that still comply with your security policy and any other organizational policies. Workstation Domain guidelines can include:

- Strong password guideline
- Document-naming guideline
- Printer use guideline
- Software installation guideline
- Handling backup media guideline
- Internet use guideline

Use operating system controls whenever possible to enforce Workstation Domain policies. These controls will not fulfill all aspects of the security policy, but they will provide a solid foundation for ensuring your information's security. Controls you will find in most current operating systems include:

- General object access permissions
- Shared object access permissions
- Private object access permissions
- Printer permissions
- Audit logging settings
- Authentication requirements
- User rights

▶ **NOTE**

Reviewing audit logs will show how users are using Workstation Domain computers and devices. The audit process uses these log files to validate that usage complies with your security policy.

Taken together, policies, procedures, and guidelines provide the instructions and limits that enable your users to comply with your security policy when using components of the Workstation Domain. Even though you design and deploy controls to limit user actions, you still should deploy additional controls to detect noncompliant behavior. Use your operating system's access audit logging features to keep log files of interesting object access requests. Carefully consider which objects you want to audit. Auditing access requests for all objects will slow your computers down and waste disk space. Identify the objects that contain sensitive or private information and enable audit logging for those objects.

A second useful technique during an audit is to compare a snapshot, or baseline, of a computer or device as it currently appears with a baseline from a previous point in time. Any differences between baselines could indicate unintended changes and possible vulnerabilities. Your audit plan should include procedures to create periodic baselines you can use to detect unwanted changes to your computers and devices. A baseline can contain many types of information, but should include the following information:

- Users and settings
- Groups and members
- File list with access permissions
- Access control lists
- Configuration settings for important applications and services
- Installed application list
- Startup/shutdown and logon scripts or batch files
- Network adapters and configuration

You should include any other information that describes the configuration of a specific computer. One of the easiest ways to create baselines is to include the commands that list the desired information in a script or batch file. You can compare saved output from any baseline to see configuration changes between snapshots. Creating periodic baselines supports the overall audit process to ensure compliance with stated security goals.

Best Practices for Workstation Domain Compliance Requirements

Workstation Domain computers and devices provide local computing resources and often provide initial access into your organization's shared resources. It is important to maintain a secure Workstation Domain both for the security of the locally stored information but also to keep other domains secure. Allowing Workstation Domain components to be insecure increases the vulnerability for other domains you access from workstations. There are many strategies for keeping the Workstation Domain secure.

Each organization should customize their Workstation Domain policies, procedures, and guidelines for their specific set of requirements. If the organization is a federal entity, compliance with the NIST 800-53 standard is mandatory. The assessment of those controls is covered in depth in guideline NIST 800-53a. Here are general guidelines and best practices to attain and maintain compliance within the Workstation Domain:

- Require unique user accounts for each person. Do not allow multiple people to use the same user account.
- Require strong passwords and train users on the importance of keeping passwords private. Require users to change passwords at a specified interval, such as every six months.
- If one person performs duties of several roles, create a unique user account for each role.
- If using DAC, assign object permissions for all shared objects to grant access only to necessary subjects.
- If using MAC, establish simple standards for assigning security classifications to objects.
- Create a backup schedule that minimizes the amount of work that would be lost if a disaster destroyed the computer just before the next backup.
- Document procedures for labeling, transporting, storing, and reusing backup media.
- Document the steps necessary to restore your system from a backup after data loss.
- Test your recovery procedure at least every six months.
- Test the power outage operation of your UPS at least monthly.
- Conduct informal monthly audits that include creating monthly baselines.
- Check for anti-malware software and signature database updates daily.
- Scan for operating system and application updates at least weekly.
- Audit users, groups, and access permissions/data classification at least quarterly.

Although this list of best practices is not exhaustive, it is a good foundation to keep Workstation Domain computers and devices secure.

CHAPTER SUMMARY

The Workstation Domain contains computers and devices that provide the primary interface for most users. Many information systems users access local and networked resources from computers in the Workstation Domain. Securing components in this domain has a dual effect of securing information on individual workstations and helping to avoid introducing vulnerabilities into the organization's network.

You learned about the importance of access controls, maximizing the A-I-C properties of security, and backing up and restoring information. You also learned strategies for staying malware-free and keeping the operating system and application software up to date. The tasks necessary to keep the Workstation Domain secure cover several areas and require diligence. The result is a domain that supports your organization's business functions and keeps your information secure.

KEY CONCEPTS AND TERMS

A-I-C	Identification	Type II authentication (what you have)
Access control lists (ACLs)	Multifactor authentication	
Authentication	Object	Type III authentication (what you are)
Authorization	Owner	
Availability	Permission	Uninterruptible power supply (UPS)
Card Verification Value (CVV)	Subject	
CIA	Two-factor authentication	War dialing
Due diligence	Type I authentication (what you know)	
Fingerprinting		

CHAPTER 9 ASSESSMENT

1. _____ means the ongoing attention and care an organization places on security and compliance.

2. PCI DSS allows merchants to store the CVV number.

   A. True
   B. False

3. Which of the following choices protect your system from users transferring private data files from a server to a workstation? (Select two.)

   A. Increase the frequency of object access audits.
   B. Deliver current security policy training.
   C. Place access control to prohibit inappropriate actions.
   D. Enable access auditing for all private data files.

4. Some attackers use the process of _____ to find modems that may be used to attack a computer.

5. Which security-related act requires organizations to protect all personal medical information?

   A. HIPAA
   B. GLBA
   C. SOX
   D. SCM

6. A data DVD can store up to 256 GB of data.

   A. True
   B. False

7. Which of the following is the process of verifying credentials of a specific user?

   A. Authorization
   B. Identification
   C. Authentication
   D. Revocation

8. Which of the following is the process of providing additional private credentials that match the user ID or username?

   A. Authorization
   B. Identification
   C. Authentication
   D. Revocation

9. A security token is an example of _____, or "what you have," authentication.

10. Which access control method is based on granting permissions?

    A. DAC
    B. MAC
    C. RBAC
    D. OAC

11. The _____ property of the A-I-C triad provides the assurance the information cannot be changed by unauthorized users.

12. What are the types of malware? (Select two.)

    A. Programs that actively spread or infect
    B. Programs that slow down data transfer
    C. Programs that cause damage
    D. Programs that hide

13. A _____ is a type of malware that is a self-contained program which replicates and sends copies of itself to other computers.

Compliance Within the LAN Domain

S TANDALONE COMPUTERS can be very useful, but they are far more effective when they are able to communicate with one another. Computers that can communicate and exchange information have the ability to assume specific roles that make your organization's computing environment more efficient and effective. Unfortunately, connecting computers also makes accessing your organization's information easier for both authorized and unauthorized users. That means you have to be diligent to ensure the availability, integrity, and confidentiality of your data.

In this chapter, you'll learn about techniques many organizations use to ensure information is secure within locally connected computers. The controls and techniques that can help meet compliance requirements are also explained. You'll learn how to connect computers together without risking the organization's information to loss, alteration, or disclosure.

Chapter 10 Topics

This chapter covers the following topics and concepts:

- How compliance law requirements and business drivers relate to one another
- Which devices and components are commonly found in the LAN Domain
- What LAN traffic and performance monitoring and analysis are
- What LAN configuration and change management are
- Which LAN management tools and systems are commonly used
- What access rights and access controls in the LAN Domain are
- How to maximize A-I-C
- How to manage the vulnerability of LAN components
- How to ensure adherence to documented IT security policies, standards, procedures, and guidelines
- What best practices for LAN Domain compliance requirements are

Compliance Law Requirements and Business Drivers

Users generally use their workstations to access other resources that are connected to an organization's local area network (LAN). A LAN is a network that covers a small physical area, such as an office or building. Resources that are connected to a LAN are potentially available to users using workstations also connected to the LAN. Because LANs increase the number of potential users that can access any resource on the LAN, it becomes even more important to control access to resources and monitor LAN activity to ensure controls are doing their job. For example, the Payment Card Industry Data Security Standard (PCI DSS) requires additional controls to protect credit card information. The Health Insurance Portability and Accountability Act (HIPAA) requires controls on personal health information. As LANs become more and more useful to authorized users and attackers, it is more important than ever to ensure compliance within the LAN Domain. Figure 10-1 shows the LAN Domain in the context of the seven domains in the IT infrastructure.

Organizations rely on networked resources more than ever in today's environments. LANs make it possible to share expensive resources, such as color printers and high-performance disk subsystems. In fact, LANs enable more efficiency in critical business functions by supporting faster information transfer and resource sharing. These benefits often result in direct cost reductions and productivity increases. Organizations rely on LAN resources to maintain cost-efficient operations. Protecting the LAN-based services directly affects costs and efficiency. A solid security policy that includes compliance with all appropriate requirements should support efficient and cost-effective operation. Implementing the controls necessary to support your security policy in the LAN Domain makes your organization more secure and more effective.

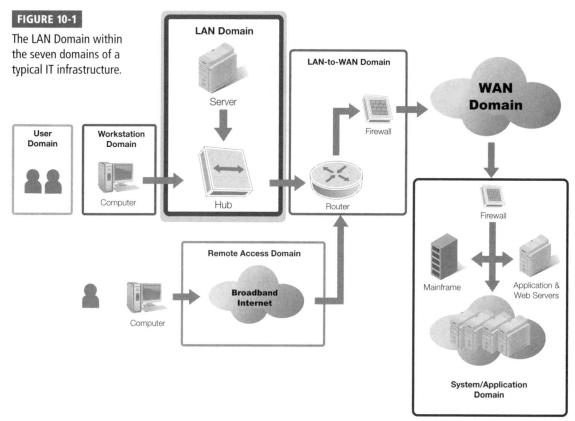

FIGURE 10-1

The LAN Domain within the seven domains of a typical IT infrastructure.

Protecting Data Privacy

At this point in the book, you are starting to see how the various domains work together in the IT infrastructure. You learned about the first two domains in Chapters 8 and 9. You learned about the controls that are appropriate when a user in the User Domain logs on to a workstation in the Workstation Domain. Now, you'll continue the model and learn about the user accessing shared resources connected to a LAN. Just because you're accessing multiple domains, you still must consider the security requirements and control needs for each domain independently of other domains. Users still have the responsibility to act in a manner that is acceptable under your organization's security policy, and Workstation Domain controls must still protect local resources. Controls from different domains are distinct but work together to provide a solid defense-in-depth approach to securing your environment.

Now you must consider another domain. Ensuring your organization's private data means designing a layer of controls that protect LAN resources from destruction, alteration, or disclosure by unauthorized users. That means you must define an authorized user in the context of the LAN Domain. A user who is authorized to access local resources might not be authorized to access LAN resources on another computer. Compliance with current legislation, regulations, and other requirements means placing appropriate controls in the LAN Domain to ensure all components are secure.

Implementing Proper Security Controls for the LAN Domain

LAN Domain controls often focus on limiting access to remote resources. A **local resource** is any resource attached to a local computer—the same computer to which the user has logged on. A **remote resource** is any resource accessible across the LAN. Of course, the user's computer and the remote resource have to be connected to a network to provide access to the remote resource.

The security controls you'll find in the LAN Domain are similar to controls you'll find in other domains. The main types of security controls in the LAN Domain include:

- Access controls for protected resources, such as printers and shared folders
- Communication controls to limit the spread of malicious software
- Anti-malware software on all computers in the LAN Domain to detect and eradicate malware
- Recovery plans, including backups, for all computers and devices in the LAN Domain
- Procedures to control configuration changes
- Monitoring tools and other detective controls to help detect suspicious LAN Domain activity
- Software patch management for all computers and devices in the LAN Domain

Good LAN Domain security controls will directly support one or more of the three pillars of security in the A-I-C triad, while not interfering with your organization's business functions. A secure system that doesn't support your organization's critical business functions isn't of much use. You will always have to balance security with functionality. Search for compensating controls as often as possible to identify the best controls for both security and functionality. Avoid controls that do not balance these two crucial needs.

Good Control, Bad Control

Assume you have an expensive color printer connected to your LAN. The printing costs are far more than the amount budgeted because employees use the printer for personal use. One way to solve the problem is to severely restrict access to the printer to only a few individuals. This approach would solve the printing cost issue but would not allow most users to use the printer for valid business purposes. In this case, the security control gets in the way of regular business functions.

Another way to address the problem is to limit which applications can generate output for the color printer. You could also log all print jobs and audit the printer activity frequently to ensure your users are only submitting valid print jobs. Conducting user training for color printer use would make these controls (in the User Domain) more effective. These controls working together will be more effective by achieving the original goal without affecting proper business use of the printer.

Devices and Components Commonly Found in the LAN Domain

The LAN Domain's primary responsibility is to provide your users with the ability to connect to, and share, resources. To fulfill this goal, the LAN Domain contains four main types of components. These components work together to allow users to share resources on the network and reduce the need for multiple dedicated resources, such as printers, file storage systems, and backup devices. The four main types of components in the LAN Domain include:

- **Connection media**—The adapters and wires (sometimes) that connect components together in the LAN Domain. Not all connection methods use wires. Wireless devices use radio waves to transmit data instead of wires. So, connection media includes wireless adapters.
- **Networking devices**—The hardware devices that connect other devices and computers using connection media.
- **Server computers and services devices**—The hardware that provides one or more services to users, such as server computers, printers, and network storage devices.
- **Networking services software**—The software that provides connection and communication services for users and devices.

Many physical devices in the LAN Domain are actually combinations of several types of components. These components should work together to provide easy access to desired resources and still maintain the security of your organization's information. Figure 10-2 shows common components you'll find in the LAN Domain.

Connection Media

The purpose of any network is to allow multiple computers or devices to communicate with each other. By definition, networked computers and devices are connected to one another and have the appropriate software to communicate. In the past, networked computers and devices were connected using some type of cable. Many of today's networks contain a mix of cables and wireless connections. The cables or devices you use to connect computers and devices to form a network are collectively called **connection media**. Although the technical details of network connections are beyond the scope of this discussion, it is important to have a general understanding of a network's components.

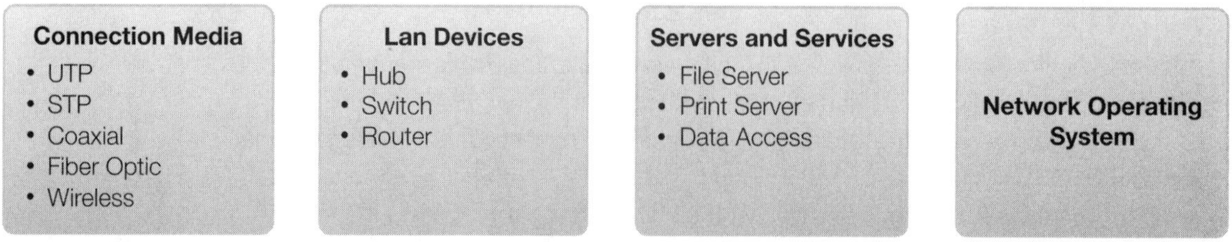

Connection Media	Lan Devices	Servers and Services	Network Operating System
• UTP • STP • Coaxial • Fiber Optic • Wireless	• Hub • Switch • Router	• File Server • Print Server • Data Access	

FIGURE 10-2

Common components in the LAN Domain.

TABLE 10-1 Basic network cabling options.

CABLE TYPE	DESCRIPTION	ADVANTAGES AND DISADVANTAGES
Unshielded twisted pair (UTP)	The most common type of network cable. UTP generally consists of two or four pairs of wires. Pairs of wires are twisted around each other to reduce interference with other pairs. The most common type of UTP is Category 5 UTP that supports 100 megabits per second (Mbps) for two pairs of wires and 1,000 Mbps for four pairs.	Lowest cost Easy to install Susceptible to interference Limited transmission speeds and distances
Shielded twisted pair (STP)	Same as UTP, but with foil shielding around each pair and optionally around the entire wire group to protect the cable from external radio and electrical interference.	Low cost Easy to install More resistant to interference than UTP Same speed limitations but supports longer run lengths
Coaxial	A single copper conductor surrounded with a plastic sheath, then a braided copper shield, and then the external insulation.	Higher cost Difficult to install Very resistant to interference Higher speeds and longer run lengths
Fiber optic	A glass core surrounded by several layers of protective materials.	Highest cost Easy to run cable, installing end connectors require special tools Immune to radio and electrical interference Extremely high speeds and long run lengths

Wired LAN Connections

There are four basic cabling options for physical network connections. Each option has its own advantages and disadvantages. If you choose to use physical cables for part, or all, of your network, you will have to run cables to each device. Running cables between devices takes careful planning to do it right. Make sure when you explore cabling options that you evaluate the cost of installing all of the cables and connection hardware to support both your current and future needs. Table 10-1 lists the four basic cable options, along with the advantages and disadvantages of each one.

Communication Protocol

A communication protocol isn't as complex as the name implies. The technical details of each protocol can be quite complex but the concept is simple. A protocol is just a set of rules that parties use to communicate. You use protocol rules every day. For example, suppose you want to invite a person to attend a meeting. If that person is a close friend, you would use an informal greeting and style of conversation. If, on the other hand, the person is an elected official, you would likely use a far more formal greeting and conversation style. You decide how to communicate based on your own protocol rules.

Wireless LAN Connections

Wireless connections are very popular in today's LAN environments where flexibility is an important design factor. Wireless connections allow devices to connect to your LAN without having to physically connect to a cable. This flexibility makes it easy to connect computers, or devices, in situations where running cables is either difficult or not practical for temporary connections. The **Institute of Electrical and Electronics Engineers (IEEE)** defines standards for many aspects of computing and communications. The **IEEE 802.11** defines standards for **wireless local area network (WLAN)** communication protocols. A **protocol** is a set of rules that governs communication.

There are four main protocols currently in the 802.11 standard. As with the discussion of wired LAN connections, the technical details are beyond the scope of this discussion, but it is important to know the basic differences among different wireless protocols. Table 10-2 lists the four most common wireless LAN protocols.

TABLE 10-2 Common 802.11 wireless LAN standards.

PROTOCOL	MAXIMUM TRANSMISSION SPEED	RANGE (FT) INDOOR/ OUTDOOR	FREQUENCY*
802.11a	54 Mbps	115/390	5 GHz
802.11b	11 Mbps	125/460	2.4 GHz
802.11g	54 Mbps	125/460	2.4 GHz
802.11n	150+ Mbps	230/820	2.4 GHz/5 GHz

Generally, hardware that supports protocols with faster speeds with higher range cost more than slower protocols. Your choice of wireless LAN protocol will likely be based on cost, transmission speed requirements, and other devices that might cause interference in a specific frequency.

> ⚠ **WARNING**
>
> Regardless of the protocol you choose, wireless connections increase the likelihood that unauthorized users will connect to your network. If you choose to implement wireless connections, you must ensure you are using strong access controls and strong wireless encryption.

Networking Devices

Once you decide on the types of connections you'll use for your network, you have to decide how your components connect to one another. Few networks have every component connected to every other component. That would make managing your network connections extremely difficult. LANs in today's environments use several types of **networking devices** to help keep connections manageable. You'll see many different types of networking devices, but the following two sections discuss the ones you'll commonly use in the LAN Domain.

Hub

The simplest network device is a hub. A hub is a box with several connectors, or ports, that allows multiple network cables to attach to it. Common hubs have 4, 8, 16, or even 32 ports. A hub is basically a hardware repeater. A hub takes input from any port and repeats the transmission, sending it as output on every port, including the original input port. Hubs make it easy to connect many devices to a network by just connecting each device to a hub. Figure 10-3 shows a simple network created using a single hub.

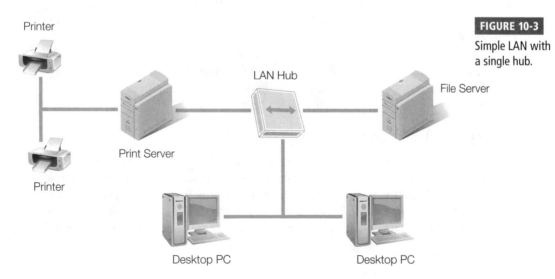

FIGURE 10-3

Simple LAN with a single hub.

Switch

Hubs are very inexpensive devices you can use to connect many computers and devices to a LAN. One problem with hubs is that they repeat all network traffic to all ports. This can cause message collisions and a frequent need to resend messages. Hubs also tend to contribute to network congestion because everyone gets all network traffic. Networks are designed to handle collisions and congestion but at the cost of slowing down the network. A switch can help avoid many collision and congestion issues and actually speed up networks. A switch is a hardware device that forwards input it receives only to the appropriate output port.

For example, if computer A wants to send a message to computer B, a switch will only send the message from computer A to the port to which computer B is attached. No other computers ever see the message. As an additional benefit, if computer C wants to send a message to computer F at the same time computers A and B are talking, the switch can handle both connections at the same time without causing a collision. Switches are also more secure because the only computers that actually see information exchanged over the network are the computers involved in the transfer. This is more secure than a hub that repeats messages to all connected computers.

Router

A router is another network device that connects two or more separate networks. A router can connect a LAN to another LAN or to devices in another domain in the IT infrastructure. Routers are more intelligent than switches and actually inspect the address portion of the packets on your network. The router examines the destination address and then forwards the packet to the correct outbound port. Routers can be standalone hardware devices or computers with multiple network interfaces running routing software.

Routers also provide an important security capability. You can define rules for each router that tell the router how to filter network traffic. You can restrict which packets you allow to flow through your networks. Routers give you the ability to aggressively control how users and applications use your LANs.

Server Computers and Services Devices

LANs provide easy access to shared resources and shared services. Shared centralized services make it possible for multiple users to share information and physical resources at a lower cost than duplicating information or purchasing devices for every workstation. Shared resources can include both **server computers and services devices**. Both offer value to a group, rather than as a dedicated resource. Examples of shared resources include:

- Shared file storage
- Shared printer and print services
- Central database and document management systems

LAN File Server

One common service present in the earliest LANs is the file-sharing service. A file server is a computer or hardware device that has at least three distinct components:

- One or more connected hard disk drives
- A network interface
- Software to provide network access to files and folders on the attached disks

In the past, most file servers were computers that managed shared folders or file systems. The file server would manage connections and support authorized read/write access to its disks by remote users. Computer-based file servers are still in widespread use, but standalone hardware devices with internal hard disk drives are becoming more popular. Regardless of whether you choose to use a computer or standalone device, a file server's main purpose is to provide secure access to its disk drives for remote users.

LAN Print Server

A print server provides the interface between the LAN and one or more printers. Like file servers, the actual server can be a computer or a standalone hardware device. In either case, the print server accepts print jobs from authorized users and processes them. That means the print server may contain the intelligence to store multiple print jobs and provide advanced abilities to manage the printing process. Print servers vary widely in capabilities but all generally exist to allow multiple remote users to share printers.

LAN Data Storage

LAN data storage might sound like the service the file server provides but the two services are distinct. A file server just stores files. A data storage server organizes data and attempts to make it more accessible than just a list of files. Data storage software includes database management systems and document management systems. Both types of software provide efficient, effective centralized access to data and documents for remote users.

Another substantial difference you'll notice between file servers and data storage products is that data storage products generally provide far greater control over access authorization. File servers can control access to individual folders and files, but data storage software can control access to the contents of files. Database management systems and document management systems often provide their own features to maintain and authorize users and requests. These systems manage large amounts of data and can grant or deny access to individual pieces of information stored inside very large files. The advantage of data management systems is they can provide fast and efficient access to large amounts of data while maintaining the security of the data down to a very specific level.

> **technical TIP**
>
> Novell was a leader in early NOS products and many early LANs ran Novell NetWare as their NOS. Today's Novell NOS product is Open Enterprise Server and is based on the SUSE distribution of Linux.

Networking Services Software

The last category of components in the LAN Domain is **networking services software**. This category consists of components that really aren't connection or hardware components. All of the network computers and components don't do anything without the network software to provide the ability to communicate. The networking services software changes a group of connected devices into a network of devices that communicate to accomplish tasks.

A **network operating system (NOS)** provides the interface between the hardware and the application layer software. The NOS provides many of the same functions an operating system provides on a standalone computer. In fact, the roles of the operating system and NOS are so similar that nearly all of today's operating systems contain NOS functionality. Today's networking components generally run either a version of Windows or UNIX/Linux operating systems.

NOS products provide extensive support for resource access and management, as well as credential management at various levels. NOSs support low-level authorization as well as higher-level standards such as Kerberos and Active Directory. Choose the NOS that fits in best with your existing IT infrastructure.

LAN Traffic and Performance Monitoring and Analysis

Once you start using a LAN to share resources, how do you know if you are upholding your security policy? You'll learn how to use preventive controls in later sections, but you should also use detective controls to validate how your users are using your LAN. Traffic and performance monitoring utilities allow you to watch the traffic flowing across your network. You can watch the traffic in real time or collect it in log files for later analysis.

> **FYI**
>
> Monitoring any resource requires system resources. You will impact your network's performance any time you collect traffic to analyze. Also, you must save a copy of network messages you plan to analyze at a later time. Because networks transport potentially high volumes of information, your saved network messages can require large amounts of disk space to store. It is generally a bad idea to save all network traffic. You should only save complete copies of network traffic when you are investigating a problem and need the extended detail for your analysis.

technical TIP

If you're interested in getting more technical information on packet sniffers and packet analyzers, you can find a list of popular tools at *http://sectools.org/sniffers.html*.

There are two common types of monitoring tools available for monitoring LANs, packet sniffers and network software log files. A **packet sniffer** is software that copies specified packets from a network interface to an output device, generally a file. A sniffer may copy all packets or may select certain packets based on a specific filter, such as source, destination, or protocol. Because sniffers copy the actual packets from the network, you get to see all of the addressing and routing information as well as the contents of each message. If the message is encrypted, you won't be able to read the contents but you will see the encrypted data.

The other common option is to change settings in network software to create audit logging entries for certain packets. You can change configuration settings to log all traffic or just certain conditions. You should only log information you must record to avoid slowing down your network.

Once you have a collection of packets, you can use packet analysis software to make sifting through the sniffer output or log files easier. Most analysis software allows you to sort and query data according to your own requirements. You can analyze packets originating from a specific computer, destined for a specific port, or you can analyze queries based on any of the packet's attributes. Using monitoring and analysis tools helps verify appropriate LAN use and identify inappropriate LAN use.

LAN Configuration and Change Management

Suppose you found inappropriate network packets during your LAN traffic analysis. Assume your traffic analysis revealed a collection of packets originating from an Internet Protocol address that is not valid for your network. In most cases, LAN controls should only allow traffic originating from, and addressed to, valid addresses. If you initially set up your LAN controls to properly filter network addresses, something is wrong.

One of the first things you should check is the current settings of your routing rules. You should be able to tell if you have defined your routing rules properly. If you find that the rules have changed, determine when the rules changed, who changed them, and why were they changed.

One attack method is to access network devices and change packet filter rules to permit malicious traffic. Another important control in the LAN Domain is network device configuration control and change management. You should implement a formal process to change network configuration settings. A change control board should approve each change and you should only allow a small number of privileged users to access network devices with the authority to change settings. You should also define your network devices to create audit log entries any time you change a configuration setting.

A formal change procedure and configuration change audit will limit unexpected changes to your network configuration and provide an audit trail when changes allow unwanted network traffic.

LAN Management, Tools, and Systems

Managing a LAN means ensuring it fulfills the goals for which it was designed. It also means to continually update the LAN's configuration to satisfy new and updated goals. LAN management covers several related activities, including:

- Monitoring LAN performance
- Changing configuration settings to optimize performance
- Changing configuration to support new requirements
- Adding necessary controls to address security issues
- Maintaining components of a current recovery process
- Adding, changing, and removing hardware components as requirements dictate
- Mapping LAN components

Although it is possible to manually keep up with the documentation and activities that accompany monitoring and changing your LAN, automated tools can greatly simplify your tasks. In fact, many open source and commercial software packages provide network monitoring and network management functionality. Many networks even have dedicated computers on the LAN running network management software. These dedicated servers are often called **network monitoring platforms (NMPs)**. Because NMP software runs on dedicated servers, it can help manage a LAN by providing monitoring and configuration assistance without having a negative performance impact on other LAN computers and devices. Explore options for network monitoring and management software for your operating system. Software that assists your network administrators will likely simplify managing your LAN and make it easier to validate compliance with your stated security goals.

---

technical TIP

For more information on network monitoring and management software, you can visit these sites:

- Stanford Linear Accelerator Center network monitoring tools, *http://www.slac.stanford .edu/xorg/nmtf/nmtf-tools.html*
- SolarWinds free network management tools, *http://www.solarwinds.com/ downloads/#free_tools*

FYI

Recall from a previous discussion how many organizations implement object access controls:

- **Discretionary access control (DAC)**—Defines access permissions based on roles, or groups. Object owners and administrators can grant access rights at their discretion.
- **Mandatory access control (MAC)**—Defines access permissions based on data classification and user clearance. Access control is based on object and subject attributes and not on anyone's discretion.

Access Rights and Access Controls in the LAN Domain

LAN access controls limit which subjects can access LAN-based objects. There are generally two levels of controls, computers or devices, and users. The first level of control ensures only authorized computers or devices can establish a connection with a target computer or device. The second level of control ensures only authorized subjects can access protected objects.

In the context of networks, any computer or device that is connected to the network is called a **node**. Switches and LAN routers are common places for the first layer of controls. Because these devices establish the network connection between a source node and a target node, this is a good place to make authorization decisions. Most LAN access controls for nodes look at the identification credentials and compare those with stored authentication information. Identification credentials for nodes can include the interface's **Media Access Control (MAC)** address, Internet Protocol (IP) address, or even a digital certificate. The idea is to select a method to uniquely identify a specific node.

The software running on your switch or router will examine connection requests and compare identification credentials with its own stored credentials to make an authorization decision. A simple way to identify nodes is to use the MAC and IP address the same way user authentication uses an ID and a password. Although not rock solid, it does help identify unauthorized nodes. If your organization requires stronger node identification and authentication, you can use digital certificates. Digital certificates require more administrative work but provide greater security.

Once your LAN establishes a connection between nodes, the second layer of access controls makes an authorization decision for the target object access request. In other words, just because computer A can connect to computer F doesn't mean that all users on computer A are authorized to access files in any shared folder on computer F. At this point, access controls look very much like object-level access controls in other domains. Your node's operating system grants or denies access to objects according to your organization's access control method. In most cases, organizations use either DAC or MAC to define access controls.

> **technical TIP**
>
> You can find an example of switch-level network access control software in the open source product FreeNAC. For more information on FreeNAC, go to *http://www.freenac.org/en/solutions/lanaccesscontrol*.

At the object level, operating systems grant access based on the requestor's identity. When moving from a single, standalone computer to a network, the concept of user ID becomes a little less concrete. To authorize an access request, the target operating system needs a user ID. There are two main methods you can use to satisfy this requirement:

- Provide identification and authentication with every resource request.
- Provide a secure identification object with every request.

The first approach is simpler but requires that the target environment authenticate the user for each request. This also means you have the problem of whether to replicate all authentication credentials to each target node or to develop a central authentication method. The second approach depends on a central authentication method. Each target node just validates the identification object and proceeds with the authorization process. Common central authentication methods include **Kerberos**, popular in UNIX/Linux environments, and Active Directory domain accounts, which use Kerberos by default. Both options allow a user to only sign in once and use the same credentials for all network resource requests.

From a compliance perspective, it is important to control node connections and object permissions by user or group. You should monitor connections and accesses for any unusual activity and watch for excessive failures in either connection requests or access requests. Carefully design LAN access controls and monitor for both exceptions and any changes to your control's rules. Either type of unusual activity could indicate an attacker is trying to perform unauthorized actions.

Maximizing A-I-C

One common goal in all domains is the pursuit of the most secure environment possible. Because maximizing the availability, integrity, and confidentiality of your organization's information leads to a secure environment, all of your activities should be to maximize A-I-C.

Maximizing Availability

It is important to develop and maintain a comprehensive recovery plan to replace lost or damaged data. As you use LANs to store more information in central repositories, it becomes more important to ensure the data is available when users request it.

A crucial part of your security plan is creating secondary copies, or backups, of your data in case the primary copy is damaged or deleted. Because more users are sharing the same set of data, any loss impacts a larger portion of your organization.

A solid recovery plan contains a schedule for creating backups, as well as the procedures for recovering lost or damaged data. All current NOS products include capable utilities to back up and recover data. Third-party vendors also provide solutions that make enterprise-wide backups easier than managing individual computers. Explore the backup solutions available for your choice of server computers and select the one that meets your security needs with minimal administrative oversight.

Most backup and recovery solutions target networked computers. Don't forget to include any network devices with valuable data in your backup and recovery plan. Some network devices store configuration settings and performance data. Backing up these devices can save valuable log and performance data and make reconfiguring a device after a failure much faster. In nearly all cases, it is faster to load backed-up configuration data than to re-enter it manually. Make sure your backup plan includes any devices with data you'll need if a device fails.

Another important aspect of availability is to ensure your users can access LAN resources in an acceptable time frame. If the network is too slow, users can't get to their requested information and you are not supporting data availability. In some cases, this problem is just due to excessive network use or a lack of network capacity for normal use. In both cases, you must examine the behavior and either reduce the load on your network or increase its capacity, or both.

In other cases, a lack of availability results from an attack. Suppose your organization sells automobile insurance. You attract new customers by offering to analyze their existing coverage and providing a competitive quote showing how your coverage saves them money. You depend on your database of coverage costs to generate the analysis report. You cannot conduct business if you cannot access your database. In this case, an attacker that renders your network unusable effectively stops your ability to conduct business. The type of attack that denies access to a critical resource or service is called a **denial of service (DoS)** attack.

The best defense from DoS attacks is to aggressively enforce access controls and monitor your network for unusual or excessive traffic. You'll need to provide evidence that you've implemented both preventive and detective controls to combat DoS attacks.

Maximizing Integrity

LAN nodes are just as susceptible to malicious software as any other computers. As LAN nodes become more powerful and based more on standard operating systems, they become more attractive targets. A compromised LAN node can be just a starting point. Once an attacker gets a foothold in your network, it becomes far easier to compromise other parts of your infrastructure.

10

Compliance Within the LAN Domain

> ⚠ **WARNING**
>
> Don't forget that malware can enter your LAN Domain in other ways. Computers and devices in the LAN Domain often have USB ports, CD/DVD drives, and other ports an attacker can use to introduce malware. Just as in the Workstation Domain, ensure you control access to external media. Don't allow external media except when you absolutely need it.

You should use the malicious code policies and procedures from the Workstation Domain in the LAN Domain as well. The issues are the same. Ensure you have anti-malware software installed on every computer in the LAN Domain. Establish procedures to ensure all anti-malware software and data are kept up to date. Because some components in the LAN Domain are devices and not general-purpose computers, you should explore anti-malware features on each device and enable any available features. Your goal is to prevent malicious software from entering your LAN Domain.

Malware is not the only integrity concern. Users can also violate data integrity. Users can be malicious or unaware of their actions. Either way, it is important to control changes to critical data. Good access controls should stop any data changes by unauthorized users; furthermore, you can also audit changes to critical data by authorized users. Audit data can provide valuable audit trails for later analysis. Good audit trails can help trace unauthorized changes back to their source. Getting to the root of unauthorized changes should provide the input needed to modify or add controls to keep the damage from happening again.

Maximizing Confidentiality

Ensuring confidentiality in the LAN Domain is one of the simpler tasks. There are basically four steps to ensuring only authorized users can see confidential data:

1. Identify confidential data.
2. Require positive identification for all access requests and define strict access controls for all confidential data you identified in Step 1.
3. Use encryption to store all confidential data you identified in Step 1.
4. Use encryption to transfer all confidential data you identified in Step 1.

You should already be enforcing identification and access controls in the LAN Domain. The new controls involve using encryption. **Encryption** is the process of scrambling data in such a way that it is unreadable by unauthorized users but can be unscrambled by authorized users to be readable again. Encrypting stored data is easy. Today's operating systems either support encryption directly or through integrated software. You can encrypt individual files, folders, volumes, or entire disk drives. Once you decide how much data you want to encrypt, explore the various encryption options available for your operating system.

Transmission encryption means never sending information across the network in the clear. The term **in the clear** means in a format anyone can read. You can use encryption at the application level or by only allowing encrypted connections between source and destination nodes. Many database management systems and document management systems can also refuse to transmit confidential data over unencrypted connections.

Regardless of how you implement encryption, you should validate your controls to enforce encryption and use a packet analyzer to verify your traffic is actually encrypted.

LAN File/Print/Communication Server Vulnerability Management

Attackers never stop exploring new ways to compromise information systems. It is crucial that you constantly make efforts to stay ahead of the attackers. As soon as new attacks surface, most hardware and software developers make changes to their products to address the new attacks. Nearly every hardware and software vendor releases updates to address vulnerabilities in their products. You should establish procedures to ensure all components in the LAN Domain are up to date.

Operating System Patch Management

Because operating systems play such a crucial role in granting or denying access to resources, they are a prized target for attackers. If an attacker can compromise the operating system, many attacks are possible. To keep your operating system as secure as possible, you should ensure you acquire and install all security-related patches, updates, and service packs. All current operating systems provide methods for automatically identifying, downloading, and installing updates. Either use your operating system's capability for automatic updates or develop procedures to keep your operating systems as current as possible.

Application Software Patch Management

Applications are also prime targets for attackers. Database management systems and document management systems commonly control access to critical data through application access controls. Attackers who compromise applications can often bypass these controls and compromise your data. Just as with your operating systems, you should establish procedures to frequently identify any security updates and install those on your applications to keep your LAN Domain as secure as possible.

Adherence to Documented IT Security Policies, Standards, Procedures, and Guidelines

Compliance in the LAN Domain depends on implementing the best controls. As with all domains, you can meet some goals using different controls. Don't just accept the common controls. Take the time to explore alternate controls for each security goal. Some controls have more of an impact on your organization than others. If two controls provide the same assurance but have different impacts on your organization, choose the one that has less of an impact.

TABLE 10-3 Preventive, detective, and corrective controls in the LAN Domain.

CATEGORY OF CONTROL	TYPE OF CONTROL	DESCRIPTION
Preventive	Node-based access controls for LAN nodes	Only allow authorized nodes to establish connections.
	User-based access controls for LAN resources	Only allow authorized users to access resources.
	Configuration change control	Limit changes to network device configuration settings and filtering rules.
	Encryption	Enforce encryption for stored data and transmitted data for confidential information.
Detective	Connection request auditing	Log connection failures for all connections and successes for high-value targets.
	Object access auditing	Log access failures for most objects and successes for critical objects.
	Performance monitoring	Frequently sample network traffic flow metrics and alert for any unusual activity.
	Packet analysis	Examine packets for known attack signatures and to ensure necessary data is encrypted.
	Configuration settings monitoring	Compare LAN device configuration settings with stored baselines to detect any unauthorized changes.
Corrective	Operating system and application patching	Keep applications and operating systems patched to the latest available level.
	Attack intervention	Automatically modify filtering rules to deny traffic from sources generating known attack signature packets.

As you analyze controls in the LAN Domain to meet compliance requirements, ensure each control satisfies your security policy. If a control does not support any part of your security policy, you should question its value to your organization. Although different legislation, regulations, and vendor standards have different requirements, Table 10-3 lists some types of controls you'll likely need to ensure components in your LAN Domain are compliant.

Implementing multiple types of controls decreases the likelihood an attack will be successful and makes your LAN Domain more secure.

Best Practices for LAN Domain Compliance Requirements

The LAN Domain for any organization often contains the bulk of an organization's sensitive information. Most organizations want to make their information available to as many users as need it, while still keeping it secure. Protecting information in the LAN Domain focuses on maintaining the balance between easy access and solid security. In reality, solid planning can provide both.

The following best practices represent what many organizations have learned. Plan well and you can enjoy a functional LAN Domain that makes information available for use. Here are general best practices for securing your LAN Domain:

- Map your proposed LAN architecture before installing any hardware. Use one of the several available network-mapping software products to make the process easier.
  - Identify all of the components and connection media you'll need for now and for future growth.
  - Update the network map any time you make changes to your network.
- Implement a single sign-on strategy for your environment to keep users from signing on multiple times as they use network resources.
- Identify critical resources and establish detailed access controls.
- Develop a backup and recovery plan for each component in the LAN Domain. Include recovery plans for damaged or destroyed connection media.
  - Don't forget to include configuration settings for network devices in your backup and recovery plan.
- Implement frequent update procedures for all operating systems, applications, and network device software and firmware.
- Define routing and filtering rules to only allow necessary traffic in the LAN Domain.
- Monitor LAN traffic for performance and packets for suspicious content.
- Carefully control any configuration setting changes or physical changes to your LAN.
  - Update your network map after any changes.
- Enable connection and object access auditing on items of interest.
- Use automated tools whenever possible to map, configure, monitor, and manage the LAN Domain.
- If your components support active attack intervention, configure devices to terminate connections when a suspected attack is in progress.

As with all best practices, these are only a starting point. Implement the points that are appropriate for your environment. Doing so will get you started toward establishing and maintaining a secure LAN Domain.

CHAPTER SUMMARY

In this chapter, you learned about how important the LAN Domain is to any organization. Because you probably store much of your organization's shared information in the LAN Domain, it is crucial you secure all components in the domain. You learned about the components commonly found in the LAN Domain and the importance of monitoring and configuring components properly. You learned about some of the most important security controls and how to maximize A-I-C in the LAN Domain.

All of the domains in the IT infrastructure are important. Although it might be difficult to highlight any one domain over the others, the LAN Domain does tend to be where much of an organization's critical data resides. Along with securing other domains, your organization's information security depends on securing the LAN Domain.

KEY CONCEPTS AND TERMS

Connection media	Media Access Control (MAC)	Protocol
Denial of service (DoS)	Network monitoring platforms	Remote resource
Encryption	(NMPs)	Server computers and services
IEEE 802.11	Network operating system	devices
In the clear	(NOS)	Wireless local area network
Institute of Electrical and	Networking devices	(WLAN)
Electronics Engineers (IEEE)	Networking services software	
Kerberos	Node	
Local resource	Packet sniffer	

CHAPTER 10 ASSESSMENT

1. A LAN is a network that generally spans several city blocks.

A. True
B. False

2. A local resource is any resource connected to the local LAN.

A. True
B. False

3. Which of the following devices repeats input received to all ports?

A. Switch
B. Hub
C. Gateway
D. Router

4. _____ cabling provides excellent protection from interference but can be expensive.

5. Even the newest wireless protocols are slower than using high-quality physical cable.

A. True
B. False

6. Which LAN device commonly has the ability to filter packets and deny traffic based on the destination address?

A. Router
B. Gateway
C. Hub
D. Switch

7. Which of the following would be the best use for a packet sniffer?

A. To approve or deny traffic based on the destination address
B. To encrypt confidential data
C. To analyze packet contents for known inappropriate traffic
D. To track configuration changes to specific LAN devices

8. Why is LAN device configuration control important?

A. Configuration control helps to detect violations of LAN resource access controls.
B. Configuration control can detect changes an attacker might have made to allow harmful traffic in a LAN.
C. It reduces the frequency of changes because they are more difficult to implement with configuration control.
D. Configuration control ensures LAN devices are set up once and never changed.

9. A(n) _____ is a dedicated computer on a LAN that runs network management software.

10. Which of the following controls would comply with the directive to limit access to payroll data to computers in the HR department?

A. User-based authorization
B. Group-based authorization
C. Media Access Control-based authorization
D. Smartcard-based authorization

11. You should back up LAN device configuration settings as part of a LAN backup.

A. True
B. False

12. A successful DoS attack violates the _____ property of A-I-C.

13. Where must sensitive information be encrypted to ensure its confidentiality? (Select two.)

A. While in use on a workstation
B. During transmission over the network
C. As it is stored on disk
D. In memory

14. Why is mapping a LAN a productive exercise?

A. Visual maps help to identify unnecessary controls.
B. Visual maps help in understanding your LAN design.
C. A LAN map is required before physically installing any hardware or connection media.
D. A visual map is the only way to define paths between devices.

15. How can some smart routers attempt to stop a DoS attack in progress?

A. Alert an attack responder.
B. Log all traffic coming from the source of the attack.
C. Terminate any connections with the source of the attack.
D. Reset all connections.

Compliance Within the LAN-to-WAN Domain

TODAY'S INFORMATION SYSTEM ENVIRONMENTS are becoming more and more reliant on distributed architectures. In the past, clients, application software, and data tended to exist close to one another. As networks grew to be faster and more stable, clients and applications began to move away from centralized data storage. Now, networks are mature enough to support larger and larger spans between different elements that make up an application. It is common to see enterprise applications in which data, clients, and even segmented applications reside in completely different network environments.

The key to supporting such an environment depends on the ability to connect local resources on a local area network (LAN) to resources on another network. The most popular mechanism is the wide area network (WAN). The purpose of the LAN-to-WAN Domain is to provide stable and controlled access from LAN resources to a WAN. You must ensure your data is secure in the LAN-to-WAN Domain as well as in all other domains. In this chapter, you'll learn about the LAN-to-WAN Domain and how to ensure compliance in this domain.

Chapter 11 Topics

This chapter covers the following topics and concepts:

- How compliance law requirements and business drivers relate to one another
- Which devices and components are commonly found in the LAN-to-WAN Domain
- What LAN-to-WAN traffic and performance monitoring and analysis are
- What LAN-to-WAN configuration and change management are
- Which LAN-to-WAN management tools and systems are commonly used
- What access rights and access controls in the LAN-to-WAN Domain are

- How to maximize A-I-C
- How to validate LAN-to-WAN configuration and perform penetration testing
- How to ensure adherence to documented IT security policies, standards, procedures, and guidelines
- What best practices for LAN-to-WAN Domain compliance requirements are

Chapter 11 Goals

When you complete this chapter, you will be able to:

- Examine compliance law requirements and business drivers
- Compare how devices and components found in the LAN-to-WAN Domain contribute to compliance
- Describe methods of ensuring compliance in the LAN-to-WAN Domain
- Summarize best practices for LAN-to-WAN Domain compliance

Compliance Law Requirements and Business Drivers

You learned in the introduction how more and more organizations rely on distributed architectures. Many of today's applications are deployed as **distributed applications**. Although the actual applications and resources belong in other domains, you'll need to govern access and data flow to and from your LAN Domain. That is the purpose of the LAN-to-WAN Domain. A distributed application is one in which the components that make up an application reside on different computers. In many cases, the components reside in different networks. As distributed applications and remote resources connected using WANs are becoming more and more useful to authorized users and attackers, it is more important than ever to ensure compliance within the LAN-to-WAN Domain. Figure 11-1 shows the LAN-to-WAN Domain in the context of the seven domains in the IT infrastructure.

Keeping your information secure means keeping it secure at all times. This is especially true as it moves between domains in the IT infrastructure. As organizations rely on remote resources and applications more and more, it becomes crucial to ensure your data is secure as it travels from location to location. A solid security policy that includes compliance with all appropriate requirements should support efficient and cost-effective operation. Implementing the controls necessary to support your security policy in the LAN-to-WAN Domain makes your organization more secure and more effective.

Protecting Data Privacy

Your organization may implement applications you develop or applications someone outside your organization developed. In either case, different parts of the application likely exchange data with other parts of the application to perform intended functions. The current architecture of many distributed applications involves a client sending input data to a remote program, or service, and then receiving the results returned from the remote program. A **service** is a set of software functionality that a client accesses using a prescribed interface. Figure 11-2 shows the exchange of data in a remote service call.

One of the most important concerns when sending data across public networks is confidentiality. Although not all data is confidential, any data you exchange with a remote resource using a WAN is potentially available for anyone else to see. Consider all WANs to be hostile and insecure. Your organization likely controls the access to your LANs and has some measure of assurance of how private the LANs are. WANs are different. You don't have control over who accesses them or who can access data traveling across a WAN. You must deploy sufficient controls to protect the privacy of any data in the LAN-to-WAN Domain.

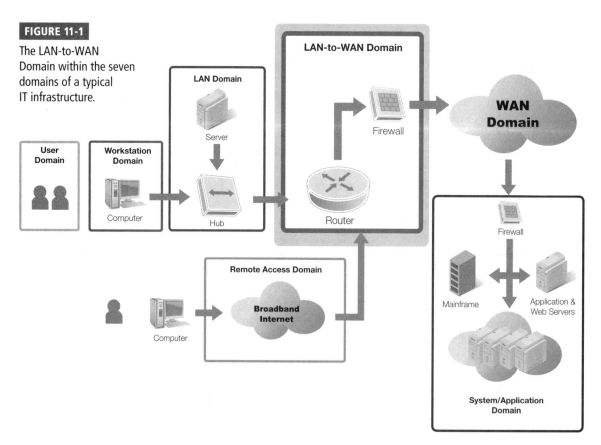

FIGURE 11-1

The LAN-to-WAN Domain within the seven domains of a typical IT infrastructure.

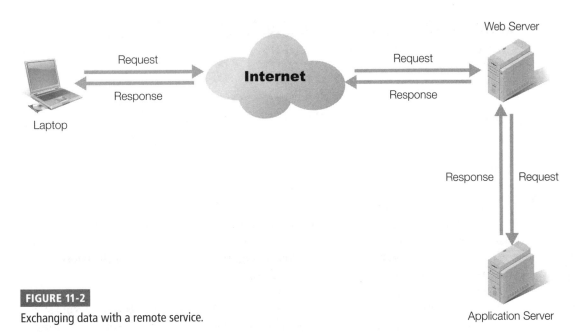

FIGURE 11-2

Exchanging data with a remote service.

Implementing Proper Security Controls for the LAN-to-WAN Domain

The primary control type you'll use in the LAN-to-WAN Domain for any data passing through the domain is traffic filtering. You'll learn that there are different devices and types of filtering, but make sure you aggressively use filtering to stop any inappropriate traffic from flowing in, out, or through your LAN-to-WAN Domain. A collection of well-placed and well-configured firewall devices can dramatically increase your network's ability to withstand attacks.

Another important control anytime data flows in or out of the LAN-to-WAN Domain is encryption. There are many encryption choices, and the right control depends on how you'll use the data and which component applies the encryption method. Your application may encrypt your data in another domain. You'll learn about different approaches later in this chapter. Some solutions require multiple layers of controls. You select the best controls that support a few general principles:

- No data in the LAN-to-WAN Domain should ever be transmitted in the clear. In-the-clear data is data that is readable by anyone.
- When using encryption, select the algorithm based on needs; don't just select the largest key.
- Assume an attacker can intercept and examine any network messages.

Devices and Components Commonly Found in the LAN-to-WAN Domain

The LAN-to-WAN Domain represents a point of transition between more secure LANs and far less secure WANs. In this section, you'll learn about the devices and components you'll commonly find in the LAN-to-WAN Domain. Once you've learned about the devices and components, you'll learn about controls to ensure compliance in the LAN-to-WAN Domain.

Router

A router is a network device that connects two or more separate networks. In the context of the LAN-to-WAN Domain, a router makes the actual connection between the LAN and the WAN. A router can be a standalone network device or it can be software that runs on a computer. In either case, the hardware must contain at least two network interfaces, one for each network. A router works by inspecting the address portion of the packet and forwarding the packet to the correct network.

The process of examining each packet is time consuming and can slow your network down. Newer network devices and software often contain support for **Multi-Protocol Label Switching (MPLS)**. MPLS networks add a simple label to each network packet. The routing devices in the network forward packets based on the address in the label, as opposed to data in the header portion of the packet. MPLS can dramatically increase the speed and usefulness of your network in two important ways:

- MPLS takes less time to process each packet because the router only has to look at the packet's label.
- MPLS devices create virtual links between nodes that can transport higher-level encrypted packets.

 NOTE

The term "firewall" refers to the fireproof wall that separates sections of buildings. The purpose of a firewall in construction is to limit the damage a fire can cause. If one section of a building catches fire, the fire will not spread beyond the firewalls and will be contained. Firewalls don't minimize damage to the section of the building that is burning—they just keep the fire from spreading and causing more damage.

Firewall

A firewall is a network security measure designed to filter out undesirable network traffic. Like a router, a firewall can be a network device or software running on a computer. Firewalls provide an important security capability. You can define rules for each firewall that tell the firewall how to filter network traffic. You can restrict which packets you allow to flow through the LAN-to-WAN Domain. Firewalls give you the ability to aggressively control what types of information can travel between your LANs and WANs.

The simplest type of firewall is a packet-filtering firewall. The firewall examines each packet and decides on an action to take after comparing the packet's attributes with the firewall rules. Rules commonly instruct firewalls to deny or forward packets based on destination protocol, Internet Protocol (IP)

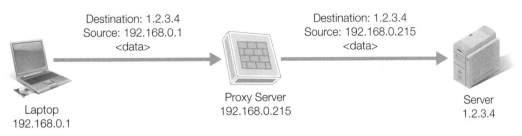

Destination: 1.2.3.4
Source: 192.168.0.1
<data>

Destination: 1.2.3.4
Source: 192.168.0.215
<data>

Laptop
192.168.0.1

Proxy Server
192.168.0.215

Server
1.2.3.4

FIGURE 11-3

Network request using a proxy server.

address, and port. You can create rules based on other criteria as well. However, protocol, IP address, and port filtering gives you the ability to restrict most unwanted traffic from passing through the firewall.

Proxy Server

A **proxy server** is a type of firewall that makes requests for remote services on behalf of local clients. The proxy server receives a request from a client and evaluates the request based on its defined rules. If it determines that the request is authorized, the proxy server forwards the packets to the remote server, using its own IP address as the source address. In this way, a proxy server hides the true source's identity. The remote server only sees the IP address of the proxy server. Figure 11-3 shows how a proxy server forwards requests to remote resources.

The proxy server keeps a record of sent messages in an internal table. Unless an error occurs, the remote server should send a response to the initial request. When the proxy server receives the response, it looks up the true address of the client that sent the original request and forwards the response to the client.

Proxy servers have several uses. Because they process all network traffic between clients and remote servers, they work well as content filters. Proxy servers can filter unwanted or inappropriate content using many different types of rules. Web content filters examine Web-based traffic and can block Web content that does not adhere to your organization's Internet or Web acceptable use policy (AUP).

Demilitarized Zone (DMZ)

The LAN-to-WAN Domain marks an important transition for data. Data flowing from a WAN to your LAN moves from an insecure domain to a secure domain. It is generally a poor idea to allow any users to access resources inside your secure LANs. It is important to positively identify users to properly control access to your organization's resources. On the other hand, many organizations do want to provide internal information to anonymous users. For example, most online retailers want anonymous users from the Internet to visit their sites and browse through their products. How do you allow anonymous users to access your data without compromising it?

FIGURE 11-4

Simple DMZ with
one firewall.

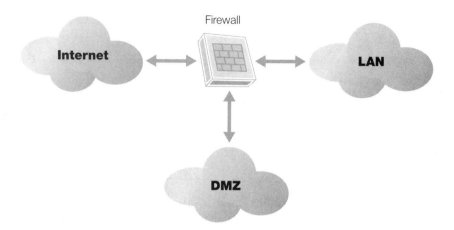

The answer lies in creating an area of your IT infrastructure that allows access for anonymous users but aggressively controls information exchanges with internal resources. This special "zone" is connected to both the Internet and your internal secure network. The term for this zone is a **demilitarized zone (DMZ)**. A DMZ is a separate network, or portion of a network, that is connected to a WAN and at least one LAN, with at least one firewall between the DMZ and your LAN. Figure 11-4 shows a simple DMZ with one firewall.

A very common use of DMZs is for Web servers. Users from the Internet can access your Web server and see pages generated from the Web server. The Web server can make limited connections to your application and database servers in your LAN. The firewall blocks connections from Internet users to your LAN but allows the Web server to connect.

FIGURE 11-5

DMZ with two
firewalls.

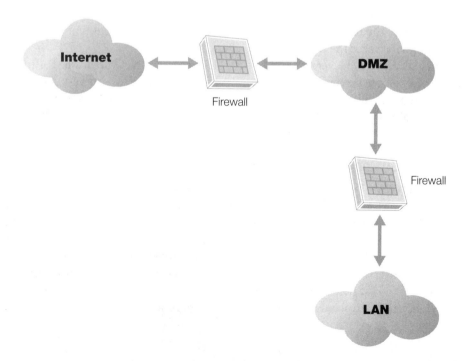

One danger is that an attacker could compromise your Web server and use it to either connect to your LAN resources or perhaps use the Web server to launch attacks on other computers. To help protect your DMZ servers from launching attacks, you can add a second firewall between the DMZ and the WAN. This firewall would filter outbound traffic and would stop attacks originating from within your DMZ. Figure 11-5 shows a DMZ with two firewalls.

Honeypots

A **honeypot** is a server deliberately set up to trap attackers. You set up a honeypot with software and data that is configured to be both insecure and interesting to attackers. The idea of a honeypot is to divert the attention of attackers away from real items of interest. You can configure the software running on the honeypot to alert you when an attacker accesses resources. This gives you the ability to track the attacker's actions and learn more about the techniques being used against legitimate targets. Perhaps you might even track down the attacker's location.

There are at least two dangers with honeypots. A honeypot that is connected to your LAN could provide an attacker with an entry point to your LAN. If the attacker successfully compromises the host, the attacker could access protected LAN resources. Second, an attacker with any skill will likely eventually realize the honeypot for what it is. An attacker might assume an organization that goes to the trouble of setting up a honeypot might have a truly valuable resource they are trying to hide. In this case, the honeypot actually draws more devoted attention to your valuable resources instead of diverting attention away.

> **⚠ WARNING**
>
> A honeypot is often viewed by attackers as a challenge. Many attackers feel they are being taunted. Given a bruised ego, attackers might execute follow-on attacks to "get even" for being tricked.

Honeypots require near-constant attention, both automated and by personnel. When a honeypot goes ignored for too long, the dangers just mentioned become real risks with dire consequences.

Internet Service Provider (ISP) Connection and Backup Connection

The purpose of the LAN-to-WAN Domain in most organizations is to provide a method to connect your LANs to the Internet. Connecting to the Internet is easier than ever before. All you have to do is establish an account with an **Internet service provider (ISP)**. The ISP provides at least one method to connect your device to their network. Once you have connected to their network, your ISP routes traffic from your environment to the Internet.

You can establish service using different connection methods. The most popular methods are:

- Dial-up
- Digital subscriber line (DSL)
- Cable modem
- Wireless
- Dedicated high-speed connection, such as a T1 or T3

FIGURE 11-6

ISP connection single
point of failure.

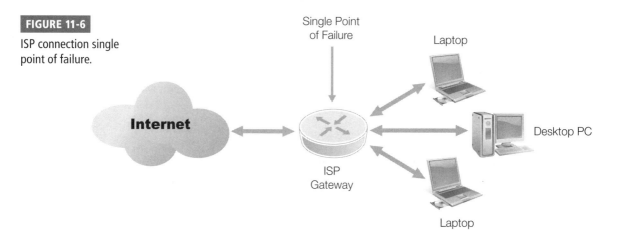

Regardless of which connection medium you choose, your network relies on the connection to your ISP to establish Internet connections. If the connection to your ISP goes down for any reason, you'll lose your connection to the Internet. A single ISP connection means a single point of failure. A **single point of failure** means many components depend on a single component. If the single component fails, all other dependent components essentially fail as well. Figure 11-6 shows a single ISP connection that represents a single point of failure.

Make sure you develop an alternate Internet connection plan to avoid a single point of failure. You'll learn how to accomplish this in the "Dual-Homed ISP Connections" section later in the chapter.

Intrusion Detection System (IDS)/Intrusion Prevention System (IPS)

Firewalls are extremely effective at filtering out known unwanted traffic. However, attackers are getting more and more sophisticated all the time. A firewall is only as good as its rules. Because most firewall rules are based on static attributes, they aren't effective at protecting a network from all types of attacks.

For example, assume an attacker compromises one of your trusted servers and installs a distributed denial of service (DDoS) agent. On command, the agent starts sending large volumes of messages to different hosts. Your firewall sees all of the messages but forwards them all because they originated from a trusted server. The result is a successful DDoS attack.

Another type of network measure that can help in this situation is an **intrusion detection system (IDS)**. An IDS is either a network hardware device or software that monitors real-time network activity. It compares the observed behavior with performance thresholds and trends to identify any unusual activity. If it does identify unusual activity, it sends a notification to someone who can explore the situation and react appropriately. Some systems provide the ability to automatically take action. An **intrusion prevention system (IPS)** extends the IDS capability by doing something to stop the attack. In the preceding example, the IPS could just modify firewall rules to deny any traffic originating from the compromised server. This simple action would stop the attack.

Data Leakage Security Appliance

As the volume of information flowing around networks increases, so does the concern that sensitive data will leak out of the protected environment into the public domain. Compliance requirements often place restrictions on data and how you must handle it. For example, Payment Card Industry Data Security Standard (PCI DSS) requires your organization to protect credit card numbers both at rest and in transit. You can ensure your applications and databases protect credit card numbers, but what about other forms of data transfer? How do you protect credit card numbers in e-mail messages?

Data leakage security appliances are network devices or software running on computers that scan network traffic for data-matching rules. The rules differ for each organization but would likely include patterns for matching credit card numbers, Social Security numbers, and other sensitive information for organizations enforcing PCI DSS compliance. Other requirements for protecting sensitive data would result in additional rules. The data leakage security appliance helps detect and prohibit data that would otherwise leak to the public due to oversight or error. It is one more layer in a multilayered approach to security.

Web Content Filtering Device

As you learned earlier, a Web content filter is a specific type of proxy server. In addition to forwarding Web requests to a remote Web server, the filter scans all traffic and applies content rules. These content rules conform to the organization's Internet AUP. Web content filters are common in many organizations that provide Internet access. The goal is to provide Internet access that is necessary or desired for appropriate users while denying inappropriate Internet use.

A Web content filter evaluates content based on several different criteria, including:

- **Blacklist**—Providing a list of uniform resource locators (URLs) or Domain Name System (DNS) entries from which all transfers are blocked
- **URL filter**—Scanning and evaluating URLs for inappropriate content using a dictionary of inappropriate search items
- **Content keyword filtering**—Evaluating text in content for inappropriate content using a dictionary of inappropriate search terms
- **Content analysis**—Evaluating text and nontext content for inappropriate content

Traffic Monitoring Device

Network traffic monitoring devices monitor traffic flowing across a network and compare performance with a baseline. Traffic monitors can help detect network issues by identifying performance problems and alerting administrators of the problem. Network problems can be caused by:

- Denial of service (DoS) or DDoS attacks
- Device or communications failure
- Bandwidth saturation

> **technical TIP**
>
> For more information on network traffic monitoring and analysis, you can refer to "LAN Traffic and Performance Monitoring and Analysis" in Chapter 10. You can also refer to *http://www .symantec.com/connect/articles/passive-network-traffic-analysis-understanding-network-through -passive-monitoring* for an interesting discussion on using passive monitoring techniques.

In any case, it is important to know when a problem develops. Traffic monitoring devices can often alert administrators to emerging problems that can be addressed before they become critical.

LAN-to-WAN Traffic and Performance Monitoring and Analysis

Monitoring the traffic that flows through the LAN-to-WAN Domain can be a demanding task, but it is one that is a vital part of ensuring your environment's security. A secure network is one that provides smooth operation and only allows authorized traffic on the network. If any part of your network were to be down even for a small period of time, productivity within your organization would decline. In the case of critical business functions, network problems could cause service interruptions and could result in noncompliance. To be proactive, it is important to monitor how traffic moves throughout the network and to verify your network is meeting your organization's security goals.

Traffic monitoring and analysis is the process of capturing network traffic and examining it to determine how users and applications are using your network. The two main monitoring techniques are network device based and non-device based. Network devices, especially routers and gateways, often include monitoring functionality you can use to keep track of your network's health. Non-device techniques require that you add additional hardware or software to capture traffic and analyze it. Any computer in the LAN-to-WAN Domain can act as a traffic capture device.

Once you capture traffic, your analysis software can examine it in real time or save it to a file for later analysis. Monitoring and analyzing network traffic in the LAN-to-WAN Domain is very similar to monitoring traffic in the LAN Domain. The goal is to detect problems before they become critical. Your efforts should focus on identifying degrading performance that might affect data availability or traffic that might indicate attack activities.

LAN-to-WAN Configuration and Change Management

The LAN-to-WAN Domain exists to provide a structured transition between your LAN and a WAN, such as the Internet. Much of the functionality in the LAN-to-WAN Domain depends on the configuration of the devices in the domain. Each device or software component operates based on configuration settings and rules. Any change to settings or rules changes the way the domain components operate.

Once you configure the components in the LAN-to-WAN Domain to operate securely, it is important to prohibit unauthorized changes to the domain configuration.

Any configuration changes you make will change the way components operate. Changes can be beneficial or detrimental. You must enforce a change management process to ensure you only make authorized changes to any configuration and that you document all changes for later auditing.

The change management process is fairly simple and contains only a few steps. Each step is important and contributes to the overall security of your environment. Here are the basic configuration management steps required to make any changes to device configuration settings or rules:

1. The requestor submits a configuration setting or rule change request. It is important to document each change and the reason for the change. Auditing configuration changes and comparing the impact of similar changes requires as much historical information as possible.

2. The **configuration control board (CCB)** reviews each request and either approves or denies the request. The CCB can be a group of people or a single person with the responsibility to evaluate changes.

3. The implementers—generally security administrators—receive approved change requests for implementation and make the approved changes.

   a. Before making any changes, security administrators should validate the current configuration against the latest authorized baseline. This step identifies any unauthorized changes.

   b. Security administrators should validate any configuration changes in a test environment whenever possible.

   c. After applying authorized changes, security administrators should create a new authorized baseline.

4. The implementers should validate the changes made to ensure any changes satisfy the original request.

Coordinated Attacks

Many attacks against enterprise data really consist of multiple coordinated attacks. Assume an attacker wants to launch a DoS attack to disable your organization's Web servers and stop you from conducting business on the Internet. The attacker attempts a direct DoS attack that your IPS devices in the LAN-to-WAN Domain immediately identify and stop.

The attacker searches for other vulnerabilities and finds a way to use social engineering to install a Trojan horse on the IPS device. The Trojan horse provides a back door the attacker can use to log on to the IPS and change configuration settings. The attacker modifies the IPS rules to not block the attacking computers. The next attack succeeds in bringing down your Web servers. This attack is successful because of a lack of controls at several levels. The last level of control that is missing is positive configuration management for the IPS.

Although it might seem like an intrusive process, requiring all configuration changes to go through a change management procedure allows you to audit all authorized changes and only deploy approved changes. The overall configuration management process should also include periodic audits of each component's configuration against the latest baseline to identify unauthorized changes. In this way, you can ensure your LAN-to-WAN components maintain a secure configuration.

LAN-to-WAN Management, Tools, and Systems

Managing the LAN-to-WAN environment basically involves the same tasks as managing the LAN environment. The differences from LAN management tasks include the efforts to ensure the additional components in the LAN-to-WAN Domain are protecting the internal domains from the external domains. The LAN Domain, as the name implies, focuses on LAN-specific topics. The LAN-to-WAN Domain includes WAN access components and security needs.

Managing the LAN-to-WAN Domain means ensuring authorized data passes smoothly through the domain's components and on to their destination. This means ensuring you have defined just the right firewall rules. Use the principle of least privilege to write firewall rules. Your rules should only allow the traffic through the firewall that is necessary to accomplish authorized business functions. In today's distributed environments, that goal is difficult to achieve. Users and applications tend to establish and use multiple connections with remote services and resources. Your firewall rules should allow all of the different connections you'll need and can take some fine-tuning to get right.

FCAPS

Managing a network involves several related tasks and can become confusing without a plan. The **Telecommunication Standardization Sector (ITU-T)** and the International Organization for Standardization (ISO) developed **FCAPS**. FCAPS is a network management functional model. FCAPS is an acronym that represents the focal tasks necessary to effectively manage a network. FCAPS stands for:

- **Fault management**—Activities to detect, log, communicate, and potentially fix network problems to keep the network running effectively. Fault management directly addresses the availability property of security by minimizing downtime.

- **Configuration management**—Activities to monitor network component configuration settings to track and manage the state of your network

- **Accounting management**—Activities to measure how your users are using your network to support regulation compliance and billing

- **Performance management**—Activities to measure and report on network performance to support optimization

- **Security management**—Activities to control access to network resources and limit access exclusively to authorized users

TABLE 11-1 Network management tools.

FCAPS AREA	TOOL	SOURCE
Fault	Nagios (open source and commercial)	*http://www.nagios.org/*
Fault	OpenNMS (open source)	*http://www.opennms.org/*
Fault	NMIS (open source)	*http://www.sins.com.au/nmis/*
Configuration	RANCID (open source)	*http://www.shrubbery.net/rancid/*
Configuration	Canner (open source framework)	*http://bangj.com*
Accounting	Lightweight Directory Access Protocol (LDAP)	Supported by many software products and available for most operating systems
Accounting	Terminal Access Controller Access Control System (TACACS)	Supported in most current operating systems
Accounting	Remote Authentication Dial-in User Service (RADIUS)	Supported in most current operating systems
Performance	Cacti (open source)	*http://www.cacti.net/*
Performance	SmokePing (open source)	*http://oss.oetiker.ch/smokeping/*
Performance	PRTG (open source)	*http://www.paessler.com/prtg/*
Performance	MRTG (open source)	*http://oss.oetiker.ch/mrtg/*
Security	Windows Firewall	Microsoft Windows operating systems
Security	IPtables	Most Linux distributions
Security	Vendor-specific firewall device	Each vendor provides specific software for their own network devices

Network Management Tools

Many tools are available to help manage your network. Look for the tools that fit into your environment best and provide the functionality you need to best manage your environment. Table 11-1 shows a list of a few network management products.

Although these tools represent functionality that is useful in the LAN-to-WAN Domain, many of them are useful to manage networks in other domains as well. Select the tools that work best to help keep your networks secure and operating smoothly.

Access Rights and Access Controls in the LAN-to-WAN Domain

You learned about the importance of controlling access to the LAN Domain in Chapter 10. In the LAN Domain context, your organization can exert substantial control over which computers and users can establish connections. The situation is slightly different in the LAN-to-WAN Domain. Although it is still possible to require strict access controls, the design of the LAN-to-WAN Domain includes active connections to a WAN. That means the components in this domain are exposed to the WAN, which in many cases is the Internet.

Internet-facing components are network components in your organization's IT infrastructure that users can access via the Internet. These components experience a higher number of threats due to this increased visibility. To make matters worse, many enterprise applications that provide Internet connectivity encourage at least some anonymous connections. This exposure to anonymous users makes it more difficult and more important to secure the components in the LAN-to-WAN Domain.

The transition nature of the LAN-to-WAN Domain calls for collections of controls to meet security needs. You need the ability to evaluate several attributes of a connection request's source before granting access to your network. You should define different access profiles based on your policies to meet the needs of different types of network users. **Network Access Control (NAC)** is a solution that defines and implements a policy that describes the requirements to access your network. NAC defines the rules a connecting node must meet to establish a secure connection with your network. It also allows you to proactively interrogate nodes that request a connection to your network to ensure they don't pose a risk. You can use NAC to classify connecting nodes based on the level of compliance with your access rules. NAC allows you to evaluate node attributes that include:

- Anti-malware protection
- Firewall status and configuration
- Operating system version and patch level
- Node role and identity
- Custom attributes for enterprise configuration

Allow Anonymous Users?

Enterprise Web-based applications generally share a common problem: How do you attract new customers to your product line before you know who they are? Historically, merchants would use advertising techniques to send information out to prospective customers. Today's model encourages prospective customers to visit online resources. Most online merchants provide the ability for casual, anonymous users to browse their Web sites and learn more about their products. Your security controls in the LAN-to-WAN Domain must provide access for these anonymous users while still ensuring the security of your data. Solid access controls can help you meet that goal.

TABLE 11-2 NAC software products.

PRODUCT	WEB SITE
PacketFence (open source)	*http://www.packetfence.org/en/home.html*
Sophos NAC Advanced	*http://www.sophos.com/products/enterprise/nac/sophos-nac/*
Symantec Network Access Control	*http://www.symantec.com/business/network-access-control*
Cisco Network Admission Control	*https://www.cisco.com/en/US/netsol/ns466/networking_solutions_package.html*
StillSecure Safe Access	*http://www.stillsecure.com/safeaccess/*
McAfee Network Access Control	*http://www.mcafee.com/us/enterprise/products/network_security/network_access_control.html*

NAC solutions enable you to exert control over which nodes can connect to your networks and what rights you'll grant to them once they connect. NAC provides a formal method to establish relationships with several types of security controls and helps you minimize threats from malware, increase LAN-to-WAN availability, and provide proof of compliance through NAC-related auditing data. NAC is a developing approach to controlling network access that several vendor products support. Table 11-2 lists some vendors that provide NAC software.

You can choose from many products to implement NAC. NAC software alone won't secure your networks, but it does give you the ability to define and enforce policies that can get you closer to your security goals.

Maximizing A-I-C

As with all other domains in the IT infrastructure, your main goal in the LAN-to-WAN Domain is to deploy and maintain controls that support all of the A-I-C properties of security for your data. The LAN-to-WAN Domain contains several components that play critical roles in providing secure access to your organization's data; maintaining that security requires diligence and the right controls.

Minimizing Single Points of Failure

One of the main functions of the LAN-to-WAN Domain is to provide access, or connectivity, between the LAN and the WAN domains. The first property in the A-I-C triad is availability. Resources and data are only available if users can successfully establish connections between the two domains. If any device in the LAN-to-WAN Domain is required to make a connection, that device must be functional 100 percent of the time to fully support data availability. Any downtime will affect the security of your environment.

To minimize any downtime due to device failure in the LAN-to-WAN Domain, ensure every node has an alternate whenever possible. Any node that does not have an alternate becomes a single point of failure. If the node fails or becomes unavailable, it affects the entire domain. Evaluate each node to see if a redundant node would remove the single point of failure. Only allow unique devices if there are no other available alternatives and implement compensating controls to protect the availability property.

Dual-Homed ISP Connections

Many organizations employ a single connection to their ISP. If the connection device goes down, so does the Internet access for the entire organization. In the preceding section, you learned to avoid single points of failure. That goal applies to your ISP connection as well. The solution is to establish at least two ISP connections, as shown in Figure 11-7. A **dual-homed ISP connection** is a design in which a network maintains two connections to its ISP. If one gateway or connection fails, the other can still connect to the Internet.

In the simplest case, you use the primary connection for normal Internet access. You only use the secondary connection if the primary connection fails. You can implement this solution easily, but it does waste the available bandwidth on the secondary connection because it sits unused most of the time. Another option is to use both connections at all times. Your ISP connection devices can decide which connection to use based on many criteria. More sophisticated connection management software can use the best ISP connection based on available bandwidth. This provides load balancing as well as fault tolerance. Less-sophisticated connection selection methods may involve simple round robin or connection count algorithms. Regardless of the method you use, having a secondary ISP connection can protect you from WAN connection failures.

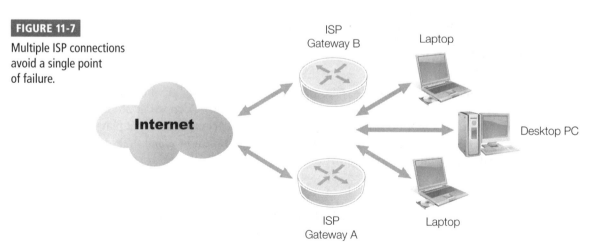

FIGURE 11-7

Multiple ISP connections avoid a single point of failure.

FYI

Methods of choosing which ISP connection to use can be very simple. The round robin method simply keeps a list of all available ISP connections. When you use one connection, the system remembers to use the next connection in the list the next time someone wants to connect. When you reach the end of the list, just start over. This method cycles through the list of ISP connections over and over.

The other simple method is to remember the number of times you have used each ISP connection. When a user wants to connect to an ISP, you select the connection with the lowest number of uses. This simple method helps you use all of your connections equally.

Once you decide to set up dual-homed ISP connections, you can choose from two different options:

- **Use two connections to the same ISP**—Two connections from the same ISP might save money but are still vulnerable to interruption if your ISP fails.

- **Use two connections from different ISPs**—Maintaining two connections from different ISPs will cost more, and require more maintenance due to working with different vendors, but will still protect your environment if one ISP goes down.

Examine using dual-homed ISP connections to maximize your data availability.

Redundant Routers and Firewalls

Another common bottleneck in any network is the router or firewall. In many networks, these devices require that all traffic pass through them. Although that practice does make maintenance and configuration easier, it introduces one or more single points of failure. If all traffic from the Internet passes through one router and that router crashes, how can your Internet users connect to you? The answer is: They can't.

The easiest way to see the most obvious single points of failures for network connections is to map your network. It is easy to see nodes on a network map where node failure means a fragmented network. Once you identify routers and firewalls that are single points of failure, you should introduce redundant nodes to your network. Every single point of failure should have at least one alternate device. Having redundant devices allows your network to continue in the case of a device failure. If there are two paths from point A to point E and one path fails, all traffic can use the other path. Implementing redundant devices addresses availability by protecting your network from device failure. However, you gain the additional benefit of spreading out traffic among the redundant devices and possibly increasing overall performance. In both cases, redundant network devices can protect the availability of your network.

Web Server Data and Hard Drive Backup and Recovery

You should have a recovery plan in place for every device and computer in your organization. Business continuity plans (BCPs) and disaster recovery plans (DRPs) enable you to recover from small to large disruptions. One crucial part of a BCP or a DRP involves recovering data and configuration settings from a secondary copy saved in case you lose your primary copy.

This secondary copy of data to be used in case of primary data loss is commonly called a "backup image" of data, or just a "backup." The value of a backup in the recovery process depends on how current it is. Because you'll lose any work that occurred after your last backup when you recover data, it makes sense to back up frequently.

One of the more common servers in the DMZ is the Web server. Web servers provide a generic front end to many enterprise applications and resources. Web servers provide the first visible point of contact for many remote clients and are necessary to bridge the outside Internet user community with the far more structured collection of application components in your organization's secure network. If your organization's Web server is down, your organization's Web presence is down, too. To maximize the availability of your organization's Web presence even in the face of disasters, it is important to ensure you have a current recovery plan for all the Web servers in the LAN-to-WAN Domain. A current recovery plan is one that you support with frequent backups—and one that you test on a regular basis. A solid schedule for backups and a plan to recover your Web servers in the case of an interruption that involves data loss will maximize your organization's Web presence uptime.

Use of Virtual Private Networks (VPNs) for Remote Access to Organizational Systems and Data

You have seen several topics that relate to data availability but nothing yet that relates to the other two properties, integrity and confidentiality. Information that travels to and from the Internet, or another WAN, can potentially be accessed by pretty much anyone. The best protection for information on a WAN is to use encryption. You can allow remote users to access resources on your LAN through the LAN-to-WAN Domain by setting up a **virtual private network (VPN)**.

A VPN is a persistent connection between two nodes. The nodes can be on the same network or on separate networks. Many VPNs also encrypt all of the traffic that flows along the connection. Because the traffic is encrypted, no unauthorized users can see the information. In this manner, encryption supports data confidentiality. Attackers can modify the data along its route, but without knowing what the data actually contains, the changes would not have a real purpose other than destroying data. When the altered data reaches the end of the VPN and gets decrypted, the VPN endpoint detects the change and takes action.

 NOTE

You'll learn more about VPNs in Chapter 13, but be aware that VPNs can provide secure access to remote users.

The endpoint can either request the data be resent or it can throw an error. Either way, you detect the unauthorized change and protect the data's integrity.

Penetration Testing and LAN-to-WAN Configuration Validation

Testing security controls and configuration settings is crucial to ensuring you have the right controls in place. One particular type of testing simulates actions an attacker would take to attack your network. This type of test is called a "penetration test" because the purpose of the test is to attempt to penetrate, or compromise, your security controls. In fact, conducting periodic penetration tests is a requirement for compliance with several standards. PCI DSS is one example that requires annual penetration tests to validate security controls.

An experienced penetration tester can simulate the actions an attacker would take and verify the strength of your security controls. Such tests validate the controls you have in place as well as indicate areas of weakness you should address. You should seek approval first, then design several types of penetration tests to ensure your security controls are doing the job.

Never conduct a penetration test unless you have written authorization from the network and system owners. Penetration tests will likely cause alarms and if you're not authorized to perform the tests, could result in liability issues and even criminal prosecution. Verbal approval is not enough—get it in writing. Before you start any penetration testing, get written approval for the specific scope of your tests. Your approval documents should include:

- Specific IP addresses or ranges of nodes you will test
- Specific IP addresses of nodes that will conduct the tests
- A list of nodes that should be excluded from the tests
- A list of the techniques used in the tests
- A schedule or time frame approved for the tests to occur
- Points of contact for the testing team and the approving organization(s)
- Procedures for handling collected test data

External to Internal

The more common type of penetration test is from the perspective of the external attacker. The penetration tester, also called the pen tester, launches a series of attacks from outside the target's network. In most cases, the pen tester conducts the tests from a computer connected to the Internet. The tester simulates the actions an attacker would take when developing an attack on your organization.

Although each penetration test is different, many tests follow similar paths. Here is a common flow a penetration tester follows to develop attacks:

1. **Reconnaissance**—Collect as much information about the target environment as possible. At this stage, the attacker is collecting both technical and nontechnical information. Both types of information can help the attacker determine how the organization operates, where it operates, and which characteristics the organization and its customers value. The purpose of an attack will drive the process. In an actual attack, if an attacker wants to extract or modify data, all efforts will be directed toward the data of interest. If the attacker wants to harm the organization, the target of the attacks will be what the organization values. An organization that markets safety to its clients would suffer from confidential data disclosure, whereas an organization that prides itself on high availability would suffer most from being shut down. Information the testers or attackers gather in the reconnaissance phase drive all subsequent activities.

2. **Footprinting**—After collecting general organizational information, the next step is to learn as much as possible about the target's technical architecture. At this point, testers use tools to query and identify as many identified nodes in the target network as possible. The process of **footprinting** means determining the operating system and version for each node. Operating system information helps identify a node's possible purpose and the next steps to learn more about the node.

3. **Scanning and enumeration**—The next step collects detailed information about each node. Testers can use automated tools to scan each node, identifying open and active ports. Testers can also query open ports to determine which services are running on a selected node. In this manner, testers can develop a detailed map of the target's technical environment and get a good picture of what hardware and software make up the target's infrastructure.

4. **Vulnerability identification**—Once the testers have all of the available information on operating systems and running software and services, the next step is to explore known vulnerabilities in the target's environment. For example, if scanning and enumeration reveals the target is running Microsoft Internet Information Services (IIS) Web server version 6.0, the testers would search for known vulnerabilities with that specific version.

5. **Attack planning**—A complete attack plan would include all identified vulnerabilities in the target environment sorted by exploit difficulty and impact. In most cases, testers will start with the easiest attacks that produce the largest impact. The attack plan is a sorted list of attacks the testers will carry out, along with the procedures to execute the attack and collect results information.

6. **Attack execution**—The execution phase follows the attack plan and launches each attack against the target environment. Testers grade the success of each attack and the effectiveness of security controls to mitigate the attack.

7. **Collect and present results**—The final step in a penetration test is to compare the attack plan with the attack results. Testers will collect all result information from each attack and present a report of overall test performance. The report should analyze the effectiveness of existing controls and make recommendations for any changes that would increase security.

Internal to External

Not all attacks occur from external sources. Many actual attacks originate from within an organization's own networks. These types of attacks can originate from compromised computers running malware or from attackers who have bypassed access controls and gained a foothold inside your network. In either case, attacks from within your organization can be more dangerous than attacks from the outside.

Internal traffic and activities are generally regarded as more trusted than external traffic. The general idea is that if a user has successfully satisfied stringent access controls, that user should be trusted. This general trust makes internal attacks dangerous if an attacker is able to circumvent access controls and operate from within your internal networks.

To measure your organization's ability to handle internal attacks, you should conduct internal penetration tests as well as external tests. There are two main types of attacks that may originate from within your organization:

- **Internal attacks on your organization**—An internal attack is one in which an attacker is able to compromise your access controls and either establish a presence inside your networks or place malware on an internal computer. In either case, the attacker has access to your resources at a higher level of trust than a general external user. Internal attacks generally target your organization.
- **Internal-to-external attacks on another organization**—An attacker might choose to use your infrastructure to launch an attack on another organization. There are two main reasons for using one organization to attack another organization. First, an attacker could use your organization to launch an attack in an attempt to hide his or her true origin. Second, the main goal of the attack could be to place the blame on your organization and cause you to incur embarrassment and possibly other consequences.

Regardless of the reasons, internal-to-external penetration testing exercises your security controls to ensure both types of attacks will not succeed. Your goal is to ensure internal attacks on your organization will not compromise your security and attacks on other organizations will not be allowed past your networks. Both external-to-internal and internal-to-external penetration testing ensure your environment is secure from attacks in both directions.

Intrusive Versus Nonintrusive Testing

Penetration tests are simulations of attacks. In most cases, attacks on information systems and infrastructures are intended to cause damage of some sort. So if you fully simulate attacks, there will likely be some impact that results. Any test that exploits an attack and results in damage is an intrusive attack. Tests that only validate the existence of a vulnerability are nonintrusive.

For example, assume your organization runs the Apache Web server. Penetration testers discover a vulnerability in the version of Apache running on your primary Web server. The vulnerability, if exploited, will cause the Web server to crash. Scanning and enumerating your Web server computers to collect data is generally a nonintrusive test, whereas exploiting the vulnerability and actually crashing the Web server is an intrusive test.

TIP

Although creating a test environment takes substantial effort, today's use of virtualization can make the process far easier. You can create a collection of virtual machines that replicate your real environment and provide a good test bed for penetration testing.

As you develop a penetration plan, assess the impact of each test and carefully consider whether you want to allow intrusive tests against your environment. If all your security controls are sufficient, even intrusive tests will fail to affect your environment. But any deficiency in your controls could allow an intrusive test to have a negative impact on your systems or networks. The best way to handle such intrusive tests in a safe manner is to perform them against a test environment that is an exact copy of your production environment.

Configuration Management Verification

You learned about the importance of managing network information earlier in this chapter. Recall the FCAPS approach to network management. The "C" in FCAPS stands for configuration. You also saw two tools in Table 11-1, RANCID and Canner, that help manage network configuration settings. It is important to aggressively control your network devices' configuration settings. RANCID and Canner, along with other available tools, can help you create baselines of configuration settings and compare changes over time. You should develop a schedule and process to frequently compare configuration baselines and verify all changes to your network's configuration.

A solid network configuration management process makes it easy to classify any configuration changes as authorized or unauthorized. You just compare baseline differences to your authorized changes list to see which changes occurred that were not authorized. Because every configuration change has some effect on what traffic flows through your LAN-to-WAN Domain, it is important to manage authorized changes and detect any unauthorized changes. Implementing the FCAPS approach will help formalize the process and make your networks more secure.

Adherence to Documented IT Security Policies, Standards, Procedures, and Guidelines

Compliance in the LAN-to-WAN Domain depends on implementing the best controls. As with other domains, explore alternate controls for each security goal. Many of the LAN-to-WAN security controls impact performance and the ability of your users to access your organization's resources. You must ensure the correct controls are in place to balance all three security properties.

As you analyze controls in the LAN-to-WAN Domain to meet compliance requirements, ensure each control satisfies your security policy. If a control does not support any part of your security policy, you should question its value to your organization. Although various legislation, regulations, and vendor standards have different requirements, Table 11-3 lists the types of controls for which you'll likely need to ensure compliance in your LAN-to-WAN Domain.

TABLE 11-3 Common compliance controls in the LAN-to-WAN Domain.

TYPE OF CONTROL	COMPONENT	DESCRIPTION
Preventive	DMZ	Use firewalls to separate resources in the LAN-to-WAN Domain from both the WAN and your LAN. A well-configured DMZ prevents unauthorized WAN users from accessing resources in your LAN.
	Firewalls	Implement firewalls between any LAN-to-WAN boundaries to filter out unauthorized traffic. A more aggressive approach is to implement firewalls between servers in the LAN-to-WAN Domain as well as on the domain boundaries.
	Network address translation (NAT)	Use NAT to hide internal IP addresses from the outside world.
	Intrusion prevention system	Use an IPS at least for each ISP connection to detect and prevent intrusions.
	User-based access controls for DMZ resources	Restrict access to DMZ resources to reduce what WAN users can access.
	Configuration change control	Limit changes to network device configuration settings and filtering rules. Require approval for all changes before deploying them.
	Encryption	Enforce encryption for all connections that span the LAN-to-WAN Domain, involve elevated authorization, or transport sensitive data of any kind.
Detective	Service exception auditing	Log failures for all service consumption requests. Failed service requests could be the signs of either an attack or reconnaissance for a future attack.
	Performance monitoring	Frequently sample network traffic flow metrics and be alert for any unusual activity.
	Packet analysis	Examine packets for known attack signatures and to ensure necessary data is encrypted.
	Configuration settings monitoring	Compare LAN-to-WAN device configuration settings to stored baselines to detect any unauthorized changes.
	Intrusion detection system	Use at least one IDS or IPS for each ISP connection to detect intrusions.
	Penetration testing	Conduct periodic penetration tests to identify security control weaknesses.

TABLE 11-3 *continued*		
TYPE OF CONTROL	**COMPONENT**	**DESCRIPTION**
Corrective	Operating system and application patching	Keep applications and operating systems patched to the latest available level.
	Attack intervention	Automatically modify filtering rules to deny traffic from sources generating known attack signature packets.
	BCP and DRP	Develop and maintain plans to survive and continue operations in the face of small or large disruptions.

Implementing multiple types of controls decreases the likelihood an attack will be successful and makes your LAN-to-WAN Domain more secure.

Best Practices for LAN-to-WAN Domain Compliance

The LAN-to-WAN Domain provides the outside world access to your data. In many ways, the domain filters authorized users from unauthorized ones. Because this domain connects your secure LAN with an untrusted WAN, you must ensure the controls protect your LAN resources. Protecting information in the LAN-to-WAN Domain focuses on maintaining the balance between easy access and solid security. Solid planning, along with aggressive management, can provide both.

The following best practices represent what many organizations have learned. Plan well and you can enjoy a functional LAN-to-WAN Domain that makes LAN information available for use to WAN users. Here are general best practices for securing your LAN-to-WAN Domain:

- Map your proposed LAN-to-WAN architecture before installing any hardware. Use one of the several available network-mapping software products to make the process easier.
  - Identify all of the components' data paths through the domain. Use the map to identify any single points of failure.
  - Update the network map any time you make physical changes to your network.
- Establish a DMZ with at least two firewalls. You should locate one firewall between your WAN connection and the DMZ perimeter and configure it to filter incoming and outgoing traffic between the WAN and the DMZ. Locate the other firewall between your LAN and the DMZ. This internal firewall should filter all incoming and outgoing traffic between the LAN and the DMZ.

- Implement at least two redundant WAN connections. Use load-balancing techniques to utilize the bandwidth of both connections.

- Configure all DMZ servers and devices to resist attacks from WAN users.

- Develop a backup and recovery plan for each component in the LAN-to-WAN Domain. Include recovery plans for damaged or destroyed connection media.
  - Don't forget to include configuration settings for network devices in your backup and recovery plans.

- Implement frequent update procedures for all operating systems, applications, and network device software and firmware.

- Define routing and filtering rules to restrict traffic passing through the LAN-to-WAN Domain. Most traffic should either terminate or originate in the LAN-to-WAN Domain.

- Monitor LAN-to-WAN traffic for performance and packets for suspicious content.

- Carefully control any configuration setting changes or physical changes to domain nodes.
  - Update your network map after any changes.

- Use automated tools whenever possible to map, configure, monitor, and manage the LAN-to-WAN Domain.

- Deploy at least one IPS for each WAN connection to detect and respond to suspected intrusions.

- Conduct complete penetration tests at least annually to evaluate security control effectiveness.

As with all best practices, these are only a starting point. Implement the points that are appropriate for your environment. Doing so will get you started toward establishing and maintaining a secure LAN-to-WAN Domain.

CHAPTER SUMMARY

In this chapter, you learned about how the LAN-to-WAN Domain provides WAN users access to your organization's LAN resources. Although it is important to secure your organization's information from internal users, it is equally important to protect your resources from attacks from WAN users. You learned about the components commonly found in the LAN-to-WAN Domain and the importance of monitoring and configuring components properly. You learned about some of the most important security controls and how to maximize A-I-C in the LAN-to-WAN Domain.

Although you learned that much of an organization's high-value information resides in the LAN Domain, the LAN-to-WAN Domain exposes that information to many WAN users. Security controls in the LAN-to-WAN Domain are crucial to protect information from threats. Solid controls and management procedures can make your organization's information available to the largest number of potential users with the minimum amount of risk.

KEY CONCEPTS AND TERMS

Configuration control board
   (CCB)
Demilitarized zone (DMZ)
Distributed application
Dual-homed ISP connection
FCAPS
Footprinting
Honeypot

Internet service provider (ISP)
Internet-facing
Intrusion detection system (IDS)
Intrusion prevention system
   (IPS)
Multi-Protocol Label Switching
   (MPLS)
Network Access Control (NAC)

Proxy server
Service
Single point of failure
Telecommunication
   Standardization Sector
   (ITU-T)
Virtual private network
   (VPN)

CHAPTER 11 ASSESSMENT

1. A distributed application is one in which the components that make up an application reside on different computers.

A. True
B. False

2. Which of the following is commonly the primary security control for data entering the LAN-to-WAN Domain?

A. Filtering
B. NAT
C. Encryption
D. Address validation

3. A _____ makes requests for remote services on behalf of local clients.

4. A _____ is an isolated part of a network that is connected both to the Internet and your internal secure network and is a common home for Internet-facing Web servers.

5. Which type of network device is most commonly used to filter network traffic?

A. Router
B. Firewall
C. Switch
D. IDS

6. If you only have one connection to the Internet and that connection fails, your organization loses its Internet connection. This is an example of a _____.

7. Which of the following devices detect potential intrusions? (Select two.)

A. Firewall
B. IPS
C. IDS
D. Load balancer

8. What is the meaning of differences between the last security configuration baseline and the current security configuration settings?

A. Unauthorized changes have occurred.
B. Authorized changes have occurred.
C. Changes have occurred (either authorized or unauthorized).
D. Unapproved changes are awaiting deployment.

9. Which of the following is a solution that defines and implements a policy that describes the requirements to access your network?

A. NAC
B. NAT
C. NIC
D. NOP

10. Which of the following best describes a dual-homed ISP connection?

A. An ISP connection using two firewalls
B. Connecting two LANs to the Internet using a single ISP connection
C. A network that maintains two ISP connections
D. Using two routers to split a single ISP connection into two subnets

11. Many organizations use a _____ to allow remote users to connect to internal network resources.

12. You only need written authorization prior to conducting a penetration test that accesses resources outside your organization.

A. True
B. False

13. NAT is helpful to hide internal IP addresses from the outside world.

A. True
B. False

14. The _____ feature speeds up routing network packets by adding a label to each packet with routing information.

15. Which of the following best describes the term "honeypot"?

A. A server that is deliberately set up as insecure to attract attackers
B. A server that contains extremely sensitive data
C. A collection of computers that are vulnerable to attack and could allow your network to be compromised
D. Vulnerable servers in your network that would not be dangerous if compromised

Compliance Within the WAN Domain

T ODAY'S ORGANIZATIONS depend on a workforce that is mobile and widely dispersed. Work has to get done regardless of where the workers might be at any one moment. An IT infrastructure that supports this type of mobility and flexibility has to include the ability for workers to connect from almost anywhere. Organizations are deploying resources and applications that are easier than ever to access from remote locations. These organizations need a framework to describe how to provide access to the organization across town or across the world and do it securely.

In Chapter 11, you learned about the LAN-to-WAN Domain and how data travels between a local area network (LAN) and a wide area network (WAN). In this chapter, you'll learn about what happens to data in the WAN Domain and how you can ensure compliance as your data travels outside your environment.

Chapter 12 Topics

This chapter covers the following topics and concepts:

- How compliance law requirements and business drivers relate to one another
- Which devices and components are commonly found in the WAN Domain
- What WAN traffic and performance monitoring and analysis are
- What WAN configuration and change management are
- Which WAN management tools and systems are commonly used
- What access rights and access controls in the WAN Domain are
- How to maximize A-I-C
- What WAN service provider SAS compliance is
- How to ensure adherence to documented IT security policies, standards, procedures, and guidelines
- What best practices for WAN Domain compliance requirements are

Chapter 12 Goals

When you complete this chapter, you will be able to:

- Examine compliance law requirements and business drivers
- Compare how devices and components found in the WAN Domain contribute to compliance
- Describe methods of ensuring compliance in the WAN Domain
- Summarize best practices for WAN Domain compliance requirements

Compliance Law Requirements and Business Drivers

You learned in the introduction how more and more organizations rely on distributed architectures. Many organizations deploy their enterprise applications as distributed applications. Although the actual applications and resources belong in other domains, clients need the ability to access resources and run distributed programs. Providing the ability to connect diverse resources is the main purpose of the WAN Domain. Although making your resources and data available to more users is a good thing, you must pay close attention to security. Keeping your data secure as it leaves your network takes advance planning. Always consider how secure your data is in each of the domains of your IT infrastructure. Figure 12-1 shows the WAN Domain in the context of the seven domains in the IT infrastructure.

Remember that your responsibility to keep your data secure doesn't stop when that data leaves the controlled area of your networks. The WAN Domain represents an area that might be largely out of your control. Your responsibility to secure data means to protect it in such a way that it is secure even when traveling across an untrusted network. Ensuring data is safe even in the WAN Domain makes it possible for your organization to deploy distributed applications that can provide unprecedented functionality to remote users. Implementing the controls necessary to support your security policy in the WAN Domain makes your organization more secure and allows you to provide a higher level of visibility to your data.

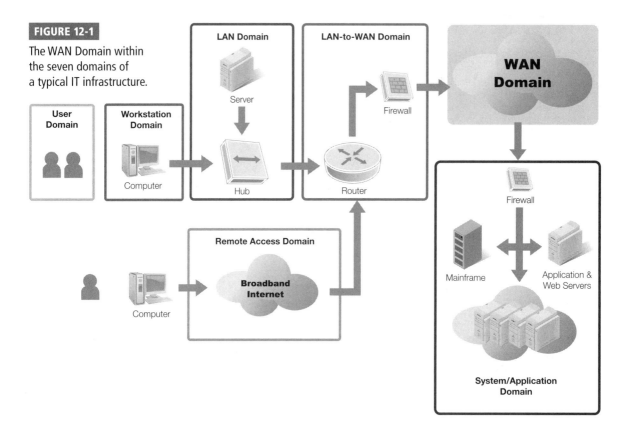

FIGURE 12-1

The WAN Domain within the seven domains of a typical IT infrastructure.

Protecting Data Privacy

WANs provide the valuable service of connecting your networks together without having to install or maintain the interconnection network media. In other words, you use someone else's network to connect your networks together. You can connect your headquarters to several branch offices using a WAN. You connect each of your networks to the WAN and all your nodes can communicate. The only problem is that you now depend on another organization to communicate. Each time you send a message from your headquarters to a branch office, that message travels across someone else's network. You no longer have control over who sees your network traffic or who can alter it. Figure 12-2 shows how data traveling from one of your nodes to another across a WAN is out of your control.

One of the most important concerns when sending data across public networks is confidentiality. Although not all data is confidential, any data you exchange with a remote resource using a WAN is potentially available for anyone else to see. Consider all WANs to be hostile and insecure. Your organization likely controls the access to your LANs and has some measure of assurance of how private the LANs are.

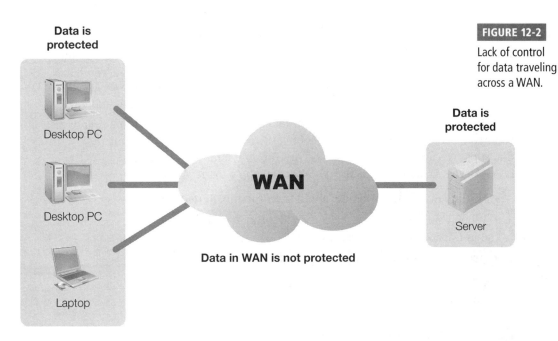

FIGURE 12-2

Lack of control
for data traveling
across a WAN.

WANs are different. You don't have control over who accesses them or who can access
data traveling across a WAN. You must deploy sufficient controls to protect the privacy
of any data in the WAN Domain.

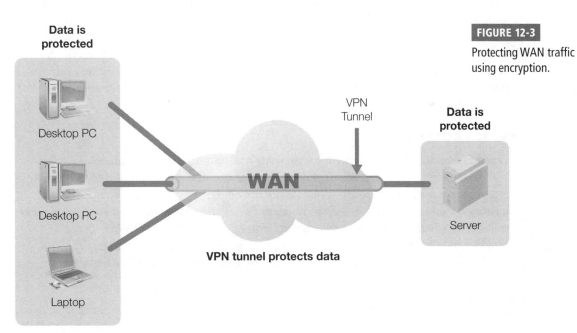

FIGURE 12-3

Protecting WAN traffic
using encryption.

Implementing Proper Security Controls for the WAN Domain

The primary control type you'll use in the WAN Domain for any data is encryption. You have many encryption choices, and the right control depends on how you'll use the data and which component applies the encryption methods. Your application may encrypt your data or another component may encrypt the connection in another domain. You'll learn about different approaches to encryption later in this chapter. Some solutions require multiple layers of controls. You select the best controls that support a few general principles. These are the same principles you saw in the LAN-to-WAN Domain in Chapter 11, and they apply to the WAN Domain as well:

- No data in the WAN Domain should ever be transmitted in the clear.
- When using encryption, select the algorithm based on needs; don't just select the largest key.
- Assume an attacker can intercept and examine any network messages.

Figure 12-3 shows a simple diagram of how a VPN tunnel protects encrypted data as it moves across the Internet.

Devices and Components Commonly Found in the WAN Domain

The WAN Domain exists to transport network messages from one node to another. In most cases, the WAN is a network that is owned and managed by some other entity. Your ability to affect the WAN's security is limited or nonexistent. You must ensure that you transmit data across the WAN in a secure fashion using secure protocols and techniques. In this section, you'll learn about the devices and components you'll commonly find in the WAN Domain that support communication, both secure and insecure. Once you've learned about the devices and components, you'll learn about controls to ensure compliance in the WAN Domain.

WAN Service Provider

Few organizations have the resources to create and manage their own global WANs. The most common approach to deploying applications and functionality across a WAN is to lease network access from a **WAN service provider**. A WAN service provider is in the business of providing WAN bandwidth to subscribing organizations. The WAN transports traffic among subscriber nodes and subscribers pay for the service. The WAN service provider handles all routing, connection media, and hardware issues within the WAN. All the subscribers do is connect to the WAN and use it to send and receive traffic.

TABLE 12-1 WAN options.		
WAN TYPE	**DESCRIPTION**	**COMMENTS**
Dedicated line/ leased line	A point-to-point connection between two physical devices	Most secure, but also one of the most expensive; exclusive access to all bandwidth
Circuit switching	A dedicated circuit established between two points for the duration of a conversation	Lower cost, but requires time to establish circuit and circuit switching is slower than the next two options
Packet switching	Messages travel in variable-length packets along point-to-point or point-to multipoint links through WAN switches	Can be substantially faster than circuit switching but media is shared and can suffer congestion
Cell relay	Similar to packet switching but with fixed-length cells	Best for transporting voice and data but overhead can reduce speed
VPN over Internet	A VPN established between two nodes	Very inexpensive but performance and stability depend on your Internet connection

12

Compliance Within the WAN Domain

The three main concerns when selecting a WAN provider are cost, speed, and stability. There are other factors to consider but these three are often the most important characteristics when selecting a WAN. Each type of WAN has its own characteristics and works best in different types of environments.

Today's WAN service providers offer several types of WANs for different budgets and performance requirements. Each type of WAN has its strengths and weaknesses. You need to evaluate each option based on your specific needs to find the best fit for your organization. Table 12-1 lists the main types of WANs available from WAN service providers.

One of the three primary considerations of how well a particular WAN fits your business requirements is stability. An inexpensive WAN that is very fast still isn't worth very much if it doesn't stay operational as often as you require. Examine the WAN service provider's **service level agreement (SLA)**. The SLA states a level of guaranteed uptime. In most cases, WAN service providers will provide several levels of service for different subscription amounts.

Pay attention to the cost for WAN service as well. Some WAN providers offer service for a fixed monthly fee, whereas other products carry a usage charge. Estimate your monthly usage and calculate your costs for each type of service.

> **NOTE**
>
> Although cost is only one factor when considering a WAN provider, it can be a determining factor.

Dedicated Lines/Circuits

Your particular WAN needs will direct you toward the best WAN choice. If your primary need for a WAN is to connect a small number of LANs to one another, dedicated lines might be the best choice. A **dedicated line**, also called a dedicated circuit, is a permanent circuit between two endpoints. A single dedicated line works very well when connecting two LANs, campus area networks (CANs), or even metropolitan area networks (MANs). You can connect more than two networks using multiple dedicated lines.

Dedicated lines are always available, fast, and secure. Because no one else shares your dedicated line with you, your organization has exclusive access to the traffic flowing along the line. Of course, the WAN service provider has access to your traffic as well, but no one else should be able to see your traffic. If your budget and connectivity needs support dedicated lines, they can return some of the best performance of all WAN options.

MPLS/VPN WAN or Metro Ethernet

If your requirements include connecting more than three or four locations, as in connecting multiple branch offices to the headquarters, dedicated lines will likely be too expensive. Another option in such a case is Multi-Protocol Label Switching (MPLS) networks supporting a virtual private network (VPN). MPLS works with many WAN technologies and provides very good overall performance using packet-switching and circuit-switching networks. Although MPLS networks are not optimal for high-bandwidth, large-volume network transfers, they work very well in most environments where you need to maintain connections between several other networks.

For high-bandwidth needs within smaller geographic regions, a hybrid of a WAN and a LAN has emerged that fills a particular niche of small WANs. Historically, MANs have been implemented as small-scale WANs using WAN protocols. Technical advances in networking hardware and connection media have enabled the deployment of the well-known Ethernet technology in larger networks. Ethernet, a longtime favorite LAN protocol, is inexpensive to deploy and provides substantial bandwidth for the low cost. This hybrid network that uses Ethernet in a MAN is called an **Ethernet MAN** or **Metro Ethernet**.

WAN Layer 2/Layer 3 Switches

Most discussions of network protocols include a discussion of the **Open Systems Interconnection (OSI) reference model**. The OSI reference model is a generic description for how computers use multiple layers of protocol rules to communicate across a network.

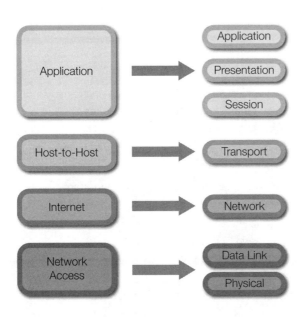

FIGURE 12-4

TCP/IP and OSI reference models.

12

Compliance Within the WAN Domain

The OSI reference model defines seven different layers of communication rules. You'll also likely encounter another popular reference model, the **TCP/IP reference model**, when discussing network protocols. The Transmission Control Protocol/Internet Protocol (TCP/IP) reference model defines four different layers of communication rules. Both models are useful to describe how protocols work and how to implement them in network communications. Figure 12-4 shows the TCP/IP reference model and the OSI reference model.

You might hear hardware devices or software protocols referred to as "layer 2 devices" or "layer 5 protocols." These references generally refer to the OSI reference model layer to describe where the referenced hardware or software operates. In the context of WANs, most WAN protocols operate at OSI layer 2. MPLS actually operates between layers 2 and 3 and is sometimes called a layer 2.5 protocol. Most traditional network switches operate at OSI layer 2, but newer devices use advanced techniques to provide more sophisticated switching capabilities at OSI layer 3.

Recall that traditional layer 2 switches use the Media Access Control (MAC) addresses in each packet to forward the packet to its proper destination. One type of layer 3 switch extends the concept of a traditional layer 2 switch by implementing fast Internet Protocol (IP) routing using hardware. Most routing using IP addresses requires software to examine each packet. Software is always slower than hardware and, thus, routing has historically been slower than switching. A layer 3 switch can greatly speed up routing by using advanced hardware to make the routing decision.

Layered Protocols in Real Life

The idea of layered protocols sounds complex, but it really reflects what happens in normal human-to-human communication. You use layers and translations in subtle ways every time you talk with a different person. Here's an example that demonstrates the obvious need for multiple layers.

Consider how ambassadors communicate in the United Nations. Assume a U.S. ambassador wants to send a written note to the ambassadors of China, Russia, and Italy. In this example, protocol requires all written messages be presented in French. Here is how the message travels through the United Nations:

1. The U.S. ambassador writes a message in English, then hands the message to a translator.
   The ambassador layer passes the message to the translator layer.

2. The translator translates the message into French, then hands it to an aide to take to the mailroom.
   The translator layer passes the message to the aide layer.

3. The aide makes three copies of the message, addresses each copy, and places the messages in the U.S. outbox in the mailroom.
   The aide layer duplicates and passes the messages to the mailroom clerk layer.

4. The mailroom clerk picks up the messages from the U.S. outbox and places them in the appropriate inboxes for China, Russia, and Italy.
   The mailroom clerk handles the physical transfer.

5. An aide for each country—China, Russia, and Italy—picks up the message and delivers it to the translator.
   The aide layer collects a message from the mailroom and passes it to the translator layer.

6. The translator translates the message from French into the country's natural language and gives it to the appropriate ambassador.
   The translator layer translates the message and passes it to the ambassador layer.

7. The ambassador for each country reads the message and takes appropriate action.

Figure 12-5 illustrates the process.

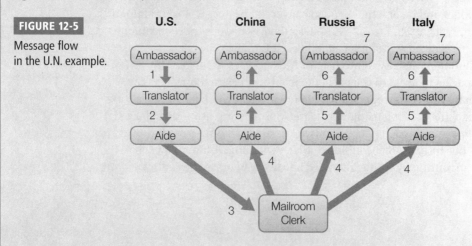

FIGURE 12-5

Message flow in the U.N. example.

WAN Backup and Redundant Links

All components in all domains can fail. It is important that each component have a backup or alternate component to replace it if it fails. Your WAN connection is no exception. If your organization relies on a single WAN connection and that connection fails, your entire access to your WAN fails.

You have already learned about the importance of redundant and alternate WAN connections in the chapter on the LAN-to-WAN Domain. The issue bears repeating here. Remember that your organization's ability to use a WAN to communicate with central resources and functions depends on the availability of your WAN to support the connection. A failure anywhere in the WAN violates your organization's data availability. Make sure you take these steps to protect the availability and security of your data across the WAN Domain:

- Ensure the SLA for each WAN service provider meets or exceeds the required uptime goals for each WAN.

- Establish backup or redundant WAN connections, either multiple connections to the same WAN or multiple connections using different WANs.

- Install backup or redundant connection devices in the WAN Domain to ensure connection hardware failure does not result in a failure to connect to your WAN.

WAN Traffic and Performance Monitoring and Analysis

Monitoring the traffic and performance of your WAN Domain can directly translate into concrete results. WAN usage might cost money, but it always costs in time. Any time you can reduce WAN usage, you are saving time and perhaps money as well. Recall that a secure network is one that provides smooth operation and only allows authorized traffic on the network. Access to your WAN is one of the necessary pieces in a distributed environment. If the WAN is down or unreachable, your distributed applications can't function. As you learned in Chapters 10 and 11, which covered the LAN and LAN-to-WAN Domains, network problems could cause service interruptions and could result in noncompliance. You need to be aware how all parts of your network are working to ensure you are compliant.

Traffic monitoring and analysis for a WAN are nearly identical to the process you learned about in Chapter 11. The WAN Domain differs from other domains in that you probably don't own or control the hardware or the software in the WAN. Your organization pays a subscription fee to connect to another organization's WAN. You generally pay the WAN service provider either by bandwidth usage or a flat fee for a specified bandwidth limit. Because you likely pay for WAN access, managing WAN traffic proactively can reduce your need for additional bandwidth and reduce your WAN costs.

You can implement WAN traffic monitoring and analysis software and devices in two ways. You can install software or devices on the perimeter of the WAN where you connect to it or rely on your WAN service provider to supply traffic flow data. You gain far more control monitoring the WAN yourself but you only have limited capability to affect the WAN's performance. One technique is to send a message to another node on the WAN and have that node echo a response. The first node can analyze the route and duration the message took for the round-trip. Comparing sample traffic with baseline data will reveal if the current performance is normal.

Several vendors provide tools to help monitor WAN traffic and optimize your WAN's throughput. Real-time WAN optimization software can analyze current WAN performance and then modify how new traffic is sent across the WAN. **WAN optimizers** can exclude unnecessary traffic, use compression to maximize bandwidth, cache data, and prioritize traffic to make the best use of your WAN. The result can be a noticeable increase in network speed. In this case, you haven't made the network any faster but you have used the available bandwidth more efficiently and increased your data throughput. Table 12-2 lists some WAN optimization products.

You can choose from many products to help optimize your WAN usage. Explore the solutions presented here, as well as other solutions, and select a product that best meets your security goals.

TABLE 12-2 WAN optimization tools.

PRODUCT	WEB SITE
Riverbed Cascade	*http://www.riverbed.com/products/cascade/*
ManageEngine OpManager	*http://www.manageengine.com/products/opmanager/ router-monitoring.html*
BlueCoat WAN Optimization product line	*http://www.bluecoat.com/solutions/businessneeds/wanoptimization*
Cisco WAN Optimization	*http://www.cisco.com/en/US/products/ps9146/products_ios _technology_home.html*
F5 WAN optimization solutions	*http://www.f5.com/solutions/acceleration/wan-optimization/*
Juniper Networks Application Acceleration Platforms	*http://www.juniper.net/us/en/products-services/ application-acceleration/wx-series/*
Expand Networks ExpandView	*http://www.expand.com/Products/expandview.aspx?enterprise*

WAN Configuration and Change Management

You learned about the importance of managing network configuration settings in the previous chapters on the LAN and LAN-to-WAN Domains. You don't have nearly the control over the WAN network components because most of the actual devices belong to your WAN service provider. However, you still need to proactively manage the components you do control. You can manage the settings of at least these WAN Domain components:

- **WAN access device**—The device or computer you use to physically connect to your WAN.

- **WAN account**—Your WAN service provider will provide access for you to configure specific settings to your WAN account. It is important that you create a backup of these settings. Even if your WAN service provider only allows you to manage your account using a Web page, saving screen shots of each configuration page is better than having no record of your settings.

- **WAN optimization device**—Any hardware or software that optimizes WAN traffic belongs to the WAN Domain and is a prime candidate for configuration management.

The strategies and techniques for managing configuration settings and controlling configuration changes should match your activities in the LAN and LAN-to-WAN Domains. Refer back to Chapters 10 and 11 for more information on proactively managing configuration setting changes. Just as with other domains, managing the configuration settings of your WAN Domain components is an important part of keeping your overall environment compliant and secure.

WAN Management, Tools, and Systems

Because the WAN service provider bears the responsibility of maintaining the actual WAN, there isn't much left to do to manage components in your WAN Domain. It is important to ensure all of the components in the WAN Domain are doing their jobs, but there isn't much you can do to manage the actual WAN. You learned about WAN optimization tools earlier in this chapter. Managing components in the WAN Domain primarily means managing how well your organization uses the WAN resources. There are three main categories of WAN management tasks, including:

- Providing the best WAN option for specific traffic
- Caring for WAN Domain components
- Optimizing WAN usage

In this respect, the WAN optimization tools from Table 12-2 are also WAN management tools. Your organization likely has different needs for WANs. As a result, you will likely use different WAN solutions. You may make the decision of which WAN to use in other domains but the actual access point exists in the WAN Domain. It is important to ensure each WAN access is configured and optimized to provide the best level of service for your needs.

Mixed WANs

Your organization doesn't have to choose only a single WAN solution. Organizations commonly use multiple WAN solutions to best meet their needs. For example, you might select dedicated lines to connect your headquarters building to your R&D facility, a packet-switching network to connect branch offices that only need data services, and a circuit-switching network for branches that need voice and data services. You could also use a metro Ethernet network for the branch office that is located in the same city as your headquarters building. Such a solution with multiple WANs can give you the best performance for your distributed enterprise needs.

Access Rights and Access Controls in the WAN Domain

Because there are limited components in the WAN Domain, there are also limited opportunities to enforce access control for the domain. There are essentially two places to control access to the WAN. First, you can deploy controls to limit access to the WAN access device. Device and user authentication and authorization controls should limit which users can access the WAN access point. The second opportunity to control WAN access is in the access device itself. The WAN access point also has the ability to enforce access controls. In this way, the WAN access device controls which users can get through the device and onto the WAN.

WAN access devices and WAN optimization devices both contain the ability to selectively grant access to the WAN. Although the WAN access device generally operates like a firewall or gateway, WAN optimization devices can make more sophisticated decisions about WAN access. Granting access may include decisions regarding time- or bandwidth-sensitive rights. Some users might only be granted WAN access during slow periods, while other users might get access on demand. You have the ability to grant or deny WAN access based on your security and functional needs.

Implementing more complex controls means you should spend more time testing the controls under different circumstances. If you implement load-based controls using WAN optimization, ensure you test the controls under different network loads, either real or simulated. Use auditing to create logging entries for repeated access denials to ensure your controls aren't degrading the ability of your users to do their jobs. As always, avoid auditing too many events. Only audit the ones you'll need to analyze your WAN's ongoing performance.

Maximizing A-I-C

You have seen in previous chapters that your main goal in all domains is to deploy and maintain controls that support all of the A-I-C properties of security for your data. The WAN Domain contains several components that play critical roles in providing secure access to your organization's data; maintaining that security requires diligence and the right controls.

WAN Service Availability SLAs

Each WAN service contract includes specific promises of stated levels of service called service level agreements, or SLAs. SLAs state what your WAN service provider promises to deliver in terms of various types of service. The first of two main SLAs addresses the availability property of data security. You should subscribe to a WAN service that guarantees the level of availability your organization requires to conduct business.

Availability SLA terms depend on the type of service you purchase. Most WAN service providers offer customers a choice of service guarantees for different costs to meet different customers' needs. Table 12-3 shows a sample list of availability service choices. Note that the differences in levels of service differ based on the reliability or recovery options selected.

The level of availability you choose will dictate the cost and hardware requirements for your WAN service. Examine the impact of expected or scheduled annual downtime and select the level of service that fits your organization.

WAN Recovery and Restoration SLAs

Most WAN service provider SLAs also include provisions for recovering from major interruptions due to hardware or carrier failure. Each SLA should contain a commitment for the maximum amount of time it should take to restore your organization's WAN service after a failure. The **Time To Recover (TTR)**, or Time To Repair, commitment states the acceptable amount of time that is allowed to repair or replace failed components. For global networks, WAN service providers often employ the services of local technicians to decrease response time. The WAN service provider would have their own SLAs with their subcontractors.

As with the availability SLA, you should select a recovery SLA that meets your organizational goals for data availability. Review your own plans to ensure that when your WAN service provider restores their service, you are ready to connect and use the WAN to continue your business operations.

TABLE 12-3 Availability service choices.

SERVICE	AVAILABILITY	COMMENT
Dual routers/dual circuits	100%	Redundant hardware and connections provide uninterrupted service.
Single router with backup	99.95%	Backup hardware can replace primary router with very little downtime; estimated annual downtime is 4.4 hours.
Single router	99.5%	A single router is a single point of failure— and you must replace failed hardware; estimated annual downtime is 43.8 hours.

TABLE 12-4 Common VPN protocols.	
PROTOCOL	**DESCRIPTION**
Layer 2 Tunneling Protocol (L2TP)	Common tunneling protocol that defines a connection between two endpoints. You need another protocol, such as Internet Protocol Security (IPSec), to provide encryption services.
Point-to-Point Tunneling Protocol (PPTP)	A layer 2 protocol that defines a tunnel between two endpoints. PPTP is older and generally less secure than L2TP.
Secure Sockets Layer/ Transport Layer Security (SSL/TLS)	Common protocol used to transport encrypted Hypertext Transfer Protocol (HTTP) traffic. Can also be used to create an encrypted tunnel.
Datagram Transport Layer Security (DTLS)	New protocol used by Cisco hardware to create a generic VPN that works well in most network architectures.
Secure Socket Tunneling Protocol (SSTP)	New protocol from Microsoft for Windows Server 2008 and Windows Vista Service Pack 2. SSTP works at the transport layer to provide a VPN that works with most firewalls.

WAN Traffic Encryption/VPNs

SLAs define levels of service that protect the availability property of data. Additional concerns when sending data across any WAN include integrity and confidentiality. The main type of control you can use to ensure the integrity and confidentiality of your data is encryption. One of the more common types of encryption in use in the WAN Domain is encrypted traffic over a VPN.

A VPN is a persistent connection between two endpoints commonly created over a WAN. Although not limited to WANs, VPNs make it easy to establish what appears to be a dedicated connection over a shared-access WAN. VPNs work well in creating persistent connections, also called tunnels, over the Internet or other types of WANs. Many VPNs also encrypt the traffic in the tunnel, making it an attractive option for WAN traffic that may contain sensitive data. Encrypted VPNs are also called **secure VPNs**. Even though others might be able to see the traffic as it travels through the WAN, no one can read it or even change it undetected because the data is encrypted.

NOTE

You'll learn more about VPNs in Chapter 13, which addresses the Remote Access Domain.

Today's networks often support multiple VPN protocols. Consult your WAN service provider for information on which VPN protocols your WAN supports. Use VPNs anytime you need to ensure integrity and confidentiality for sending sensitive data over a WAN. Table 12-4 lists some of the more common VPN protocols in use today.

WAN Service Provider SAS Compliance

Statement on Auditing Standards (SAS) 70, Service Organizations is an internationally recognized auditing standard developed by the **American Institute of Certified Public Accountants (AICPA)**.

A SAS 70 statement of compliance signifies that a service organization has had its control objectives and control activities examined by an independent auditing firm. Because so much emphasis is placed on security and compliance with multiple sources of requirements, service providers must demonstrate that they have adequate controls in place to securely handle their customers' data. In addition, the requirements of Section 404 of the Sarbanes-Oxley Act of 2002 make SAS 70 audit reports even more important to the process of reporting on the effectiveness of internal control over financial reporting.

According to the SAS 70 Web site, "SAS No. 70 is the authoritative guidance that allows service organizations to disclose their control activities and processes to their customers and their customers' auditors in a uniform reporting format. The issuance of a service auditor's report prepared in accordance with SAS No. 70 signifies that a service organization has had its control objectives and control activities examined by an independent accounting and auditing firm. The service auditor's report, which includes the service auditor's opinion, is issued to the service organization at the conclusion of a SAS 70 examination." [1]

SAS 70 defines two different types of service auditor reports, Type I and Type II. A Type I report describes the audited organization's security controls as of a specific point in time. A Type II report includes a description of the audited organization's security controls and a detailed examination of the performance of the controls over at least a six-month time period. Table 12-5 compares the contents of a SAS 70 Type I and Type II report.

A SAS 70 compliance audit demonstrates that a WAN service provider stands behind its security controls and has confidence in its ability to protect customer data. You should insist on doing business only with WAN service providers who can show evidence of a SAS 70 audit.

TABLE 12-5 Comparing a SAS 70 Type I and Type II audit report.

REPORT SECTION	TYPE I REPORT	TYPE II REPORT
Auditor's opinion of control description completeness and effectiveness	Required	Required
Description of controls	Required	Required
Time period (minimum six months) test results and statement of control effectiveness	Optional	Required
Supplemental/supporting information	Optional	Optional

TABLE 12-6 Common compliance controls in the WAN Domain.

TYPE OF CONTROL	COMPONENT	DESCRIPTION
Preventive	Enforce privacy through encryption	Deny any unencrypted traffic to travel to the WAN.
	Optimize WAN throughput	Use a WAN optimizer to identify and deny unnecessary WAN traffic.
	Assurance of WAN service provider security	Insist that all WAN service providers provide evidence of SAS 70 (or equivalent) compliance.
	Assurance of WAN availability	Establish WAN service that provides SLAs that meet or exceed your organization's uptime and recovery requirements.
	User-based access controls for WAN resources	Restrict access to WAN to reduce traffic and resource exposure.
	Configuration change control	Limit changes to all network device configuration settings and filtering rules. Require approval for all changes before deploying them.
Detective	Performance monitoring	Frequently sample WAN traffic flow metrics and alert for any unusual activity.
	Traffic analysis	Examine traffic for known attack signatures and to ensure data is encrypted.
	Configuration settings monitoring	Compare WAN device configuration settings with stored baselines to detect any unauthorized changes.
	Penetration testing	Conduct periodic penetration tests to identify security control weaknesses.
Corrective	WAN component patching	Keep WAN devices and applications patched to the latest available level.
	Attack intervention	Automatically modify filtering rules to deny traffic from sources generating known attack signature packets.
	Business continuity plan (BCP) and disaster recovery plan (DRP)	Develop and maintain plans to survive and continue operations in the face of small or large disruptions. Coordinate your BCP and DRP with your WAN service provider's SLAs.

Adherence to Documented IT Security Policies, Standards, Procedures, and Guidelines

Compliance in the WAN Domain depends on implementing the best controls you can, and ensuring your WAN service provider's controls are compliant as well. As with other domains, explore alternate controls for each security goal. You must ensure the correct controls are in place to balance each of the three A-I-C security properties.

As you analyze controls in the WAN Domain to meet compliance requirements, ensure each control satisfies your security policy. If a control does not support any part of your security policy, you should question its value to your organization. Although different legislation, regulations, and vendor standards have different requirements, Table 12-6 lists the types of controls for which you'll likely need to ensure compliance in your WAN Domain.

Implementing multiple types of controls decreases the likelihood an attack will be successful and makes your WAN Domain more secure.

Best Practices for WAN Domain Compliance Requirements

The WAN Domain allows multiple locations to establish network connections without having to manage the physical networks yourself. Because this domain connects your environment to an untrusted WAN, you must ensure the controls protect your internal resources. Solid planning, along with aggressive management, can provide both easy access across an untrusted WAN and the ability to maintain your data's security.

The following best practices represent what many organizations have learned. Plan well and you can enjoy a functional WAN Domain that makes internal information and resources available for use to WAN users. Here are general best practices for securing your WAN Domain:

- Map your proposed WAN architecture, including redundant and backup hardware and connections, before establishing WAN service. Use one of the several available network-mapping software products to make the process easier.
  - Update the network map anytime you make physical changes to your network.
- Establish multiple WAN connections to avoid any single points of failure. Use fault-tolerant hardware that can maintain WAN connectivity if the primary connection or devices fail.
- Use load-balancing techniques on the multiple WAN connections to utilize the bandwidth of both connections.
- Develop a backup and recovery plan for each component in the WAN Domain. Include recovery plans for damaged or destroyed connection media.
  - Don't forget to include configuration settings for network devices in your backup and recovery plans.

- Implement frequent update procedures for all operating systems, applications, and network device software and firmware in the WAN Domain.
- Monitor WAN traffic for performance and traffic for suspicious content.
- Carefully control any configuration setting changes or physical changes to domain nodes.
  - Update your network map after any changes.
- Use automated tools whenever possible to map, configure, monitor, and manage the WAN Domain.
- Use WAN optimization devices or software to maximize WAN utilization.

These best practices give you a brief overview of the issues you'll need to consider when implementing WAN access. Consider each of the best practices and add your own that will make your organization safer when transporting data across a WAN.

CHAPTER SUMMARY

The WAN Domain allows your users to connect to your resources and applications through a WAN from anywhere the WAN reaches. Opening your environment up to a WAN also opens new possibilities for attacks from WAN users. Connecting to a WAN offers many advantages and pitfalls. Learn about the components in the WAN Domain and how to secure them. Through solid planning, you can empower your environment with the flexibility and functionality of WAN access while minimizing the security issues.

KEY CONCEPTS AND TERMS

American Institute of Certified
   Public Accountants (AICPA)
Dedicated line
Ethernet MAN
Metro Ethernet

Open Systems Interconnection
   (OSI) reference model
Secure VPNs
Service level agreement (SLA)
TCP/IP reference model

Time To Recover (TTR)
WAN optimizers
WAN service provider

CHAPTER 12 ASSESSMENT

1. The WAN Domain commonly contains a DMZ.

A. True
B. False

2. One of the most important concerns when sending data across a WAN is confidentiality.

A. True
B. False

3. Which of the following is the primary type of control employed in the WAN Domain?

A. Firewalls
B. Encryption
C. Hashing
D. Compression

4. Who writes SLAs?

A. Subscribing organization
B. Telecom company
C. WAN service provider
D. SAS 70

5. Which type of WAN generally has the highest speed and is most secure?

A. Dedicated line
B. Circuit switching
C. Packet switching
D. MPLS network

6. The _____ contains the guaranteed availability for your WAN connection.

7. Which WAN technology is a cost-effective solution for connecting multiple locations?

A. MPLS
B. ISDN
C. MAN
D. L2TP

8. Most WAN protocols operate at which level in the OSI reference model?

A. 7
B. 3
C. 2
D. 1

9. A _____ can exclude unnecessary traffic from the WAN.

10. WAN subscription cost tends to decrease as availability increases.

A. True
B. False

11. By definition, VPN traffic is encrypted.

A. True
B. False

12. Which of the following best describes SAS 70?

A. Security specification
B. Auditing standard
C. Encryption standard
D. WAN specification

13. Both types of SAS 70 audit reports include a description of security controls.

A. True
B. False

14. A _____ makes it easy to establish what *appears* to be a dedicated connection over a WAN.

15. Which of the following describes a common LAN protocol deployed to a network the size of a city?

A. IPSec MAN
B. Urban Ethernet
C. TCP MAN
D. Metro Ethernet

ENDNOTE

1. "About SAS 70" (SAS70.com, 2009). *http://www.sas70.com* (accessed 4/30/2010).

12

Compliance Within
the WAN Domain

Compliance Within the Remote Access Domain

O RGANIZATIONS ARE BECOMING more diverse and dispersed. Many organizations that used to conduct business from a single, central location or a small number of locations are now finding themselves spread out across many areas. Employees work from home and while on the road. Customers and partners need access to central information to maintain their business relationships. Many organizations are finding that supporting remote access to their data is a primary requirement for doing business in today's global economic environment. Both applications and users are placing increasing demands to access data from remote locations, often using untrusted wide area networks (WANs). Extending trust to remote users requires more planning and effort but provides the basis for keeping data secure regardless of how far it travels.

Securing data as it travels from your protected internal network across an untrusted WAN to remote users depends on the ability to trust in the identity those users provide. Not only do you establish trust when you establish a connection, but also you establish trust throughout the conversation. You need to trust the user or entity on the other end of a connection during each data exchange. The purpose of the Remote Access Domain is to provide mechanisms to establish and maintain trust between remote users and components within other domains in your organization. In this chapter, you'll learn about the Remote Access Domain, the components commonly found in the domain, and techniques to keep the domain secure and compliant.

Chapter 13 Topics

This chapter covers the following topics and concepts:

- How compliance law requirements and business drivers relate to one another
- Which devices and components are commonly found in the Remote Access Domain
- What remote access and virtual private network (VPN) tunnel monitoring are
- What remote access traffic and performance monitoring and analysis are
- What remote access configuration and change management are
- Which remote access management tools and systems are commonly used
- What access rights and access controls in the Remote Access Domain are
- What Remote Access Domain configuration validation is
- How to ensure adherence to documented IT security policies, standards, procedures, and guidelines
- What best practices for Remote Access Domain compliance requirements are

Chapter 13 Goals

When you complete this chapter, you will be able to:

- Examine compliance law requirements and business drivers
- Compare how devices and components found in the Remote Access Domain contribute to compliance
- Describe methods of ensuring compliance in the Remote Access Domain
- Summarize best practices for Remote Access Domain compliance

Compliance Law Requirements and Business Drivers

Empowering users from many locations to use resources that might not be located near them makes economic sense. In most cases, shared resources are less costly than duplicated resources. Of course, sharing resources only makes sense if you can do it securely in a way that supports your business functions. Providing effective and secure access for remote users and resources is the primary focus of the Remote Access Domain.

This domain contains the components that can bring your distributed environment together and make its resources available and useful to remote users. When your organization provides this level of service, you are enabling remote users to operate more effectively and efficiently without having to physically be at your main location.

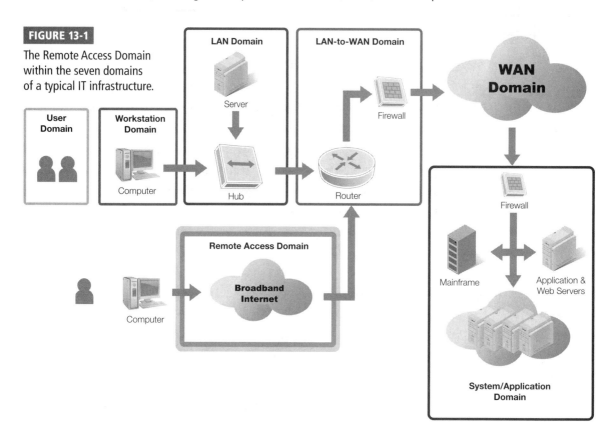

FIGURE 13-1

The Remote Access Domain within the seven domains of a typical IT infrastructure.

This capability is a benefit to users who are geographically separated from your physical resources either permanently or temporarily. Your users can do their jobs from more locations if they can access your resources remotely. The Remote Access Domain provides the access path for your remote users. Figure 13-1 shows the Remote Access Domain in the context of the seven domains in the IT infrastructure.

Take necessary steps to secure your data in all seven domains of the IT infrastructure. Distributing your data far from its secure storage locations exposes it to more threats of attack. You'll likely need to show compliance with one or more requirements that directly address sensitive data sent to remote users. For example, the Health Insurance Portability and Accountability Act (HIPAA) requires controls to protect the privacy of medical data. The Payment Card Industry (PCI) requires credit card privacy controls. Many states require privacy controls on any personal identifiable data. These are only a few of the requirements you'll need to satisfy when supporting remote users. Your security policy should include all of the necessary elements to meet compliance requirements and support efficient and cost-effective operation. Making sure you have the proper controls in place to secure the Remote Access Domain is one important part of an overall plan for data security.

Protecting Data Privacy

The primary security concern for remote access is data privacy. Although availability is important, confidentiality and integrity get far more attention in compliance requirements. The most important consideration when allowing remote users to access data is ensuring private data remains private. Ensuring data privacy essentially means only allowing authorized users to view or modify it. Because remote users commonly use public WANs to access data and applications, keeping sensitive data away from unauthorized users is difficult, if not impossible.

Your organization does not control access to your data in the WAN. The WAN service provider is responsible for controlling access to the traffic it transports. Although you should establish a level of trust with your WAN service provider, you can't enjoy the same level of privacy assurance as you do for data inside your own networks. However, you still must protect the privacy of your data even in the WAN. The specific controls you use are not important. The important goal is to ensure the privacy of your data does not suffer when it is transmitted to remote users.

Implementing Proper Security Controls for the Remote Access Domain

The most common control for protecting data privacy in untrusted environments is encryption. Recall that encryption is the process of scrambling data in such a way that it is unreadable by unauthorized users but can be unscrambled by authorized users to be readable again. Encrypted data ensures only users who possess the decryption key can properly decrypt a message. When you only provide decryption keys to authorized users, you protect data from being accessed by unauthorized users.

You must encrypt sensitive data before sending it to a remote user or location to ensure compliance with all appropriate requirements. Technically, you can send data that is not considered sensitive in the clear. However, classifying data at run time is time consuming and increases the potential to miss sensitive data and accidentally send it in the clear, or unencrypted. It is generally easier and more consistent to encrypt all data transferred in a session. Although you can use a variety of methods to decide what data to encrypt, there are three main strategies for encrypting data to send to remote users:

- **Application data encryption**—The application determines what data should be encrypted and encrypts it. The client application on the remote side decrypts the data and presents it to the user. This method of encryption requires substantial effort and overhead but can avoid encrypting data that does not need it.

- **Application connection encryption**—The application requires clients use secure connections when exchanging data that might be sensitive. An example is the payment screen of an e-commerce application. Although your application may allow customers to shop using unencrypted connections, using **Hypertext Transfer Protocol (HTTP)**, payment process requires a secure connection, using **Hypertext Transfer Protocol Secure (HTTPS)**. The application validates the connection type, not the actual data.

This strategy requires less application interaction than application data encryption and still offers assurance of data privacy. One drawback is the reliance on the connection encryption strength to ensure data privacy. If the connection is not configured well, your data could be at risk.

- **System connection encryption**—The third strategy does not require any application intervention or changes at all. The connection with the remote user handles the encryption. The most common way to implement system connection encryption is by setting up a secure virtual private network (VPN). A secure VPN encrypts all traffic on the connection. The system encrypts the data before placing it on the VPN at the endpoint and it is decrypted after it is removed from the remote endpoint. VPNs are useful because they allow any type of application to transfer data across an untrusted network without sacrificing data privacy.

Your budget and the operating systems you support will have an impact on which encryption strategy you select. Each strategy has many choices, each with benefits and challenges. Choose the best option to fit your needs. One of the most popular options to ensure data privacy for remote users is the VPN. Examine the VPN choices available for your environment and select one that meets your security needs.

Although the most common security control in the Remote Access Domain is encryption, don't forget the controls on remote users and the computers they use to access your network from a remote location. Remote users must adhere to your remote access acceptable use policy (AUP). Encryption can help protect your sensitive data, but a user who isn't careful or a poorly secured laptop can leave the data vulnerable once it gets onto the remote computer. You'll learn more about the vulnerabilities associated with each Remote Access Domain component in the next section. Make sure you protect all components with the best controls.

Devices and Components Commonly Found in the Remote Access Domain

The Remote Access Domain provides access to remote users and remote resources. It exists, in part, to provide a secure way to exchange data with remote components without sacrificing data privacy. This domain consists of several components that work together with your WAN to ensure your data is private and your environment is compliant. Figure 13-2 shows the devices and components commonly found in the Remote Access Domain.

Remote User

The first component of the Remote Access Domain is the remote user. A remote user is a person who connects to, and accesses, resources or applications from a remote location using a WAN to connect. The first remote users used dial-up connections to access computers and networks remotely. Personnel who traveled often needed to access data from the organization's central database when they were away from the office.

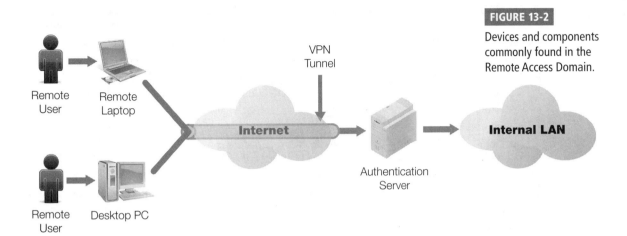

FIGURE 13-2

Devices and components commonly found in the Remote Access Domain.

This example is a classic case for remote access. The classic solution to this need was to provide a modem, or bank of modems, attached to the internal network. Users could dial in and access resources just like local users. The growth of high-speed networks and the Internet have changed the connection methods but not the basic requirements and problems.

Remote users pose several problems for data privacy. Those problems that are most common with remote users are:

- Remote users connect to an organization's resources using untrusted networks. Whether you use the Internet or some other WAN, your network traffic flows across someone else's networks and may be intercepted along the way. If there is a packet sniffer on the WAN, you won't know others are examining your traffic.

- Remote users often use public computers or terminals. Many travelers use business center computers in hotels to access the Internet and other resources. Users leave traces of their activities on computers used to access networks. It is possible that users leave traces of sensitive data after accessing it from a remote location.

- Remote users can be sloppy. You must have a strong remote access AUP in place that sets standards for how remote users handle data. Remote access introduces more risk because the data is transferred away from the protection of your organization's internal controls. Ensure you deploy controls that protect your data all the way to a remote user's computer—and once it is there.

Remote user access should require a higher standard of care than local user access. Local users enjoy the additional protection of the local environment and its security controls to protect data. Remote users do not have the additional layers of protection. You must ensure your users agree to comply with your remote access AUP and you have sufficient controls in place to protect the security of your data even in remote locations.

FYI

Be careful when allowing devices to act as remote access devices. PDAs and smartphones can cause problems. Many of these devices are not as secure as they might seem. Although most of today's smart devices that can support VPNs do so well, local data protection support is often lacking. Smaller and more compact devices are ultraportable and easy to misplace. Unfortunately, few of these devices have truly secure encryption for data at rest. These facts should encourage you to restrict the devices you allow to retrieve sensitive data or require additional controls. It is just too easy to download and store sensitive information on a device that can fall into the wrong person's hands.

Remote Workstation or Laptop

Remote users are really just normal users who access resources and applications from a remote location. They use workstations or laptops to establish the connection to the desired resources. In short, the remote user logs on to a computer. The computer accesses a WAN and uses it to establish a connection with other resources. The computer, laptop, or other device becomes the remote device. Remote devices aren't special devices—they just have the ability to connect to a WAN and establish a connection to some other resource. In fact, more and more personal digital assistants (PDAs) and smartphones contain the capability to act as remote devices.

Remote devices need two main capabilities to handle remote connections in a secure manner:

- Remote devices must be able to handle encryption. The most common type of encryption used in remote access is the secure VPN. As long as your device supports the VPN you've chosen for remote access and can establish a secure connection, the device passes the first test.

- Remote devices must be able to protect stored data. Even when using a VPN, the data gets decrypted when it arrives at the remote device. If your remote device can't ensure data privacy through its own controls, it should not be allowed to retrieve or process your confidential data.

As computers and other devices mature, it is common to see VPN support and local data privacy protection as standard features for computers. You can use operating system encryption or third-party utilities to encrypt data. Either way, most of today's computers with recent operating systems already contain the ability to act as secure remote access devices.

Remote Access Controls and Tools

Enabling remote access depends on both the remote devices and the remote servers cooperating. Because remote access depends on one endpoint at the remote location and another endpoint in your local environment, the Remote Access Domain actually spans several domains. By definition, the Remote Access Domain components use the WAN Domain to communicate. The Remote Access Domain server components also generally reside in the LAN-to-WAN Domain environment, even though they still belong to the Remote Access Domain.

When a remote user wants to access the organization's internal network, the remote device requests a connection from the remote access server. The remote access server queries the remote device for identification and authentication credentials. If the identity authenticates, the remote access server grants a connection and rights based on stored authorization information. Figure 13-3 shows the remote connection process.

The basic steps don't really differ much from a local logon process. The main difference is that the three basic steps are handled by the remote access server. Once a remote user successfully connects, the user can access resources like any other user. The three basic steps required to establish a remote connection are:

- **Identification**—The remote user provides a user ID or user name.
- **Authentication**—The remote access server prompts the remote user for authentication credentials. These credentials can be a password, a PIN, a smart card, or data from a biometric reading. The remote access server looks up the stored authentication information for the supplied user. If the authentication credentials provided by the user match the stored credentials, the user is authenticated.
- **Authorization**—Depending on the type of remote access server, the authorization information may be stored with the authentication information or may be stored in a separate location. In either case, the remote access server looks up the authorization information for the authenticated user and assigns rights and privileges based on the remote user's security settings.

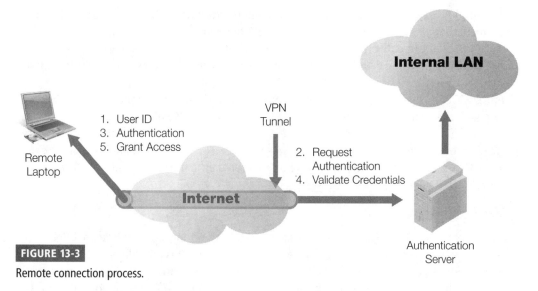

FIGURE 13-3

Remote connection process.

Authentication Servers

The process in the previous section describes how the authentication process works for remote users. There are many ways to authenticate remote users, but three main approaches are used most often. The first two, RADIUS and TACACS+, rely on centralized authentication databases and servers to handle all remote users. Either of these approaches works well when there are a large number of remote users or you need to manage remote users in a central location. You'll learn about the third method in the next section.

RADIUS

Remote Authentication Dial In User Service (RADIUS) is a network protocol that supports remote connections by centralizing the management tasks for authentication, authorization, and accounting for computers to connect and access a network. RADIUS is a popular protocol that many network software and devices support and is often used by Internet service providers (ISPs) and large enterprises to manage access to their networks.

> **NOTE**
>
> The application layer is layer 7 in the Open Systems Interconnection (OSI) reference model, or layer 4 in the Transmission Control Protocol/ Internet Protocol (TCP/IP) reference model.

RADIUS is a client/server protocol that runs in the application layer and uses User Datagram Protocol (UDP) to transport authentication and control information. Servers with RADIUS support that control access for remote users and devices communicate with the RADIUS server to authenticate devices and users before granting access. In addition to just granting access and authorizing actions, RADIUS records usage of network services for accounting purposes.

TACACS+

Terminal Access Controller Access-Control System Plus (TACACS+) is another network protocol that was developed by Cisco. TACACS+ has roots back to an earlier protocol, TACACS, but is an entirely different protocol. TACACS+ provides access control remote networked computing devices using one or more centralized servers. TACACS+ is similar to RADIUS in that it provides authentication, authorization, and accounting services, but TACACS+ separates the authentication and authorization information. TACACS+ also uses the Transmission Control Protocol (TCP) for more reliability.

One difference between RADIUS and TACACS+ is of interest to a discussion of security. RADIUS only encrypts the password when sending an access request packet to the server. TACACS+ encrypts the entire packet. That makes it a little harder to sniff data from a TACACS+ packet.

VPNs and Encryption

VPNs are one of the most popular methods to establish remote connections. A VPN appears to your software as a regular network connection. It is actually a virtual connection, also called a tunnel, that uses a regular WAN connection of many hops but looks like a direct connection to your software. Most VPNs offer the option to encrypt traffic using different modes to meet different needs.

> **technical TIP**
>
> Most people associate VPNs with encrypted traffic. Although most VPN uses include encrypting all of the traffic transported through the VPN tunnel, encryption is an option and not a part of the VPN itself. The "private" part of VPN really refers to private addressing, not data privacy.

The concept of **tunneling** is central to most VPNs. Tunneling allows applications to use any protocol to communicate with servers and services without having to worry about addressing or privacy concerns. Applications can even use protocols that aren't compatible with your WAN. Here's how tunneling works:

1. Your application sends a message to a remote address using its application layer protocol.
2. The target address your application used directs the message to the tunnel interface. The tunnel interface places each of the packets from the application layer inside another packet using an **encapsulating protocol**. This encapsulating protocol handles tunnel addressing and encryption issues.
3. The tunnel packet interface then passes the packets to the layers that handle the WAN interface for physical transfer.
4. On the receiving end, the packets go from the WAN to the remote tunnel interface where the packets are decrypted and assembled back into the application layer packets and then passed up to the remote application layer.

This arrangement provides excellent flexibility and security. Depending on your operating system and VPN solution choices, you can choose from among several encapsulating protocols, including:

- **Generic Routing Encapsulation (GRE)**—A tunneling protocol developed by Cisco Systems as an encapsulating protocol that can transport a variety of other protocols inside IP tunnels
- **Internet Protocol Security (IPSec)**—A protocol suite designed to secure IP traffic using authentication and encryption for each packet
- **Layer 2 Forwarding (L2F)**—A tunneling protocol developed by Cisco Systems to establish VPNs over the Internet. L2F does not provide encryption—it relies on other protocols for encryption.
- **Point-to-Point Tunneling Protocol (PPTP)**—A protocol used to implement VPNs using a control channel over TCP and a GRE tunnel for data. PPTP does not provide encryption.
- **Layer 2 Tunneling Protocol (L2TP)**—A tunneling protocol used to implement a VPN. L2TP is a newer protocol that traces its ancestry to L2F and PPTP. Like its predecessors, L2TP does not provide encryption itself.

The VPN you select depends on several factors. Some VPN solutions are vendor specific and rely on one type of hardware. Other types of VPNs are operating system specific. For example, the new **Secure Sockets Tunneling Protocol (SSTP)** is only available for the Windows operating system. SSTP is Microsoft's attempt to provide a solution that works on any networking hardware. SSTP uses Secure Sockets Layer (SSL) to transport PPP or L2TP traffic. Using SSL removes many of the firewall and network address translation (NAT) issues some other protocols encounter. Once you have assessed your needs and environmental restrictions, select the VPN solution that best fills your needs for functionality, security, and maintainability.

Internet Service Provider (ISP) WAN Connection

One of the more common ways to establish remote connections is using the Internet. Because it is easy to establish Internet connections and the access points are numerous, it makes sense to at least consider it for your remote connections needs. Historically, there have been several issues that must be resolved to use the Internet as a remote access WAN:

- Both sides of the connection must use the same WAN. When using the Internet as the WAN, all each side must do is establish an Internet connection. The LAN-to-WAN Domain already ensures your internal networks are connected to your WAN. All that is left is for the remote node to connect.

- Because the Internet is a public use network, encryption is an absolute necessity. VPNs work well to transport data securely over the Internet.

- Reliable access must be available for remote nodes. Internet access is becoming easier to find than ever before. Many Wi-Fi hotspots exist to allow computers and devices to connect to the Internet.

- Remote connections must be fast enough to be usable. This requirement is one that will likely cause the most potential issues. Internet service is easy to find and it is easy to use VPNs. Sometimes, especially in more remote areas, it is difficult to find high-speed Internet access. In such cases, it is important to provide access through low-bandwidth methods to ensure data availability.

Although the Internet might not be the fastest WAN, it is fast becoming the most cost-effective medium and the easiest use for remote connections.

Broadband Internet Service Provider WAN Connection

The last point in the previous section regarding Internet access was speed. Historically, most users connected to the Internet by dialing into an ISP modem. Modems are rated at speeds as high as 56 kilobits per second (kbps), although real transmissions rarely sustain the maximum data rate. Even at the highest rate, interacting with remote resources can be slow. As the volume of data that needs to be exchanged increases, dial-up connections become more and more frustrating for remote users.

The alternatives to dial-up include broadband techniques that substantially increase the network connection speed. **Broadband** refers to the technique of only using a portion of the full bandwidth of a channel. Dial-up connections use **baseband** techniques that require the entire channel's bandwidth. Broadband Internet access is defined as any customer connection that provides service at 256 kbps or higher. Many ISPs now provide asymmetric digital subscriber line (ADSL), cable, wireless, cellular, and satellite connections that classify as high-speed, or broadband, Internet service. The proliferation of broadband connections makes using the Internet for remote connections an even more attractive option.

Remote Access and VPN Tunnel Monitoring

Any time you allow remote access to your internal protected local area network (LAN) by remote users, you increase the risk of security violations. It is important that you know who is using the remote access features you've enabled to access your resources. There's a lot you can monitor with respect to remote access, but the best place to start is by identifying and validating just who is using remote access. There are at least three activities of interest you should be monitoring:

- **Create VPN connection**—Your VPN server has the ability to track both successful and unsuccessful VPN connection requests. Although auditing all connection requests can create a large amount of information, it can also provide valuable information on how remote users are accessing your resources. Know who is using your resources, where those people are connecting from, and how they are using your VPN.

- **Remote access connection**—Once a remote user establishes a VPN, it is also interesting to see what they're doing with it. You can audit resource connections to see how remote users and resources are using your VPN. You should also audit non-VPN remote connection requests. Unless you're using a non-VPN encryption solution, all non-VPN remote connection requests should be denied.

- **Remote computer logon**—Another interesting piece of information you should audit is any remote logons to your computers or devices. Each operating system contains functions to audit logons. In fact, the operating systems can audit much more than just logons. You should be auditing access to sensitive resources at some level. As with all auditing activity, don't audit more than you need. Audit log files can become very large.

The overall idea is to keep track of who is using your VPNs and what they are doing. For example, assume your primary VPN is optimized for large volumes of small messages. Your expectation when you enabled the VPN was that users would use it to access your online order management system. VPN and remote access monitoring has shown you that most VPN users are running very large custom reports from your database to analyze data. The VPN is actually transporting large volumes of data for a relatively small number of users. You find that you can change some VPN settings that make it run faster for the way your users are using the VPN. Reports run faster and your data is more available. Table 13-1 lists a few programs that help monitor remote access and VPN usage.

TABLE 13-1 Remote access and VPN monitoring tools.	
PRODUCT	**SOURCE**
CodePlex Remote Access Monitor (Open source)	*http://remoteaccessmonitor.codeplex.com/*
SoftSea Remote Access Monitor (Free)	*http://www.softsea.com/review/Remote-Access-Monitor.html*
Cisco VPN Monitor	*http://www.cisco.com/en/US/products/sw/cscowork/ps2326/ products_user_guide_chapter09186a00800e680d.html#63236*
SNMP	Not a vendor-specific product

The last entry in Table 13-1 is the **Simple Network Management Protocol (SNMP)**. SNMP is a network protocol used to monitor network devices. Most network devices include SNMP support and can run SNMP agents to report conditions that require attention by another computer or device running network management system software. SNMP uses UDP protocol messages to retrieve information from network devices and for the devices to send updates when conditions you define are met. Although there are many ways to use SNMP, you can configure devices to send an alert to the network manager when remote users connect to your network.

Remote Access Traffic and Performance Monitoring and Analysis

Monitoring connections and events related to remote access users is important to learn about who is accessing your network from remote locations. But to ensure your VPNs are configured to best utilize your VPN bandwidth, it is important to monitor the traffic flowing along your VPNs. Although you can't monitor the contents of traffic in encrypted VPN tunnels, you can monitor traffic statistics to understand how well your remote users are utilizing VPN bandwidth. You can also detect unusual VPN activity that could indicate malicious activity or excessive use.

Because both endpoints are within domains in your IT infrastructure, you can monitor decrypted packets once they emerge from the end of the VPN tunnel. It is important to note that monitoring VPN traffic does not replace any other types of network monitoring.

> **technical TIP**
>
> You should verify that all traffic flowing along your VPNs is encrypted. It is possible to configure VPN tunnels to transport data without encrypting it first. If you misconfigure your VPN or if an attacker is successful at reconfiguring your VPN, you could be sending data into the WAN unencrypted. Validate that the packets flowing along your VPN are actually encrypted.

It is still important that you monitor WAN traffic to understand how your organization uses your WAN connections. VPN traffic monitoring provides additional information on how individual tunnels are behaving within your overall WAN usage. Excessive WAN usage might indicate a network usage problem. Further investigation using VPN monitoring could reveal that one remote user using a VPN is attempting to launch a denial of service (DoS) attack on your organization. In this case, WAN traffic monitoring revealed a high-level problem and VPN traffic monitoring revealed the cause of the problem. You need to monitor at both levels to get the whole picture.

You can implement VPN traffic monitoring and analysis using the same methods as LAN and WAN traffic monitoring and analysis. You can install software or devices on the perimeter of the VPN where you establish the endpoint. You can also use any of a wide variety of network management software packages that support SNMP to monitor traffic directly from the network devices that transport VPN traffic. Regardless of the methods you employ, monitoring and analyzing VPN traffic is important to ensure your private data is secure and compliant.

Remote Access Configuration and Change Management

You learned about the importance of managing network configuration settings in the previous chapters on the LAN, LAN-to-WAN, and WAN Domains. Managing the changes to your VPN and remote access configuration is crucial to maintaining a secure environment for remote users and resources. Just as with devices and computers in other domains, ensure that you control configuration changes to Remote Access Domain components, including:

- VPN client software
- Authentication servers
- VPN servers
- Remote access servers
- Network management system servers

The strategies and techniques for managing configuration settings and controlling configuration changes should match your activities in the LAN, LAN-to-WAN, and WAN Domains. Refer to Chapters 10, 11, and 12 for more information on proactively managing configuration setting changes. Just as with other domains, managing the configuration settings of your Remote Access Domain components is an important part of keeping your overall environment compliant and secure.

Remote Access Management, Tools, and Systems

Managing remote access components means ensuring each one fulfills the goals for which it was designed. It also means to continually update your configuration to satisfy new and updated goals. Remote access management covers several related activities, including:

- Authorizing users and nodes to connect remotely
- Verifying privacy settings are in place
- Monitoring VPN performance
- Changing configuration settings to optimize performance
- Changing configuration to support new requirements
- Adding necessary controls to address security issues
- Maintaining components of a current recovery process
- Adding, changing, and removing hardware components as requirements dictate

The specific tools and procedures you use to manage remote access components depend on the operating systems and products you use. Configuring remote access users is similar to configuring local users. In fact, remote access settings are generally just additional configuration settings for regular users. For example, in Microsoft Windows Server 2008 R2, you enable remote desktop connections on the server machine and define authorized users using the "Remote" page of the System Properties window. Then you can define a Group Policy object for users or groups that define specific settings for remote sessions. Figure 13-4 shows the Start a Program on Connection setting in the Group Policy Management Editor.

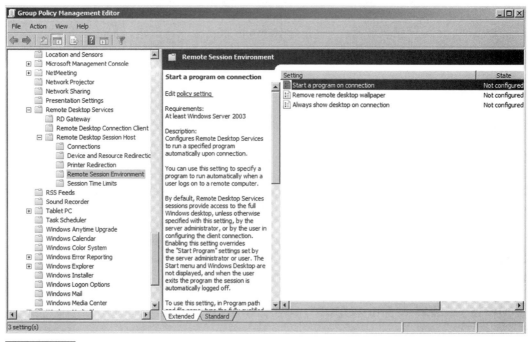

FIGURE 13-4

Windows Server 2008 R2 Group Policy Management Editor.

In addition to operating system settings, some remote access authentication and authorization products require additional configuration information. Learn what your environment requires to define and configure users and devices for remote access. Most network device vendors have their own management software. The remaining management tasks are similar to tasks in the LAN and LAN-to-WAN Domains. The main focus is on ensuring you configure each network device properly and optimally.

Explore options for VPN monitoring and management software for your operating system and network devices. Software that assists your network administrators will likely simplify managing your VPNs and make it easier to validate compliance with your stated security goals.

Access Rights and Access Controls in the Remote Access Domain

The degree to which you grant rights and permissions to remote users depends on your general access model and your operating system. In most cases, remote users accessing your environment via a VPN enjoy the same rights as users on your LAN. The idea behind a VPN is that once it is established, it operates just like a LAN. VPN users are essentially the same as other LAN users. Although it is possible to exclude some users from accessing your network using a VPN at the operating system level, it is generally easier to use the remote access authentication server to define which users can use remote access.

The main goal for all networking issues is to keep things simple. Complexity leads to an increased exposure to risk and requires more effort to maintain. Try to keep three lists of users: internal network users, remote access users, and global users. If you don't need to separate most local and remote user rights, then just defining a global user list keeps things simple. Once you create the users, you'll need to support remote access; your operating system provides the ability to define what each user can do through permissions or access control lists (ACLs). Refer to Chapter 8 for a discussion of user rights and permissions in the User Domain.

> ⚠ **WARNING**
>
> Do not include administrative users in a global user list. If you do allow remote administration, you should create administrative accounts specifically defined for remote administration. This practice makes auditing and controlling remote users with elevated privileges easier.

In addition to user rights, your remote access servers can define how you handle remote connections. You should set up VPNs to appear as networks that are separate from your physical LANs. Defining all VPNs in a specific range of subnets gives you the ability to define filtering or access rules that affect just your VPN connections. Defining rules for VPNs gives you the ability to identify and filter suspicious traffic or any traffic that is not authorized. For example, suppose you want to prohibit remote users from using **Server Message Block (SMB)** to map network resources as shares. You could set a rule in a firewall that sits between your VPN endpoint and your LAN to drop any TCP traffic for the default SMB port, 445. In this way, you prohibit any SMB access from your VPNs.

You can use user rights, permissions, ACLs, and firewall rules to restrict what remote users can do. Document what you'll allow remote users to do and use the appropriate controls to enforce your rules. The more remote users can do increases the risk to your data security. Allowing remote users to access your environment can increase your organization's effectiveness at the risk of reducing your overall security. Ensure you have the necessary controls in place to limit what remote users can do and to ensure your data is safe regardless of where it travels.

Remote Access Domain Configuration Validation

Validating compliance in the Remote Access Domain includes validating the controls that satisfy compliance requirements. With respect to the Remote Access Domain, most compliance concerns focus on data privacy. It is important to evaluate all controls to ensure all three properties of the availability, integrity, and confidentiality (A-I-C) triad are satisfied. There are three main areas of concern in the Remote Access Domain: client-side configuration, server-side configuration, and configuration management verification. Each area focuses on a slightly different component of the Remote Access Domain. Taken together, validating these three areas provides assurance that components in your Remote Access Domain are compliant with the necessary requirements.

VPN Client Definition and Access Controls

Each VPN client stores configuration details to connect to the organization's VPN server. Typically, VPN details include information such as:

- Host name or address (primary and backup)
- Logon user name
- Password (optional—dependent on authentication method)
- Authentication method
- Transport protocol
- Local address options
- Local log settings

Each of the client settings should match the server settings. In some cases, servers support multiple types of clients and will negotiate settings, such as authentication method and transport protocol. It is important that you verify each client's settings to ensure clients are in compliance with organizational VPN settings standards. One of the easiest ways to verify client settings is to restrict your server settings to deny any connection requests that fall below certain standards. If your clients meet the standards, they can connect. If not, their connections fail.

There are two types of access controls for remote access. The first are the access controls for computers or devices. These access controls define which computers or devices can establish remote connections. Your authentication servers or VPN servers store computer and device access controls. The location depends on the type of VPN and operating system you are using. The second type of access control is at the user or group level. This type of access control is the same as access control in the User Domain. Once a remote user authenticates and is authorized to access resources, the normal operating system access controls take effect.

SSL/VPN Remote Access Via Browser and SSL, 128-Bit Encryption

Most Web development languages and many applications have the ability to require secure connections. For example, you can require that a particular Web page or cookie can only be sent to a client using a secure connection. If the client attempts to render a secure Web page using an insecure protocol, the page does not render. You would have to use HTTPS to render the page. In other words, you would have to use HTTPS in the address to reach the page.

To verify compliance with data privacy for remote users, you should enforce the following:

- All Web pages that access sensitive data require secure HTTPS connections or have local host addresses.

  - Local host addresses for Web pages require VPN connections.

- Require all users authenticate before accessing any resources or data.

- Only VPN nodes can access sensitive data directly.

- Operating system– and application-specific access controls define which users can access sensitive data.

Adhering to these rules will ensure your data is safe from unauthorized remote users.

 WARNING

Consult the setup and configuration guide for your Web server. Some Web servers enable all encryption modes by default, including a debugging mode that actually doesn't encrypt traffic. If you leave this option enabled, attackers can trick your Web server into sending private data without using Secure Sockets Layer/Transport Layer Security (SSL/TLS) with encryption. Unless you're using a VPN, the Web server sends the data in the clear.

 WARNING

When using encryption between Web browsers and Web servers, always require 128-bit SSL/TLS encryption. Older algorithms only used 40-bit encryption that is easily compromised. If your Web server still supports 40-bit encryption, an attacker can force the weaker encryption and compromise your data.

13

Compliance Within the
Remote Access Domain

VPN Configuration Management Verification

You learned about the FCAPS approach to network management in Chapter 11. Recall that the "C" in FCAPS stands for configuration. You can use the same tools, such as the RANCID and Canner as mentioned in Chapter 11, to help manage VPN configuration settings. Managing all your network devices' configuration settings keep unauthorized changes from reducing your data's security. RANCID and Canner, along with other available tools, can help you create baselines of configuration settings and compare changes over time. You should develop a schedule and process to frequently compare configuration baselines and verify all changes to your network's configuration.

Recall that a solid network configuration management process includes managing changes to all configuration settings. A formal process makes it easy to classify any configuration changes as authorized or unauthorized. You just compare baseline differences to your authorized changes list to see which changes occurred that were not authorized. Implementing the FCAPS approach across all your networks will help formalize the process and make your networks more secure.

TABLE 13-2 Common compliance controls in the Remote Access Domain.

TYPE OF CONTROL	COMPONENT	DESCRIPTION
Preventive	Proxy server	Deny any unencrypted traffic to travel between remote users and your internal network
	Firewalls	Use a firewall between the VPN endpoint and your internal network to identify and deny unnecessary traffic
	User-based access controls for all resources	Restrict access to VPN to reduce traffic and resource exposure
	Configuration change control	Limit changes to all network device configuration settings and filtering rules. Require approval for all changes before deploying them.
Detective	Performance monitoring	Frequently sample VPN traffic flow metrics and alert for any unusual activity
	Traffic analysis	Examine traffic for known attack signatures and to ensure data is encrypted
	Configuration settings monitoring	Compare VPN/remote access device configuration settings to stored baselines to detect any unauthorized changes
	Penetration testing	Conduct periodic penetration tests to identify security control weaknesses
Corrective	VPN/remote access component patching	Keep VPN/remote access devices and applications patched to the latest available level
	Attack intervention	Automatically modify filtering rules to deny traffic from sources generating known attack signature packets
	Business continuity planning and disaster recovery planning	Develop and maintain plans to survive and continue operations in the face of small or large disruptions. Establish alternate WAN access plans in the case of primary WAN failure.

Adherence to Documented IT Security Policies, Standards, Procedures, and Guidelines

Security doesn't just happen. A secure environment is the result of solid plans and faithful adherence to those plans. If your organization takes the time to plan the best ways to achieve compliance and security assurance, it makes the most sense to follow the plans. Each component of your plans should address one or more of the basic A-I-C properties of data security. As you select and deploy controls, ensure each one supports your organization's security policy. Many organizations end up deploying controls that seem good but are not indicated in their policy. Such a situation indicates either the control is not needed or the policy needs amending. In either case, your controls should be the result of enacting your security policy. Above all else, it is important that your security policy be current and complete. Table 13-2 lists the types of controls you'll likely need to ensure are compliant in your Remote Access Domain.

These controls won't meet every compliance goal but will satisfy many current compliance requirements and make your Remote Access Domain more secure.

Best Practices for Remote Access Domain Compliance Requirements

The Remote Access Domain opens applications and resources to remote users. Doing so has the potential for exposing your internal environment to more threats. Because this domain commonly connects remote users to your environment using an untrusted WAN, you must ensure the controls protect your internal resources. Selecting, deploying, and managing the right security controls can provide efficient and secure access across an untrusted WAN.

This list of best practices covers the most common suggestions and goals many organizations have found helpful in securing the Remote Access Domain. These pointers will help you get started to develop a plan and select the right security controls to ensure your remote users enjoy a high level of service without sacrificing your data's security:

- Map your proposed remote access architecture, including redundant and backup connections. Use one of the several available network-mapping software products to make the process easier.
  - Update the network map any time you make physical changes to your network.
- Install at least one firewall between your VPN endpoint and your internal network.
- Select a VPN provider that your clients can easily access. If you select a vendor-specific VPN solution, develop a method to distribute and maintain the VPN client software to your users.
- Use global user accounts whenever possible.
  - Use strong authentication for all user accounts.

- Create a limited number of administrative accounts with permissions for remote administration.
- Develop a backup and recovery plan for each component in the Remote Access Domain.
    - Don't forget to include configuration settings for network devices in your backup and recovery plans.
- Implement frequent update procedures for all operating systems, applications, and network device software and firmware in the Remote Access Domain.
- Monitor VPN traffic for performance and suspicious content.
- Carefully control any configuration setting changes or physical changes to domain nodes.
    - Update your network map after any changes.
- Require encryption for all communication in the Remote Access Domain.
- Enforce anti-malware minimum standards for all remote computers as well as server computers in the Remote Access Domain. Ensure all anti-malware software and signature databases are kept up to date.

Review the suggested best practices and implement the controls that work best for your environment. Each organization has different needs and will end up with different controls to best ensure functionality and security in the Remote Access Domain.

CHAPTER SUMMARY

This chapter covered how to enable remote users to access your network's internal applications and resources by implementing components in the Remote Access Domain. You learned to address the increased risks associated with allowing remote users to access your network using untrusted WANs. You also learned about controls and strategies that work well in the Remote Access Domain to keep your environment functional without sacrificing compliance.

KEY CONCEPTS AND TERMS

Baseband	Hypertext Transfer Protocol Secure (HTTPS)	Simple Network Management Protocol (SNMP)
Broadband	Secure Sockets Tunneling Protocol (SSTP)	Tunneling
Encapsulating protocol		
Hypertext Transfer Protocol (HTTP)	Server Message Block (SMB)	

CHAPTER 13 ASSESSMENT

1. The primary concern for remote access is availability.

A. True
B. False

2. Which entity is responsible for controlling access to network traffic in the WAN?

A. WAN optimizer
B. Your organization
C. WAN service provider
D. Network Management Platform

3. _____ is the primary security control used in the Remote Access Domain.

4. All VPN traffic is encrypted.

A. True
B. False

5. Given adequate security controls, PDAs are appropriate for use as remote access devices.

A. True
B. False

6. Which of the following terms means the process to decide what a user can do?

A. Identification
B. Authentication
C. Clearance
D. Authorization

7. Which of the following protocols is used for encrypted traffic?

A. HTTPS
B. SNMP
C. IP
D. L2TP

8. _____ is a technique that creates a virtual encrypted channel that allows applications to use any protocol to communicate with servers and services without having to worry about addressing privacy concerns.

9. Which of the following protocols works well with firewalls?

A. GRE
B. SSTP
C. L2TP
D. L2F

10. Which of the following transmission techniques requires the entire bandwidth of a channel?

A. Multiband
B. Baseband
C. Broadband
D. Duplex

11. _____ is a network protocol used to monitor network devices.

12. The use of global user accounts can simplify user maintenance.

A. True
B. False

13. Which protocol is commonly used to protect data sent to Web browsers when not using VPNs?

A. IPSec
B. PPTP
C. GRE
D. SSL/TLS

14. Which of the following controls would best protect sensitive data disclosure to unauthorized users using remote computers?

A. Encryption
B. Strong passwords
C. Firewalls
D. Configuration management tools

15. Which protocol does SNMP use to transport messages?

A. TCP
B. UDP
C. SSL
D. GRE

Compliance Within the System/Application Domain

YOU LEARNED ABOUT SEVERAL DOMAINS that support distributed applications in previous chapters. You learned about how application components can run on different networks and work together to perform business functions. Some application components run in your organization's environment and others run outside your environment. You know how most of the different domains work together to provide the infrastructure to connect users to resources, but there's one more piece to the puzzle. To complete the picture, you'll need to learn about how distributed application components operate, where they fit into a seamless application design, and how to ensure you maintain your data's security as your application components process and manipulate it.

The last domain you'll cover addresses your application programs and the systems that run them. The domain responsible for application software components is the System/Application Domain. This domain provides the computers and the application programs that run on them. These application components exchange data with users or other application components and perform some function that is of value to users. In this chapter, you'll learn about the System/Application Domain and how to ensure compliance in this domain.

Chapter 14 Topics

This chapter covers the following topics and concepts:

- How compliance law requirements and business drivers relate to one another
- Which devices and components are commonly found in the System/Application Domain
- What system and application traffic and performance monitoring and analysis are
- What system and application configuration and change management are

- Which system and application management tools and systems are commonly used
- What access rights and access controls in the System/Application Domain are
- How to maximize availability, integrity, and confidentiality (A-I-C)
- What System/Application server vulnerability management is
- How to ensure adherence to documented IT security policies, standards, procedures, and guidelines
- What best practices for System/Application Domain compliance requirements are

Chapter 14 Goals

When you complete this chapter, you will be able to:

- Examine compliance law requirements and business drivers
- Compare how devices and components found in the System/Application Domain contribute to compliance
- Describe methods of ensuring compliance in the System/Application Domain
- Summarize best practices for System/Application Domain compliance

Compliance Law Requirements and Business Drivers

Although sharing resources such as printers and disk drives among network users is beneficial and can reduce costs, the real power of network environments is in distributed applications. Centralizing core business functions on networked servers can dramatically increase the security of your data in many ways. You can centrally control how you store your data and how you allow users to access it. You've learned about other domains in the IT infrastructure that provide the ability to connect computers, devices, and users together. In this chapter, you'll learn about one last domain: the System/Application Domain. The System/Application Domain provides the environment for the applications you run as clients on your network and the computer systems that house them. This domain provides the engine for today's distributed applications and empowers the concept of providing individual components of applications, as opposed to entire applications in one footprint. Figure 14-1 shows the System/Application Domain in the context of the seven domains in the IT infrastructure.

Keeping data secure in the System/Application Domain focuses on ensuring availability and controlling unauthorized access. You've already learned about many of the techniques you'll use in the System/Application Domain. Although other domains focus on keeping data secure as it travels across various networks, the System/Application Domain's main security controls ensure your data's security in storage and in use.

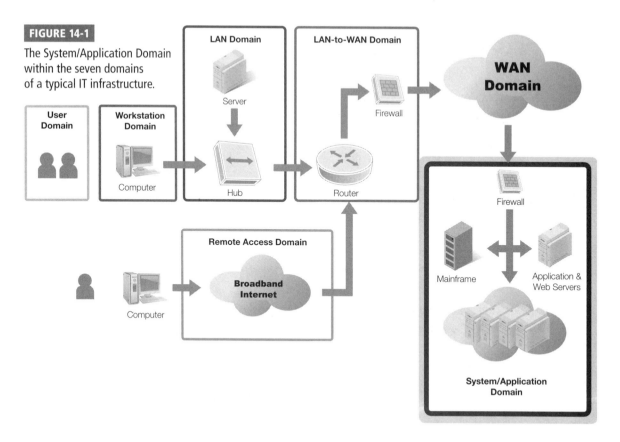

FIGURE 14-1

The System/Application Domain within the seven domains of a typical IT infrastructure.

As with other domains, you'll likely need to show compliance with one or more requirements that directly address sensitive data you store and process in the domain. The Health Insurance Portability and Accountability Act (HIPAA) requires controls to protect the privacy of medical data, PCI requires credit card privacy controls, and many states require privacy controls on any personal identifiable data. These are only a few of the requirements you'll need to satisfy when selecting security controls for storing and using data. A solid security policy that includes compliance with all appropriate requirements should not only be secure, but should support efficient and cost-effective operation. Implementing the controls necessary to support your security policy in the System/Application Domain makes your organization more effective by providing useful data that is compliant with relevant requirements.

Protecting Data Privacy

Because the System/Application Domain centralizes much of your data and the processing of that data, it is important that you protect it from disclosure or unauthorized alteration. More and more compliance requirements state that applications must ensure the privacy of different types of data. Recall that ensuring data privacy essentially means only allowing authorized users to view or modify it. Because you control all of the components in the System/Application Domain, you can deploy layers of controls to restrict access to authorized users.

Although controlling access to data and resources can be challenging, in some ways it is a little easier than trying to protect data as you send it to remote locations. You can enforce strict rules that limit which users and programs can access your data. An unauthorized user must access your network, then a server in the domain, and then run a program or access data in a database. There are several points along the way to place good security controls. You can implement several types of controls that make it difficult for unauthorized users to get to your private data. An important first step is to identify sensitive or private data and then design controls to protect that data's privacy.

Implementing Proper Security Controls for the System/Application Domain

The best security controls are simple layered controls. Try to avoid overly complex controls. Complex controls generally take more effort for configuration and maintenance and often provide more opportunities to fail. Your goal in designing security controls is to ensure they do their jobs and keep your data secure. Although deploying layered controls is generally considered to be sound security practice, be careful that you don't create so many controls that authorized users have difficulty accessing the data they need. Try to search for controls that balance security and usability needs.

Security controls in the System/Application Domain generally fall into three categories. There are many potential controls, but the most important controls should isolate data, limit access to data, or protect data from loss through redundancy. Each type of control plays a part in keeping your data secure and your organization compliant:

- **Isolate data**—Because much of an organization's sensitive data resides in one or more databases in the System/Application Domain, it is important to place barriers between sensitive data and other entities. You can use firewalls and your network design to isolate data. Your network addressing scheme can separate one or more nodes into their own subnet. A **subnet** is simply a part of a network. Other network devices, such as switches, can physically isolate subnets from other nodes.

---

technical TIP

One example of too many controls is the use of multiple logons. As environments grow and add new functionality, it is common to deploy new software applications. Many software applications use their own internal user identification, authentication, and authorization strategies. Using an application with its own defined users poses a few problems. Systems administrators face additional maintenance to keep the user list accurate. Users have to log on several times as they use different applications. One solution is to use a single sign-on (SSO) system in which a user only has to sign on, or log on, once. SSO can greatly ease user frustration. It might sound like a minor decision, but it can have a large effect on how well your users accept any new controls.

TIP

Regardless of the operating system or controls you use, limit access to your sensitive data. Know which users and which nodes can access your data.

- **Limit access to data**—Node and user access controls in the System/Application Domain are similar to access controls you learned about in previous chapters. Operating systems provide mechanisms to restrict object access by users or groups. You can also use network authentication to restrict which computers and devices can connect to servers that contain sensitive data.

- **Protect data from loss through redundancy**—Because the System/Application Domain exists to provide applications and data to your users, it has to be functional. You'll need plans to ensure users can access your applications and data regardless of what happens. That means you'll need to create redundant copies of data or other strategies to protect your organization from data or functionality loss.

Several of the other domains you've studied support users and their ability to access applications and data. In one view, you can look at the System/Application Domain as the central repository of the data you are trying to protect. The System/Application Domain provides the security controls closest to your data. An attacker who has compromised enough controls to reach this domain doesn't have much farther to go. The controls you place in the System/Application Domain could be the controls that make the difference between secure data and loss. Take the time to plan your security controls well.

Devices and Components Commonly Found in the System/Application Domain

The System/Application Domain contains the application components that your organization runs and the computer systems on which the applications reside. This domain also contains computers, devices, and software components that support the domain's application software. The rest of this section lists the devices and components you'll commonly find in the System/Application Domain and some of the controls to ensure compliance. Figure 14-2 shows the devices and components commonly found in the System/Application Domain.

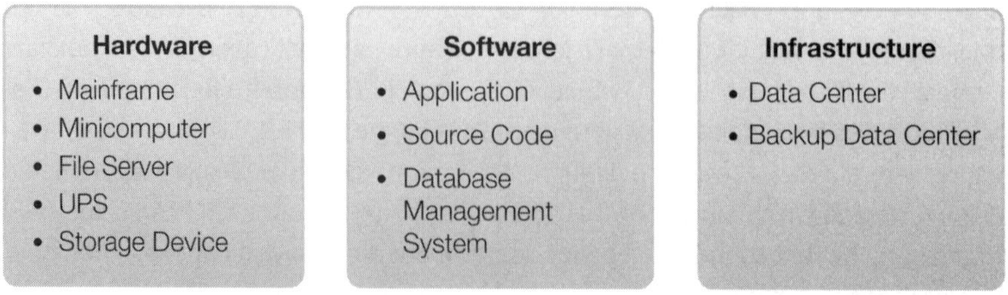

FIGURE 14-2

Devices and components commonly found in the System/Application Domain.

Hardware	Software	Infrastructure
• Mainframe	• Application	• Data Center
• Minicomputer	• Source Code	• Backup Data Center
• File Server	• Database Management System	
• UPS		
• Storage Device		

Computer Room/Data Center

The components in the System/Application Domain commonly reside in the same room. The room in which central server computers and hardware reside is called a **data center**, or just a computer room. Because the software and data in this domain are central to your organization's operation, it is imperative that the hardware stays operational. A well-equipped data center generally has at least the following characteristics:

- **Physical access control**—Secure data centers have doors with locks that only a limited number of people can open. Electronic locks or combination locks are common to easily enable a group of people access to the room. Physical access control reduces the likelihood an attacker could physically damage data center hardware or launch an attack using removable media. Inserting a universal serial bus (USB) drive that is infected with malware is a real type of attack. Limiting physical access to critical hardware can mitigate that type of attack.

- **Controlled environment**—Heating, ventilating, and air conditioning (HVAC) service controls the temperature and humidity of a secure data center. Data centers routinely have dozens, or even hundreds, of computers and devices all running at the same time. Keeping the temperature and humidity at proper levels allows the hardware to operate without overheating. Data centers also need dependable electrical power. A data center requires enough reliable power to run all computers and devices currently located in the data center as well as room for growth.

- **Fire suppression equipment**—A data center fire has the potential to wipe out large amounts of secure data and hardware. Extinguishing a fire helps protect the hardware assets and the data they contain. Unfortunately, water could damage computing hardware as much as fire, so sprinklers aren't appropriate in data centers. A common solution is a roomwide fire suppression gas that deploys to displace the oxygen in the entire room.

- **Easy access to hardware and wiring**—Data center components tend to change frequently. Data center personnel must upgrade old hardware, add new hardware, reconfigure existing hardware, and fix broken hardware. Each of these tasks generally involves moving hardware components from one place to another and attaching necessary wires and cables. Data center computers generally don't have cases like desktop computers do. Many times, they look like bare components on rails. The design allows them to be used in rack systems. A **rack system** is an open cabinet with tracks into which multiple computers can be mounted instead of individual cases. You can slide computers in and out like drawers. Using rack systems makes it easy to manage hardware. Because there tends to be a lot of wiring in a data center, many use a raised floor design. Using raised floors with removable access panels makes accessing wires easy and increases overall airflow throughout the data center.

> **technical TIP**
>
> When designing a disaster recovery plan, *always* protect people first. Computers, devices, and data can all be replaced. People cannot. A common gas used for years in data center fire suppression systems is **halon**. Although halon works well to suppress fire, halon is hazardous to humans and the environment. Due to the dangers associated with halon, other gas fire suppression options have emerged and are replacing halon. In fact, the manufacture of a common type of halon, Halon 1301, is banned and all new fire suppression systems must use an alternative substance.

- **High-speed internal LAN**—Many computers in the data center are high-performance server computers. To optimize communication between servers, high-bandwidth networks, such as fiber optic networks, are common within the data center.

When designing a data center, make sure it has the ability to support all the components you need today and in the foreseeable future. Data centers that are flexible and scalable allow your organization to change and grow to reflect business demands.

Redundant Computer Room/Data Center

A disaster recovery plan contains the steps to restore your IT infrastructure to a point where your organization can continue operations. If a disaster occurs that causes damage and interrupts your business functions, it is important to return to productive activities as soon as possible. If your organization can't carry out its main business functions, it cannot fulfill its purpose. A solid **disaster recovery plan (DRP)** carefully identifies each component of your IT infrastructure that is critical to your primary business functions. Then, the plan states the steps you can take to replace damaged or destroyed components.

Several options are available for serious disasters that damage or destroy major IT infrastructure components. These are a few of the most common options, starting with the most expensive option with the shortest cutover time:

- **Hot site**—A complete copy of your environment at a remote site. Hot sites are kept as current as possible with replicated data so switching from your original environment to the alternate environment can occur with a minimum of downtime.
- **Warm site**—A complete copy of your environment at a remote site. Warm sites are updated with current data only periodically, normally daily or even weekly. When a disaster occurs, there will be a short delay while a switchover team prepares the warm site with the latest data updates.
- **Cold site**—A site that may have hardware in place, but it will not likely be set up or configured. Cold sites take more time to bring into operation because of the extensive amount of configuration work required for hardware and software.
- **Service level agreement (SLA)**—A contract with a vendor that guarantees replacement hardware or software within a specific amount of time.

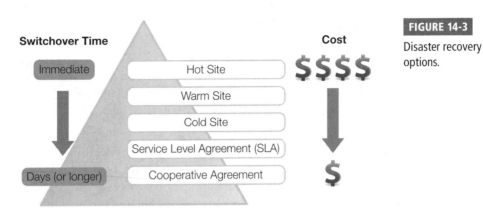

FIGURE 14-3

Disaster recovery options.

- **Cooperative agreement**—A cooperative agreement is between two or more organizations to help one another in case a disaster hits one of the parties. The organization that is not affected by the disaster agrees to allow the other organization to use part of its own IT infrastructure capacity to conduct minimal business operations. There is usually a specified time limit that allows the organization that suffered damage time to rebuild its IT infrastructure.

Figure 14-3 shows disaster recovery options in terms of switchover time and cost.

Regardless of which option best suits your organization, the purpose of a disaster recovery plan is to repair or replace damaged IT infrastructure components as quickly as possible to allow the business to continue in operation.

UPS Power Supplies and Diesel Generators to Maintain Operations

There is a lot of confusion between a DRP and a **business continuity plan (BCP)**. The two plans work closely with one another and depend on one another for success. You can summarize the difference between the two plans into three main points:

- A DRP for IT ensures the IT infrastructure is operational and ready to support primary business functions. A DRP for IT focuses mainly on the IT department.
- A BCP is an organizational plan. It doesn't focus only on IT. The BCP ensures the organization can survive any disruption and continue operating. If the disruption is major, the BCP will rely on the DRP to provide an IT infrastructure the organization can use.
- A DRP is a component of a comprehensive BCP.

To summarize, a comprehensive BCP will take effect any time there is a disruption to business functions. An example is a water main break that interrupts water flow to your main office. A DRP takes effect when an event causes a major disruption. A major disruption is one where you must intervene and take some action to restore a functional IT infrastructure. A fire that damages your data center is an example of a disaster.

One type of interruption a BCP addresses is a power outage. Losing power for a data center means computers cannot operate and the environment can no longer support the hardware. With no power, there is no HVAC, lights, or anything that relies on electricity. It is important to plan for power outages and place corrective controls to address a loss of power. There are two main methods that address a power outage. The first method addresses short-term outages, whereas the second method addresses longer-term outages:

- **Uninterruptible power supply (UPS)**—A UPS provides continuous usable power to one or more devices. UPS units for data centers are typically much larger than workstation UPS units and can support several devices for longer periods of time. A UPS protects data center devices from power fluctuations and outages from several minutes to even several hours for large, expensive units.

- **Power generator**—Generators that commonly use diesel fuel to create electricity can deliver power to critical data center components for long periods of time. When a power outage lasts longer than a UPS can power devices, generators can produce electricity as long as they have fuel. Generators are generally not extremely long-term solutions. They will provide power until either regular power is restored or you can move to an alternate data center that has reliable power. In a case in which you must locate a data center in a place that does not have reliable power, however, generators can become the primary power source.

Mission-critical data centers require multiple levels of protection to ensure continuous operation. UPS devices and generators are integral parts of a BCP that keep an organization in operation.

Mainframe Computers

Several types of computers make their homes in data centers. The largest type of computer is the mainframe computer. The term "mainframe" dates back to the early days of computers and originally referred to the large cabinets that housed the processing units and memory modules of early computers. The term came to be used to describe large and extremely powerful computers that can run many applications supporting thousands of users simultaneously. Mainframe computers also have the characteristic of being extremely reliable. Most mainframe computers run without interruption, and can even be serviced and upgraded while still operating.

Because the hardware, software, environmental requirements, and maintenance for mainframe computers are all expensive, only the largest organizations typically can justify their expense. Mainframe environmental and power requirements created the need for the early dedicated data centers. Today's mainframe computers are powerful hosts for multiple operating systems that run as **virtual machines**. A virtual machine is a software program that looks and runs like a physical computer. A large mainframe computer can run many virtual machines and provide the services of many physical computers.

Computing in the Cloud

Cloud computing is becoming one of the fastest growing trends in IT. The term **cloud computing** means Internet-based computing. For years, many networks and the Internet have been depicted in print using cloud diagrams. Cloud computing draws from this historical mental picture. The idea behind the cloud is that instead of owning computing resources, an organization can rent it from a provider. The provider maintains the data center and continuous connectivity to your rented servers. Most cloud providers use computers, including mainframe computers, running many virtual machines to provide cloud services to their customers. There are multiple cloud models available from providers and your choice of models will depend on your budget and compliance requirements.

Sometimes the choice of deployment mode depends on your compliance requirements. The hybrid or community deployment modes are the two supported choices if your organization must comply with any of the following:

- Federal Information Security Management Act (FISMA)
- HIPAA
- Sarbanes-Oxley (SOX)
- European Union's Data Protection Directive
- Payment Card Industry Data Security Standard (PCI DSS)

The hybrid and community deployment modes do support compliance requirements but are generally more expensive and restrictive. Carefully examine your compliance requirements before moving to the cloud.

Minicomputers

Many organizations realize they need more computing power than basic workstations or PC-based hardware but aren't ready for the commitment to a mainframe computer. The first minicomputers started appearing in data centers in the 1960s as an alternative to mainframe computers. Minicomputers are more powerful than workstations but less powerful than mainframe computers. They fit somewhere in the middle and address the needs of medium-sized businesses.

Before the 1980s, minicomputers and mainframe computers were the only types of computers that could handle multiple users and multiple applications at the same time. Smaller computers of the time could only handle single users and one application at a time. The 1980s saw the growth of more capable hardware and operating systems for low-cost computers. These small, inexpensive computers are called "microcomputers" and still dominate the personal computer and workstation markets.

Minicomputers still exist to address the needs of medium-sized businesses, but they aren't as distinct as they were in the past. Some of today's minicomputers are distinct hardware platforms and some are actually high-end microcomputers running operating system versions that cater to high performance and reliability. Either way, minicomputer performance and cost fill a need between workstations and mainframe computers.

Server Computers

Some computers in a data center aren't multipurpose computers but fill specific roles. Computer roles most commonly focus on satisfying client needs for specific services. Computers that perform specific functions for clients are generally called "server computers," or just servers. Common servers you'll find in today's environments may include:

- File server
- Web server
- Authentication server
- Database server
- Application server
- Mail server
- Media server

These are only a few of the types of servers in many data centers. Server computers help organizations by allowing a computer to focus all of its resources on a single task, providing a specific service to clients. A collection of separate server computers that each provides a different service can increase the performance of the entire environment by removing interservice conflicts and competition for a single computer's resources. Isolating services on separate server computers can also limit the effects of attacks. An attack that compromises a server computer running a single service will have less impact than a compromise of a single computer running many applications and services.

Data Storage Devices

Data centers are convenient places to locate shared storage devices. The central location, managed environment, and higher general level of security make the data center an ideal environment for protected shared storage. Many networks offer managed storage devices that are shared among network users. Shared devices can be attached to file servers or be separate from server computers. Shared storage devices can be disk drives, tape libraries, optical jukeboxes, solid state storage, or any other mechanism used to store data.

One common method to provide shared storage capability to network users is through the use of a **storage area network (SAN)**. A SAN is a collection of storage devices that is attached to a network in such a way that the devices appear to be local storage devices.

In effect, the storage devices form their own network that the operating system accesses just like local drives. The SAN devices protect the data by limiting how clients can access the storage devices. SANs can make it easy to keep shared data available and secure.

Applications

Computer applications have matured along with computer hardware capability. Early computing systems placed all data and software capabilities on a central host computer. Clients used simple terminals to connect directly to the host computer to run applications. Application design has changed through several generations to its current level of maturity, the distributed application model. Each architectural change depended on advances in networking support and changed the way applications use networks and resources. Application architectures mainly differ in the location of critical resources. Critical application resources are:

- **Data storage**—The interface to physical storage devices, such as disk drives
- **Data access**—Software to access stored data, such as database management systems or document management systems
- **Business logic**—Application software that accesses and processes data
- **User interface**—Application software that interacts with end users

Table 14-1 lists major application architectures and their impact on network resources.

Although not all applications are fully distributed, the trend for new development efforts is to deploy distributed applications. More and more applications are specifically written to run on application server computers. This move toward distributed applications has an impact on security and compliance. Although many organizations use application servers in a secure data center to run application components, others may just run applications on a generic network computer. Each application must ensure it protects the security of the data it handles.

Source Code

Application software is a collection of computer programs that fulfills some purpose. Programs that computers can run are the result of a process that starts with programmers creating text files for programs, called **source code**. Source code files are then compiled into programs that computers can run.

---

technical TIP

Not all source code files are compiled into programs computers can run. Some languages actually interpret source code files while other environments just assemble source code instructions into machine-readable instructions. Regardless of your particular environment, all programs start off as source code files.

TABLE 14-1 Application architectures.					
ARCHITECTURE	**SERVICE LOCATION**				**COMMENTS**
	Data Storage	**Data Access**	**Business Logic**	**User Interface**	
Host based	Host	Host	Host	Host	Everything runs on the host. Host-based applications are easy to maintain and secure but are not very scalable.
Client based	Server	Client	Client	Client	This architecture is also called diskless workstations. This architecture didn't last too long because even a few clients can saturate a network with all disk accesses occurring over a network.
Client/server	Server	Server	Client	Client	This common model attempts to separate application execution from data access and storage. In a classic client/server model, the client runs all of the application code. Although workstations have become powerful, this model is slow when the application needs large amounts of data that must be transferred across the network.
Distributed	Server	Server	Server	Client	Distributed computing attempts to solve the network saturation problem by reducing the amount of information transferred across the network. Large volumes of data can be transferred between a database server and an application server in the data center without having to use the rest of the network. Reduced network usage can result in much better performance. Keeping more data within the data center's network increases the data's security as well.

The best way to secure applications from unintended changes is to keep your development environment separate from your production, or live, environment. You'll learn more about how to do this in the section that covers configuration and change management. Separating the different environments is mandatory for SOX compliance.

The process of changing how an application program runs starts with changing the source code files that correspond to the program you want to change. The programmer would then follow the prescribed procedure to convert the source code into a program the computer can run. This process works for attackers as well. Although it is possible to modify a computer program directly, it is far more difficult than modifying the source code. An important step in securing applications is to remove the source code. Without source code, it is very difficult to modify an application.

Databases and Privacy Data

Very few applications run as standalone programs. Nearly every application accesses data of some sort. Enterprise applications may access databases that are hundreds of gigabytes or even terabytes in size. Databases that store this much data are valuable targets for attackers and should be the focus of your security efforts in the System/Application Domain. Data is a crucial asset in many of today's organizations. An organization's ability to keep its data secure is crucial to its public image and is mandatory to maintain compliance with many requirements.

Because the database is where many organizations store sensitive data, it is the last barrier an attacker must compromise. In a secure environment, an attacker must compromise several layers of security controls to get to the actual database. Even though the hope is that an attacker never gets that far, you should implement additional controls to ensure you protect the data in your database from local attacks. The database should be the center of your security control efforts. You should take every opportunity to restrict access to the sensitive data in your database, including using controls provided by your database management system as well.

You'll learn about specific database controls in the "Access Rights and Access Controls to the System/Application Domain" section later in this chapter. Just because your database resides in a secure data center, you shouldn't assume it is safe. Use the security controls available to you at every level possible. Your job is to make an attacker's job as difficult as possible.

System and Application Traffic and Performance Monitoring and Analysis

The main goals for implementing distributed applications are to make the components that access and manipulate your data secure, easy, and fast. Making components secure depends on a secure infrastructure and deploying the best security controls. Components that are easy to run depend on a solid interface design. The third goal, to make application components fast, depends on both good design and proper configuration of the underlying infrastructure.

Once you deploy application components, good performance depends on identifying configuration problems and usage issues and addressing them. The most efficient way to identify problems is by monitoring application traffic and performance and comparing sampled metrics with expected performance. There are two main methods you can use to monitor application traffic and performance. The first method uses monitoring tools to sample application network traffic and analyze the packets to ensure your applications are exchanging data efficiently with clients. **Application performance monitoring** software can measure end-user response time for server requests as well as end-user traffic volume. You can set thresholds in the monitoring software's configuration to alert you if your application or your network slows down. Application monitoring software installed on the most important application servers can ensure your applications are servicing end-user requests efficiently and making your data available in a timely fashion. Table 14-2 lists several application monitoring software solutions that work with many different types of applications.

The second method to monitor and manage application performance requires specific knowledge of your application and of the tools available to manage it. Most applications,

TABLE 14-2 Application performance monitoring software.

PRODUCT	WEB SITE
SolarWinds Orion APM	*http://www.solarwinds.com/products/orion/application_monitor/info.aspx*
NetQoS SuperAgent	*http://www.netqos.com/solutions/superagent/*
NetScout nGenius Performance Manager	*http://www.netscout.com/products/performance_manager.asp*
Blue Coat Application Performance Monitoring	*http://www.bluecoat.com/solutions/businessneeds/appmonitor*
Radware Application Performance Monitoring	*http://www.radware.com/Products/Management/AppPerformancemonitoring.aspx*
ManageEngine Applications Manager	*http://www.manageengine.com/products/applications_manager/index.html?mtad*

development languages, and database management systems have tools available to monitor how well the application platform is performing. Explore your application and the tools available to monitor how well it is operating. Application or development language-specific tools might take more time to learn but might also provide far more detailed internal information you can use to enhance your application's performance.

Regardless of the method you employ, application monitoring software and application-specific tools can only help identify problems. Solving the problems requires that you first understand why the problem exists and then how to address it. Poor performance can originate from several different sources. Finding the source of a slow application component can be time consuming and difficult. In many cases, solving application performance problems requires input from analysts, developers, network administrators, and database administrators. The problem can be in any of several places. Application monitoring software and application-specific tools serve to identify the problems that affect your application's availability. Your organization's application performance issue resolution plan should direct the next steps.

System and Application Configuration and Change Management

Any organization that develops or modifies software applications must follow a configuration management method to ensure the integrity of their software. Far too many organizations lack the formal procedures to control changes to their software. Compliance requires formal change procedures. For example, SOX requires that any changes made to software be documented and tracked in such a way that changes can be undone. Further, SOX requires that all development activities and personnel be completely separate from your production environment. Although compliance requires these actions, they are really just good practices.

Software development and maintenance has evolved as more of an art than a science in many organizations. Small organizations with a very few software developers commonly approach the development process informally because it is easy to keep track of a few programs and a few people. As any organization grows, the software development and maintenance activities become more complex. As an organization grows from a small to medium size, it becomes evident that informal procedures no longer provide the level of control needed to maintain a dynamic application's integrity. One formal method to control the software development life cycle is **software configuration management (SCM)**. SCM provides the activities and requirements to formalize the entire software development process.

SCM requires that all development occur in a separate environment from production. In the most secure environments, the development area is on a server separate from where the completed application runs in production. Once developers complete software changes, the changes should move to an isolated testing and quality assurance (QA) environment. Testing and QA personnel test modified software to ensure it complies with the change request requirements and with existing application requirements. Many software changes to fix bugs or add functionality actually cause unintended problems. It is the responsibility of the testing and QA personnel to validate that the newly modified software performs as intended.

Once software changes have been tested and approved, they can be moved into production. Sarbanes-Oxley requires complete separation between developers and the production environment. Software developers are not allowed to access the production environment at all. Another role, such as a configuration gatekeeper, must move the software to the production environment. This security control limits the ability for software developers to accidentally place untested software in production. Untested code could violate any or all of the three A-I-C properties of data security. The separation between developers and production also stops malicious software developers from placing unauthorized software in production environments.

Regardless of your operating or development environment, it is imperative that your organization implement software configuration management software and controls to manage any changes to software. A solid set of tools will help manage changes, keep untested software from harming your data, and make it far easier to remove and replace offending software if an undiscovered bug does end up in the production environment.

System and Application Management, Tools, and Systems

Managing the components of the System/Application Domain means ensuring the computers and devices are operating properly and that the application components are running efficiently. These tasks can be grouped into the following goals:

- Ensure your computers and devices are operating properly.
- Ensure your data center network is operating properly, including interfaces to the networks outside your data center.
- Ensure your application components are operating properly.

Proactive monitoring provides assurance that everything is working as planned and raises alerts anytime issues are identified. Application performance monitoring software is the highest-level monitoring and analysis tool. If your application performance monitoring software reports that all is well, you have the assurance that application components, networks, and computers and devices are all operating properly. If a component has issues, your applications won't operate properly. Although it is possible that an issue can develop that does not immediately manifest an application problem, most application performance monitors can periodically run basic tests on idle applications to ensure all is well.

If your application performance monitoring software does indicate a problem, the course of action may include any of the following actions:

- Alert appropriate personnel to initiate troubleshooting procedures on the problematic application.
- Launch network monitoring and analysis software to evaluate network components and connections.
- Launch system monitors or interrogators to evaluate data center computers.

The tools you can use include the application performance monitoring software you read about in the "System and Application Traffic and Performance Monitoring and Analysis" section earlier in this chapter, as well as system and network monitoring software you saw listed in previous chapters. Managing computers, devices, networks, and software in the System/Application Domain doesn't introduce any new tools or topics. The practice of ensuring domain components are operating properly consists of tools and techniques that are appropriate and in use for other domains as well. Using these tools and techniques can help ensure the System/Application Domain is providing your users with application components to fulfill business requirements.

Access Rights and Access Controls in the System/Application Domain

The System/Application Domain is perhaps the most protected domain in relation to users. Both local and remote users must pass through several domains to access any components in the System/Application Domain. That means it is reasonable to expect users and attackers have already encountered several layers of security controls to even make it this far. Recall that a good security plan involves several layers of controls. You should deploy solid controls that protect each domain. However, it isn't good enough to rely on security controls in other domains. Although it is reasonable to expect the System/Application Domain components to be relatively safer than Internet-facing components, you still must protect all components in each domain.

What happens if an attacker is able to compromise the security controls in other domains and access the System/Application Domain components? How can you stop an attempted attack? The answer to both questions is to ensure you limit access to each component in the System/Application Domain using security controls. Although this might seem obvious, it is important to secure each domain's components and resist relying on controls in any other domain. Even if you properly secure your environment using multiple layers of controls, always assume the current domain must protect each component. When each domain provides security controls that protect its components without interfering with business processes, you automatically implement a layered approach to security that makes your environment more secure.

In spite of the fact that the System/Application Domain is farther away from users and tends to be more protected than some other domains, it does have a particular weakness. Distributed applications commonly depend on the Internet to expose application components to the widest number of remote users. By far, the most common method to make application components available to remote users is through a Web server. The Web server allows Internet users to send requests for services. Your application design dictates whether your application is public or private. Private applications tend to be easier to protect because you have the option of requiring a secure VPN to access your application. Most public applications allow non-VPN users to request services.

14

Within the System/
Application Domain

FIGURE 14-4

Remote user request for a service from a distributed application.

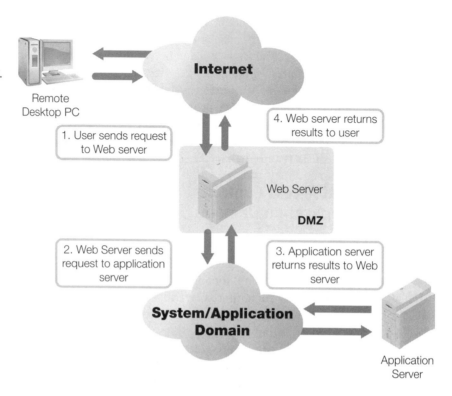

Allowing anonymous Internet users into your network poses a potential problem. To illustrate, Figure 14-4 shows a remote user requesting and receiving service from a distributed application:

1. Anonymous users can send an application request directly to your Web server. Your Web server likely resides in the demilitarized zone (DMZ) in your LAN-to-WAN Domain.

2. The Web server then launches a program that establishes a connection to an application server in the System/Application Domain.

3. The application server runs the requested program on behalf of the remote user and returns the results back through the Web server.

4. The Web server returns the results to the user.

Following the path, it is easy to see that an attacker can get right to your Web server in the DMZ. To make your distributed application available to the maximum number of people, your firewalls will likely leave your Web server ports wide open. All an attacker has to do is compromise your Web server to potentially connect right to your application server. So, one well-placed attack can threaten your System/Application Domain. That's why layered security controls in every domain are essential.

Your System/Application Domain should implement access controls for nodes and users. You should use Network Access Control (NAC) software, such as PacketFence or Sophos NAC Advanced, with positive authentication to ensure no rogue nodes are allowed to access System/Application Domain components. To address attacks from your Web server, your application server should enforce user access controls and your application should also enforce its own user access controls. You should define one set of users for remote access through a Web server and another set of users for internal access. That way, you can separate the rights and permissions and also audit remote user access more aggressively. The most secure position is to assume all access requests are potentially hostile and then evaluate each one with aggressive access controls.

Maximizing A-I-C

Identifying security controls to protect data can be confusing. As with other domains, one effective way to ensure you have the right controls in place is to review how well you are maximizing the A-I-C properties of data security. If you can demonstrate that your controls are addressing the needs for data availability, integrity, and confidentiality, you have addressed the basic needs for data security.

> **NOTE**
>
> In many cases, addressing the A-I-C properties of data security meets compliance requirements as well. Don't neglect to review your compliance requirements when examining security controls as some requirements might call for additional security controls.

BCP and DRP

The first concern for your System/Application Domain is that the data is available to authorized users on demand. That means all of the necessary computers, devices, and networking components must be operating properly and any software required for your application should be up and running. When your data is not available, you need to have a plan in place to address the problem. Most security-related legislation, regulations, and standards require some type of business continuity plan to ensure data availability.

A BCP takes effect any time some event interrupts your business operation. Events can be minor, such as a brief power outage, or major, such as a fire in the data center. In either case, your BCP should contain the steps to restore business operations back to normal. In some cases, a disaster causes damage to one or more infrastructure components that interrupt your BCP activities. For example, a fire in the data center might destroy a server. Until you replace or repair the server, it cannot contribute to your business operation. You need another plan to address disasters that restores your operating environment to a state where it can contribute to your business operation. The disaster recovery plan is a separate plan that responds to disasters and restores the infrastructure components to a point where the BCP can restore business operation.

Both plans are important and you must ensure you provide recovery teams with the material and information they need to execute a DRP and BCP when needed. The most important two resources any recovery team needs are well-documented procedures and redundant, undamaged domain components. Redundant, undamaged domain components can be any of the following items:

14

Within the System/
Application Domain

> **technical TIP**
>
> Your access controls should carefully limit which users can connect to servers in the System/ Application Domain from a Web server. Do not allow users with escalated privileges to connect from your DMZ. Only allow escalated privilege users to connect from a protected Web server that can only be reached by VPN. These controls reduce the potential for an attacker to connect to sensitive servers from Internet-facing components.

- Current valid backup images of data and other files
- Current replicated images of data and other files
- Identical copies of hardware and devices, either individual components or an entire duplicate data center
- Replacement hardware and devices
- Replacement parts for hardware and devices
- Repaired hardware and devices

As long as the recovery team has access to the domain components it needs to restore operation, team members can follow a well-documented plan. Make sure you protect every domain with a comprehensive BCP and DRP.

Access Controls

Access controls play an important part in the System/Application Domain. Earlier in this chapter, you learned how an attacker could potentially compromise your Web server and attempt to access System/Application Domain components directly. If an attacker is able to compromise a computer in your DMZ and able to exploit a vulnerability that provides access into another domain, solid access controls can limit the damage that attack can do. Many attackers will attempt to escalate user privileges to establish a connection to another computer or another domain to alter or disclose data.

In addition to NAC devices limiting connections to the System/Application Domain components and operating system access controls for user logons, all applications should implement access controls as well. Application access controls can limit access for specific data elements. In a database environment, applications can employ access controls at the record or row level. For even more fine-tuned control, some applications and databases support access control at the field or column level. Application controls can limit which users can read data and which users can write data. Proper use of access controls at all levels can protect the confidentiality and integrity of your data. As long as you employ strong authentication techniques, user identity and access controls help keep your data secure.

Database and Drive Encryption

Access controls protect the confidentiality and integrity of data as long as the operating system enforces the controls. If an attacker is able to acquire a copy of data outside the scope of the operating system, access control cannot protect the data's security. There are two main approaches to acquire data outside the scope of the operating system.

The first attack method is to boot the computer that contains the data using removable media. Removable media, such as a CD, DVD, or USB drive, can contain an alternate operating system that allows the attacker to access any file with no access controls. A successful attack such as this allows an attacker to copy any desired data, regardless of how confidential it is. There are two main defenses to this type of attack. The first defense is to limit physical access to critical servers. Most data centers employ physical controls such as locked access doors that only a select few people can open. If an attacker cannot physically access a computer, this type of attack fails. The second defense is to employ operating system-level encryption.

A second type of attack can result in disclosing large amounts of confidential data. This second type of attack involves acquiring a copy of a backup image. Many organizations make the mistake of not securing backups once they are created. You should transport backup media to another physical location to protect it from a physical disaster. The purpose of creating backup images is to provide a redundant copy of your data if a disaster destroys the primary copy. Suppose a flood destroys your entire data center. If your backup images were stored in the data center, they could be destroyed as well. Transporting backups to remote locations for storage increases the likelihood they'll be usable even after a disaster at the main data center.

If an attacker can steal a copy of your backup media as they are being transported from the data center to the storage location, all of your data could be disclosed. Data on backup media is easy to access. There are at least two controls to stop this type of attack as well. The first control is to secure all backup media during transport. Treat backups with care and respect the value to your organization. Investing in a method of secure transportation is far less expensive than one security breach. Many companies provide secure transportation and storage for backup media. Consider using such a service to ensure your backups don't fall into the wrong hands.

The second control to protect backups is to use encryption. Several types of encryption are available for different needs. Some types of encryption help protect backup media and others help protect files on disk. Table 14-3 compares the six most common options for data encryption.

Storing data encrypted can help ensure only authorized users can decrypt it. This type of control assists you in protecting the confidentiality and integrity of your data.

System/Application Server Vulnerability Management

No software is perfect. All application software and operating system software are susceptible to software vulnerabilities. Because today's applications and operating systems are so complex, it is likely that multiple vulnerabilities exist in any version. Attackers know how difficult it is to develop secure software and they spend substantial effort trying to find vulnerabilities to exploit.

TABLE 14-3 Common options to encrypt data.

ENCRYPTION TYPE	DESCRIPTION	WHAT IT PROTECTS
File	Encrypt individual files. If part of the operating system, such as Windows Encrypting File System (EFS), the encryption key is derived from the user password and files are not readable when the user is not logged on.	Alternate boot attacks or any access that bypasses operating system access controls
Folder/directory	Encrypt entire folders/directories. An example is Windows EFS in folder encryption mode.	Alternate boot attacks or any attack that bypasses system access controls
Volume/drive	Encrypt entire volume or drive, such as Windows BitLocker or TruCrypt.	Alternate boot attacks or any attack that bypasses system access controls
Application	Encrypt individual pieces of data based on the application's requirements.	Any attack that bypasses the application access controls; also protects backups from attack
Database	Encrypt the entire database. If implemented by the database management system, this is often called **Transparent Data Encryption (TDE)**.	Any attack that bypasses the database management system access controls; also protects backups from attack
Backup	Encrypt backup media as you create the backup image.	Protects backups from attack

Software developers are engaged in a continuous cycle to keep their software as secure as possible. Attackers run exhaustive tests against software to uncover any vulnerabilities. When they find a vulnerability, they develop an attack that exploits it. They launch an attack and some computer systems become victims. The victims report what has happened to the software provider and the software provider modifies their software to remove the vulnerability. They test their new software and release it as a patch. Then the cycle repeats itself. Attackers are continuously looking for vulnerabilities and software providers are continuously fixing the vulnerabilities they find.

Operating System Patch Management

Operating systems have substantial access to the hardware they control. Compromising an operating system basically means owning that computer. An attacker who successfully compromises an operating system can often use that computer for other attacks as well.

You should frequently check your operating system's Web site for newly released patches and apply those patches. An operating system that has the latest available patches is less vulnerable to the newest attacks.

Set up each computer to either download and apply patches automatically or set up a procedure that ensures you apply operating system patches to all computers as soon as they are available. The longer you delay patching any computer, the longer that computer remains vulnerable to newly released attacks.

Application Software Patch Management

Application software can contain vulnerabilities as well. Just as with operating systems, it is advisable that you acquire the latest application software patches from your application software vendor and apply them as soon as possible. This process is relatively easy for off-the-shelf software. It can be more difficult for software you have modified. Regardless of the role you play in modifying application software, it is important to have a plan in place to keep your software free from known vulnerabilities. Always remember that if you know about a vulnerability, the chances are that some attacker knows about it too.

Adherence to Documented IT Security Policies, Standards, Procedures, and Guidelines

You've learned in previous chapters how important adherence to documented policies, standards, procedures, and guidelines is to achieve compliance and a secure environment. That goal is just as important in the System/Application Domain. Although most of the other domains in the IT infrastructure are similar to domains in other organizations, the components in the System/Application Domain tend to be very specific to each organization. The applications any organization runs define the services that organization can provide. In some ways, the System/Application Domain defines the organization to the outside world.

Because the components in this domain are so specific to the organization and not generic, in many cases it is imperative to create specific documents to direct actions that apply to the System/Application Domain. Security policies state high-level goals for security. Standards state specific performance metrics to meet goals. Procedures document the steps to meet stated performance metrics, and guidelines provide general direction for situations that don't have specific procedures. Develop documents that address each of the three A-I-C data security properties and each compliance requirement. Plan how you're going to meet compliance requirements before taking action.

Once you take the time to create the documents to direct IT activities, you should make every effort to follow the documents. If they have errors or need to be updated, make the necessary changes to keep them as current as possible. Following documented actions will always result in behavior that is more secure and compliant than simply making it up as you go.

Best Practices for System/Application Domain Compliance Requirements

The System/Application Domain is the engine for your organization's distributed applications. Although other domains are crucial to supporting your organization, the System/Application Domain houses most of your organization's data and the programs that access it. You can consider this domain to be the last chance you have to protect your organization's data from attackers. Although a good layered security plan should prevent attackers from ever getting this far, never assume this domain is safe. Treat it like all other domains and select security controls as if this was the only domain.

Although no single list can include all controls your organization will implement for the System/Application Domain, there are some best practices that organizations have developed through experience. These provide a good starting point for you to plan for a secure and compliant domain. Here are general best practices for securing your System/Application Domain:

- Establish physical controls to protect the data center.
  - Use door locks to limit access to authorized individuals.
  - Install a fire suppression system.
  - Ensure electrical and HVAC facilities meet or exceed your equipment's requirements.
- Use at least one firewall to limit network traffic from other domains to only authorized traffic.
- Use NAC devices to restrict which computers and devices can connect to System/Application Domain components.
- Connect critical server computers using high-speed network media, such as fiber optic, for servers that require large network transfers. An example is the connection between an application server and a database server.
- Define user- or group-based access controls for each computer in the domain.
- Use application-defined access controls to limit access to data.
- Only allow low-privilege users to establish connections between Internet-facing servers in the DMZ and System/Application Domain servers.
- Only allow escalated privilege user connections that originate from protected Web servers where users can only connect using a secure VPN.
- Frequently update operating systems with the latest security patches on all computers.
- Frequently update all application software with the latest security patches.

- If your organization engages in software development or software modifications, follow these best practices:
  - Use software configuration management software to control software changes.
  - Create separate environments for development, testing, and production.
  - Prohibit developers from accessing the production environment.
  - Follow formal procedures for approving software to move from development to testing, and from testing to production.
- Create a BCP and DRP that includes each component in the System/Application Domain.
  - Keep the BCP and DRP up to date to reflect any changes to the domain.
  - Test the BCP and DRP at least annually.
- Protect all backup media in transit and storage.
- Ensure all backup media is encrypted.
- Encrypt all sensitive data when it is stored on disks.
- Use application monitoring software to identify performance or availability issues.

CHAPTER SUMMARY

A secure distributed application is the result of careful planning and the right security controls deployed in all domains. Because the System/Application Domain is where much of your data and applications reside, it is a good starting point for security controls. If you carefully ensure each component is protected from attacks, you can greatly increase the ability of your organization to support the three A-I-C properties of data security. Ensuring your data is secure in the System/Application Domain is the first step in ensuring its security throughout its life. Follow the best practices and you'll be on your way to creating and maintaining secure data and processes that meet your compliance requirements.

14

Within the System/
Application Domain

KEY CONCEPTS AND TERMS

Application performance monitoring	Halon	Subnet
Business continuity plan (BCP)	Rack system	Transparent Data Encryption (TDE)
Cloud computing	Software configuration management (SCM)	Virtual machine
Data center	Source code	
Disaster recovery plan (DRP)	Storage area network (SAN)	

CHAPTER 14 ASSESSMENT

1. The main concern of data security in the System/Application Domain is integrity.

A. True
B. False

2. Because the System/Application Domain is the innermost domain, security controls are not as important.

A. True
B. False

3. A solid multilayered security plan means that an attacker will likely encounter several security controls before reaching the System/Application Domain components.

A. True
B. False

4. A _____ is a subdivision or part of a network.

5. Which of the following is *not* a common feature of a data center?

A. Controlled environment
B. Limited physical access
C. In-room generator
D. Raised floor

6. Every disaster recovery plan should protect _____ first.

7. Which type of plan contains instructions on how to recover from a power failure?

A. DRP
B. BCP
C. SLA
D. TDE

8. Which of the following is true?

A. A BCP is normally part of a DRP.
B. A BCP addresses only IT issues.
C. A DRP is normally part of a BCP.
D. A DRP should address even minor interruptions.

9. Which common term originally referred to the large cabinets that housed the processing units and memory modules of early computers?

A. Core rack
B. Rack system
C. Mainframe
D. Minicomputer

10. Which term refers to Internet-based computing services where computational services are rented?

A. Virtual machine
B. Cloud computing
C. Minicomputer
D. Multiplexing

11. A _____ generally resides in the DMZ and provides the interface between remote users and an application server.

12. Which type of full database encryption doesn't require any user interaction?

A. TDE
B. OLE
C. AES
D. DES

13. Which benefits do application performance monitoring software provide? (Select two.)

A. Measure end-user response time.
B. Measure senior management browsing habits.
C. Measure end-user traffic volume.
D. Measure application-installed code base.

14. According to SOX requirements, which type of user accounts are prohibited from access to the production environment?

A. Database administrators
B. Software developers
C. Network administrators
D. End users

PART THREE

Ethics, Education, and Certification for IT Auditors

Ethics, Education, and Certification for IT Auditors

A CAREER IN INFORMATION TECHNOLOGY (IT) AUDITING is both rewarding and demanding. The field continuously evolves and changes. Corporate events of the past decade, such as the WorldCom and Enron scandals, have forced auditors to adapt to new laws and regulations. As you've learned throughout this book, organizations depend on people and data. Employees process, store, and transmit data every day. Organizations must protect the data they use and create, either by law or as a best practice. Therefore, IT information security touches nearly all parts of an organization, and auditing is an important part of security.

The combination of IT and business acumen will continue to drive the auditing profession. Many IT professionals routinely work with IT auditors. At the same time, IT auditors continue to become more technically savvy. Even traditional auditors are increasingly working together with IT auditors and IT professionals.

The need for IT auditors with strong values and ethics is more important than ever. IT auditors require in-depth knowledge and skills in the areas of auditing and IT. In addition, IT auditors require traditional soft skills. The IT auditing profession draws on a wealth of resources beyond formal college coursework. A number of professional bodies provide standards and guidance as well as educational and certification programs. The Certified Information Systems Auditor (CISA) and Certified Information Systems Security Professional (CISSP) certifications are two commonly held credentials by IT auditors.

In this chapter, you will learn about certifications and careers in the auditing profession. You will also examine professional ethics and codes of conduct that auditors are required to uphold.

This chapter covers the following topics and concepts:

- What IT auditing career opportunities are available
- Why professional ethics and integrity of IT auditors are important
- What codes of conduct are, and how employees and IT auditors must follow them
- How to become certified or accredited for IT auditing

Chapter 15 Goals

When you complete this chapter, you will be able to:

- Understand the required skills and knowledge required for a career in IT auditing
- Understand what makes up a code of conduct and a code of ethics
- Identify codes of ethics from various professional organizations
- Identify the components that make up a mature code of conduct and why organizations establish them
- Understand the differences between auditing associations and other professional bodies
- Differentiate between certifications available to auditors and IT professionals
- Identify educational opportunities and resources available to IT auditors

IT Auditing Career Opportunities

The growth of IT auditing careers over the last decade is a result of several factors. Two primary factors are new legislative requirements and the use of IT throughout the business. Many organizations must prove they have reasonable controls in place as mandated by legislation such as the Sarbanes-Oxley (SOX) Act and the Health Insurance Portability and Accountability Act (HIPAA). In addition, organizations increasingly rely on computer systems to create, process, and store sensitive data. As a result, new risks and greater challenges have emerged.

Traditionally, organizations relied on **certified public accountants (CPAs)** or auditors associated with accounting to review their financial controls. With the increased use of computing systems, IT departments also began reviewing the adequacy of internal controls. Today, the accounting and information security (IS) fields are common paths to IT auditing careers. Other common paths come via risk management and project management.

TIP

ISACA is a member-based organization for information governance, control, security, and audit professionals. Membership in ISACA provides networking opportunities with a like-minded community. Full-time students can join ISACA at reduced rates. Those interested in IT auditing or IT careers in governance, risk management, control, and compliance might want to consider a membership in ISACA.

Many universities now offer specialized programs in information systems and audit. Degree-granting programs in information systems security are more common than in the past, as are business accounting programs with a focus on technology. ISACA provides "Model Curricula for IS Audit and Control" to foster information system auditing degrees through universities. It provides a framework for schools to map courses to topics that provide graduates with the skills and capabilities to enter the profession.

In addition to accredited programs, there are numerous professional certifications and associations. These associations provide continuing education and opportunities. Many of these will be covered later in this chapter, including details about certification programs.

One organization, the **Institute of Internal Auditors (IIA)**, provides a fellowship program for experienced auditors to develop their careers. This program encourages audit executives and leaders to send high-achieving auditors through a six-month rotational fellowship program. Participants use their knowledge and desire to support the IIA to conduct research, develop guidance, and create tools and services for the internal auditing profession.

Participants must meet the following requirements:

- At least five years of professional experience in internal auditing
- An active IIA membership or a professional certification
- A bachelor's or higher degree
- Two professional recommendations
- A personal letter of interest
- A minimum of two writing samples
- A completed application

A successful career in IT auditing requires knowledge and skills in both IT and auditing. Numerous certifications exist that focus on IT auditing. Certification exams provide goals for those entering the field, as well as proof of knowledge for experienced auditors. IT auditors should also have an understanding of business concepts. This includes financial and operational controls. Beyond IT and auditing skills, IT auditors require the following soft skills:

- **Analytical**—For analyzing procedural and technical controls, procedures, and processes
- **Communication**—For discussing and presenting audit scope, findings, and recommendations
- **Interviewing**—For gathering required documentation and evidence to conduct an audit
- **Negotiation**—For discussing with management the need to implement identified recommendations

- **Business writing**—For writing effective reports
- **Behavioral**—For dealing with all levels of personnel within an organization throughout the audit process
- **Project management**—For managing the audit process, which is essentially a project
- **Leadership**—For managing a team of IT auditors

In addition to technical, audit, and soft skills, other attributes are helpful. The profession demands that IT auditors appreciate learning and be intellectually curious. In addition, an IT auditor should be objective and highly ethical.

With changing regulations, business challenges, and technology that evolves at a rapid pace, the demand for IT auditors will likely continue. Organizations' increased attention on IT governance, compliance, and risk-management practices will provide many opportunities for the IT auditor.

For college graduates, a career in IT auditing presents a welcome opportunity. In fact, all of the Big Four audit firms have hiring programs for college graduates. These organizations are among the world's largest recruiters of college graduates! If you find you lean more to the technical side, many consulting and security assessment firms offer auditing positions. These positions tend to focus more on the technical aspects of controls and compliance.

Professional Ethics and Integrity of IT Auditors

Ethics are generally moral beliefs and rules about what is right and what is wrong. Professional ethics relate to any professional field, not just IT auditing. An individual within a professional role has special knowledge. This knowledge can be abused or used for morally unjust purposes. As a result, ethics helps guide the use of these skills and knowledge.

A **code of ethics** for IT auditors and organizations is important for outlining clear expectations. It also provides the grounds for complaints and possible follow-on disciplinary action. Expectations provide morally acceptable values and principles to help shape behaviors. A code of ethics isn't always enough, however. Consider Enron and the corresponding case study in Chapter 1. Both Enron and its accounting firm, Arthur Andersen, had detailed codes of ethics. Although having codified ethics is important, organizations need to promote ethical behavior as part of the work culture. Having dedicated ethics officers and conducting regular ethics training is a start.

> **WARNING**
>
> Enron is one example of an organization in which much ethical wrongdoing occurred. When scandals such as Enron are uncovered, the results include prison time, fines, and/or bankruptcy. They also negatively impact the lives of the victims affected by ethical and legal violations.

IT auditors need to practice strong ethical behavior and demonstrate integrity and objectivity. Nearly all organizations that provide IT auditing services have their own codes of conduct and ethical standards. Professional organizations for IT auditors, such as ISACA and the IIA, also have codes of ethics.

The IIA's "Professional Practices Framework," for example, includes a code of ethics, among other professional guidance. The IIA Code of Ethics has four principles:

- **Integrity**—Honesty and standing firm to moral obligations helps to establish trust. This is critical as organizations rely on auditors' professional judgment.

- **Objectivity**—Auditors need to make a fair assessment of activities and processes being examined, without being unjustifiably influenced by their own or others' interests.

- **Confidentiality**—Like therapists who are privy to the personal details of their clients, auditors are entrusted with access to valuable information about their client organizations. This information should not be disclosed without proper authority or other legal obligation.

- **Competency**—Auditors are successful in their duties by applying their knowledge, skills, and experience to their work.

The IIA Rules of Conduct provide further interpretive guidance of the principles to help guide ethical behavior.

The ISACA Code of Professional Ethics has the same intent as the IIA Code of Ethics, and shares similar concepts and terminology. ISACA's ethical code helps guide both the professional and personal conduct of its members as well as holders of ISACA credentials. ISACA certifications are discussed later in this chapter. The ISACA Code of Professional Ethics contains seven guiding principles. The ISACA published principles state that members and ISACA certification holders shall:[1]

- Support the implementation of, and encourage compliance with, appropriate standards, procedures and controls for information systems.

- Perform their duties with objectivity, due diligence and professional care, in accordance with professional standards and best practices.

- Serve in the interest of stakeholders in a lawful and honest manner, while maintaining high standards of conduct and character, and not engage in acts discreditable to the profession.

- Maintain the privacy and confidentiality of information obtained in the course of their duties unless disclosure is required by legal authority. Such information shall not be used for personal benefit or released to inappropriate parties.

- Maintain competency in their respective fields and agree to undertake only those activities which they can reasonably expect to complete with professional competence.

- Inform appropriate parties of the results of work performed; revealing all significant facts known to them.

- Support the professional education of stakeholders in enhancing their understanding of information systems security and control.

Source: COBIT 4.1. © 1996–2007 ITGI. All rights reserved. Used by permission.

Failure to comply with this Code of Professional Ethics can result in an investigation into a member's and/or certification holder's conduct and, ultimately, in disciplinary measures.

ISACA also publishes "Professional Ethics and Standards Document #S3" as part of its Information Technology Assurance Framework (ITAF). The S3 standard provides further rules regarding expected behavior. If, for example, adherence to professional ethics is "impaired or appears impaired," the auditor should consider withdrawing from the assignment. In addition, auditors and ISACA members should make sure the rest of their team adheres to the Code of Professional Ethics. This standard also references additional information system auditing guidelines from ISACA for further information on professional ethics and standards.

Codes of Conduct for Employees and IT Auditors

A **code of conduct** and a "code of ethics" are terms often used interchangeably. There are subtle differences, however.

The Sarbanes-Oxley Act defines in Section 406 a code of ethics as "such standards as are reasonably necessary to promote: 1) honest and ethical conduct, including the ethical handling of actual or apparent conflicts of interest between personal and professional relationships; 2) full, fair, accurate, timely and understandable disclosure in the periodic reports required to be filed by the issuer; and 3) compliance with applicable government rules and regulations." [2]

The International Federation of Accountants (IFAC) provides a working definition of a code of conduct in its *International Good Practice Guidance: Defining and Developing an Effective Code of Conduct for Organizations*. IFAC defines a code of conduct as "Principles, values, standards, or rules of behavior that guide the decisions, procedures, and systems of an organization in a way that: a) contributes to the welfare of its key stakeholders and b) respects the rights of all constituents affected by its operations." [3]

A code of conduct should be consistent with the code of ethics. The code of conduct is often part of the larger ethics and compliance program within an organization. A well-rounded code of conduct does the following:

- Clearly states the company's mission in the beginning
- Includes a statement from senior management early in the document
- Stresses the company's values and principles
- Provides guidelines on ethical and expected conduct including rules of conduct
- Provides examples of ethical and unethical behavior

IT auditors belonging to professional organizations or holding certifications are required to adhere to professional codes of ethics. Standards set forth by these organizations further guide the conduct of IT auditors. In addition, most organizations, including all of the major accounting and consulting firms, have employer-driven codes of conducts.

Employer/Organization Driven

Companies listed on public stock exchanges are, in many cases, required to adopt a code of conduct. Both the NASDAQ and the New York Stock Exchange (NYSE) require this. Specifically, they require that listed companies implement and make available to the public their code of conduct for all directors, officers, and employees.

Requirements aside, a code of conduct provides organizations with several benefits. First, it enhances the organization's values and beliefs, and it helps establish a strong culture based on the vision and mission of the organization. Next, a well-implemented code of conduct will build respect as well as enhance the organization's reputation. Finally, it will help guide the organization and its people away from unethical and illegal behavior.

> **NOTE**
>
> All employees, including auditors, are expected to comply with their organization's code of conduct. Auditors, however, are also responsible for verifying and testing their clients' codes of conduct.

An organizational code of conduct might be included in the employee handbook. Additionally, policy should establish that employees confirm they have read and will comply with the code of conduct. Organizations should reinforce the code occasionally. Many organizations accomplish this through annual verification as well as ongoing training.

For example, KPMG is one of the largest auditing firms in the world. The company's code of conduct states that it "sets forth our core values, shared responsibilities, global commitments and promises. Additionally, the Code provides you with general guidance about the firm's expectations, situations that may require particular attention, additional resources and channels of communication, as well as illustrative questions and answers."[4] The guide is a colorful, easy-to-read pamphlet available for download from *http://www.us.kpmg.com/microsite/attachments/kpmg-code-of-conduct.pdf*. The 2008 Code of Conduct includes the following key sections:

- **Letter from the Chairman**—Introduces the goal of KPMG to be regarded as the best Big Four public accounting firm. It further reiterates the strong corporate commitment to an ethics and compliance program to achieve that goal. The letter also introduces the company's "values-based" culture.

- **Our Code and Our Commitment**—Introduces the commitment to the Code by another senior executive. It also summarizes the importance of the Code, and to whom it applies.

- **Our Core Values**—Describes the "KPMG way," which defines the company's culture by identifying values that reflect who they are, what they do, and how they do it.

- **Our Shared Responsibilities**—Provides key policies and responsibilities for which individuals and management are held accountable. This section describes ethics and integrity as the foundation of business conduct.

- **Getting Help**—Sets the expectation that help should be sought if necessary and that unethical and illegal activity must be reported. It also reiterates the conduct, policies, and processes around providing an environment that fosters such expectations.
- **Our People**—Reiterates the importance and value of the people and the need to embrace diversity and treat each other with respect.
- **Our Firm**—Outlines expected behaviors for maintaining professional licenses and certifications, as well as protecting the organization's physical, electronic, and intellectual property assets.
- **Clients and the Marketplace**—Describes commitments and standards around behaving lawfully and ethically and delivering quality service. It also includes other important expectations of conduct including importance of maintaining independence and maintaining client confidentiality.
- **Public and Community**—Describes the corporate expectation that all employees behave as responsible corporate citizens and the importance of building strong communities with other organizations and charities.

Employee Handbook and Employment Policies

Many organizations also drive expected standards of conduct through corporate policies such as acceptable use policies. The organization may also include these expectations within an employee handbook. In many cases, an organization's code of conduct and acceptable use policies also apply to vendors or other organizations with which they do business. In fact, in describing the "KPMG Way" from the previous section, KPMG describes its core values as representative of "how our people relate to each other, what we expect of our clients and vendors, and what our clients, vendors, and the marketplace should expect of us."[5] This also means that IT auditors, who may spend a considerable amount of time at a client organization, not only must represent themselves consistently with their own code, but also must be aware of their client's expectations.

(ISC)² Code of Ethics

The **International Information Systems Security Certification Consortium (ISC)²** is a nonprofit organization that provides education and certification programs for IS professionals. It develops and maintains a **Common Body of Knowledge (CBK)** that consists of 10 information security domains or high-level topics. The certifications that (ISC)² offers are based on these 10 domains. The (ISC)² certifications are described as follows:

- The **Systems Security Certified Practitioner (SSCP)** is an ideal certification for security engineers, analysts, and administrators. It is also popular for those without primary duties as an IS professional but who would benefit from understanding security. This includes information system auditors, programmers, and database administrators.

▶**TIP**

Those without the years of experience required of (ISC)² certifications may obtain the Associate of (ISC)² status. This program is ideal for those switching careers and college students. This achievement requires candidates to pass the CISSP or SSCP certification and adhere to the (ISC)² Code of Ethics. This program provides various opportunities as benefits. For many, it provides an ideal opportunity to attract potential employers.

- The **Certification and Accreditation Professional (CAP)** is a certification for professionals involved in certifying and accrediting the security of information systems.
- The **Certified Secure Software Lifecycle Professional (CSSLP)** is a certification for those involved with ensuring security throughout the software life cycle.
- The **Certified Information Systems Security Professional (CISSP)** is arguably the most recognized information security certification. This certification is ideal for information security management professionals or those who develop policies and procedures for information security. The CISSP includes three concentrations in architecture, engineering, and management.

A goal of (ISC)² is to protect the integrity and value of these certifications as well as the professionalism of the information security industry. As a result, the organization requires credential holders and candidates to adhere to the (ISC)² Code of Ethics. There are four mandatory principles, or Code of Ethics Canons:[6]

- Protect society, the commonwealth, and the infrastructure.
- Act honorably, honestly, justly, responsibly, and legally.
- Provide diligent and competent service to principals.
- Advance and protect the profession.

▶**NOTE**

Fear, uncertainty, and doubt, or **FUD**, is a common expression within IT circles. FUD is a tactic often seen in politics, sales, and marketing. People use FUD to encourage unfavorable opinions and speculation about a particular topic, often for self-serving interests.

The four principles of ethical behavior come with additional guidelines to help resolve good versus bad situations. The goal is to encourage correct behavior through research, teaching, advancing the profession, and valuing the certifications. The guidelines also discourage certain behaviors. For example, they discourage associating or appearing to associate with criminals or criminal behavior. They also discourage attaching vulnerable systems to the public network, providing unwarranted reassurance, and promoting unnecessary fear, uncertainty, and doubt.

The guiding principles for each requirement are listed on the (ISC)² Web site at *http://www.isc2.org/ethics/default.aspx*. The Code of Ethics states that complying with these guiding principles is not required, nor does compliance ensure ethical conduct. (ISC)² provides the principles to help members resolve ethical dilemmas they may face during the course of their careers. The (ISC)² board of directors, however, may use the principles to judge the behavior of members.

To protect the reputation of the profession, (ISC)² provides a procedure for ethics complaints. (ISC)² will only consider complaints directly related to one of the four principles. The board of directors established the Ethics Committee to oversee the process and provide recommendations to the board.

(ISC)² also participates in the **Ethics Working Group**. The purpose of this group is twofold. First, it defines information security as a recognized profession within IT. Second, it establishes a generally accepted framework of ethical behavior. The Ethics Working Group notes that professions have common characteristics. Having a code of ethics with appropriate oversight is one such characteristic. Others include a common body of knowledge, a governing body, and a certification authority within the profession.

> **NOTE**
>
> Other participants in the Ethics Working Group include the International Information Systems Security Association (ISSA) and the Global Information Assurance Certification (GIAC). GAIC is covered later in this chapter.

(ISC)², along with other member organizations, reviewed their respective codes of ethics with the goal of unifying them through the Ethics Working Group. Each organization found many commonalities and consistencies among the various codes. As a result, the group completed the Unified Framework of Professional Ethics for Security Professionals. This framework is in draft and currently available for review. This framework is organized by four high-level goals, with accompanying details. A summary of the framework includes:

- **Integrity**—Act in compliance with laws and apply the highest moral principles.
- **Objectivity**—Act fairly and without prejudice.
- **Professional competence and due care**—Act with professionalism and perform duties diligently.
- **Confidentiality**—Act with respect, protect confidential information, and use **due care** to prevent inappropriate disclosure.

Certification and Accreditation for IT Auditing

Auditors have an important duty to evaluate organizational controls. These controls impact the confidentiality, integrity, and availability of IT assets and information. As a result, it is vital that IT auditing professionals understand both technology and accounting concepts. In many cases, it's not just desirable but necessary for IT auditing professionals to demonstrate certain levels of competence. If you choose to become certified, you will demonstrate your willingness to improve your knowledge and skills. This provides career benefits as well. It proves your expertise in specific areas to your organization, prospective employer, and clients.

Certification programs are available that focus solely on IT. Certification programs are also available that focus on auditing. Additionally, certifications exist that blend the two. Such certifications are more aligned to information system auditing and assurance.

> **NOTE**
>
> Certification is not the same as licensure. Licensure gives permission to practice within a specific field. Licensure is required for fields that involve a high level of specialization, and which may pose a danger to the individual or the public. Both, however, indicate that an individual has demonstrated a certain level of knowledge or ability. Consider that a license is required to drive a vehicle. Common professions that require licensure include medical practitioners and aviation pilots.

Professional certifications have been around for a long time across many different fields. In the IT field, the number of certifications has skyrocketed over the past decade. This is due, in part, to the many vendor certification programs that are oriented toward specific technologies. These programs are managed by the corresponding vendors, and the programs benefit the vendors from a marketing aspect.

There are also many nonvendor, also called vendor-neutral, certifications. The **Computing Technology Industry Association (CompTIA)** provides one of the oldest nonvendor IT-related certification programs. CompTIA is a nonprofit organization that provides vendor-neutral certification exams. In addition, the organization provides educational programs and market research, and has been involved in activities to advance the IT profession. CompTIA's beginnings go back to 1982. It introduced its first exam, the A+ certification, in 1993. CompTIA was truly a pioneer in the IT security industry. CompTIA certifications include the following:

- **A+**—Recommended for entry-level technicians. Covers basic operating systems and computer installation, troubleshooting, and communication.
- **Network+**—Recommended for those with at least nine months of networking experience. Covers managing and maintaining basic network infrastructure.
- **Security+**—Recommended for those with at least two years of IT networking experience, with an emphasis on security. Covers computer and network security, cryptography, and assessments and audits.
- **Server+**—Recommended for those who have already achieved the A+ certification. Covers the more advanced computing concepts related to servers.
- **Linux+**—Recommended for those who have already achieved the A+ and Network+ certification, or those who have equivalent knowledge. Covers the management of Linux operating systems.
- **PDI+**—Recommended for entry-level technicians. Covers printer and document imaging technology.
- **RFID+**—Recommended for those with 6 to 24 months of related experience. Covers the installation and maintenance of radio frequency identification (RFID) solutions.
- **Convergence+**—Recommended for those with 18 to 24 months of experience with voice and/or data networking technologies. Covers the design, implementation, and management of voice and data networks.
- **CTT+**—Recommended for technical instructors. Covers presentation and communications skills for both traditional classes and virtual class environments.
- **CDIA+**—Recommended for those who sell document imaging solutions. Covers planning and designing of document imaging management systems.
- **Project+**—Recommended for those with at least one year of managing or participating in small to medium-size projects. Covers the process of project management.

Those interested in IT auditing and assessment may find the **Project+** and the **Security+** certifications especially beneficial. Unlike some of the more advanced certifications discussed in the next section, these certifications are a great starting point. The other certifications that CompTIA offers can also benefit auditing and assessment professionals required to prove knowledge in more specialized areas.

Many certification programs are increasingly seeking **American National Standards Institute (ANSI)** accreditation. ANSI accreditation is based on ISO/IEC international standards to ensure certification programs are of high quality. ANSI accreditation helps maintain the value of certification programs as ANSI accreditation is recognized as a stamp of approval for a quality certification program.

> **NOTE**
>
> In 2007, ANSI accredited the CompTIA A+, Network+, and Security+ certifications.

The following sections discuss three well-known and respected organizations that offer programs that require a candidate to sufficiently demonstrate competences in the auditing of information systems. The complete list of professional certifications is beyond the scope of this chapter.

IIA

Established in 1941, long before the Internet, when most processes were performed manually, the Institute of Internal Auditors (IIA) is an international professional association for auditors. The IIA's mission is to "provide dynamic leadership for the global profession of internal auditing." To achieve this mission, the IIA supports many activities that promote the value of the internal audit function. Activities include a wide range of educational and developmental opportunities. The IIA is well known for its published standards and guidance provided to internal auditors.

The IIA provides guidance through the **International Professional Practices Framework (IPPF)**. The IPPF includes mandatory and strongly recommended guidance. Mandatory guidance includes the definition of internal auditing, the code of ethics discussed earlier, and various standards. Standards provide the framework for performing internal auditing functions. They include the basic requirements of internal auditing including further explanations to clarify terms and concepts.

The IIA's recommended guidance includes position papers, practice advisories, and practice guides. The position papers include general topics on governance, risk, and control.

▶ **NOTE**

For many years, the IIA provided a Web site and publication named *ITAudit*. The publication is now called *Internal Auditor* magazine. The Web site is located at *http://www.theiia.org/intauditor/*. It includes archived issues of ITAudit dating back to 1998.

They also include explanations of the different roles and responsibilities within the auditing community. The practice advisories assist auditors in applying the standards specific to approaches and methodologies. Finally, the practice guides provide details for internal audit activities. Pertaining to the IT auditor, the IIA provides a series of audit guides specific to IT called **Global Technology Audit Guide (GTAG)**. These guides provide audit-related guidance pertaining to technology management, control, and security. A related series of guides deals with specific areas related to IT risk and control and is called **Guide to the Assessment of IT Risk (GAIT)**.

In addition, the IIA provides audit-related certifications. These include the following:

* Certified Internal Auditor (CIA)
* Certification in Control Self-Assessment (CCSA)
* Certified Government Auditing Professional (CGAP)
* Certified Financial Services Auditor (CFSA)

Certified Internal Auditor (CIA) Certification

The **Certified Internal Auditor (CIA)** certification, according to the IIA, is "the only globally accepted certification for internal auditors and remains the standard by which individuals demonstrate their competency and professionalism in the internal auditing field."[7] The CIA exam covers internal auditing practices and issues, as well as risks and solutions. The CIA certification is made up of four parts. The first three parts are modeled on the IPPF. A candidate may receive credit for the fourth part if he or she has obtained another related specialty certification. This includes one of the other three IIA certifications or a number of other non-IIA certifications. The Certified Public Accountant (CPA) designation from the American Institute of Certified Public Accountants (AICPA) qualifies, for example. Another example is the Certified Information Systems Auditor (CISA) certification from ISACA, which is explored further in the next section.

The four parts of the CIA exam process include:

* **Part 1**—The Internal Audit Activity's Role in Governance, Risk, and Control
* **Part 2**—Conducting the Internal Audit Engagement
* **Part 3**—Business Analysis and Information Technology
* **Part 4**—Business Management Skills

To become certified, candidates must meet the following requirements:

* **Exam requirements**—Candidates must complete the exam with a passing score.
* **Educational requirements**—Candidates must have a bachelor's degree or higher from an accredited school or an educational equivalent.

- **Experience requirements**—Candidates must have a minimum of 24 months of experience with internal auditing.
- **Professional conduct requirements**—Candidates must abide by the IIA Code of Ethics. They must also provide a completed IIA Character Reference Form.

The IIA makes exceptions for experience and educational requirements for certain equivalents. In both cases, proper documentation is required.

Like the CIA certification, the following three specialty certifications offered by the IIA also require a bachelor's degree or higher, adherence to the IIA Code of Conduct, and a completed Character Reference Form.

Certification in Control Self-Assessment (CCSA)

The **Certification in Control Self-Assessment (CCSA)** certification is for practitioners of **control self-assessments (CSAs)**. A CSA provides a method for those internal to an organization to assess risks and controls on their own. Internal auditors are often involved from a more consultative standpoint and can use the CSA program for focusing audit work on more high-risk areas. Candidates for the CCSA exam must obtain one year of control-related business experience, which could be experience with CSA, auditing, or risk management. The CSA exam covers the following six domains:

- CSA Fundamentals
- CSA Program Integration
- Elements of the CSA Process
- Business Objectives/Organizational Performance
- Risk Identification and Assessment
- Control Theory and Application

Certified Government Auditing Professional (CGAP) Certification

The **Certified Government Auditing Professional (CGAP)** certification is for public sector internal auditors. This exam tests areas of audit knowledge unique to the public sector. This includes grants and legislative oversight. Candidates must obtain two years of auditing experience in a government environment. This can include federal, state, or local government. The CGAP exam covers the following four domains:

- Standards, Governance, and Risk/Control Frameworks
- Government Auditing Practice
- Government Auditing Skills and Techniques
- Government Auditing Environment

Certified Financial Services Auditor (CFSA) Certification

The **Certified Financial Services Auditor (CFSA)** exam tests candidate's audit knowledge and abilities with regard to financial services. Candidates must obtain two years of auditing experience in a financial services environment. The exam covers the following four domains:

- Financial Services Auditing
- Auditing Financial Services Products
- Auditing Financial Services Processes
- The Regulatory Environment

In addition to testing on these four domains, the candidate must choose from one of three financial service areas. These include banking, insurance, or securities. The exam includes additional questions specific to the chosen discipline covering the relevant products, processes, and regulatory environments.

ISACA

ISACA, first introduced in Chapter 4, is a professional association that provides many resources for information systems auditors and IT security and governance professionals. ISACA publishes technical journals, standards, guidelines, and procedures. The organization also promotes research and provides education programs as well as several professional certifications. ISACA is widely recognized as a result of its popular CISA exam.

ISACA publishes several best-practice framework guidelines, which were covered in Chapter 4. These include COBIT, ITAF, Risk IT, and Val IT. In addition, ISACA provides several other educational opportunities and professional resources:

- **Standards**—For IT audit as well as information systems control professionals. The standards provide mandatory requirements for IT audit.

- **Research**—Includes research papers to promote the development of timely topics relevant to IT governance, control, assurance, and security professionals.

- **Publications**—Include the ISACA Journal, a bimonthly publication for audit, control, security, and IT governance professionals. Additionally, ISACA offers a bookstore containing professional development and reference material. This also includes an online library, which provides Web access to a wide collection of books.

- **Chapter membership**—Includes membership in local chapters around the world that sponsor local education events and seminars and conduct regular meetings.

- **Training and conferences**—Include various conferences that appeal to those new to the field as well as experienced professionals. Additionally, ISACA provides different training opportunities such as certification review courses, onsite training, and online courses.

- **Certifications**—Include a handful of certifications for information governance, risk, security, and auditing.

Each ISACA certification requires experience, ethics, education, and an exam. The candidate must pass an administered exam, adhere to the Code of Professional Ethics, and prove relevant experience. Upon certification, the candidate must also adhere to the continuing professional education program. The continuing education program ensures that certification holders maintain competency of knowledge and skills within the certified area. Each exam is based on a "job practice." The job practice provides the basis for the experience requirements and is the basis of the exam. The job practice is organized by a series of statements that test both knowledge and skills. These are known as task and knowledge statements, which are grouped together and make up parts of the exam, known as domains.

> **NOTE**
> ISACA offers its certification exams only twice a year. The exams are available in various cities around the world.

> **NOTE**
> Of the ISACA certifications, only the CISA is specifically focused on the IT auditing profession. This does not mean that an IT auditor would not be eligible or benefit from the other certifications. In fact, all the exams cover areas that are relevant to IT auditors.

Certified Information Systems Auditor (CISA) Certification

The **Certified Information Systems Auditor (CISA)** program is well accepted and mature; it's been available since 1978. This certification program is arguably the benchmark for an information systems audit certification for audit, control, and security professionals. In fact, ISACA lists several facts recognizing the significance and importance of the CISA certification. Examples include the following:

- In 2009, CISA won the Best Professional Certification Program from *SC Magazine*. Finalists also included ISACA's CISM program and the (ISC)² CISSP.
- The National Stock Exchange of India requires CISA certification to conduct system audits.
- CISA is an approved certification for the U.S. Department of Defense Information Assurance Workforce Improvement Program.
- Payment Card Industry Data Security Standard (PCI DSS) accepts CISA as a validation requirement for qualified security assessors.
- The U.S. Federal Reserve Bank requires all assistant examiners to pass the CISA exam before they can be eligible for commissioning.

To qualify, a candidate needs at least five years of professional information systems auditing or security work experience. ISACA provides a list of available substitutions. Candidates may substitute a maximum of one year of information systems experience. Certification holders are also required to adhere to the ISACA information systems auditing standards. The CISA covers the following domains:

- **Information Systems Audit Process**—Provides assurance that IT and associated data is protected and controlled. Specifically, this includes making sure that system audit services are within audit standards, guidelines, and best practices.

- **IT Governance**—Provides assurance that a governing program is in place. This includes the structure, policies, processes, and monitoring to achieve effective governance.
- **Systems and Infrastructure Life Cycle Management**—Provides assurance that practices from systems development and acquisition to disposal are adequately in place.
    - **IT Service Delivery and Support**—Provides assurance that practices are in place to deliver adequate service levels in line with the business objectives.

> **NOTE**
>
> As of 2010, over 70,000 professionals have earned the CISA designation. ANSI accredits both CISA and CISM.

- **Protection of Information Assets**—Provides assurance that a security policy framework is in place. This also includes assurance that appropriate controls are in place to protect the confidentiality, integrity, and availability of information systems and data.
- **Business Continuity and Disaster Recovery**—Provides assurance that the business continues in spite of disruptions.

Certified Information Security Manager (CISM) Certification

The **Certified Information Security Manager (CISM)** certification is designed for information security managers. Candidates also need to prove a minimum of five years of information security experience, which must include three years of experience in three or more of the focus areas or domains. This exam also allows for substitutions. For example, two years may be substituted for a CISA, a CISSP, or a postgraduate degree in information security. The CISM covers the following domains:

- Information Security Governance
- Information Risk Management
- Information Security Program Development
- Information Security Program Management
- Incident Management & Response

Certified in Risk and Information Systems Control (CRISC) Certification

Certified in Risk and Information Systems and Control (CRISC) is a broad certification program, appealing mostly to IT professionals. CRISC tests for knowledge of enterprise risk as well as the life cycle of information systems controls to mitigate risk. Candidates also need to prove at least five years of IT or business experience and at least three years of experience in one or more of the CRISC focus areas, which include:

- Risk identification, assessment, and evaluation
- Risk response
- Risk monitoring
- Information systems control design and implementation
- Information systems control monitoring and maintenance

Certified in the Governance of Enterprise IT (CGEIT) Certification

The **Certified in the Governance of Enterprise IT (CGEIT)** certification is targeted to IT governance professionals. This includes those involved in the leadership and processes to help make sure that the IT organization is aligned with an organization's strategies. Candidates need to prove at least five years experience in a governance support role of an organization's IT. The CGEIT covers the following domains:

- Information Technology Governance Framework
- Strategic Alignment
- Value Delivery
- Risk Management

In addition to ISACA, the SANS Institute in conjunction with Global Information Assurance Certification offers IT audit certifications as well as many security-related certifications.

SANS Institute

The **SANS Institute** was founded in 1989 and is a popular source for information security knowledge, training, and certification. Unlike the other organizations, SANS is a for-profit institute and is owned by The Escal Institute of Advanced Technologies.

SANS offers training and certification programs to a wide range of IT professionals. The training spans different groups such as audit, network, and security as well as positions from system administrators to chief information security officers (CISOs). In addition, SANS also provides a variety of free resources, including a large collection of research documents within their online Reading Room. The Reading Room features computer security technical papers in dozens of categories.

SANS offers a wide selection of training programs and a variety of delivery methods. These include:

- **Classroom training events**—These are offered many times throughout the year across major cities globally. These SANS events are similar to professional conferences in that they also offer networking opportunities, vendor product information, and guest speakers.
- **SANS WhatWorks Summit**—These unique two-day events provide information on current topics in computer security.
- **Community training events**—Similar to the classroom training events, the community events provide the same content but in small classroom settings within local communities.
- **Mentor sessions**—Mentor sessions provide a multiweek program to learn from an assigned mentor the same material offered in the classroom training and community training events.

15

Ethics, Education, and Certification

- **Onsite training**—Training can be provided at your workplace. This is ideal for organizations that would like to train a large number of personnel.
- **Partnership series**—This series provides discounted training to specific groups where classes will be more than 125 people. These groups include, for example, those whose work impacts national security or groups that have budget constraints.
- **SANS vLive!**—This program provides live instructor-led training over the Web.
- **SANS OnDemand**—This program provides training similar to SANS vLive over the Web, but not in a live environment. Rather, it includes on-demand integrated courseware.
- **Self study**—Similar to SANS OnDemand, self study is more focused on certification study. This program provides the learner with printed course books, CDs, and practice questions.

In 1999, SANS established the **Global Information Assurance Certification (GIAC)**. GIAC operates as a separate entity, although like SANS, it is a trademark name of The Escal Institute of Advanced Technologies. GIAC provides many different vendor-neutral information security certifications. These certifications are grouped within four different tracks. These tracks include:

- IT audit
- Security administration
- Security management
- Software security

GIAC Certifications

GIAC certifications include those listed in Table 15-1. After attaining one of these certifications, the certification holder can achieve Gold certification or Expert Level certification by demonstrating a deeper level of knowledge. The GIAC Gold program requires the candidate to work with an assigned advisor while writing a detailed technical report. These papers are subsequently published by SANS into the Reading Room. The GIAC Expert Level certification program involves a multiday experience in which the candidate must demonstrate individual- and group-based exercises. This includes, for example, presentations, research, essays, and hands-on testing exams.

 NOTE

There was another audit-related GIAC certification named GIAC Security Audit Essentials (GSAE). This exam has been retired and is no longer available.

Of the many different exams, GIAC provides two exams focused on IT auditing. These include the G7799 and the GSNA. All of the GIAC certifications are tied to specific SANS training courses. SANS training, however, is not required. Experienced candidates have the option to instead purchase a GIAC Exam Challenge. This includes access to two practice tests and the certification exam.

TABLE 15-1 GIAC certification programs.

CERTIFICATION	DESIGNATION	TRACK	LEVEL
GIAC Certified ISO-17799 Specialist	G7799	Audit	Intermediate
GIAC Systems and Network Auditor	GSNA	Audit	Advanced
GIAC Secure Software Programmer—.NET	GSSP-NET	Software Security	Advanced
GIAC Secure Software Programmer—Java	GSSP-JAVA	Software Security	Advanced
GIAC Legal Issues	GLEG	Legal	Advanced
GIAC Information Security Professional	GISP	Management	Intermediate
GIAC Security Leadership Certification	GSLC	Management	Advanced
GIAC Certified Manager Certification	GCPM	Management	Advanced
GIAC Information Security Fundamentals	GISF	Security Administration	Introductory
GIAC Security Essentials Certification	GSEC	Security Administration	Intermediate
GIAC Certified Forensic Analyst	GCFA	Security Administration	Advanced
GIAC Certified Firewall Analyst	GCFW	Security Administration	Advanced
GIAC Certified Incident Handler	GCIH	Security Administration	Advanced
GIAC Certified UNIX Security Administrator	GCUX	Security Administration	Advanced
GIAC Certified Windows Security Administrator	GCWN	Security Administration	Advanced
GIAC Certified Enterprise Defender	GCED	Security Administration	Advanced
GIAC Certified Penetration Tester	GPEN	Security Administration	Advanced
GIAC Web Application Penetration Tester	GWAPT	Security Administration	Advanced
GIAC Assessing Wireless Networks	GAWN	Security Administration	Highly Advanced
GIAC Reverse Engineering Malware	GREM	Security Administration	Highly Advanced

GIAC Systems and Network Auditor (GSNA) Certification

The **GIAC Systems and Network Auditor (GSNA)** certification assesses the candidate's understanding of more than three dozen exam certification objectives. The following is an abridged list of these objectives and expectations:

- Understand basic auditing terms as well as strategies for baseline security controls.
- Understand defense in depth as it applies to critical systems and methods to audit them.
- Demonstrate the ability to identify perimeter systems and firewall architecture as well as the ability to plan and manage a perimeter audit.
- Understand how a risk assessment is used to identify necessary controls.
- Describe the auditing process from planning to the final report to management.
- Understand the concepts of auditing databases and understanding SQL basics.
- Understand router configurations and access controls lists as well as demonstrate an understanding of secure switch architecture.
- Demonstrate basic operating system knowledge of UNIX and Windows systems, including audit, logging, and security fundamentals.
- Understand the tools and methodologies for conducting a vulnerability assessment.
- Understand how to identify and audit wireless devices and modems.
- Understand various aspects of Web technology, including Web applications and Web vulnerabilities and security.

> **TIP**
>
> Both the CISA and the GSNA demonstrate competencies in regard to both IT and auditing. The CISA, however, tends to be more audit focused, while the GSNA is more technically focused.

GIAC Certified ISO-17799 Specialist (G7799) Certification

The **GIAC Certified ISO-17799 Specialist (G7799)** certification is named after ISO/IEC 17799, which has been renamed to ISO/IEC 27002. This exam tests the candidate on the ISO/IEC 27001 and 27002 frameworks and is designed for management professionals. The candidate is tested on his or her understanding of the ISO/IEC 27002 framework and his or her ability to put the framework into practice. G17799 covers the sections with the ISO/IEC standard as well as the following:

- **ISO 27001/27002 background**—Understanding ISO 27000 series standards and the purpose of audit controls and the security management program
- **Policy writing**—Understanding common security principles involved in creating policies
- **Process improvement and site security**—Familiarity with implementing a continual process improvement program
- **Risk analysis techniques and methods**—Understanding of terminology, process, and tools associated with risk analysis
- **Specifying controls**—Understanding the role of security and audit controls
- **Twelve steps**—Understanding the steps for scoping, implementing, and maintaining a security system as specified in ISO 27001

SANS continued its growth in 2008 with the introduction of the **SANS Technology Institute**. The institute provides graduate-level educational programs, which grant master's degrees in information security. The SANS Technology Institute has been authorized by the Maryland Higher Education Commission to grant such a degree. As of 2010, it has not been granted regional accreditation, but is a candidate for accreditation.

Admission into the institute requires successful completion of undergraduate work as well as additional requirements related to information security. This includes professional experience in the field; in addition, candidates must hold a major GIAC Gold Certification.

CHAPTER SUMMARY

The IT audit profession continues to grow, and is supported by several professional organizations. IT auditors need to strongly adhere to ethical codes and be in constant pursuit of continued education. There are numerous educational opportunities for those just entering the profession or those looking for growth. Organizations such as the IIA and ISACA provide a tremendous amount of resources for the profession. Practitioners within audit, IT, or a combination of both should strongly consider membership and take advantage of the educational and certification opportunities.

KEY CONCEPTS AND TERMS

American National Standards Institute (ANSI)

Certification and Accreditation Professional (CAP)

Certification in Control Self-Assessment (CCSA)

Certified Financial Services Auditor (CFSA)

Certified Government Auditing Professional (CGAP)

Certified in Risk and Information Systems and Control (CRISC)

Certified in the Governance of Enterprise IT (CGEIT)

Certified Information Security Manager (CISM)

Certified Information Systems Auditor (CISA)

Certified Information Systems Security Professional (CISSP)

Certified Internal Auditor (CIA)

Certified public accountants (CPAs)

Certified Secure Software Lifecycle Professional (CSSLP)

Code of conduct

Code of ethics

Common Body of Knowledge (CBK)

Computing Technology Industry Association (CompTIA)

Continuing education units (CEUs)

Control self-assessments (CSAs)

Due care

Ethics

Ethics Working Group

FUD

GIAC Certified ISO-17799 Specialist (G7799).

GIAC Systems and Network Auditor (GSNA)

Global Information Assurance Certification (GIAC)

Global Technology Audit Guide (GTAG)

Guide to the Assessment of IT Risk (GAIT)

Institute of Internal Auditors (IIA)

International Information Systems Security Certification Consortium (ISC)[2]

International Professional Practices Framework (IPPF)

Project+

SANS Institute

SANS Technology Institute

Security+

Systems Security Certified Practitioner (SSCP)

CHAPTER 15 ASSESSMENT

1. Which of the following is *not* considered a soft skill needed by IT auditors?

A. Penetration testing skills
B. Negotiation skills
C. Business writing skills
D. Behavior skills
E. Communication skills
F. Leadership skills

2. A _____ of ethics for IT auditors is important for outlining clear ethical expectations.

3. The Sarbanes-Oxley Act does *not* attempt to define a code of ethics, but rather it references the code of ethics established by the IIA.

A. True
B. False

4. According to IFAC, the rules of behavior that guide the decisions of an organization should do which of the following? (Select the two best answers.)

A. Contribute to the personal fortunes of IT vendors.
B. Contribute to the welfare of key stakeholders.
C. Respect the rights of all constituents affected by the organization's operations.
D. Consider what is best for the organization's stock price.
E. Respect that each individual has a different moral code.

5. A thorough code of conduct would include which of the following?

A. The company mission
B. The company's values
C. Examples of ethical and unethical behavior
D. All of the above

6. The NYSE requires that companies listed on its exchange publicly make available a code of conduct.

A. True
B. False

7. An individual holding which of the following certifications should be familiar with the (ISC)² code of ethics?

A. SSCP
B. CISA
C. CISSP
D. Answers A and C
E. None of the above

8. Which of the following is *not* a mandatory principle or canon of the (ISC)² Code of Ethics?

A. Protect society, the commonwealth, and the infrastructure.
B. Act honorably, honestly, justly, responsibly, and legally.
C. Provide diligent and competent service to principals.
D. Advance and protect the profession.
E. Serve justly, competently, and with pretense.

9. Certification and licensure are essentially the same thing.

A. True
B. False

10. Which of the following organizations provides IT-related professional certifications?

A. CompTIA
B. ISACA
C. ANSI
D. All of the above
E. Answers A and B only

11. Which of the following is *not* professional guidance provided by the IIA?

A. COBIT
B. GAIT
C. GTAG
D. IPPF

12. A candidate for the Certified Internal Auditor certification must first achieve the Certified Information Systems Auditor certification.

A. True
B. False

15

Ethics, Education, and Certification

13. To become an ISACA Certified Information Systems Auditor, which of the following are required?

A. Successfully pass an examination
B. Adhere to an ethical code
C. Experience
D. All of the above

14. The SANS Institute is a nonprofit organization that provides free certification exams across four different information security tracks.

A. True
B. False

15. Which of the following is a GIAC certification that would most likely appeal to an IT auditor?

A. GSNA
B. GLEG
C. GCFA
D. CISSP
E. CISA

ENDNOTES

1. "Code of Professional Ethics" (ISACA, 2010). *http://www.isaca.org/Content/ContentGroups/ Standards2/Code_of_Ethics2/ISACA_Code_of _Professional_Ethics.htm* (accessed April 3, 2010).

2. Pub. L. 107-204, title IV, Sec. 406, July 30, 2002, 116 Stat. 789. *http://uscode.house.gov/ download/pls/15C98.txt* (accessed April 7, 2010).

3. "International Good Practice Guidance: Defining and Developing an Effective Code of Conduct for Organizations" (International Federation of Accounts, June 2007). *http://web.ifac.org/publica- tions/professional-accountants-in-business-committee/ international-good-practice#evaluating-and-improving-co* (accessed April 3, 2010).

4. "KPMG's Code of Conduct—Our Promise of Professionalism" (KPMG, July 9, 2008). *http://www.us.kpmg.com/microsite/attachments/ kpmg-code-of-conduct.pdf* (accessed April 8, 2010).

5. Ibid.

6. "(ISC)² Code of Ethics" ((ISC)2, 2010). *http://www.isc2.org/ethics/default.aspx* (accessed April 3, 2010).

7. "Certified Internal Auditor (CIA)" (The Institute of Internal Auditors, 2010). *http://www.theiia.org/certification/certified-internal -auditor/* (accessed April 8, 2010).

Answer Key

CHAPTER 1 The Need for Information Systems Security Compliance

1. B   2. Risk-based approach   3. A   4. A guide for assessing security controls   5. D   6. B   7. Independent   8. C   9. A   10. D
11. E   12. E   13. D   14. E   15. Strict liability

CHAPTER 2 Overview of U.S. Compliance Laws

1. A   2. C   3. Accreditation   4. A   5. B   6. B   7. C   8. E
9. D   10. A   11. B   12. C   13. B   14. B   15. F

CHAPTER 3 What Is the Scope of an IT Infrastructure Audit for Compliance?

1. Gap   2. C   3. A   4. A   5. B   6. C   7. E   8. B   9. D
10. Framework   11. D   12. A, B, and C   13. A, B, and E   14. Identity

CHAPTER 4 Auditing Standards and Frameworks

1. Framework   2. A   3. B   4. A, B, and C   5. A   6. B   7. Goal
8. B   9. B   10. B   11. B   12. Practice   13. D   14. C   15. B

CHAPTER 5 Planning an IT Infrastructure Audit for Compliance

1. E   2. C   3. B   4. Threat   5. C   6. A   7. D   8. Scope
9. A   10. A   11. E   12. B   13. A   14. C   15. D

CHAPTER 6 Conducting an IT Infrastructure Audit for Compliance

1. A   2. C   3. B   4. B   5. Penetration test   6. A   7. A
8. Computer assisted audit tools and techniques   9. D   10. A
11. Management   12. A   13. A   14. A   15. C

CHAPTER 7 Writing the IT Infrastructure Audit Report

1. A   2. B   3. B   4. B   5. Nonexistent   6. Threat likelihood ×
Impact level = Risk   7. A   8. C   9. A   10. A

CHAPTER 8 Compliance Within the User Domain

1. B   2. Business drivers   3. C   4. A   5. Need to know   6. B
7. D   8. B   9. C   10. A   11. C   12. B   13. C   14. B   15. A

CHAPTER 9 Compliance Within the Workstation Domain

1. Due diligence   2. B   3. B and C   4. War dialing   5. A   6. B
7. C   8. C   9. Type II   10. A   11. Integrity   12. A and D
13. Worm

CHAPTER 10 Compliance Within the LAN Domain

1. B   2. B   3. B   4. Fiber optic   5. A   6. A   7. C   8. B
9. Network monitoring platform, or NMP   10. C   11. A   12. Availability
13. B and C   14. B   15. C

CHAPTER 11 Compliance Within the LAN-to-WAN Domain

1. A   2. A   3. Proxy server   4. Demilitarized zone (DMZ)   5. B
6. Single point of failure   7. B and C   8. C   9. A   10. C
11. Virtual private network (VPN)   12. B   13. A   14. Multi-Protocol
Label Switching (MPLS)   15. A

CHAPTER 12 Compliance Within the WAN Domain

1. B   2. A   3. B   4. C   5. A   6. Service level agreement (SLA)
7. A   8. C   9. WAN optimizer   10. B   11. B   12. B   13. A
14. Virtual private network, or VPN   15. D

CHAPTER 13 Compliance Within the Remote Access Domain

1. B   2. C   3. Encryption   4. B   5. A   6. D   7. A
8. Tunneling   9. B   10. B   11. SNMP   12. A   13. D
14. B   15. B

CHAPTER 14 Compliance Within the System/Application Domain

1. B   2. B   3. A   4. Subnet   5. C   6. People   7. B   8. C
9. C   10. B   11. Web server   12. A   13. A and C   14. B

CHAPTER 15 Ethics, Education, and Certification for IT Auditors

1. A   2. Code   3. B   4. B and C   5. D   6. A   7. D   8. E
9. B   10. E   11. A   12. A   13. D   14. B   15. A

Standard Acronyms

3DES	triple data encryption standard	**DMZ**	demilitarized zone
ACD	automatic call distributor	**DoS**	denial of service
AES	Advanced Encryption Standard	**DPI**	deep packet inspection
ANSI	American National Standards Institute	**DRP**	disaster recovery plan
AP	access point	**DSL**	digital subscriber line
API	application programming interface	**DSS**	Digital Signature Standard
B2B	business to business	**DSU**	data service unit
B2C	business to consumer	**EDI**	Electronic Data Interchange
BBB	Better Business Bureau	**EIDE**	Enhanced IDE
BCP	business continuity planning	**FACTA**	Fair and Accurate Credit Transactions Act
C2C	consumer to consumer	**FAR**	false acceptance rate
CA	certificate authority	**FBI**	Federal Bureau of Investigation
CAP	Certification and Accreditation Professional	**FDIC**	Federal Deposit Insurance Corporation
CAUCE	Coalition Against Unsolicited Commercial Email	**FEP**	front-end processor
		FRCP	Federal Rules of Civil Procedure
CCC	CERT Coordination Center	**FRR**	false rejection rate
CCNA	Cisco Certified Network Associate	**FTC**	Federal Trade Commission
CERT	Computer Emergency Response Team	**FTP**	file transfer protocol
CFE	Certified Fraud Examiner	**GIAC**	Global Information Assurance Certification
CISA	Certified Information Systems Auditor	**GLBA**	Gramm-Leach-Bliley Act
CISM	Certified Information Security Manager	**HIDS**	host-based intrusion detection system
CISSP	Certified Information System Security Professional	**HIPAA**	Health Insurance Portability and Accountability Act
CMIP	common management information protocol	**HIPS**	host-based intrusion prevention system
COPPA	Children's Online Privacy Protection	**HTTP**	hypertext transfer protocol
CRC	cyclic redundancy check	**HTTPS**	HTTP over Secure Socket Layer
CSI	Computer Security Institute	**HTML**	hypertext markup language
CTI	Computer Telephony Integration	**IAB**	Internet Activities Board
DBMS	database management system	**IDEA**	International Data Encryption Algorithm
DDoS	distributed denial of service	**IDPS**	intrusion detection and prevention
DES	Data Encryption Standard	**IDS**	intrusion detection system

IEEE	Institute of Electrical and Electronics Engineers
IETF	Internet Engineering Task Force
InfoSec	information security
IPS	intrusion prevention system
IPSec	IP Security
IPv4	Internet protocol version 4
IPv6	Internet protocol version 6
IRS	Internal Revenue Service
(ISC)²	International Information System Security Certification Consortium
ISO	International Organization for Standardization
ISP	Internet service provider
ISS	Internet security systems
ITRC	Identity Theft Resource Center
IVR	interactive voice response
LAN	local area network
MAN	metropolitan area network
MD5	Message Digest 5
modem	modulator demodulator
NFIC	National Fraud Information Center
NIDS	network intrusion detection system
NIPS	network intrusion prevention system
NIST	National Institute of Standards and Technology
NMS	network management system
OS	operating system
OSI	open system interconnection
PBX	private branch exchange
PCI	Payment Card Industry
PGP	Pretty Good Privacy
PKI	public-key infrastructure
RAID	redundant array of independent disks
RFC	Request for Comments
RSA	Rivest, Shamir, and Adleman (algorithm)

SAN	storage area network
SANCP	Security Analyst Network Connection Profiler
SANS	SysAdmin, Audit, Network, Security
SAP	service access point
SCSI	small computer system interface
SET	Secure electronic transaction
SGC	server-gated cryptography
SHA	Secure Hash Algorithm
S-HTTP	secure HTTP
SLA	service level agreement
SMFA	specific management functional area
SNMP	simple network management protocol
SOX	Sarbanes-Oxley Act of 2002 (also Sarbox)
SSA	Social Security Administration
SSCP	Systems Security Certified Practitioner
SSL	Secure Socket Layer
SSO	single system sign-on
STP	shielded twisted cable
TCP/IP	Transmission Control Protocol/Internet Protocol
TCSEC	Trusted Computer System Evaluation Criteria
TFTP	Trivial File Transfer Protocol
TNI	Trusted Network Interpretation
UDP	User Datagram Protocol
UPS	uninterruptible power supply
UTP	unshielded twisted cable
VLAN	virtual local area network
VOIP	Voice over Internet Protocol
VPN	virtual private network
WAN	wide area network
WLAN	wireless local area network
WNIC	wireless network interface card
W3C	World Wide Web Consortium
WWW	World Wide Web

Glossary of Key Terms

A

Acceptable use policies (AUPs) | Policies that define what actions are acceptable and which ones aren't.

Access control lists (ACLs) | The lists of permissions that define which users or groups can access an object.

Act of Congress | A statute or public law enacted by Congress.

A-I-C | The availability, integrity, and confidentiality properties that describe a secure object. Also referred to as confidentiality, integrity, and availability (CIA).

American Institute of Certified Public Accountants (AICPA) | The organization that developed the SAS 70 standard.

American National Standards Institute | A nonprofit accrediting organization that overseas the development of standards.

Application performance monitoring | Software that can measure end-user response time for application software server requests as well as end-user traffic volume.

Approved Scanning Vendor (ASV) | A qualified and approved company able to perform Payment Card Industry (PCI) vulnerability scans and assessment.

Assurance | A level of confidence that appropriate and effective IT controls are in place.

Audit | An independent assessment that takes a well-defined approach to examining an organization's internal policies, controls, and activities.

Audit frequency | The rate of occurrence for an audit.

Audit objective | The goal of an audit.

Audit scope | The range of the organization to be included in an audit within a defined time frame.

Auditing Standard No. 5 | An audit of internal control of financial reporting that is integrated with an audit of financial statements.

Auditing Standards Board of the American Institute of Certified Public Accounts (AICPA) | An organization that issues and maintains auditing standards.

Authentication | The process of providing additional credentials that match the user ID or user name.

Authorization | The process of granting rights and permissions to access objects to a subject.

Availability | The assurance that information is available to authorized users in an acceptable time frame when the information is requested.

B

Background check | An investigation to divulge evidence of past behavior that may indicate a prospect is a security risk.

Baseband | A transmission technique that uses the entire channel's bandwidth.

Baseline controls | Countermeasures that apply broadly to the entire IT infrastructure.

Broadband | A transmission technique that only uses a portion of the full bandwidth of a channel.

Business continuity plan (BCP) | A plan that documents the steps to restore business operation after an interruption.

Business drivers | The components, including people, information, and conditions, that support business objectives.

C

Card Verification Value (CVV) | A number printed on credit cards that provides additional authentication when rendering payment for online transactions.

Certification and Accreditation (C&A) | An audit of federal systems prior to being placed into a production environment.

Certification and Accreditation Professional (CAP) | An (ISC)^2 certification the tests a candidates knowledge of the process of certifying and accrediting the security of information systems.

Certification in Control Self-Assessment (CCSA) | A IIA certification that tests professional knowledge of control self-assessments.

Certified Financial Services Auditor (CFSA) | A IIA certification that tests audit knowledge and abilities of financial services.

Certified Government Auditing Professional (CGAP) | An IIA certification that tests audit knowledge unique to the public sector.

Certified in Risk and Information Systems and Control (CRISC) | An ISACA certification that tests knowledge of enterprise risk and control.

Certified in the Governance of Enterprise IT (CGEIT) | An ISACA certification that tests knowledge of IT governance concepts.

Certified Information Security Manager (CISM) | An ISACA certification that tests required knowledge of information security managers.

Certified Information Systems Auditor (CISA) | An ISACA certification exam considered by many as the "gold standard" for IT auditing.

Certified Information Systems Security Professional (CISSP) | An (ISC)^2 certification considered by many as the "gold standard" for information security management.

Certified Internal Auditor (CIA) | A IIA certification exam that covers internal auditing practices and issues.

Certified public accountant (CPA) | A designation for earned by qualified accounts in the United States passing an accounting certification exam and meeting other professional requirements.

Certified Secure Software Lifecycle Professional (CSSLP) | An (ISC)^2 certification that tests candidates on IT security throughout the software life cycle.

Chief privacy officer (CPO) | A senior-level position responsible for the overall management of an organization's privacy program.

Children's Internet Protection Act (CIPA) | An act of Congress to address concerns about minors' access to explicit online content.

CIA | The confidentiality, integrity, and availability (CIA) properties that describe a secure object. Also referred to as availability, integrity, and confidentiality (A-I-C).

Cloud computing | A computing model in that instead of owning computing resources, an organization can rent it from a provider. The provider maintains the data center and continuous connectivity to your rented servers.

Code of conduct | a statement of procedures and guiding principles to influence the culture and behavior of an organization's employees.

Code of ethics | A statement of general principles that pertain to an organization and its constituents.

Committee of Sponsoring Organizations (COSO) of the Treadway Commission | An organization that provides guidance to executive management on organizational governance, internal controls, and risk management.

Common Body of Knowledge (CBK) | A (ISC)^2 term that describes the 10 topics that form the knowledge areas of its members.

Compensating controls | Alternative countermeasures to minimize risk.

Compliance | The act of adhering to internal policies, as well as applicable laws, regulations, and industry requirements.

Computer assisted audit tools and techniques (CAATT) | Automated computerized tools and techniques auditors used to aid them in their auditing function.

Computing Technology Industry Association (CompTIA) | A nonprofit professional association known for its many certifications covering a wide range of topics.

Confidentiality | Assurance that information is not disclosed to unauthorized sources.

Confidentiality agreement | A legally binding document in which the parties agree that certain types of information will pass among the parties and must remain confidential and not divulged—also commonly called a non-disclosure agreement (NDA).

Configuration and change management | The detailed recording, management, and updating regarding the details of an information system.

Configuration control board (CCB) | A person or group of people that reviews each change request and either approves or denies the request.

Configuration management database (CMDB) | A central repository of system configuration items.

Connection media | The adapters and wires, or wireless media, that connects components together in the LAN Domain.

Consensus Audit Guidelines (CAG) | A listing of the top 20 critical security controls, published by SANS.

Continuing education unit (CEU) | A measurement used in continuing education programs such as certifications.

Control activities | Provide the details on how to achieve control objectives.

Control objectives | State the high-level organizational goal of information system measures.

Control Objectives for Information and related Technology (COBIT) | A framework providing best practices for IT governance and control.

Control self-assessment (CSA) | A method for organizations to assess risk and controls on their own.

Controls | Actions or changes put in place to reduce a weakness or potential loss. A control is also referred to as a countermeasure.

Corrective controls | Mechanisms that repair damage caused by an undesired action and limit further damage, such as the procedure to remove detected viruses or using a firewall to block an attacking system.

Cyber, Identity, and Information Assurance (CIAA) | A Department of Defense (DoD) information security strategy.

D

Data center | One or more rooms with protected access and controlled environment for computers and other IT devices. Another common term is simply a computer room.

Dedicated line | A permanent circuit between two endpoints.

Demilitarized zone (DMZ) | A separate network, or portion of a network, that is connected to a WAN and at least one LAN, with at least one firewall between the DMZ and your LAN.

Denial of service (DoS) | An attack that generally floods a network with traffic. A successful attack renders the network unusable and effectively stops the ability to conduct business.

Descriptive control | Measures to be applied to a system that are high level and provide a lot of flexibility.

Detective controls | Mechanisms that recognize when an undesired action has occurred, such as motion detectors or usage log analysis tools.

Disaster recovery plan (DRP) | A plan that documents the steps you can take to replace damaged or destroyed components due to a disaster to restore the integrity of your IT infrastructure.

Discretionary access control (DAC) | Access permissions based on roles, or groups, that allows object owners and administrators to grant access rights at their discretion.

Distributed application | An environment in which the components that make up an application reside on different computers.

Dual-homed ISP connection | A design in which a network maintains two connections to its ISP.

Due care | The level of effort IT security professionals owe their employers and colleagues.

Due diligence | The ongoing attention and care an organization places on security and compliance.

E

Encapsulating protocol | A protocol that encrypts each message for transport by a nonencrypting protocol.

Encryption | The process of scrambling data in such a way that it is unreadable by unauthorized users but can be unscrambled by authorized users to be readable again.

Enron | A large U.S.–based energy company that went bankrupt in 2001 and has become a symbol of corporate fraud and corruption.

Enterprise risk management (ERM) | The governing process for managing risks and opportunities.

Enterprise risk management (ERM) framework | The process organizations use to manage risks related to achieving their goals.

Ethernet MAN | A hybrid network that uses Ethernet on a MAN, also called Metro Ethernet.

Ethics | Moral beliefs and rules around what is right and wrong.

Ethics Working Group | A consortium to define information security as a recognized profession within IT, and establish a generally accepted framework of ethical behavior.

Executive summary | A concise yet informative review intended for senior level management or those with decision-making power.

F

Fair Credit Reporting Act (FCRA) | U.S. legislation that defines national standards for all consumer reports.

Family Educational Rights and Privacy Act (FERPA) | An act of Congress to protect the privacy of education records.

FCAPS | The acronym for a network management functional model that stands for Fault, Configuration, Accounting, Performance, and Security.

Federal Information Processing Standards (FIPS) | Technical standards published by NIST and approved by the secretary of commerce.

Federal Information Security Management Act of 2002 (FISMA) | An act of Congress to recognize the importance of information security United States interests.

Finding | A documented conclusion that highlights deficiencies, abuse, fraud or other questionable acts.

Fingerprinting | The process of identifying the operating system and general configuration of a computer.

Footprinting | The process of determining the operating system and version of a network node.

Framework | A conceptual set of rules and ideas that provide structure to a complex and challenging situation.

FUD | An acronym used to describe fear, uncertainty, and doubt.

G

Gap analysis | A comparison between the actual and desired outcome.

Generally Accepted Privacy Principles (GAPP) | A set of principles developed to provide guidance for privacy audits.

GIAC Certified ISO 17799 Specialist (G7799) | A GIAC certification that tests knowledge of the ISO/IEC 27000 series frameworks.

GIAC Systems and Network Auditor (GSNA) | A GIAC certification that tests technically focused knowledge of information systems auditing.

Global Information Assurance Certification (GIAC) | A SANS associated organization that provides an assortment of information assurance certifications.

Global Technology Audit Guide (GTAG) | IIA-published documents that provide audit guidance for IT auditors.

Governance | The process through which an organization's processes and assets are directed and controlled.

Gramm-Leach-Bliley Act (GLBA) | An act of Congress to protect the financial information of consumer information held by financial agencies.

Guide to the Assessment of IT Risk (GAIT) | IIA-published documents that provide guidance related to IT risk and control.

H

Halon | A gas commonly used in data center fire suppression systems. Due to halon's toxic properties, one type of halon has been banned and is no longer produced. Alternative gases are becoming more common.

Health Information Technology for Economic and Clinical Health Act (HITECH) | Builds upon HIPAA by providing for increased enforcement and breach notification.

Health Insurance Portability and Accountability Act (HIPAA) | An act of Congress that helps citizens maintain their health coverage as well as improve the efficiency and effectiveness of the American health care system.

Honeypot | A server deliberately set up as insecure in an effort to trap or track attackers.

Hypertext Transfer Protocol (HTTP) | A protocol used to transport hypertext files, or Web pages.

Hypertext Transfer Protocol Secure (HTTPS) | A protocol used to transport encrypted hypertext files, or Web pages.

I

Identification | The process of providing user credentials or claiming to be a specific user.

Identity theft | The taking of one's personal information for unauthorized use.

IEEE 802.11 | A standard that defines standards for WLAN communication protocols.

In the clear | Information that is not encrypted and is readable by anyone.

Information assurance (IA) | Protection of the confidentiality, integrity, and availability of data, and providing for authentication and nonrepudiation of services.

Information resource management | A process of managing information to improve performance.

Information Security Management System (ISMS) | A set of policies governing information security management.

Information Systems Security Assessment Framework (ISSAF) | A method for evaluating networks, systems, and applications.

Information Technology Assurance Framework (ITAF) | A living document from ISACA that addresses audit and assurance standards, as well as the body of knowledge that IT audit professionals must be aware of.

Information Technology Governance Institute (ITGI) | A research think tank that provides resources on IT governance.

Information Technology Laboratory (ITL) Bulletins | NIST publications that provide in-depth coverage of important topics.

Institute of Electrical and Electronics Engineers (IEEE) | An organization that defines standards for many aspects of computing and communications.

Institute of Internal Auditors (IIA) | A guidance setting professional body for internal audit professionals.

Integrated audit | An audit that combines the assessment of financial reporting along with the assessment of related IT controls.

Integrity | Assurance against unauthorized modification or destruction.

Intellectual property rights (IPRs) | The exclusive privilege to intangible assets.

International Electrotechnical Commission (IEC) | An international, nonprofit organization that publishes global standards on electrotechnology, or all things electronic and electric.

International Information Systems Security Certification Consortium (ISC)[2] | A nonprofit professional and certification body that provides related programs for information security professionals.

International Organization for Standardization (ISO) | The world's largest publisher of worldwide standards.

International Professional Practices Framework (IPFF) | Mandatory practices and strongly recommended guidance published by the IIA.

Internet Protocol (IP) address | A numerical representation that identifies a system node on a computer network.

Internet service provider (ISP) | An organization that provides a connection to the Internet.

Internet-facing | The network components in your organization's IT infrastructure that users can access via the Internet.

Intrusion detection system (IDS) | A network hardware device or software that monitors real-time network activity and compares the observed behavior with performance thresholds and trends to detect unusual activity that might represent an intrusion.

Intrusion prevention system (IPS) | A network hardware device or software that monitors real-time network activity, compares the observed behavior with performance thresholds and trends to detect unusual activity that might represent an intrusion, and takes action to stop the attack.

GLOSSARY

ISACA | A global professional organization that provides resources and guidance around IT governance.

ISO/IEC 27001 | Accepted good practices providing an accepted baseline from which IT auditors can audit against.

ISO/IEC 27002 | An information security code of practice that provides good practices for information security management.

ISO/IEC 27005 | A security risk-management framework developed by ISO/IEC.

IT Assurance Framework (ITAF) | A framework for IT assurance, created by ISACA.

IT universe | All the resources or auditable components within an organization.

K

Kerberos | A popular computer network authentication protocol that allows nodes to prove their identities to one another.

L

LAN Domain | An IT domain that comprises the equipment making up the local area network.

LAN-to-WAN Domain | An IT domain that bridges between the LAN and the WAN.

Least privilege | *See* principle of least privilege.

Local area network (LAN) | A computer network for communications between systems covering a small physical area.

Local resource | Any resource attached to a local computer—the same computer to which the user has logged on.

M

Mandatory access control (MAC) | Access control method based on data classification and user clearance.

Media Access Control (MAC) | A unique identifier assigned to most network adapters.

Metro Ethernet | Another name for an Ethernet MAN.

Multifactor authentication | A type of authentication that uses more than two types of authentication to authenticate a user.

Multi-Protocol Label Switching (MPLS) | A network mechanism that adds a simple label to each network packet, making routing of the packet faster than routing based on data in the header portion of the packet.

N

National Checklist Program (NCP) | A government repository of baseline security checklists.

National Institute of Standards and Technology (NIST) | An organization with the mission of promoting innovation and competitiveness through the advancement of science, standards, and technology to improve economic security and quality of life.

Need to know | A subject has a need to access an object to complete a task.

Network Access Control (NAC) | A combination of security controls that defines and implements a policy that describes the requirements to access your network.

Network monitoring platforms (NMPs) | A dedicated computer on the LAN running network management software.

Network operating system (NOS) | Software that provides the interface between the hardware and the application layer software.

Network scan | An automated method for discovering host systems on a network.

Networking devices | Hardware devices that connect other devices and computers using connection media.

Networking services software | Software that provides connection and communication services for users and devices.

NIST 800-15 | A NIST published technical guide to conducting information security tests and assessments.

NIST 800-30 | A guide developed by NIST for the management of risk for IT systems.

NIST 800-53 | Recommended security controls developed by NIST.

NIST 800-53A | A guide for assessing security controls developed by NIST.

NIST Internal Reports (NISTIR) | NIST publications that describe niche technical research.

Node | Any computer or device that is connected to the network.

O

Object | The target of an access request, such as a file, folder, or other resource.

Objectives | A set of goals. Used as part of an assessment to determine what needs to be accomplished to validate a control.

Open Source Security Testing Methodology Manual (OSSTMM) | A method that takes a scientific approach to security testing.

Open Systems Interconnection (OSI) reference model | A generic description for how computers use multiple layers of protocol rules to communicate across a network. The OSI reference model defines seven distinct layers.

Owner | A user who has complete control of an object, including the right to grant access to other users or groups.

P

Packet sniffer | Software that copies specified packets from a network interface to an output device, generally a file.

Payment Card Industry Data Security Council (PCI DSC) | The organization responsible for the development and maintenance of security standards for the payment card industry.

Payment Card Industry Data Security Standard (PCI DSS) | Industry-created standards to prevent payment card theft and fraud.

Penetration testing | A method for assessing information systems in an attempt to bypass controls and gain access.

Permission | The definition of what object access actions are permitted for a specific user or group.

Plan-Do-Check-Act (PDCA) | An iterative process for continuous improvement.

Prescriptive control | Detailed and specific measures to be applied to a system.

Pretexting | The act of using false pretenses to obtain confidential information.

Preventive controls | Mechanisms that keep an undesired action from happening, such as locked doors or computer access controls.

Principle of least privilege | A principle that states that users should not have access above what is required to perform their duties.

Privacy management | The rights and obligations of individuals and organizations in regard to how they manage personal information.

Privacy officer | Senior-level management position within an organization with responsibility for privacy laws and the impact to the organization.

Project+ certification | A CompTIA certification that tests knowledge of project management.

Protected health information (PHI) | Individually identifiable health information.

Protocol | A protocol is a set of rules that governs communication.

Proxy server | A type of firewall that makes requests for remote services on behalf of local clients.

Public Company Accounting Oversight Board (PCAOB) | An organization that provides oversight for public accounting firms and defines the process for compliance audits.

Q

Qualified Security Assessor | An organization qualified and authorized to perform PCI compliance assessment.

R

RACI matrix | A table used to document the Responsibility, Accountability, Consulted, and Informed characteristics for tasks and roles.

Rack system | An open cabinet with tracks into which multiple computers can be mounted instead of individual cases.

Red Flags Rule | A rule established by the Fair and Accurate Credit Transactions Act and implemented to prevent identity theft.

Regulatory agencies | Oversight agencies that deal with administrative law, codifying, and enforcing rules.

Remote Access Domain | An IT domain that covers the access infrastructure for users accessing remote systems.

Remote resource | Any resource accessible across the LAN.

Responsible, Accountable, Consulted, and Informed (RACI) | A component of COBIT that defines who is responsible, accountable, consulted, or informed of COBIT-related processes.

Risk | An uncertainty that might lead to a loss. Losses occur when a threat exploits vulnerability.

Risk appetite | The degree of risk that an organization is willing to accept to achieve its goals.

Risk assessment | An analysis of threats and vulnerabilities against assets. A risk assessment allows the risks to be prioritized.

Risk IT | A framework based upon guiding principles to effectively manage risk. Developed by ISACA.

Risk management | The practice of identifying, assessing, controlling, and mitigating risks. Techniques to manage risk include avoid, transfer, mitigate, and accept the risk.

Risk tolerance | The range of acceptance of risks to keep an organization within their appetite for risk.

Rotation of duties | The process of rotating employees into different functions or job roles.

S

SANS Institute | A popular source for information security knowledge, training, and certification. SANS is a for-profit institute owned by the Escal Institute of Advanced Technologies.

SANS Technology Institute | A SANS related organization that provides graduate level educational programs.

Sarbanes-Oxley (SOX) Act of 2002 | An act that was created in the wake of accounting scandals from the likes of Enron and WorldCom. This act set new accountability and corporate responsibility standards for public companies and accounting firms.

Secure Sockets Tunneling Protocol (SSTP) | A VPN protocol developed by Microsoft to provide a solution that works on any networking hardware. SSTP uses Secure Sockets Layer (SSL) to transport Point-to-Point Protocol (PPP) or Layer 2 Tunneling Protocol (L2TP) traffic.

Secure VPNs | VPNs in which all traffic is encrypted.

Security configuration management (SCM) | The process and techniques around managing security-related configuration items that directly relate to controls or settings.

Security+ certification | A CompTIA certification that tests basic IT security concepts.

Separation of duties | The process of dividing roles and responsibilities so a single individual can't undermine a critical process.

Server computers and services devices | Hardware that provides one or more services to users, such as server computers, printers, and network storage devices.

Server Message Block (SMB) | A protocol used to map network resources as shared resources, allowing multiple computers to share the same resource.

Service level agreement (SLA) | A portion of a service contract that promises specific levels of service.

Service | A set of software functionality that a client accesses using a prescribed interface.

Simple Network Management Protocol (SNMP) | A network protocol used to monitor network devices.

Single point of failure | Any component on which service relies; if the single component fails, all other dependent components essentially fail as well.

Social engineering | An act of manipulating people into divulging information.

Software configuration management (SCM) | A formal method for managing changes to a software application.

Source code | Text files of programs that developers compile into application programs computers can run.

Special Publications | A series of standards developed by NIST.

Statement on Auditing Standards (SAS) 70, Service Organizations | A widely recognized and accepted auditing standard for service organizations.

Storage area network (SAN) | A collection of storage devices that is attached to a network in such a way that the devices appear to be local storage devices.

Subject | A user or principle object that requests to access a file, folder, or other resource.

Subnet | A subsection, or part, of a network.

System Security Certified Practitioner (SSCP) | An (ISC)² certification that tests candidates for knowledge of security concepts appropriate for IT security practitioners.

System/Application Domain | An IT domain that covers network systems, applications, and software for users.

TCP/IP reference model | A generic description for how computers use multiple layers of protocol rules to communicate across a network. The TCP/IP reference model defines four different layers of communication rules.

Telecommunication Standardization Sector (ITU-T) | An international organization that produces global telecommunications standards.

Threat actions | The methods of carrying out a particular threat.

Threat identification | The process of identifying all threats and those with the ability to threaten the organization.

Time To Recover (TTR) | The acceptable amount of time that is allowed to repair or replace failed components, also called Time To Repair.

The TJX Companies, Incorporated | A large off-price retailer of apparel and home fashions that suffered one of the most severe breaches of private data in history.

Transmission Control Protocol/Internet Protocol (TCP/IP) | A suite of protocols consisting of four layers, which describes how nodes on networks, including the Internet, interact and communicate.

Transparent Data Encryption (TDE) | A method of encrypting an entire database that is transparent to the user and requires no input or action.

Tunneling | A technique that creates a virtual encrypted connection and allows applications to use any protocol to communicate with servers and services without having to worry about addressing or privacy concerns.

Two-factor authentication | A type of authentication that uses two types of authentication to authenticate a user.

Type I authentication (what you know) | The information that only a valid user knows. The most common examples of Type I authentication are a password or PIN.

Type II authentication (what you have) | A physical object that contains identity information, such as a token, card, or other device.

Type III authentication (what you are) | A physical characteristic (biometric), such as a fingerprint, handprint, or retina characteristic.

Uninterruptible power supply (UPS) | A device that provides continuous usable power to one or more devices.

User Domain | An IT domain that covers the end users of information systems.

Val IT | A framework that governs IT investments, created by ISACA.

Virtual machine | A software program that looks and runs like a physical computer.

Virtual private network (VPN) | A persistent connection between two nodes that allows bidirectional communication as if the connection were a direct connection with both nodes in the same network.

Vulnerability analysis | The examination of weaknesses or flaws.

Vulnerability scan | An automated method for testing a system's services and applications for known security holes.

W

WAN Domain | An IT domain that covers the equipment and activities outside of the LAN and beyond the LAN-to-WAN Domain.

WAN optimizers | The network devices or software that can analyze current WAN performance and then modify how new traffic is sent across the WAN.

WAN service provider | An organization that provides access to their wide area network for a fee.

War dialing | The process of instructing a computer to dial many telephone numbers looking for modems on the other end.

Wide area network (WAN) | A network covering a large area often connecting multiple LANs.

Wireless local area network (WLAN) | A LAN where network components communicate using radio frequency transmissions.

Workstation Domain | The operating environment of an end user.

WorldCom | A large U.S.-based telecommunications company involved in a massive accounting scandal, which ultimately forced it to file bankruptcy in 2002.

References

AICPA Information Technology Center. "SAS No. 70, Service Organizations," 2009. http://infotech.aicpa.org/Resources/Assurance+Services/Standards/SAS+No.+70+Service+Organizations.htm (accessed March 4, 2010).

Beresford, Dennis R., Nicholas deB. Katzenbach, and C. B. Rogers, Jr. "Report of Investigation by the Special Investigative Committee of the Board of Directors of WorldCom, Inc.," March 13, 2003. http://www.sec.gov/Archives/edgar/data/723527/000093176303001862/dex991.htm (accessed February 15, 2010).

Cannings, Rich, Himanshu Dwivedi, and Zane Lackey. *Hacking Exposed Web 2.0: Web 2.0 Security Secrets and Solutions*. New York: McGraw-Hill Professional, 2008.

Cannon, David L., Timothy S. Bergmann, and Brady Pamplin. CISA: *Certified Information Systems Auditor Study Guide*. Indianapolis: Sybex, Wiley Publishing, 2006.

Celender, Jennifer. "Information Privacy Topics, A Discussion," SANS Institute, 2002. http://www.sans.org/reading_room/whitepapers/privacy/information_privacy_topics_a_discussion_687 (accessed April 1, 2010).

Clarke, Steve. *End-user Computing: Concepts, Methodologies, Tools, and Applications*. Hershey, PA: IGI Publishing, 2008.

Contesti, Diana-Lynn, Douglas Andre, Eric Waxvik, Paul A. Henry, and Bonnie A. Goins. *Official (ISC)² Guide to the SSCP CBK*. Boca Raton, FL: Auerbach Publications, Taylor & Francis Group, 2007.

COSO. "About Us," 2010. http://www.coso.org/aboutus.htm (accessed March 3, 2010).

———. "Guidance," 2010. http://www.coso.org/guidance.htm (accessed March 2, 2010).

Davis, Chris, Mike Schiller, and Kevin Wheeler. *IT Auditing: Using Controls to Protect Information Assets*. 1st ed. New York: The Mcgraw-Hill Companies, 2007.

The Ethics Working Group. "Ethics Working Group," n.d. http://ethics-wg.org/ (accessed April 5, 2010).

Federal Trade Commission. "Fighting Fraud with the Red Flags Rule: A How-To Guide for Business," n.d. http://ftc.gov/redflagsrule (accessed February 21, 2010).

———. "Gramm-Leach-Bliley Act: Subchapter I: Disclosure of Nonpublic Personal Information," n.d. http://www.ftc.gov/privacy/glbact/glbsub1.htm (accessed February 21, 2010).

Gallegos, Frederick, and Sandra Senft. *Information Technology Control and Audit*, 3rd ed. Boca Raton, FL: Auerbach Publications, Taylor & Francis Group, 2008.

GIAC—Global Information Assurance Certification. "Information Security Certification for IT Security Professionals," 2010. http://www.giac.org/ (accessed April 7, 2010).

Hamid, Rafidah Abdul. "Wireless LAN: Security Issues and Solutions," SANS Institute, 2003. http://www.sans.org/reading_room/whitepapers/wireless/wireless-lan-security-issues-solutions_1009 (accessed April 12, 2010).

Herzog, Pete. "OSSTMM—Open Source Security Testing Methodology Manual," ISECOM, 2010. http://www.isecom.org/osstmm/ (accessed March 19, 2010).

Heschl, Jimmy. "COBIT in Relation to Other International Standards," ISACA—Serving IT Governance Professionals, 2004. http://www.isaca.org/Template.cfm?Section=Home&Template=/ContentManagement/ContentDisplay.cfm&ContentID=21326 (accessed February 27, 2010).

IETF Tools. "RFC 1087—Ethics and the Internet," January 1989. http://tools.ietf.org/html/rfc1087 (accessed April 10, 2010).

Information Assurance Support Environment. "Policy and Guidance," 2010. http://iase.disa.mil/policy-guidance/index.html (accessed February 19, 2010).

The Institute of Internal Auditors (IIA). "Code of Ethics—English," 2010. http://www.theiia.org/guidance/standards-and-guidance/ippf/code-of-ethics/ (accessed April 3, 2010).

———. "IIA Reference Library: Audit Software," n.d. http://www.theiia.org/itauditarchive/index.cfm?act=ITAudit.reflibcategory&catid=7 (accessed March 19, 2010).

———. "Welcome to the IIA," 2010. http://www.theiia.org/ (accessed March 13, 2010).

International Federation of Accountants. "International Good Practice Guidance: Defining and Developing an Effective Code of Conduct for Organizations," June 2007. http://web.ifac.org/publications/professional-accountants-in-business-committee/international-good-practice#evaluating-and-improving-co (accessed April 3, 2010).

Internet Free Expression Alliance. "Children's Internet Protection Act," 2001. ifea.net/cipa.pdf (accessed February 20, 2010).

ISACA. "Code of Professional Ethics," 2010. http://www.isaca.org/Template.cfm?Section=Home&CONTENTID=55498&TEMPLATE=/ContentManagement/ContentDisplay.cfm (accessed April 3, 2010).

———. "Risk IT, Based on COBIT," n.d. http://www.isaca.org/Template.cfm?Section=Risk_IT7&Template=/TaggedPage/TaggedPageDisplay.cfm&TPLID=79&ContentID=48749 (accessed March 13, 2010).

———. "Security Assessment—Penetration Testing and Vulnerability Assessment, Document P8," July 2004. http://www.isaca.org/ContentManagement/ContentDisplay.cfm?ContentID=31608 (accessed March 20, 2010).

———. "Standards for IT Audit and Assurance (English)," 2010. http://www.isaca.org/Template.cfm?Section=Standards&Template=/ContentManagement/ContentDisplay.cfm&ContentID=18248 (accessed March 28, 2010).

ISACA/ITGI. "COBIT 4.1," 2010. http://www.isaca.org/Template.cfm?Section=COBIT6&Template=/TaggedPage/TaggedPageDisplay.cfm&TPLID=55&ContentID=7981 (accessed March 28, 2010).

(ISC)². "(ISC)² Code of Ethics," 2010. http://www.isc2.org/ethics/default.aspx (accessed April 3, 2010).

ISO Standards Development. "Committee ISO/IEC JTC 001 'Information technology,'" 2010. http://isotc.iso.org/livelink/livelink/open/jtc1 (accessed March 3, 2010).

IT Governance Institute (ITGI). http://itgi.org/ (accessed March 21, 2010).

———. "Unlocking Value: An Executive Primer on the Critical Role of IT Governance." http://www.isaca.org/ContentManagement/ContentDisplay.cfm?ContentID=48247 (accessed February 13, 2010).

Kidder, Rushworth. *How Good People Make Tough Choices Resolving the Dilemmas of Ethical Living*. Clovis, CA: Quill, 2003.

King, Tom. "Packet Sniffing in a Switched Environment," SANS Institute, June/July 2006. http://www.sans.org/reading_room/whitepapers/networkdevs/packet-sniffing-switched-environment_244 (accessed April 12, 2010).

KPMG. "KPMG's Code of Conduct—Our Promise of Professionalism," July 9, 2008. http://www.us.kpmg.com/microsite/attachments/kpmg-code-of-conduct.pdf (accessed April 8, 2010).

Kurihara, Yutaka, et al. *Information Technology and Economic Development*. Hershey, PA: IGI Publishing, 2008.

"LAN Switch Security: What the Hackers Know That You Don't." *Network World* 24, no. 45 (2007): 8.

Leo, Ross. *The HIPAA Program Reference Handbook*. Boca Raton, FL: CRC Press, 2005.

Littman, Marlyn Kemper. *Building Broadband Networks*. Boca Raton, FL: CRC Press, 2002.

National Institute of Standards and Technology (NIST). "Computer Security Division—Computer Security Resource Center," March 2010. http://csrc.nist.gov/ (accessed March 10, 2010).

———. "Publications," 2010. http://csrc.nist.gov/publications/PubsSPs.html (accessed March 4, 2010).

National Institute of Standards and Technology (NIST), Computer Security Division. "Federal Information Security Management Act (FISMA) Implementation Project," 2010. http://csrc.nist.gov/groups/SMA/fisma/index.html (accessed February 19, 2010).

———. "Information Security Handbook: A Guide for Managers," October 2006. http://csrc.nist.gov/publications/nistpubs/800-100/SP800-100-Mar07-2007.pdf (accessed February 22, 2010).

———. "Recommended Security Controls for Federal Information Systems and Organizations," August 2009. http://csrc.nist.gov/publications/nistpubs/800-53-Rev3/sp800-53-rev3-final-errata.pdf (accessed February 23, 2010).

———. "Risk Management Guide for Information Technology Systems," June 2002. http://csrc.nist.gov/publications/nistpubs/800-30/sp800-30.pdf (accessed March 24, 2010).

NIST.gov—Computer Security Division—Computer Security Resource Center. http://csrc.nist.gov/ (accessed March 21, 2010).

Open Information Systems Security Group (OISSG). http://www.oissg.org/issaf (accessed March 20, 2010).

Oud, Ernst. "The Value to IT of Using International Standards," ISACA—Serving IT Governance Professionals, 2005. http://www.isaca.org/Content/ContentGroups/Journal1/20058/jpdf053-The-Value-to-IT-Using.pdf (accessed February 26, 2010).

PCI Security Standards Council. "About the PCI Data Security Standard (PCI DSS)," 2010. https://www.pcisecuritystandards.org/security_standards/pci_dss.shtml (accessed February 21, 2010).

Powers, Jr., William C., Raymond S. Troubh, and Herbert S. Winokur, Jr. "Report of Investigation by the Special Investigative Committee of the Board of Directors of Enron Corp." news.findlaw .com/wp/docs/enron/specinv020102rpt1.pdf (accessed February 15, 2010).

Public Company Accounting Oversight Board. "Auditing Standard No. 5," 2010. http://pcaobus .org/Standards/Auditing/Pages/Auditing_Standard_5.aspx (accessed February 22, 2010).

———. "Auditing," 2010. http://pcaobus.org/Standards/Auditing/Pages/default.aspx (accessed February 27, 2010).

Ross, Ron, Stu Katzke, Arnold Johnson, Marianne Swanson, Gary Stoneburner, and George Rogers. "Recommended Security Controls for Federal Information Systems." NIST Special Publication 800-53, revision 2. http://csrc.nist.gov/publications/nistpubs/800-53-Rev2/ sp800-53-rev2-final.pdf (accessed February 11, 2010).

SANS InfoSec Resources. "20 Critical Security Controls," 2010. http://www.sans.org/critical -security-controls/ (accessed March 13, 2010).

SANS Institute. "SANS: Computer Security Training, Network Research & Resources," 2010. http://www.sans.org/ (accessed April 7, 2010).

The SANS Technology Institute. "Earn Your Masters Degree in Information Security from SANS Technology Institute, a Security Graduate School," 2010. http://www.sans.edu/ (accessed April 10, 2010).

Sayana, S. Anantha. "Using CAATs to Support IS Audit," vol. 1, 2003. ISACAA—Serving IT Governance Professionals, 2010. http://www.isaca.org/Template.cfm?Section=K -NET3&CONTENTID=16190&TEMPLATE=/ContentManagement/ContentDisplay.cfm (accessed March 19, 2010).

Subramanian, Ramesh. *Computer Security, Privacy, and Politics: Current Issues, Challenges and Solutions*. Hershey, PA: IGI Publishing, 2008.

Sweren, Scott. "ISO 17799: Then, Now and in the Future," ISACA—Serving IT Governance Professionals, 2006. http://www.isaca.org/Template.cfm?Section=Home&Template=/ ContentManagement/ContentDisplay.cfm&ContentID=30703 (accessed February 27, 2010).

Talukder, Asoke K., and Manish Chaitanya. *Architecting Secure Software Systems*. Boca Raton, FL: CRC Press, 2008.

Tipton, Harold F., and Micki Krause. *Information Security Management Handbook*. 6th ed. Boca Raton, FL: Auerbach Publications, Taylor & Francis Group, 2007.

Tipton, Harold, and Micki Krause. *Information Security Management Handbook*, 6th ed., vol. 3. Chicago: Auerbach Publications, 2009.

Tyson, Jeff. "How LAN Switches Work," Howstuffworks.com, 2010. http://www.howstuffworks. com/lan-switch.htm (accessed April 12, 2010).

U.S. Department of Education. "Family Educational Rights and Privacy Act (FERPA)," February 2010. http://www2.ed.gov/policy/gen/guid/fpco/ferpa/index.html (accessed February 18, 2010).

U.S. Department of Health and Human Services. "HIPAA Administrative Simplification Statute and Rules," n.d. http://www.hhs.gov/ocr/privacy/hipaa/administrative/index.html (accessed February 21, 2010).

U.S. Government Accountability Office. "GAO/PCIE Financial Audit Manual (FAM)," vols. 1 and 2, July 2008; vol. 3, August 2007. http://www.gao.gov/special.pubs/gaopcie/ (accessed March 25, 2010).

U.S. Securities and Exchange Commission. "The Laws That Govern the Securities Industry," January 29, 2010. http://www.sec.gov/about/laws.shtml (accessed February 19, 2010).

Wakefield, Robin L. "Employee Monitoring and Surveillance—The Growing Trend," ISACA, 2004. http://www.isaca.org/Template.cfm?Section=Home&Template=/ContentManagement/ContentDisplay.cfm&ContentID=16758 (accessed April 1, 2010).

Wright, Craig S. *The IT Regulatory and Standards Compliance Handbook: How to Survive Information Systems Audit and Assessments*. Burlington, MA: Syngress, 2008.

Index